THE
MEDIA
AND THE
GULF WAR

THE
MEDIA
AND THE
GULF WAR

Edited by Hedrick Smith

Seven Locks Press

© 1992 by the Foreign Policy Institute of the School of Advanced International Studies, Johns Hopkins University.
All rights reserved.
Printed in the United States of America.

Library of Congress Cataloging-in-Publication Data

The Media and the Gulf War / edited by Hedrick Smith.
    p. cm.
    Includes bibliographical references.
    ISBN   0-932020-99-2   : $24.95
    1. Persian Gulf War, 1991—Press coverage—United States.
I. Smith, Hedrick.
DS79.739.M43   1992 25.00
070.4'4995670442—dc20

DS	92-18303
79.739	CIP
M43 1992	

ISBN 0-932020-99-2

The publisher wishes to tha   editors, and publishers who
permitted us to use material. F   ar on page 434.

Seven Locks Press
Washington, D.C.

Contents

I. Pentagon Policy:
Censorship and the Pools

The Ground Rules and the Protest

The Rationale of Policy: Pros and Cons

Clash of Cultures: The Press Versus the Military

Government Control of Information: Precedents and Parallels

How the Government Policy
Worked During Combat

What We Missed

II. The Performance of the Press

Washington and Saudi Arabia: How Good Was the Press?

Baghdad: Reporting from the Other Side

Press Neutrality?

Implications for the Future

Appendices

Preface

When I was a Moscow correspondent for *The New York Times* in the early 1970s, during the dictatorship of Soviet leader Leonid Brezhnev, Americans used to ask me what it was like to operate under censorship. Many pictured me passing dispatches through a slit in the wall to anonymous agents in airless offices who would scan every line, every word, for dangerous meaning and then redline offending paragraphs, sentences, and adjectives.

"Officially, there is no censorship," I would reply. "No Soviet official examines my stories before I send them. I communicate with our New York and London offices directly by telex. Sometimes, when I have just had a meeting with a prominent dissident like Aleksandr Solzhenitsyn or Andrei Sakharov, I notice that my telex keeps breaking down, or disconnecting, or garbling words and sentences—as if some gremlins in the Kremlin, reading my messages, were so offended that they interfered with my communications lines. These nuisances come and go, and I never know whether they are my imagination or Soviet malevolence. I have no official censor assigned to me. But there is something worse."

Then I would explain that the most effective censorship of all is not the deleting of words, sentences, and paragraphs but the denial of access—stopping information at the source before I could learn it, simply putting 40 percent of the country off-limits to American and other Western reporters, and in the other 60 percent, simply shutting reporters off from contact with Soviet officials and intimidating ordinary citizens so they would not dare talk with foreign reporters. I learned that the Iron Curtain was at my fingertips.

The Foreign Ministry had an Information Department, but we could never get any information from it—not if Khrushchev died, or there was a huge fire on the outskirts of Moscow sending smoke billowing over the city; not if there was a Soviet invasion of Czechoslovakia, or if we simply wanted to know in advance what time Fidel

Castro's plane would land at Moscow Airport. The occasional briefings run by the Foreign Ministry were exercises in futility, guaranteed to produce pure propaganda. We would attend and try to penetrate the wall of noninformation with thoughtful, probing, or provocative questions. But the briefers repeated their formula answers, so we rarely learned anything of value.

To travel more than 25 miles from the Kremlin we needed special permission. We had to tell the government our exact movements—the cities we would travel to, the time our trains and planes left and landed, the hotels we would use, the institutions and people we wanted to see. Generally, the government insisted that we travel with escorts from official Soviet news agencies, such as Press Agency Novosti; sometimes we had to pay for their travel costs as well as our own. Theoretically, the escorts were there to ease the way, to help us make contact with the Soviet people; but it was immediately obvious that they were there for the opposite purpose—to seal us off, to block us from normal, open discourse with ordinary Russians. So we nicknamed them "babysitters." Sometimes we had a different babysitter in each city we visited. Sometimes, on visits to large regions such as Siberia or Central Asia, we traveled in groups (rather like American press pools) and had several babysitters monitoring our movements and our conversations throughout the whole trip.

Of course, we managed to break away at times, pretending to go for a stroll or attending a local theater performance and ducking out during intermission. Sometimes, our babysitters got lax; occasionally they even spilled revealing stories or confessions themselves. In Moscow, Leningrad, and other cities where we spent a lot of time, we got to know Soviet citizens who were unafraid to talk to us despite the risks of official disapproval or arrest. Over time, we formed friendships and evaded the restrictions. But the blanket denial of access to most of Soviet life was a very effective form of precensorship; it simply cut off information at the source, and we were left in the dark about many fundamental facts of life—economic inefficiency, poor medical care, how many people smoked cigarettes, infant mortality, the advantages of class and rank, the degree of political disagreement. For the most part, we had to rely on what American reporters call "the handout," the official version of reality, the party line parroted in the controlled Soviet media.

In the Persian Gulf War, hundreds of American reporters protested that they were being forced to work under similar or worse conditions than those my compatriots and I had known in Moscow.

For one thing, the war reporters actually faced censorship—that is, military officers reviewed, delayed, or edited their stories, changing words or simply holding up the dispatches until they were no longer timely and thus no longer worth printing. They posed more interference than my Kremlin gremlins.

But more important was the basic parallel to Moscow: access was radically confined, gingerly rationed to a tiny fraction of the press corps. Freedom of movement, opportunities for independent conversation and reporting, for simply developing one's own view of reality were all severely restricted. Press movements were controlled; reporters and camera crews had to travel with official escorts or risk losing accreditation to the entire war zone or even being shot at by "friendly" fire. Getting to any military units meant moving in "pools"—that is, small, selected groups, with transportation, contact, and conversation all officially arranged, monitored, and managed. Except when Iraqi Scud missiles threatened TV correspondents reporting live, reality was as sanitized as it had been for us in Moscow.

Few modern wars have lent themselves as readily to controlled access and information management as the Gulf War. The battlefield was remote. For all but a few days at the end, it consisted of an unseen air war fought many miles from and thousands of feet above the 1,300 or so earth-bound reporters who were there to cover it. Their main view of the conflict in Iraq—like the public's—consisted of the videotapes the Pentagon chose to release. All facts were sanitized to suit the Defense Department and then funneled through a narrow tube of official briefers.

The weapons were exotic, poorly understood by many reporters who were inexperienced in the technology of modern warfare and therefore totally dependent on the military's explanations and evaluations of its own performance. The war was so swift that few had enough time to gain either much substantive knowledge or independent sources of information. The size of the operation and the wide use of reserve units affected a larger portion of the American public than most modern wars, and this personal stake made the public impatient when the press showed skepticism about the war effort or went about its normal business of probing for shortcomings, inconsistencies, and mistakes. This combination left many reporters feeling trapped by physical obstacles, an unsympathetic public, and a suspicious and disciplined military. For many, the principal outcome was press coverage that glorified American and allied triumphs, fueling a surge of public patriotism. Pete Williams, the Pentagon spokesman, applauded the press for giving "the American people the best war coverage they ever had." But a minority of Americans accused the press of cheerleading for the Pentagon, of being manipulated and co-opted by the government, and of failing in its role as the independent eyes and ears of the American public.

Legions of reporters and editors protested in outrage against the pervasive tightness of the military's restrictions and carried a stream of complaints to the Pentagon, to the White House, to Congress, even in a constitutional lawsuit to the courts. News organizations vowed after the war that they would never again submit to such restrictive and undemocratic rules of engagement from their own government.

So the war ended triumphantly, but a central issue of democracy was joined powerfully and now demands examination and debate. The sheer volume of coverage and the immediacy of round-the-clock television coverage gave force to the clash between press and military. Live coverage brought the institutional conflict into all our living rooms.

War always tests democracy—its cohesion, its staying power, its sense of purpose. Bloodshed tests not only a people's determination and willingness to sacrifice for a common cause, but the wisdom of

xiv

national leadership in embarking on bloody combat and its skill in the prosecution of that conflict.

War also tests democracy's commitment to its central values of freedom, openness, independent inquiry, dissent, and lusty public debate, all of which undergird the essential ingredient that most distinguishes democracy from dictatorship: the consent of the governed, especially when the issue is a policy of war that asks the ultimate sacrifice of its youth. The popularity of the quick and easy victory in the Persian Gulf War cannot brush aside these issues. It cannot resolve the continuing tensions between the clashing demands of discipline and freedom, secrecy and honesty, cohesion and dissent, the military and the press, the First Amendment and national security.

It is these issues this volume examines, mainly through the writings, speeches, and discussions of those on the front lines. The central debate is immediately framed and joined. Point-counterpoint: Pentagon regulations interposed against immediate objections from the American Society of Newspaper Editors. After these documents come the arguments by Defense Secretary Dick Cheney and his spokesman, Pete Williams, setting out the military rationale for corralling the media. The military view was vehemently denounced by, among others, Walter Cronkite (see "What Is There to Hide?"), invoking the precedent of press loyalty and closeness of press and troops in World War II, and former Indochina correspondent-now-columnist Sydney Schanberg (see "Censoring for Political Security"), invoking the broken-field, free reporting of the Vietnam War as the proper precedent for all modern conflicts.

Quite obviously, the breach between the Pentagon and the press that appeared during the Persian Gulf War was not opened suddenly. In modern times, communal antagonisms run in a historical line from Vietnam to the gulf. In Vietnam, it was the military that felt the press had unfairly maligned those in uniform and undermined the conduct of the war by showing its negative side and turning public opinion against the war. By the time of the Grenada invasion in October 1983, it was the press that howled that it had been both misled by the White

House about the imminent attack and then kept off the island by the Pentagon during the initial assault—a painful experience repeated in the brief war in Panama, where the practice of press pools was used to keep a small press corps cooped up and out of the way of the military.

But the roots of the antagonism run much deeper. The most celebrated example of the military's institutional mistrust of reporters was voiced during the Civil War by Gen. William T. Sherman, who seemed to feel that reporters ought to be shot on sight as spies. Like many modern commanders, Sherman worried not only about the enemy's gaining useful information from war dispatches of reporters, but about the disastrous impact on public morale in the Yankee North of reports of military bungling.

My own most vivid personal recollection of the institutional confrontation between government and press is of a Friday afternoon background session at the State Department in 1968. Those were dark days in the Vietnam War, a time of raw and rancid feelings in Washington. Secretary of State Dean Rusk, normally softspoken if unwavering in his defense of the war, suddenly challenged reporters to stop raising embarrassing questions and fall in behind the government. Fed up with the tough questioning, Rusk wheeled on the semicircle of us reporters around him and exploded: "Whose side are you on?" John Scali of ABC News had been peppering the secretary with questions and took Rusk's jab as an assault on his own patriotism. He leapt up toward Rusk, as if to defend himself, but was restrained by others. (See Bill Monroe, "Rusk to John Scali: Whose Side Are You On?")

But if Rusk and others found the relentless probing and criticism of the war by the press cause to question the motives and loyalties of reporters, the Johnson administration's seemingly endless string of lies and deceptions during the Vietnam War generated a new level of distrust among reporters toward the government in general and official briefings in particular. The gulf between press and officials created in the Vietnam era has become a permanent legacy in

Washington. (See Thomas Lippman, "The Briefers and the Press.")

Vietnam, and now the Persian Gulf, have certainly aggravated military-press relations, but the roots of tension lie beyond specific historical experience. By now, it is a commonplace observation that there is an inevitable clash of cultures between the disciplined, hierarchical military, responding to the call of duty, patriotism, and team instincts, and the free-wheeling, individualistic press, instinctively mistrustful of officialdom and authority, and motivated to break news and make headlines.

Lt. Gen. Bernard Trainor, a career Marine officer who later became a military analyst for *The New York Times* and for ABC, wrote with insight (see "The Military and the Media") about character traits and feelings that had become deeply inbred in the two opposing camps:

> Oddly enough, I have found striking similarities between my colleagues in both camps. Both are idealistic, bright, totally dedicated to their professions, and technically proficient. They work long hours willingly under arduous conditions, crave recognition, and feel they are underpaid. The strain on family life is equally severe in both professions. But there are notable differences as well. A journalist tends to be creative, while a soldier is more content with traditional approaches. Reporters are independent, while military men are team players. And of course one tends to be liberal and skeptical, the other conservative and accepting.
>
> There is another big difference which bears directly on their interrelationship. The military is hostile toward the journalist, while the journalist is indifferent toward the military. To the journalist, the military is just another huge bureaucracy to report on, no different from Exxon or Congress. But whereas businessmen and politicians try to enlist journalists for their own purposes, the military man tries to avoid them, and when he cannot, he

faces the prospect defensively with a mixture of fear, dread, and contempt.

Given those feelings, the most natural reflex in the military is to corral and handcuff the press. American history, not to mention global politics, carries precedents for the kind of press restrictions imposed during the Persian Gulf War, though the numbers of reporters obviously aggravated the collective sense of grievance. Reporters never like to be forced to operate through pools, with a handful of reporters getting to see the action, pooling their notes, and then circulating a report from which all the press draws its stories. Reporters are trained to go see for themselves. So pools are accepted only in extremis, for limited purposes; but in the Gulf War, they became the essential mode of operation, and that rubbed the press corps's collective nerves.

Actually, the pool system was an outgrowth of reporters' earlier frustration at being totally excluded from the assault on Grenada. The Pentagon's response was to offer access to small "pools" of reporters as its only feasible means for moving representatives of the press corps around hot battlefields, especially early in operations. But retired Army Maj. Gen. Winant Sidle, who had drafted the plan for limited pools in extreme situations, such as the start of battle, opposed their prolonged and pervasive use in the Persian Gulf (see Senate testimony). Gara LaMarche of The Fund for Free Expression argued that the Pentagon's policy put the United States "In Bad Company," with dictatorships or governments ill-disposed to American-style democracy.

In practice, one reporter after another had horror stories to tell about how their movements were restricted, their conversations monitored, and their dispatches delayed (see Christoper Hanson, "The Pool"). In testimony before the U.S. Senate Governmental Affairs Committee, Malcolm Browne of *The New York Times* told of filing a dispatch of an American air triumph—raids against Saddam Hussein's nuclear weapons facilities—only to have it held for military clearance while the French Press Agency broke the story and then Gen. Norman Schwarzkopf announced it. By the time Browne's dispatch was released by the military, it was old news. Some correspondents broke away from the pool system and were branded by the military as "unilaterals" who were risking being shot in the war zone; nonetheless, some of the best (Robert Fisk, "Out of the Pool," and Chris Hedges, "The Unilaterals") managed to get some of the best stories of the war through their daring and enterprise. After the war, Michael Getler of *The Washington Post* summed up the feelings of many in the press, deploring what he called "the most thorough and sophisticated wartime control of American reporters in modern times." In rebuttal, at the National Press Club, Pete Williams, the Pentagon spokesman, replied that "there simply was no way for us to open up a rapidly moving front to reporters roaming the battlefield."

In the aftermath of the war, public attention was immediately captured by the uprisings against Saddam Hussein inside Iraq and the Iraqi military's persecution of the Kurds. But with the curtain of military censorship lifted, some reporters and analysts turned to the issue of stories that the public missed during wartime because the information had been blocked (see Tom Wicker, "An Unknown Casualty"). In place of the impression conveyed by the selective release of videotapes displaying American technological wizardry—showing American "smart weapons" unerringly hitting high priority targets in the early days of the air war—the Defense Department now disclosed that "U.S. Bombs Missed 70 Percent of the Time" (see Barton Gellman) because most of the ordnance the United States had used, especially against Iraqi troops, were old-fashioned bombs guided by gravity, not computers. Stuart Auerbach of *The Washington Post* found out that nearly 30 times during the war, the Bush administration had to make urgent pleas to the Japanese, German, French, and Thai governments for rush shipments of high technology components—which U.S. industry could not supply and without which the American military machine would have been crippled (see "U.S. Relied on Foreign-Made Parts for Weapons"). Eric Schmitt of *The New York Times* reported that the failure of an American computer system allowed an Iraqi Scud missile to hit an American barracks in Dhahran, causing the worst American casualties (see "Army Is Blaming Patriot's Computer for Failure to Stop the Dhahran Scud").

The second section of this volume is devoted to the other half of the story—the performance of the press itself, from the knowledge and experience of the reporters and the caliber of their questions at military briefings, the impact of instantaneous television coverage of the air war, especially Peter Arnett's broadcasts from Baghdad, to whether the press was too much the cheerleader for the war, too readily co-opted and manipulated by the military.

In *Media Monitor*, Robert Lichter provided a detailed statistical breakdown of television coverage during the war, what topics got how much attention, week by week (see "The Instant Replay War"). Reuven Frank, former President of NBC News, mocked the television claims of "live" coverage: "Bullshit. . . . What we're getting 'live' is briefings about events that are from 12 to 24 hours old—and reporters talking to each other live" (see Richard Valeriani, "Talking Back to the Tube.") Lewis Lapham, editor of *Harper's*, mocked the press as "Trained Seals and Sitting Ducks" for the Pentagon. In *The Washington Post* ("The Gulf Between the Military and the Media"), Henry Allen delivered the scathing judgment that "The Persian Gulf press briefings are making reporters look like fools, nitpickers, and egomaniacs." Some suggested that television was pushing too fast to get on the air with raw information, but the print media were doing a better job (see Howard Kurtz, "Newspapers, Getting It Late but Right"). But others, such as Gene Ruffini, Scott Armstrong, and Eqbal Ahmad, offered more sweeping criticisms of press performance. Ruffini, in *Washington Journalism Review*, charged that the press had been too compliant a tool of the president and had "Failed to Challenge the Rush to War." At a National Press Club panel discussion, Armstrong asserted that the press had simply ignored the big stories, such as secret Saudi-American agreements on the conduct of the war. Ahmad charged the American media with a broader cultural myopia about the Arab world—failing to address seriously such questions as what

Western policy miscues fed Saddam Hussein's ambition, why some Arab popular opinion opposed military intervention, the politics and economics of oil, why the United States should spend so much on "strategic alliance" with Israel if Israel's greatest role in the Gulf War was to stay out (see "What the Media Missed"). For all these criticisms, a Los Angeles Times-Mirror poll showed the public's general approval of the press performance, and Lt. Gen. Thomas Kelly, the Pentagon briefer, bowed out with words of praise for the professionalism of the press: ". . . as you know, I hold a lot of you in great respect" (see "Kelly Exits with Praise for Media").

Of all the press exploits during the Gulf War, none was more controversial than Peter Arnett's dramatic reporting from Baghdad for CNN—drawing accolades from many of his colleagues in the press and stinging charges from much of the Bush administration and its supporters. At the annual dinner of the press's Gridiron Club in Washington, where many figures are introduced to applause—President Bush stopped clapping when Arnett was introduced. That captured the feeling of the war's most ardent advocates in Washington. Sen. Alan Simpson of Wyoming called Arnett a "sympathizer" of Saddam Hussein for staying in Baghdad and allowing himself to be used for Iraqi propaganda, and suggested that in the Vietnam War Arnett had had family ties to the Vietcong (see Howard Kurtz, "Senator Simpson Calls Arnett 'Sympathizer'"). After condemnations from press columnists (see Jim Hoagland, "Simpson's Scud Attack") and Arnett's son, Simpson apologized in *The New York Times* for labeling Arnett a "sympathizer" and retracted the charge about Arnett's family (see Simpson's "Letter to Editor"). But the senator stuck to his critical view of Arnett's presence in Baghdad and insisted that Arnett had been too dependent on his Iraqi "handlers" for information.

Both NBC reporter Ed Rabel, in "Baghdad: The Ugly Dateline," and Arnett, in a lengthy question-and-answer session at the National Press Club, described in graphic and important detail what it was like to work in Baghdad during the war. Arnett was both amusing and revealing of the real limitations imposed on him, about his constant game of wits with his Iraqi handlers, trying to slip tidbits of forbidden information across to viewers around the world, and about the famous episode of his report on a baby milk factory that the Pentagon claimed was a military target. He came to the session with some plastic-wrapped powdered milk. "If you believe me, you will join me later," he teased. "We will open this packet and we will put it in our coffee." And he tweaked Senator Simpson for having chastised Arnett and other Western journalists before the Persian Gulf War for being too harsh on Saddam Hussein, with whom the Bush administration had had friendly terms at the time.

But as was pointed out by Stephen Hess, a Brookings Institution expert on the media (quoted in Jeff Kamen, "CNN's Breakthrough in Baghdad"), the real issue was not Arnett's reporting but CNN's new role. "What is new in this war is not censorship," Hess asserted. "What is totally different is an instantaneous, continuous, and international network. CNN really is the story. And it's clear that we all have a lot to learn about this new phenomenon." What Hess was alluding to is CNN President Ted Turner's One World philosophy, which moti-vated Turner to ban the word "foreign" from CNN's broadcasts and the thinking of his news staff. Ed Turner, CNN's vice president, put it this way: "You must avoid the appearance of cheerleading. We are, after all, at CNN, a global network." Echoes came from other American journalists (Dan Rather and Mike Wallace of CBS, Bernard Shaw of CNN). Shaw, CNN's anchor, explained: "There's no 'en-emy,' there's no 'friendly'; I can't take sides and I don't take sides. As an American, how I feel privately, that's personal. But professionally, I do not take sides . . . As a reporter I am neutral." This concept of neutrality was sharply attacked by John Corry in *Commentary* both in principle and in practice, declaring that this would have been unthink-able for Edward R. Murrow in London during World War II (see "The Issue of Neutrality"). Stephen Aubin, in *Defense Media Review*, said it was impossible "because the media are not neutral observers—they are players, maybe even weapons of war" (see "Bashing the Media:

Why the Public Outrage?"). Unquestionably, the debate over this issue will far outlive the Persian Gulf War.

So will the controversy over the policies applied by the Pentagon in the Persian Gulf War. As Jason DeParle reports, the Defense Department thinks it has a winning strategy and is inclined to stick with the formula in future conflicts (see "Keeping the News in Step: Are the Pentagon Rules Here to Stay?"). The press corps, on the other hand, is in an uproar. Washington bureau chiefs of 15 major news organizations have sent a collective message to the Pentagon asserting that their organizations will never again submit to or cooperate with such restrictive rules. ("Our organizations are committed to the proposition that this should not be allowed to happen again.") They vow an ongoing struggle to persuade the Pentagon to throw out the pooling system and adopt more open procedures.

What is more, this is now more than an intramural squabble reflecting the institutional tensions between the press and the Pentagon. The argument has broadened into a question of legal rights and of what the United States Constitution guarantees; for during the Persian Gulf War, some members of the press went to court to assert a constitutional right of access to American battlefields in wartime— a right, they argued, that cannot be abridged by the military. Led by *The Nation* magazine, 15 news organizations and individual writers or reporters challenged the pool system and asserted the constitutional right of access to the battlefield for the press. It was a stunning argument.

As precedents, the legal brief of the press cited a long history of press activities in wartime from the American Revolution through the Civil War, World War II, and into the modern era. These were all conflicts, the press argued, where reporters had accompanied the American military into battle. In rebuttal, the Pentagon gave a very different version of American military history, citing examples of military censorship accepted by the press from the Revolutionary period forward, and asserting that even when the press had gone into battle, its numbers had been very limited.

The two sides clashed not only over history but over the implications of using pools: the press made the case that pools were a Pentagon technique for keeping the vast majority of reporters away from the battlefield, while the Defense Department argued that pools were the only feasible vehicle for getting some reporters to the front. One side saw exclusion; the other, inclusion. Moreover, the Pentagon objected to the very idea of making this a debate of legal rights. Its brief urged that the press case be thrown out of court and contended that the courts had no jurisdiction in such matters.

Federal District Judge Leonard Sand, accepting what he acknowledged was a "novel" assertion of press rights under the First Amendment of the Constitution, denied the military argument that the courts had no jurisdiction. But the war ended before he issued his ruling. In his judgment, he called the issue moot because there was no longer any alleged wrong to be remedied. Judge Sand declined to issue a sweeping declaratory judgment against future use of pools, asserting that it was not clear whether the Pentagon's pooling system would be applied in its present form in some future conflict. He dismissed the immediate case on grounds that the underlying constitutional issues "are not sufficiently in focus at this time" for a judicial decision. But in so doing, Judge Sand asserted that "important constitutional issues [are] at stake," and they would beg settlement in law in some future conflict.

So this war and its outcome—and the government's satisfaction with its policy—have not stilled the debate. This was almost inevitable, because the war was so short and American casualties were so light. A longer and more bloody war might well have found American public opinion much more divided and the Bush administration facing conflicting political pressures on its tight information policy. Yet even in this short war, the most fundamental issues of law and policy have been thrust to the fore by the Pentagon's restrictive policies. One sad legacy is the scar of unresolved tensions between the media and military, each now feeling aggrieved by a conflict in which it feels its interests were unfairly overridden. As a society, we have no resolution to the question of proper press access to battlefields where Americans are called to die for their country, or to the vital issue of what constitutes adequate and timely information for American democracy during wartime. These are issues that future generals and journalists will have to confront and try to resolve.

Hedrick Smith
Chevy Chase, Maryland

Acknowledgments

This book speaks with many voices about a common concern. Like the proverbial group of blind men who each described what an elephant is, based on the part he encountered, the authors of the pieces collected here each contributed a valuable perspective of a necessarily unwieldy whole. This is their book, and the credit for it is theirs, not mine. I should also credit the authors of the dozens of pieces that I would like to have included but could not for lack of space. Their insights and observations helped me to shape the structure of the book and to define and sharpen the questions raised in the book.

I wish to extend particular thanks to all those who generously granted permission to reproduce the many articles, comments, and transcribed speeches and panel discussions that follow.

I owe a special debt to the Foreign Policy Institute of the Paul H. Nitze School of Advanced International Studies, the Johns Hopkins University, in Washington, D.C., which provided funding and patient support for this project. The FPI Fellows and institute director Steve Szabo all took an interest in the project and offered helpful advice as well as material.

Finally, I am most grateful to James McCall, who tracked down, helped organize, and assembled the materials that went into this project. His many hours of intelligent and devoted work gathered the substance of this book.

—H.S.

Pentagon Policy:
Censorship and
the Pools

Chapter One

The Ground Rules and the Protest

What were the restrictions that sparked controversy? What was the reaction of U.S. news editors?

Ground Rules and Guidelines for Desert Shield

Pete Williams

Memorandum for Washington Bureau Chiefs of the Pentagon Press Corps

SUBJ: Ground rules and guidelines for correspondents in the event of hostilities in the Persian Gulf

Last Monday, I sent you copies of our revised ground rules for press coverage of combat operations and guidelines for correspondents that are intended to meet the specific operational environment of the Persian Gulf. I appreciate the comments I have received from some of you and understand your concerns, particularly with respect to security review and pooling in general. I also was pleased by the general consensus that the one-page version of the ground rules was an improvement.

The ground rules have been reviewed and approved with no major changes. They became effective today.

The guidelines were revised to comply with operational concerns in Saudi Arabia. We added a provision that media representatives will not be permitted to carry weapons, clarified the escort requirement, added a sentence giving medical personnel the authority to determine media guidelines at medical facilities, and deleted the sentence saying the [Joint Information Bureau] JIB in Dhahran would verify next of kin notification on casualties. We also added a section, in response to many questions, which clarifies our policy on unilateral media coverage of the forward areas during the period when the pools are operational.

Last Saturday, I conducted a conference call with the majority of the CENTCOM public affairs officers, who were gathered in Riyadh

4

and Dhahran, and discussed the ground rules and guidelines to ensure that the intent and purpose of the ground rules is clearly understood.

I appreciate your counsel and remain ready to discuss any problems or questions you may have.

Pete Williams
Assistant Secretary of Defense
(Public Affairs)

Operation Desert Shield Ground Rules

The following information should not be reported because its publication or broadcast could jeopardize operations and endanger lives:

(1) For U.S. or coalition units, specific numerical information on troop strength, aircraft, weapons systems, on-hand equipment, or supplies (e.g., artillery tanks, radars, missiles, trucks, water), including amounts of ammunition or fuel moved by or on hand in support and combat units. Unit size may be described in general terms such as "company-size," "multibattalion," "multidivision," "naval task force," and "carrier battle group." Number or amount of equipment and supplies may described in general terms such as "large," "small," or "many."

(2) Any information that reveals details of future plans, operations, or strikes, including postponed or canceled operations.

(3) Information, photography, and imagery that would reveal the specific location of military forces or show the level of security at military installations or encampments. Locations may be described as follows: all navy embark stories can identify the ship upon which embarked as a dateline and will state that the report is coming from the "Persian Gulf," "Red Sea," or "North Arabian Sea." Stories written in Saudi Arabia may be datelined "Eastern Saudi Arabia," "Near the

5

Kuwaiti border," etc. For specific countries outside Saudi Arabia, stories will state that the report is coming from the Persian Gulf region unless that country has acknowledged its participation.

(4) Rules of engagement details.

(5) Information on intelligence collection activities, including targets, methods, and results.

(6) During an operation, specific information on friendly force troop movements, tactical deployments, and dispositions that would jeopardize operational security or lives. This would include unit designations, names of operations, and size of friendly forces involved, until released by CENTCOM.

(7) Identification of mission aircraft points of origin, other than as land- or carrier-based.

(8) Information on the effectiveness or ineffectiveness of enemy camouflage, cover, deception, targeting, direct and indirect fire, intelligence collection, or security measures.

(9) Specific identifying information on missing or downed aircraft or ships while search and rescue operations are planned or underway.

(10) Special operations forces' methods, unique equipment, or tactics.

(11) Specific operating methods and tactics (e.g., air angles of attack or speeds, or naval tactics and evasive maneuvers). General terms such as "low" or "fast" may be used.

(12) Information on operational or support vulnerabilities that could be used against U.S. forces, such as details of major battle damage or major personnel losses of specific U.S. or coalition units, until that information no longer provides tactical advantage to the enemy and is, therefore, released by CENTCOM. Damage and casualties may be described as "light," "moderate," or "heavy."

Guidelines for News Media

News media personnel must carry and support any personal and professional gear they take with them, including protective cases for professional equipment, batteries, cables, converters, etc.

Night Operations—Light discipline restrictions will be followed. The only approved light source is a flashlight with a red lens. No visible light source, including flash or television lights, will be used when operating with forces at night unless specifically approved by the on-scene commander.

Because of host-nation requirements, you must stay with your public affairs escort while on Saudi bases. At other U.S. tactical or field locations and encampments, a public affairs escort may be required because of security, safety, and mission requirements as determined by the host commander.

Casualty information, because of concern of the notification of the next of kin, is extremely sensitive. By executive directive, next of kin of all military fatalities must be notified in person by a uniformed member of the appropriate service. There have been instances in which the next of kin have first learned of the death or wounding of a loved one through the news media. The problem is particularly difficult for visual media. Casualty photographs showing a recognizable face, name tag, or other identifying feature or item should not be used before the next of kin have been notified. The anguish that sudden recognition at home can cause far outweighs the news value of the photograph, film, or videotape. News coverage of casualties in medical centers will be in strict compliance with the instructions of doctors and medical officials.

To the extent that individuals in the news media seek access to the U.S. area of operation, the following rule applies: Prior to or upon commencement of hostilities, media pools will be established to provide initial combat coverage of U.S. forces. U.S. news media personnel present in Saudi Arabia will be given the opportunity to join CENTCOM media pools, providing they agree to pool their products. News media personnel who are not members of the official CENTCOM media pools will not be permitted into forward areas. Reporters are strongly discouraged from attempting to link up on their own with combat units. U.S. commanders will maintain extremely tight security throughout the operational area and will exclude from the area of operation all unauthorized individuals.

For news media personnel participating in designated CENTCOM media pools:

(1) Upon registering with the JIB, news media should contact their respective pool coordinator for an explanation of pool operations.

(2) In the event of hostilities, pool products will be subject to review before release to determine if they contain sensitive information about military plans, capabilities, operation, or vulnerabilities (see attached ground rules) that would jeopardize the outcome of an operation or the safety of U.S. or coalition forces. Material will be examined solely for its conformance to the attached ground rules, not for its potential to express criticism or cause embarrassment. The public affairs escort officer on scene will review pool reports, discuss ground rule problems with the reporter, and in the limited circumstances when no agreement can be reached with a reporter about disputed materials, immediately send the disputed materials to JIB Dhahran for review by the JIB Director and the appropriate news media representative. If no agreement can be reached, the issue will be immediately forwarded to OASD(PA) for review with the appropriate bureau chief. The ultimate decision on publication will be made by the originating reporter's news organization.

(3) Correspondents may not carry a personal weapon.

CENTCOM Pool Membership and Operating Procedures

General. The following procedures pertain to the CENTCOM news media pool concept for providing news to the widest possible American audience during the initial stages of U.S. military activities in the Arabian Gulf area. The CENTCOM pools will be drawn from news media within Saudi Arabia. Their composition and operation should not be confused with that of the Department of Defense National Media Pool. The pools are a cooperative arrangement designed to balance the media's desire for unilateral coverage with the logistics realities of the military operation, which make it impossible for every media representative to cover every activity of his or her choice, and with CENTCOM's responsibility to maintain operational security, protect the safety of the troops, and prevent interference with military operations. There is no intention to discriminate among media representatives on the basis of reporting content or viewpoint. Favoritism or disparate treatment of the media in pool operations by pool coordinators will not be tolerated. The purpose and intention of the pool concept is to get media representatives to and from the scene of military action, to get their reports back to the Joint Information Bureau-Dhahran for filing—rapidly and safely, and to permit unilateral media coverage of combat and combat-related activity as soon as possible. There will be two types of pools: 18-member pools for ground combat operations and smaller, 7-member pools for ground combat and other coverage. Pools will be formed and governed by the media organizations that are qualified to participate and will be administered through pool-appointed coordinators working in conjunction with the JIB-Dhahran. The media will operate under the ground rules issued by CENTCOM on January 15, 1991.

Pool participation. Due to logistics and space limitations, participation in the pools will be limited to media that principally serve the American public and that have had a long-term presence covering Department of Defense military operations, except for pool positions specifically designated as "Saudi" or "international." Pool positions will be divided among the following categories of media: television, radio, wire service, news magazine, newspaper, pencil, photo, Saudi, and international. Media that do not principally serve the American public are qualified to participate in the CENTCOM media pool in the international category.

Pool procedures. Because of the extensive media presence in the Arabian Gulf, the fact that some media organizations are represented by many individuals, and the likelihood that more organizations and individuals will arrive in the future, membership in all categories

9

except pencil will be by organization rather than specific individual. An organization will be eligible to participate in pool activities only after being a member of the appropriate media pool category for three continuous weeks. Members of a single-medium pool may use their discretion to allow participation by organizations which have had a significant stay in country, but which have had breaks in their stay that would otherwise cause them to be ineligible to participate under the three-continuous-weeks rule.

The single-medium pools will be formed and governed by the members. The members of each category will appoint a pool coordinator who will serve as the spokesperson and single point of contact for that medium. The print media will select a coordinator who will serve as the point of contact for the pencil category. Any disputes about membership in or operation of the pool shall be resolved by the pool coordinator.

Each single-medium pool coordinator will maintain a current list of members and a waiting list prioritized in the order in which they should be placed on the pools. The same order will be used to replace pool members during normal rotations and those individual members who return from the field prematurely and who do not have another individual in Dhahran from their organization to replace them.

Membership of standing pools will rotate approximately every two to three weeks as the situation permits.

Pool categories and composition

Television: The television category will be open to the major television networks.

Radio: The radio category will be open to those radio networks that serve a general (nonprivate) listening audience.

Wire Service: The wire service category will be open to the major wire services.

News Magazine: The news magazine category will be open to those major national news magazines that serve a general news function.

Newspaper: The newspaper category will be divided into two subcategories for participation in the 18-member pools. One will be open to those major papers and newspaper groups that have made a commitment since the early stages of Operation Desert Shield to cover U.S. military activities in Saudi Arabia and which have had a continuous or near-continuous presence in Saudi Arabia since the early stages of the operation, such as *The New York Times*, Cox, Knight-Ridder, *The Wall Street Journal*, *Chicago Tribune*, the *Los Angeles Times*, *The Washington Post*, *USA Today* and *Boston Globe*. The second category will include all other newspapers.

Pencil: The general category of "pencil" (print reporter) may be used by the print media pool coordinator in assigning print reporters to the smaller pools. All eligible print reporters may participate.

Photo: The photography category will be divided into the four subcategories of wire, newspaper, magazine, and photo agency. Participants may take part in only one subcategory.

Saudi: The Saudi category will be open to Saudi reporters as determined by the Saudi Ministry of Information liaison in the JIB-Dhahran. They must speak and write English and must file their reports in English.

International: The international category will be open to reporters from organizations which do not principally serve the American public from any news medium. They must speak and write English and must file their reports in English.

Sharing of Media Products
Within the CENTCOM Pools

Pool participants and media organizations eligible to participate in the pools will share all media products within their medium; e.g., television products will be shared by all other television pool members and photo products will be shared with other photo pool members. The procedures for sharing those products and the operating expenses of the pool will be determined by the participants of each medium.

Alert Procedures for Combat
Correspondent Pool Activation

When the pools are to be activated, the JIB-Dhahran director or his designated representative will call each of the pool coordinators and announce the activation of the pools. The pool coordinators will be told when and where the pool members are to report (the reporting time will be within—but not later than—two hours of alert notification).

Operational security (OPSEC) considerations are of the utmost concern. JIB personnel, pool coordinators, and pool members need to be especially cognizant of OPSEC. All involved with the activation of the pools need to remain calm and unexcited. Voice inflection, nervous behavior, etc., are all indicators that something extraordinary is underway and could signal that operations are imminent.

Neither pool coordinators nor pool members will be told if the activation is an "exercise" or actual "alert."

Pool members should report to the predesignated assembly area dressed for deployment, with the appropriate equipment and supplies.

Recommendations for changes to pool membership or other procedures will be considered on a case-by-case basis.

The Protest

Letters from the American Society of Newspaper Editors (ASNE)

January 8, 1991

Dear Mr. Williams:

The newly revised (January 7) set of ground rules and guidelines for news media coverage in the gulf are a major improvement over the previous proposals. Still, we have concern in two areas.

First, we must strongly protest the use of a "security review" of any type. Even though you have told us that "material will not be withheld just because it is embarrassing or contains criticism" there is no guarantee that on-site commanders will not do what was done in July, 1987, when the commodore in charge during the reflagging of Kuwaiti tankers insisted on censoring material that in no way violated news media ground rules but merely embarrassed him.

In a world where "spin control" of the news has become commonplace, this form of prior restraint is a tool to gain control over what the American public sees or hears from the battlefield. There was no such prior review in Vietnam, and there were few security breaches of any consequence.

Finally, we are concerned that the entire emphasis of your ground rules is on the pool coverage, over which you will assert direct control. Our view of a pool situation is that it should be in effect only as long as it absolutely has to be, say for the first day or so of fighting, because of the logistical difficulty of getting the press in quickly. But as soon as possible the press should be allowed coverage that would be free of many of the pool restraints. We see no evidence of any attempt to prepare for that circumstance.

13

There are 250 U.S. reporters on site in Saudi Arabia today. The American public would be best served by a system that allows them to do their job as quickly as possible after hostilities break out.

We ask that you devote more time to preparation for that situation.

Sincerely,

Burl Osborne   Larry Kramer
President, ASNE   ASNE Press, Bar & Public Affairs Committee

January 25, 1991

Dear Mr. Williams:

Now that we are in the second week of the war, I ask on behalf of my colleagues in the American Society of Newspaper Editors that you consider changes in ground rules for coverage of the war in order to better balance the need for timely reporting with the need for security. We propose changes in two areas about which most concern has been expressed.

We recognize, as a predicate, that security ought to be a paramount in your considerations. Reporters have demonstrated in the past that they will abide by reasonable security guidelines. As has been pointed out frequently, they did so in Vietnam, and there were very, very few breaches of security. The experience of the past two weeks tends to confirm that even in this new environment of instant communications capability, journalists recognize the need to maintain military security. In these circumstances, we believe the requirement for "security review" is neither necessary nor helpful to the military, and it unnecessarily restrains the ability of journalists to do their jobs properly.

We propose that you at least try out a ground rule that provides security guidelines for journalists, but does not impose the require-

14

ment of prior review. We believe that the military and the press, and by extension the American public, all would benefit.

The second area of major concern is access. We understand that the initial circumstance of the war may have dictated pool coverage as the only practical way for reporters to be present. We also appreciate your willingness to consider and implement some modifications to the original plan.

It does seem that it now is appropriate to find a way to expand access to the various areas of operation, and we ask that you permit this to happen. We believe that all interests are best served if access to and distribution of news from the gulf is expanded. If a system of rotation is required to avoid overburdening some locations, that is fine. If some areas require military escorts to get there, that is fine too. But we ask that escorts be limited to escorting, and that journalists be permitted to do their work once on the scene without the inhibiting presence of a public affairs officer looking over their shoulders. The sight of a PAO declaring chaplains to be off-limits to journalists doesn't do anyone any good.

We ask that you give these proposals serious consideration and that you call on us if we can be of any help in further discussions.

With best wishes.

Sincerely,

Burl Osborne
President, ASNE

Chapter Two

The Rationale of Policy: Pros and Cons

Why did the administration and the military impose restrictions? Was there sufficient justification for the restrictions, or did they impose controls that were too tight? Was each side fighting the last war? Did each side overreact as they expected a return to the confrontations of Vietnam?

Military Decisions Leading to Gulf War News Censorship

Jason DeParle

The American military operation in the Persian Gulf was still in its frantic, tentative youth on August 14, 1990, when Capt. Ron Wildermuth of the navy sat in his office at United States Central Command headquarters in Tampa, Florida, and sent a classified message flashing across military computers on three continents.

As Gen. H. Norman Schwarzkopf's chief aide for public affairs, Captain Wildermuth had spent days drafting the message, a 10-page document known as Annex Foxtrot, which laid out a blueprint for the operation's public information policy. The movement of troops, weapons, and matériel was to become the largest since the humiliating—and televised—Vietnam War defeat. And in the officer's mind, one point bore repetition.

"News media representatives," he wrote, "will be escorted at all times. Repeat, at all times."

The drafting of Annex Foxtrot was one step in a long march of decisions that, by war's end, left the government with a dramatically changed policy on press coverage of military operations.

The Gulf War marked this century's first major conflict where the policy was to confine reporters to escorted pools that sharply curtailed when and how they could talk to troops. And within months, Americans were receiving news accompanied by words that had not been connected with combat accounts for nearly 50 years: "Reports reviewed by military censors."

The policy began with a decision by the administration's most senior officials, including President Bush, to manage the information flow in a way that supported the operation's political goals and avoided the perceived mistakes of Vietnam.

But the elaboration of this approach took place incrementally, with the main oversight responsibility delegated to Defense Secretary Dick Cheney, whose press policy during the Panama invasion had been faulted by an official Pentagon inquiry for its "excessive concern for secrecy."

And Mr. Cheney, in turn, left many decisions in the hands of field commanders, many of whom had left Vietnam deeply suspicious of reporters, who were relatively free to cover American forces in action.

While critics of the policy have argued that the restrictions on independent reporting were intended to produce a sanitized view of the war, top officials have said they were necessary to prevent security lapses in a new era of instant communications.

"It isn't like World War II, when George Patton would sit around in his tent with six or seven reporters and muse," with the result "transcribed and reviewed for eventual release," said Gen. Colin L. Powell, the Chairman of the Joint Chiefs of Staff.

If a commander "in Desert Shield sat around in his tent and mused with a few CNN guys and pool guys and other guys, it's in 105 capitals a minute later," General Powell said in an interview.

Dozens of interviews with civilian and military officials and a review of major planning documents disclose the following points:

■ The White House, while delegating most decisions to Mr. Cheney, closely monitored some details. Mr. Bush watched virtually every briefing, while his aides urged that certain officers be swept from television screens and promoted Lt. Gen. Thomas W. Kelly as a briefer with star potential. The Pentagon, once it realized the power of televised briefings, set up daily rehearsal sessions for General Kelly, and happened onto a system for learning the questions that reporters would throw at him.

■ The military, assuming that correspondents from the small-town press would write sympathetic articles, provided free transportation to Saudi Arabia and special access to servicemen and women from their areas. Aides also analyzed articles written by

19

other reporters to determine their interests and to screen out interview requests from those likely to focus on mistakes by the military.

■ Pentagon officials decided early in the operation to radically change the purpose of press pools, taking what had been set up as a temporary device to get reporters to a combat zone and turning it into the sole means of combat coverage. Despite that decision, Mr. Cheney's spokesman, Pete Williams, held a series of autumn meetings with news executives that encouraged them to believe that traditional independent reporting would follow.

■ White House officials, in the face of criticism, wavered at one point but dropped the idea of easing press restrictions after a "Saturday Night Live" sketch lampooning the press convinced them and the president that the public was on their side.

Striding into his press secretary's office during an interview about war coverage last month, Mr. Bush stamped the policy with his own seal of approval. "I think that the American people stand behind us," he said. "I think they felt they got a lot of information about this war."

Public opinion polls have shown overwhelming majorities backing the military over the press.

In separate interviews, Mr. Cheney and John H. Sununu, the White House chief of staff, called the policy a model for the future. The only time information was withheld, Mr. Sununu said, was when it would compromise military security. "There was never an effort not to give information out," he said. "There was never an effort not to focus on things."

And Mr. Cheney, the policy's chief architect, said, "there was better coverage, more extensive coverage, more elaborate coverage, greater knowledge on the part of the American people, about this war, as it unfolded, than any other war in history." But few journalists agree.

"I'm not sure the public's interest is served by seeing what seems to have been such a painless war, when 50,000 to 100,000 people may have died on the other side," said Ted Koppel, host of the ABC News program "Nightline."

"Obviously this was done so they could maintain the closest possible control over public opinion, to increase support for the war."

Guiding Principles

No Accidents in This Campaign. Early in the troop buildup, the president and the group of top advisers discussed past military endeavors in which they felt press policy was handled poorly, including Vietnam, Panama, and the May 1975 seizure of the American merchant ship *Mayaguez* off Cambodia. The group instructed Mr. Cheney, one of its members, to take charge.

"Nobody dwelled on it," one official at the meeting said. "The sense was, 'Set it up over there, pay attention to it—don't have things happen by accident, take control of it.'"

In an interview, Mr. Cheney said he was guided by two overarching principles. One was that military needs had to take precedence over journalistic rights, and so the "lore" of past practice needed to be disregarded.

Another was to guard government credibility. "There was ample precedent that one of the really great ways to screw up an operation— certainly was one of the lessons learned in Southeast Asia—is don't get out there making claims you can't back up," Mr. Cheney said.

Indeed, one of the reasons that the government lost public support for the conflict in Vietnam was the much-discussed credibility gap, attributed to the Johnson administration's failure to be candid with the public about its policy.

President Lyndon B. Johnson for a time tried to hide the extent of the American military buildup and repeatedly cast an optimistic gloss on the military effort and on the ability of the South Vietnamese to govern in the face of on-the-scene reporting showing the opposite.

The military had been thinking about the press long before the Iraqi invasion of Kuwait. "One thing Vietnam did to us is nobody says, 'Oh,

21

don't worry about public affairs,'" said retired Maj. Gen. Winant Sidle, who served as the chief military spokesman there.

While some commanders had simply left the press behind, as was the case in Grenada and Panama, a more sophisticated approach had also been developing. "Seek out the media and try to bring them in to write stories and produce television shows or clips in support of the organization's goals," a War College textbook suggests. Many air force generals receive a course in briefing style, during which their presentations are videotaped and critiqued.

While Mr. Cheney and other leaders were explicit in saying they were shaped by the lessons of Vietnam, General Powell said, "I never gave it the first thought."

Calling Vietnam references "a cheap shot," General Powell said that whenever reporters were unhappy, "you take out your little branding iron with the 'V' and heat it up and burn it into our foreheads."

Emphasizing that he was just a captain in Vietnam, General Powell said that his experiences as a top commander or national security adviser during the Beirut crisis of 1983 and in Grenada and Panama taught him much more about "how we had to handle the information."

General Powell did say that one of his top priorities in training commanders has been to make "them understand the proper role of media." While some have pointed to such training to argue that the military has grown more skilled at manipulating the press, General Powell said, "I spin it differently."

"Sure, you want to see if you can get the press to support the goals, but that's not why you work with the press," he said. "You work with the press because it is your obligation."

When he arrived in Saudi Arabia, Captain Wildermuth, the Schwarzkopf aide, compiled a list of ground rules that journalists were required to sign in exchange for credentials. From the correspondents' standpoint, the trouble began with these words: "You MUST remain with your military escort at all times."

Captain Wildermuth said he added that provision on his own. "You needed an escort to provide a liaison with the units," he said. "That military guy speaks military. It's just smart." For that reason, he said, escorts were a standard part of press pools.

But critics say this decision fundamentally changed coverage of military operations, by transforming escorts into a permanent part of the news gathering process.

Fred S. Hoffman, a former Pentagon spokesman who helped design the pool system in the mid-1980s, said the new rule was "far more restrictive than anything we'd ever tried to do."

Captain Wildermuth said he did not directly consult General Schwarzkopf about the rules. But, he added, he was careful to make them reflect the commander's general philosophy. General Schwarzkopf declined to be interviewed for this article.

Rules at Work

Better Treatment for Local Press. Without the independent movement they had in Vietnam, reporters covering the buildup last fall said they were rarely able to talk to the troops. The escorted visits were conducted infrequently and typically lasted one night.

Public affairs officials said the presence of reporters would distract units from their war preparations.

But under the military's Hometown News Program, about 960 journalists from generally small papers and television stations near units' home bases along with a handful from larger organizations including *The New York Times*, flew to Saudi Arabia free on military aircraft. They spent up to four nights in the field with their hometown units.

Why didn't those reporters pose a problem?

"There was just a safer feeling," said Lt. Col. Michael Cox of the air force, who ran the program. "If they know that they're getting a free ride and they can't afford the $2,000 ticket, there's probably going to be a tendency to say, 'We'll do good stuff here.'"

On the one occasion the Pentagon suggested giving the major news organizations more time in the field, General Schwarzkopf vetoed the suggestion. That was in October, after planners sent to Saudi Arabia by Mr. Williams, Mr. Cheney's spokesman, recommended sending four six-member pools to the front lines and treating reporters as "de facto members of the units." The first pools were not in place until January 14, three days before the start of the air war.

While lack of access to troops brought one set of reporters' complaints, the conduct of escorts brought another. The escorts helped choose whom reporters could talk to. Some hovered over interviews and others stepped in front of cameras to interrupt ones they did not like.

Mr. Williams has described such incidents as isolated, involving inexperienced officers. "That's not the way it's supposed to work," he told a congressional committee in February.

But others argue that leaders set a restrictive tone by design. After this newspaper quoted a private criticizing President Bush, General Schwarzkopf called the enlisted man's commanding general, asking for an explanation.

Aides to General Schwarzkopf said they screened requests for interviews by researching the reporter's past articles "to be aware of what the person's interests were," as one said, adding that such research is standard peacetime procedure.

Stories about angry commanders traveled quickly, and Mr. Hoffman, the former Pentagon spokesman whom Mr. Williams consulted during the run-up to the war, said escorts understood that they risked being called to task for negative stories. "If it's not what they intended," Mr. Hoffman said "there was ample time to straighten out the situation."

Pool Coverage

Some Assumptions and the Deception. The autumn skirmishes between reporters and escorts were followed by perhaps the most important information-policy decision of the war: the order to limit battle coverage to officially sanctioned pools.

"There's a huge gaggle of reporters out there, and the press has absolutely no capacity to police itself," Mr. Cheney said in the interview. "There was no way we were ever going to put 100 percent of the reporters who wanted to go cover the war out with the troops."

But the decision to confine reporting to official pools represented a departure not only from Vietnam, but also from World War II, where reporters had generally been given wide access to combat action and to commanders, with their dispatches reviewed by military censors for security violations.

It was also a departure from the pool system conceived after the 1983 invasion of Grenada, which led to reporters' protests at being left behind. Pool members were to accompany troops into combat on a moment's notice, sharing their reports, then quickly dissolving as soon as other reporters could arrive. Then, independent, or "unilateral," coverage would follow.

But Mr. Cheney scrapped the system in Panama by delaying the pool's departure when United States forces invaded in 1989. He later said he feared security breaches; the inquiry commissioned by the Pentagon found that fear "excessive."

A group of news executives that met with Mr. Williams in the fall to discuss visas say he reassured them that any pool coverage of actual combat would be short-lived.

"It was, 'Don't worry about it, boys, we understand your concerns—we're going to have unilateral coverage,'" said George Watson, Washington bureau chief of ABC News.

But by his own account, Mr. Williams left the last of those meetings, on November 28, and briefed Mr. Cheney and General Powell on precisely the opposite approach—a plan to make pools the sole means of combat coverage, which they accepted. On December 14, Mr. Williams made that plan public.

"Obviously we didn't make it as clear as we should have," Mr.

Williams said of the news executives' angry reaction. "But fully a month before the war started, we submitted a draft to them."

After making only minor modifications, he issued a final order imposing pools on January 15, less than 46 hours before the start of the air war.

The journalists involved in the meetings have been accused by colleagues—and some have accused themselves—of failing to exercise sufficient vigilance.

But Mr. Williams says that while the journalists may have felt they were in a negotiation, he never considered them equal partners.

"This was not a decision made by a committee," he said. "They bear no responsibility for the decision."

Statement to the Press

Dick Cheney

Just a short time ago, you heard the president announce that coalition forces of Operation Desert Storm have begun a large-scale ground operation against Iraqi forces inside Kuwait. This phase of the combined air, land, and sea campaign has been carefully planned to force Iraq out of Kuwait, with a minimum number of casualties to allied forces.

Up to now, we've been as forthcoming as possible about military operations. But from this point forward, we must limit what we say. We've now undertaken a major military operation. Allied military units are on the move. Their positions, movements, and plans must be carefully safeguarded. We must assume that the enemy is confused about what is happening on the battlefield, and it is absolutely essential that we not do anything inadvertently ourselves to clarify the picture for him.

Everything we say about the operation from this point forward, every detail we offer, would increase the likelihood that the military forces of Iraq could learn more about our operations.

Such information would put military operations at risk, and even the most innocent sounding information could be used directly against the men and women whose lives are on the line carrying out these operations.

We cannot permit the Iraqi forces to know anything about what we're doing. For that reason, I will not say anything tonight about the operation that is currently underway. We will have nothing to say about it for many more hours. When it is safe to begin discussing the operation we will do so in as much detail as we prudently can.

But for now, our regular briefing schedule here at the Pentagon and in Riyadh [Saudi Arabia] is suspended until further notice.

I want to assure all of you that we understand our solemn obligation to the American people to keep them informed of developments. But I am confident that they understand that this policy is necessary to save lives and to reduce American casualties, as well as those of coalition forces.

I will be happy to take a few questions about the background to the decision that's been made. But let me reemphasize once again: I will not answer any questions about the military operation underway, and at the end of my remarks, we will then, as I indicated previously, suspend all further briefings for the time being.

When did the president make the decision to go ahead with the ground war, and to give [Gen. H. Norman] Schwarzkopf [commander of the coalition forces] the authority?

The final decision, of course, to go forward wasn't really resolved until it was clear today that the deadline had come and gone, and [Iraqi President] Saddam Hussein had refused to comply with the UN resolutions. But this has obviously been a massive undertaking, with hundreds of thousands of people involved, enormous logistical planning, a great deal of preparation required to undertake this kind of operation. So, for some period of time now, we've had a planning date, and a planning hour that was selected by General Schwarzkopf— based upon when he believed his forces would be ready, based upon when he felt we would have accomplished all we could with the air phase of the campaign by itself, based upon preparations of coalition forces, and that became a planning date.

It was subject to change, up to the last minute, based upon such considerations as weather and the changes in the diplomatic situation. If Saddam Hussein had come into compliance with the deadline, had announced by noon today that he was prepared to withdraw unconditionally his forces from Kuwait, then we would have stopped preparations for and execution of the operation. So, in that sense, up until noon today, the president had the option to say, stop.

He had approved the original date, again, based upon the planning decisions that I indicated.

28

You're saying, was the original date today?

That's correct, to the extent that we, to the extent that we had a specific planning date in mind for some period of time now, it was this particular day and a partcular hour.

How long had you been planning—

But because there are different, different units involved going at different times, I don't want to be any more precise than I've already been.

You mentioned that this was a large-scale ground operation against Iraqi forces inside Kuwait. By that, did you mean to say that the ground operation will take place only inside Kuwait?

I simply am not going to talk about the operation. I am not in a position to be able to say anything about the operation without compromising the security of the operation, and I simply am going to refuse to accept all such questions.

Do you know yet to the extent that the Iraqi forces are resisting?

I do not have any detailed reporting at this point on the operation. It's still very early, the early stages of the operation, and I would not expect that we will receive any comprehensive reporting here in the Pentagon for some period of time.

You had repeatedly said that the ground operation would not begin until you were confident that the air campaign had gotten to a point where much of the risk had been eliminated for the ground troops. Can you share with us what the progress the last 38 days has been, and why you are now confident that there is a minimal risk, or however you want to characterize it for our ground troops?

I would not say that there is minimal risk. This is a major military operation against a well-equipped, well-fortified opponent. I would not want to underestimate the difficulties of the task at all. What we

29

have said repeatedly was that we wanted to conduct an air campaign for as long as possible, to destroy as much as possible of the Iraqi force, and to make it easier for us to undertake the ground phase of the operation when that became possible. We obviously have reached that point, where we think it's appropriate to kick in the next phase of the campaign.

The president said he has consulted with all the allied coalition members. Can you give us a rough percentage of how many coalition members actually have committed ground forces and are actually on the move?
I don't want to do that tonight. That, again, gets us into the business of talking about specific forces, specific units, and what they might be doing in connection with the operation. A significant number of our allies are, in fact, participating in this phase of the campaign.

Can you tell us about the process of consulting with them, or at least informing them before we went ahead with the ground mission? Can you give us a little bit of the sense of the reaction when you told them we're going in?
There's really been work at two levels. There's been work at the military level, between General Schwarzkopf and the other commanders in the field, in terms of planning the details of the operation and preparing the forces to carry them out. There has also been extensive consultation by the president and Secretary of State James A. Baker [III] with the political leadership of those nations involved.

The goal of this operation was to free Kuwait, and the Soviets up to the last moment had an agreement by the Iraqis to pull out of Kuwait. What was the sense of urgency to move now, to extract Saddam Hussein from Kuwait, in light of that agreement?
It's been stated repeatedly, but I'll state it again, that the only acceptable solution to this conflict is for complete compliance by the Iraqis with the UN Security Council resolutions. That includes the

immediate, unconditional withdrawal of their forces from Kuwait. As made clear by the president yesterday, we wanted an indication from them that they would begin that withdrawal by noon today, and we gave them seven days in which to complete it.

They refused to do that. It included, as well, consideration for the fact that the offer you talk about, the proposition that the Soviets and the Iraqis developed, involved a cease-fire prior to any Iraqi withdrawal. We made it clear repeatedly we were not interested in any cease-fires, that a cease-fire would simply have allowed Saddam Hussein to regroup his forces, resupply them, and could conceivably have cost even more casualties.

It's also true that that propostition embodied within it the repeal of all the other UN sanctions and resolutions that had been voted by the Security Council. We felt that was totally unacceptable. We've seen just in the last 72 hours what would appear to be a deliberate effort on the part of the Iraqis to further destroy what's left of Kuwait, to put the torch to the oil fields. There were reports of executions of Kuwaiti citizens inside Kuwait City. And under the circumstances the notion that Saddam Hussein should be permitted to get away scot-free, without being held accountable for his actions, or without having to pay reparations, for example, was unacceptable from the standpoint of the coalition.

The president's statement yesterday was very clear. It was very concise in terms of what we wanted from Saddam Hussein by way of compliance with these resolutions. It was agreed upon by the coalition. It was consistent with the UN Security Council resolutions. He would have been wise to accept it. He refused to do so.

Again, can you put yourself in the position of disavowing any effort to change the governance, the leadership, the political structure of Iraq by means of fully enforcing the UN resolutions? Suppose you knock him out of Kuwait and he says I'm still not going to pay reparations? Do you then go on to Baghdad to set up a government that will pay the reparations?

31

We've made it clear repeatedly that if Saddam Hussein were to be replaced by another government, we would not shed a tear over his demise. But we've also made it clear that it is not an objective of U.S. policy to change the government of Iraq. If that happens, so be it. With respect to the future application of the sanctions that have already been voted by the UN Security Council, how they would be applied or altered, with respect to this government of Iraq, or some future government of Iraq, is really a matter that the UN Security Council will have to address in due course once they're driven out of Kuwait.

I'll do one more, one more question.

Have you had any sort of communication whatsoever today from Saddam Hussein in any form?

None that I'm aware of.

Again, let me, by way of closing, emphasize what I mentioned at the outset, that we recognize we have an obligation to provide as much information as we possibly can to the press and to the American people, but we are currently engaged in an extremely complex military undertaking. The lives of literally thousands of Americans and allied personnel are at stake, and we simply have to operate on the basis that we are going to, for the time being, put a lid on further briefings about the operation.

As soon as it's possible to do so, General Schwarzkopf in Riyadh, General [Colin L.] Powell here at the Pentagon will be happy to provide as much detail as possible about the campaign itself. But that's going to have to await developments.

Thank you very much.

Statement Before the U.S. Senate Committee on Governmental Affairs

Pete Williams

Some of the most enduring news reports during World War II came from Edward R. Murrow, who stood on a London rooftop and reported the German bombing raids. Fifty years later, Americans watched reporters on the rooftops of hotels in Riyadh and Dhahran—and their colleagues with gas masks on in Tel Aviv—describing incoming Scud missile attacks from Iraq.

It was the writer Henry Tomlinson who said, "The war the generals always get ready for is the previous one." The same might be said of journalists: the coverage arrangements for military operations in the Persian Gulf are frequently compared to what's remembered from Vietnam, Korea, or World War II.

But Edward R. Murrow's proposal to talk without a script so concerned the military that he had to record a series of trial runs on phonograph discs. He submitted them for approval, but they were lost. So he had to record six more before he persuaded the authorities that he could speak off the cuff without violating the censorship rules. Today, Arthur Kent, Sam Donaldson, Eric Engberg, and Charles Jaco can describe what they see—and show it on television—with no military censorship of any kind. And there are two other notable differences: they are live, and, at least in the case of CNN, their reports can been seen by the commanders of enemy forces just as easily as they can be seen by American viewers at home in their living rooms.

Operation Desert Storm isn't taking place in the jungles of Vietnam, or the hills of Korea, or across the continents and oceans of World War II. The campaign on the Arabian Peninsula has been designed to get a specific and unique job done. The press arrangements are also suited to the peculiar conditions there. But our goal is

33

the same as those of our predecessors—to get as much information as possible to the American people about their military without jeopardizing the lives of the troops or the success of the operation.

Origin of the Persian Gulf Press Arrangements

Saddam Hussein stunned the world when his troops rolled across the northern border of Kuwait last August 2. Within five hours, his army had taken Kuwait City. And from that day forward, the number of Iraqi troops in occupied Kuwait continued to grow and to move south, stopping only at Kuwait's southern border with Saudi Arabia.

That weekend, August 5, President Bush sent Secretary Cheney to Saudi Arabia for discussions with King Fahd on how best to defend Saudi Arabia and the stability of the Persian Gulf. As history now knows, the first U.S. forces began to arrive a few days after their meeting, joining U.S. Navy ships already in the region. On Wednesday, as the first U.S. Air Force F-15s landed on sovereign Saudi territory, there were no Western reporters in the kingdom. We urged the Saudi government to begin granting visas to U.S. news organizations, so that reporters could cover the arrival of the U.S. military.

On Friday of that week, Secretary Cheney again called Prince Bandar, the Saudi Ambassador to the United States, to inquire about the progress for issuing visas. Prince Bandar said the Saudis were studying the question but agreed in the meantime to accept a pool of U.S. reporters if the U.S. military could get them in. So we activated the DoD National Media Pool, a structure that had been in use since 1983.

The National Media Pool

The pool was set up after the 1983 U.S. military operation in Grenada. While Grenada was a military success, it was a journalistic disaster because reporters were kept off the island until the fighting was over. So a retired army major general, Winant Sidle, from whom this committee will hear later today, was asked to head up a panel of military officers and journalists to work out a plan for news coverage of future military operations. The result of their work was the Department of Defense National Media Pool, a rotating list of correspondents, photographers, and technicians who could be called up on short notice to cover the early stages of military missions.

It was this pool that covered the U.S. Navy's escort of oil tankers in the Persian Gulf in 1987. Its first big test in ground combat came in December of 1989, during Operation Just Cause in Panama. Just Cause was a mixed success for the pool. It arrived within four hours of when the shooting started, but it took too long to get reporters to the scene of the action. I think we learned some important lessons from what happened in Panama, and we've applied them to what's going on in the gulf.

The true purpose of the National Media Pool is to enable reporters to cover the earliest possible action of a U.S. military operation in a remote area where there is no other presence of the American press, while still protecting the element of surprise—an essential part of what military people call operational security. Of course, Operation Desert Shield was no secret. The president made a public announcement that he was ordering U.S. forces to the gulf. But because there were no Western reporters in Saudi Arabia, we flew in the DoD media pool.

First Reporters Came on the DoD Pool

We moved quickly, once we received permission from the Saudi government on Friday, August 10. We notified the news organizations in the pool rotation that Friday night. They brought in their passports Saturday morning, and I took them to the Saudi embassy myself that afternoon, where the appropriate staff had been brought in to issue the necessary visas. One reporter had run out of pages in his passport, so we carried it across town so that the State Department could add some more.

The pool left Andrews Air Force base early Sunday morning, August 12, stopping off to see the U.S. Central Command operation in Tampa, Florida. The reporters interviewed General Schwarzkopf, who had not yet moved his headquarters to Riyadh. So the press pool got to Saudi Arabia before the commander of the operation had even set up shop there. The reporters arrived Monday afternoon, August 13, and continued to act as a pool until August 26. After the pool began filing its reports, the Saudis started to issue visas to other reporters. But the news organizations in the Pentagon pool asked that we keep it going until the visa picture cleared up.

Jay Peterzell was *Time* magazine's representative on the pool. Afterward, he wrote this: "The Pentagon people worked hard to keep the press in the country." And he offered this assessment:

> The pool did give U.S. journalists a way of getting into Saudi Arabia and seeing at least part of what was going on at a time when there was no other way of doing either of those things. Also, in the first two weeks after the wave of TV, newspaper, and magazine correspondents flooded into the country, they did not produce any story that was essentially different from what we in the pool had filed.

Starting with those initial 17—representing AP, UPI, Reuters, CNN, National Public Radio, *Time*, Scripps-Howard, the *Los Angeles Times*, and the *Milwaukee Journal*—the number of reporters, editors, photographers, producers, and technicians grew to nearly 800 by December. Except during the first two weeks of the pool, those reporters all filed their stories independently, directly to their own news organizations. They visited ships at sea, air bases, marines up north, and soldiers training in the desert. They went aboard AWACS radar warning planes. They quoted generals who said their forces were ready and privates who said they were not. They wrote about helicopter pilots crashing into the sand because they couldn't judge distances in the flat desert light. And reporters described the remarkable speed with which the U.S. military moved so many men and women to the gulf with so much of their equipment.

Planning for Combat Coverage

The mission given U.S. forces in Operation Desert Shield was to deter further aggression from Iraq and to defend Saudi Arabia if deterrence failed. After the president in mid-November announced a further buildup in U.S. forces, to give the coalition a true offensive option, my office began working on a plan that would allow reporters to cover combat while maintaining the operational security necessary to assure tactical surprise and save American lives.

One of the first concerns of news organizations in the Pentagon press corps was that they did not have enough staff in the Persian Gulf to cover hostilities. Since they did not know how the Saudi government would respond to their request for more visas, and since they couldn't predict what restrictions might be imposed on commercial air traffic in the event of a war, they asked us whether we'd be willing to use a military plane to take in a group of reporters to act as journalistic reinforcements. We agreed to do so.

A U.S. Air Force C-141 cargo plane left Andrews Air Force base on January 17, the morning after the bombing began, with 127 news media personnel on board. That plane left at the onset of hostilities, during the most intensive airlift since the Berlin blockade. The fact that senior military commanders dedicated one of their cargo airplanes to the job of transporting another 127 journalists to Saudi Arabia demonstrated the military's commitment to take reporters to the scene of the action so they could get the story out to the American people.

The plan for combat coverage was not drawn up in a vacuum. We worked closely with the military and with the news media to develop a plan that would meet the needs of both. We had several meetings at the Pentagon with the bureau chiefs of the Pentagon press corps. We talked with the reporters who cover the military regularly. And we

37

consulted with some of the people you'll hear from later today — General Sidle and Mr. Hoffman — and several of my predessors in the public affairs office at the Pentagon. Because an important part of our planning was working with the news media, our drafts and proposals frequently became public. We did our planning in Macy's window, which meant that our false starts and stumbles were in full view.

Safeguarding Military Security

The main concern of the military is that information not be published that would jeopardize a military operation or endanger the lives of the troops who must carry it out. The preamble to the rules for reporters covering World War II summarized the issue by saying that editors, in wondering what can be published, should ask themselves, "Is this information I would like to have if I were the enemy?"

In formulating the ground rules and guidelines for covering Operation Desert Storm, we looked at the rules developed in 1942 for World War II, at those handed down by General Eisenhower's chief of staff for the reporters who covered the D-Day landings, and at the ground rules established by General MacArthur for covering the Korean War. We carefully studied the rules drawn up for covering the war in Vietnam.

The rules are not intended to prevent journalists from reporting on incidents that might embarrass the military or to make military operations look sanitized. Instead, they are intended to prevent publication of details that could jeopardize a military operation or endanger the lives of U.S. troops.

Some of the things that must not be reported are:

- details of future operations;
- specific information about troop strengths or locations;
- details of troop movements or tactics while a specific operation is underway;

- specific information on missing or downed airplanes or ships while search and rescue operations are underway; and,
- information on operational weaknesses that could be used against U.S. forces.

American reporters understand the reasoning behind these ground rules. They are patriotic citizens, and they don't want anything they write to endanger lives. The ground rules are the least controversial aspect of the coverage plan for the war in the Persian Gulf. Mr. Chairman, I'd like to ask that a copy of the ground rules and the guidelines be inserted at this point in the record.

The Ground Rule Appeal Process

The reporters covering World War II wrote their stories and submitted them to a military censor. The censors cut out anything they felt broke their rules and sent the stories on. The decisions of the censors were final. There is no such system of censorship in Operation Desert Storm. There is, instead, a procedure that allows us to appeal to news organizations — before the harm is done — when we think material in their stories would violate the ground rules. And the final decisions belong to journalists.

Stories written by reporters who are out with troops in the field are reviewed by military public affairs officers to ensure troop safety and operational security, then sent on to the press center in Dhahran, Saudi Arabia, for release. If, after talking things over with the reporter, the field public affairs officer believes information in a story violates the ground rules, public affairs officers at the press center review it before release. If they, too, believe the story would break the ground rules, they appeal it to us at the Pentagon for our opinion.

If we, too, think there's a problem, we call bureau chiefs or editors stateside and discuss the story with them. We understand that news must move quickly, and we act as fast as we can. Our appeal process is intended only to allow us to discuss potential ground rule violations

39

with editors and bureau chiefs and to remind them of the need to protect sensitive information. But unlike a system of censorship, the system now in place leaves the final decision to publish or broadcast in the hands of journalists, not the military.

Since Operation Desert Storm began on January 16, over 820 print pool reports have been written. Of those, only five have been submitted for our review in Washington. We quickly cleared four of them. The fifth appeal came to us over the weekend, involving a story that dealt in considerable detail with the methods of intelligence operations in the field. We called the reporter's editor-in-chief, and he agreed that the story should be changed to protect sensitive intelligence procedures. This aspect of the coverage plan is also working well.

Only the pool stories, from reporters in the field, are subject to this review, not live television and radio reports or the thousands of other stories written in Dhahran and Riyadh, based on pool reports, original reporting, and the military briefings.

Getting Access to the Troops

As the number of troops in the desert grew, so did the number of reporters to cover them. The U.S. and international press corps went from zero on August 2, to 17 on the first pool, rising to 800 by December. Most of those reporters, the good ones anyway, want to be out where the action is, just as they've done in previous conflicts. But with hundreds of fiercely independent reporters seeking to join up with combat units, we concluded that when the combat started, we'd have to rely on pools.

Before the air phase of the operation began a month ago, news organizations were afraid that we wouldn't get the job done. They reminded us of their experience in Panama. But as viewers, readers, and listeners know, we had the pools in place before the operation started. Reporters were on an aircraft carrier in the Red Sea to witness the launching of air strikes, onboard a battleship in the Persian Gulf that fired the first cruise missiles ever used in combat, on the air force bases where the fighter planes and bombers were taking off around the clock, and with several ground units in the desert.

Carl Rochelle of CNN was asked on the air if he felt he had been allowed access to everything he wanted onboard the ships, and he said, "I must tell you I am more satisfied with the pool shoot I just came off than any of the others I've been on." Four days into the air campaign, Molly Moore of *The Washington Post* said, "It's gone a lot smoother than any of us thought."

Those first days were not without problems. We know of cases where stories were approved in the field only to be delayed for over a day on their trip back to the press center in Dhahran. The first stories written about the Stealth fighters were, for some reason, sent all the way back to the F-117's home base in Nevada to be cleared. I'm sure some of the reporters you'll hear from later today will have examples of their own.

The biggest complaint from journalists right now is that more of them want to get out into the field. They are worried about how much access they'll have to the army and the marines in the event the President decides to proceed with the next phase of the campaign, intensifying action on the ground. And here's where the contrasts with World War II and Vietnam are especially strong.

Access to the Ground Troops

Unlike World War II, this will not be an operation in which reporters can ride around in jeeps going from one part of the front to another, or like Vietnam where reporters could hop a helicopter to specific points of action. If a ground war begins on the Arabian Peninsula, the battlefield will be chaotic and the action will be violent. This will be modern, intense warfare.

Reporters at the front will have to be in armored vehicles or on helicopters. They'll have to carry their own gas masks and chemical protective suits along with all their other gear. Those with frontline troops will be part of a highly mobile operation. It will be deadly serious business, and our frontline units simply will not have the capacity to accommodate large numbers of reporters.

To cover the conflict, reporters will have to be part of a unit, able to move with it. Each commander has an assigned number of vehicles with only so many seats. While he can take care of the reporters he knows are coming, he cannot keep absorbing those who arrive on their own, unexpectedly, in their own rented four wheel drives. The pool system allows us to tell the divisional commanders how many reporters they'll be responsible for. And the reporters in these pools are allowed to stay with the military units they're covering, learning as much as they can about the unit's plans and tactics.

Our latest count shows that over 1,400 reporters, editors, producers, photographers, and technicians are now registered with the joint information bureaus in Dhahran and Riyadh, representing the U.S. and the international press. Not all of them want to go to the front. But more want to go than we can possibly accommodate. That's why we've had to rely on pools of reporters — rotating groups whose stories and pictures are available to all.

Of course, the ground war hasn't started yet. U.S. military units are repositioning, some of them moving nearly every day. And if the ground war does start, it won't be like Vietnam, with minor skirmishes here and there and a major offensive every now and then. It will be a set-piece operation, as carefully orchestrated as possible. In this sense, it will be like D-Day. It's useful to remember that 461 reporters were signed up at the Supreme Headquarters, Allied Expeditionary Force to cover D-Day. Of that number, only 27 U.S. reporters actually went ashore with the first wave of forces.

So the situation on the ground in the Arabian Peninsula is a little like the picture before D-Day, with reporters waiting for the action to start. Even so, when Desert Storm began, 43 reporters were already out with ground units, and the number has been growing. By the end of this week, 100 reporters will be with army units, 33 with the marines on land, and 18 more will be out with the marines on amphibious ships.

That's in addition to the 19 covering the navy on ships at sea, the 14 who have been roving around to air bases, covering the air force part of the campaign, and 8 more covering the medical part of the story. So that's a total of 192 reporters who will be out with combat forces by the end of the week.

Pools Are a Compromise

The news business is an intensely competitive one. Journalists are accustomed to working on their own. The best are especially independent. In the setup imposed now in the Persian Gulf, each correspondent files a story that becomes available to everyone else. Pools rub reporters the wrong way, but there is simply no way for us to open up a rapidly moving front to reporters who roam the battlefield. We believe the pool system does three things: it gets reporters out to see the action, it guarantees that Americans at home get reports from the scene of the action, and it allows the military to accommodate a reasonable number of journalists without overwhelming the units that are fighting the enemy.

The system we have now in Operation Desert Storm — with two briefings a day in Riyadh and one in the Pentagon, pools of reporters out with the troops, a set of clear ground rules, and a procedure of ground rule appeal — is intended to permit the most open possible coverage of a new kind of warfare. When it's all over, we very much want to sit down with representatives of the military and the news media to see how well it worked and how it might be improved.

I cannot deny that there have been problems. I know reporters are frustrated that they can't all get out to see the troops. But I believe the system we have now is fair, that it gets a reasonable number of journalists out to see the action, and that the American people will get the accounting they deserve of what their husbands and wives, and sons and daughters, are doing under arms half a world away.

When reporters arrived at General Eisenhower's headquarters in 1944, they were handed a book called *Regulations for War Corre-*

spondents. In the foreword, he spelled out in three sentences the logic for the kind of system I've described to you today. Here's what he said to those journalists: "The first essential in military operations is that no information of value should be given to the enemy. The first essential in newspaper work and broadcasting is wide-open publicity. It is your job and mine to try to reconcile these sometimes diverse considerations."

What Is There to Hide?

Walter Cronkite

With an arrogance foreign to the democratic system, the U.S. military in Saudi Arabia is trampling on the American people's right to know. It is doing a disservice not only to the home front but also to history and its own best interests. Recent polls indicate the public sides with the military in its so far successful effort to control the press. This can only be because the press has failed to make clear the public's stake in the matter.

It is drummed into us, and we take pride in the fact, that these are "our boys (and girls)," "our troops," "our forces" in the gulf. They are, indeed, and it is our war. Our elected representatives in Congress gave our elected president permission to wage it. We had better darned well know what they are doing in our name.

After World War II most Germans protested that they did not know what went on in the heinous Nazi concentration camps. It is just possible that they did not. But this claim of ignorance did not absolve them from blame: they had complacently permitted Hitler to do his dirty business in the dark. They raised little objection, most even applauded, when he closed their newspapers and clamped down on free speech. Certainly our leaders are not to be compared with Hitler, but today, because of onerous, unnecessary rules, Americans are not being permitted to see and hear the full story of what their military forces are doing in an action that will reverberate long into the nation's future.

The military is acting on a generally discredited Pentagon myth that the Vietnam War was lost because of the uncensored press coverage. The military would do better to pattern its PR after its handling of the press in World War II, a war we won.

As in World War II, there should be censorship of all dispatches, film, and tape leaving the battle area. The troops' security must be protected against inadvertent disclosures about particular weaponry, disposition of forces, tactical plans, and the like. In World War II most press material was sent by courier back to division headquarters where a designated intelligence officer cleared it for transmission back to the communications facilities. Usually this officer was a civilian called to wartime duty. In most cases, he was as concerned with the public's right to know as the military's right to certain secrets. In all cases, he was open to appeal by correspondents who thought their stories were being held up for political reasons.

We often won those arguments, usually by making the case that the enemy already had the information our army wanted to censor. Once in England the censors held up my report that the Eighth Air Force had bombed Germany through a solid cloud cover. This was politically sensitive; our air staff maintained we were practicing only precision bombing on military targets. But the censors released my story when I pointed out the obvious—Germans on the ground and the Luftwaffe attacking bombers knew the clouds were there. The truth was not being withheld from Germans but Americans.

With a rational censorship system in place, the press should be free to go where it wants, when it wants, to see, hear, and photograph what it believes is in the public interest. The number of correspondents wandering freely behind the lines must be controlled, but this was handled in World War II by the simple expedient of accreditation, and as long as this is applied liberally for established reporters of major organizations, the public's rights are protected. Incidentally, war correspondents should be put in uniform. Regular military gear, without insignia and with a clearly identifiable "war correspondent" badge, worked well in World War II. Such gear, in most cases, was enough to assure transportation, food, and shelter—and to identify the holder's noncombatant status in case of capture.

The military also has the responsibility of giving all the information it possibly can to the press, and the press has every right, to the point of insolence, to demand this. The gulf briefings are ridiculously inadequate. Why should we not be told what bridges have been hit? Don't the Iraqis know? Material from the briefings should be subject to the same censorship as battlefield reports. The reporters would get a much more candid appraisal of the fighting. The TV coverage would be delayed, but of what serious consequence is that?

It would be helpful if all sides agreed that live battlefield coverage is not an issue. The promise of such coverage was nothing but science fiction, despite our early experience of seeing Baghdad, Tel Aviv, and Dhahran under attack, live in our living rooms. But it simply can't be. Imagine the Iraqi commander monitoring American troop movements via CNN!

The greatest mistake of our military so far is its attempt to control coverage by assigning a few pool reporters and photographers to be taken to locations determined by the military with supervising officers monitoring all their conversations with the troops in the field. An American citizen is entitled to ask: "What are they trying to hide?" The answer might be casualties from shelling, collapsing morale, disaffection, insurrection, incompetent officers, poorly trained troops, malfunctioning equipment, widespread illness—who knows? But the fact that we don't know, the fact that the military apparently feels there is *something* it must hide, can only lead eventually to a breakdown in home-front confidence and the very echoes from Vietnam that the Pentagon fears the most.

Censoring for Political Security

Sydney H. Schanberg

"This will not be another Vietnam." That oft-repeated pledge by President Bush is his maxim for the war in the Persian Gulf. He and his men leave no doubt as to what it means, for they quickly explain that this time our troops will not have "their hands tied behind their backs." But there's an addendum to that promise which, though clear from the administration's acts, has not been spoken: "This time, the hands of the press will be tied."

So far (as of this writing, February 12 [1991]), it would appear from polls and general reaction that a lot of Americans are not displeased by the government's handcuffing of the press. We journalists are not a very popular bunch. Some people see us as whiny and self-important, and some even see us as unpatriotic because we take it upon ourselves to challenge and question the government in difficult times like these. I can't say we haven't invited some of this disapproval through occasional lapses from professionalism. But I don't think this suggests we should hunker down timidly now and wait for our ratings to rise. We are required to be responsible, not popular.

Let's look at what the administration has done to control and manipulate press coverage of this war and why it has done it.

First, the why. This is easy. The answer is Vietnam. Many politicians and senior military men cling tenaciously to the myth that the press, through pessimistic reporting, tipped public opinion and cost us the war in Vietnam. There's no factual support for this theory, but scapegoats are useful when the historical evidence is painful. And that evidence suggests that a misguided and ill-conceived policy got America bogged down in a foreign war where the national interest was not fundamentally at stake. Eventually the public grew disheartened over the gap between the promises of success the White House kept

48

making and the actuality of failure. Our losses, human and material, were what tipped public opinion.

This time around the White House isn't taking any chances. All reporters in the American portion of the gulf war zone have to operate under a system of controls that goes far beyond anything imposed in any other modern war—unless you include Grenada and Panama, where reporters were essentially kept away from the action. Those were the dress rehearsals for the press muzzling in the gulf—test runs, so to speak, to see if either the public or major news organizations would raise much of an outcry (they didn't).

The new controls go like this. To begin with, there is a list of security guidelines laying down the categories of sensitive military information (details of future operations, specifics on troop units, etc.) that the press cannot report because it might jeopardize American or allied lives. No reporter has any objection to these restrictions. They are essentially the same ground rules the press abided by in World War II, Korea, and Vietnam.

It's what has been added to these traditional ground rules, however, that constitutes the muzzle. First, the only way a reporter can visit a frontline unit is by qualifying for the "pool" system, whereby a handful of reporters represents the entire press corps and shares the story with everybody. Only a fraction of the reporters, mostly those from the largest news organizations, can qualify for the pools. The rest are permitted to forage on their own, doing rear-echelon stories, but the rules forbid them to go to the forward areas and warn that if they make the attempt they will be "excluded"—taken into custody and shipped back. (By February 12, as this article went to press, at least two dozen journalists had been detained in this fashion. In some cases their credentials were lifted, though returned later. One reporter, Chris Hedges of *The New York Times*, was grabbed and decredentialized by the American military for conducting what it termed "unauthorized" interviews without an escort. He had been interviewing Saudi shopkeepers along a road 50 miles from the Kuwaiti border.)

It gets worse. Though the pool reporters are allowed at the front, their visits are anything but spontaneous. The pools get taken only where the military decides to take them. They are accompanied at all times by an escort officer, even when interviewing troops, which means that truth and candor on the part of the interviewees often become instant casualties. When a pool gets back from its guided visit, all stories and footage must be submitted to a "security review"—a euphemism for censorship.

Of the two controls—the pool system and the review of stories for possible security violations—it is the former that is the more odious, for this is tantamount to prior restraint. If reporters can go only where their babysitters decide to take them and can stay only a short time, they have already been subjected to the ultimate censorship. Since they've been allowed to see nothing, what possible "secrets" can they be carrying? The system has worked all too well. The press has been crippled, rendered unable to provide the public with a credible picture of what war is like in all its guises. What has been delivered to the public instead are superficial brush strokes across the sanitized surface of war. Bombs fall remotely and perfectly, and no one seems to be bleeding.

The "security review" at the end of the pool process merely applies the final, harassing, delaying, cosmeticizing touches on the information and completes the subjugation of the press corps and, by extension, the public. In a typical incident, one of the censors had a problem with the word "giddy," the use of which he decided was a breach of military security. Fred Bruni of the *Detroit Free Press* had used the word to describe some young Stealth bomber pilots who were buoyant as they returned from their first combat mission. Without consulting Bruni, the censor changed "giddy" to "proud." No reality, please, not even when it's innocuous. When Bruni noticed the change, he protested and got the censor to accept "pumped up." Then the military, giving no reason, held the story for two days before sending it to the Detroit paper.

As anyone can see, the security issue is almost entirely a red herring. With very rare exceptions, the press has never breached any of the security rules—not in World War II, not in Korea, and not in Vietnam. Barry Zorthian, who was the official spokesman for the United States Mission in Saigon from 1964 to 1968, said recently that though roughly 2,000 correspondents were accredited to cover Vietnam in those years and hundreds of thousands of stories were filed, only five or six violations of the security guidelines occurred. He recalled most of these as accidental or based on misunderstanding. To his knowledge, he said, none of them actually jeopardized any military operations or the lives of personnel.

Henry Kissinger, who has certainly shown no tolerance for press criticism, was asked on television the other day whether he could recall even one journalist breaching security in Vietnam. He replied:

"I can think of some reporting that jeopardized national security, but none in the field." The reports he referred to were leaks out of Washington.

So it's all too clear that the current restrictions have nothing to do with military security and everything to do with political security. Political security requires that the government do as complete a job as possible at blacking out stories that might lead to embarrassment or criticism of the government or to questions from ordinary Americans about the war policy. The press controls in the gulf are preemptive strikes against the possibility of such stories coming from the front.

But the control and manipulation of information has done something else, too. It has debased the press.

Consider these depressing excerpts from a powerful story from the gulf by Robert Fisk for the British paper, *The Independent*:

> Most of the journalists with the military now wear uniforms. . . . They are dependent on the troops and their officers for communications, perhaps for their lives. And there is thus the profound desire to fit in, to "work the system," a frequent absence of critical faculties.

This was painfully illustrated last week when Iraqi troops captured the abandoned Saudi border town of Khafji. Pool reporters were first kept up to 15 miles from the [fighting] and—misled by their U.S. military minders—filed stores reporting the recapture of the town. But when *The Independent* traveled to the scene to investigate, an American NBC television reporter— a member of the military pool— responded: "You asshole, you'll prevent us from working. You're not allowed here. Get out. Go back to Dhahran." He then called over an American Marine public affairs officer, who announced: "You're not allowed to talk to U.S. Marines, and they're not allowed to talk to you."

It was a disturbing moment. By traveling to Khafji, *The Independent* discovered that the Iraqis were still fighting in the town long after the prime minister had claimed outside No. 10 Downing Street that it had been liberated. For the American reporter, however, the privileges of the pool . . . were more important than the right of a journalist to do his job.

The American and British military have thus been able to set reporters up against reporters, to divide journalists on the grounds that those who try to work outside the pool will destroy the opportunities of those who are working—under military restriction— within it.

Privately, some government officials have tried to justify the restraints as a necessary counter-tactic against Saddam Hussein's strategy—i.e., his presumed belief that a prolonged war with steady casualties will erode public support of the president. But a president who is seen to be withholding information is also likely to lose public support over time. It may sound corny, but our democracy relies on openness for its strength. It's a messy system, often inefficient and clumsy, but it functions because the public is included, not kept in the dark. It's worth reminding ourselves that the most supremely efficient systems in the world are dictatorships where the press is completely controlled.

When George Bush decided he wasn't going to let the press have a front-row seat for this war, he was deciding against the public—even though at this point many Americans not only seem unaware they're being deprived of anything important to their lives but have even applauded the president's quarantining of the press. Again, the press can't sit around chewing its nails over its popularity ratings. For better or worse, with all of our fallibilities, we are the only professional, independent witnesses who have an established role in our system. And we can't abdicate that role, even if the public at some given moment in time doesn't want to hear what we have witnessed.

As I write, more than 800 journalists have been accredited by the military in Saudi Arabia, roughly 80 percent of them Americans or working for American news organizations. Only about 125 have been allowed into the pools. The rest can do other reporting but are officially banned from the front lines. The press guidelines say: "News media personnel who are not members of the official CENTCOM media pools will not be permitted into forward areas. . . . U.S. commanders will maintain extremely tight security throughout the operational areas and will exclude from the area of operation all unauthorized individuals."

When a reporter at a Pentagon briefing asked if this meant that commanders had received an "operational order to detain reporters who show up unescorted out in the battlefield and remove them to the rear" the Pentagon spokesman, Pete Williams, replied: "There is a general order right now."

Contrast this with World War II, when General Dwight Eisenhower issued a quite different order, directing all unit commanders of the Allied Expeditionary Force to give correspondents "the greatest possible latitude in the gathering of legitimate news." The order went on: "They should be allowed to talk freely with officers and enlisted personnel and to see the machinery of war in operation in order to visualize and transmit to the public the conditions under which the men from their countries are waging war against the enemy."

Eisenhower's order went out on May 11, 1944, just before D-Day. This makes the comparison with World War II even more appropriate, because President Bush and his men, in trying to erase the Vietnam image, have called upon Americans to think of the Gulf War as D-Day at Normandy. Fine, Mr. President, call this war what you like, but please remember that American journalists were allowed to hit the Normandy beaches alongside the troops. And there were no Pentagon babysitters with them.

Also unlike World War II (and Korea and Vietnam), reporters are not being assigned to units and permitted to stay with them for extended periods. They're not even being allowed to fly on bombing missions in those planes where there is room. One such plane is the eight-engine B-52 Stratofortress. It flies in formations of three, each carrying roughly 30 tons of bombs. Such bombloads inflict a tremendous pounding over a wide area and are usually directed at troop concentrations rather than buildings and installations. Military briefers in Vietnam called it carpet bombing, but the briefers in this war have bridled when reporters have used the phrase. Apparently carpet bombing has a harsh sound and must be deodorized.

In fact, there's a concerted attempt to try to edit out all reminders of Vietnam. It's hard to believe, but the Pentagon has gone so far as prohibiting the filming, or any news coverage at all, of the arrival of war dead at Dover Air Force Base, the main military mortuary. So much for the contention that the press restrictions are necessary for security reasons.

It's not that I don't understand the thinking behind the restrictions. There's hardly a government extant, ours or anyone else's, that wants people not under its control traveling to the front and witnessing a war and then telling everybody else about it—especially telling and showing the terribleness of war. Because the government fears that the terrible images might shape people's opinions.

This doesn't mean our politicians and generals are telling us a pack of lies. Not at all. They're just not telling us anything approaching a complete story. That's not their job as they perceive it. But it is the job of an independent press.

Which brings us, finally, to the issue of what the press has been doing for itself to try to reverse the new restraints. Darned little, sadly.

The break with this country's tradition of relatively open access to military operations began in Grenada in October 1983, when the Reagan White House kept the press out until the fighting was over. The major news organizations complained. To quiet us, the White House and Pentagon threw us a bone—the odious pool system. Oddly, we took it with barely a whimper. Then, on the first test of the system—the 1989 Panama invasion—pool reporters were barred from observing the military engagement all through the first and decisive day of fighting. The rest of the press corps, 500 strong, was virtually interned on a military base, even during the aftermath of the combat. As a result, we still have only the sketchiest picture of what took place and how many civilians and soldiers were killed.

And now we have our sanitized coverage of the war with Iraq. When the consequences of the press controls became obvious during the troop buildup prior to the war, a lawsuit was filed on January 10 in federal court in New York to overturn the restrictions on constitutional grounds. It was prepared by the Center for Constitutional Rights, an established civil liberties group, on behalf of 11 news organizations and 5 writers. The news organizations are for the most part small, liberal, alternative publications—*The Nation, In These Times, Mother Jones, L.A. Weekly, The Progressive, Texas Observer, The Guardian* and *The Village Voice*—plus *Harper's*, Pacifica Radio, Pacific News Service and writers E.L. Doctorow, William Styron, Michael Klare, Scott Armstrong, and myself. Agence France-Presse, the French news agency, having been excluded from the press pool, has filed a companion suit.

All the major media organizations were aware of the lawsuit before it was filed, yet as I write, not one has joined it. The suit is about prior restraint of information, a constitutional issue that normally sets the television networks and leading newspapers into instant legal motion. I truly hope they will find their voices soon.

How to explain their inaction now? It's my belief that the press is still living with its own scars from Vietnam. And Watergate. We were accused, mostly by ideologues, of being less than patriotic, of bringing down a presidency, of therefore not being on the American team. And as a professional community we grew timid, worried about offending the political establishment. And that establishment, sensing we had gone under the blankets, moved in to tame us in a big and permanent way. These new press controls are, for me, a reflection of that move.

In late January CBS asked me to appear on "America Tonight" for a program on the press controls. Pete Williams, the Pentagon spokesman, agreed to appear opposite me, which created the potential for a good debate. Then the program's producer called. He said they had to disinvite me because Williams had called back to say the Pentagon's chief counsel had ruled that no Pentagon official could appear with anyone associated with the lawsuit.

The producer explained: "Our feeling was, after much deliberation and discussion, that we felt there was greater value in getting the Pentagon spokesman on and confronting him and pressing him on the air than it was to get you on without the Pentagon. You can understand our position, can't you?"

I said yes, I understood it intellectually, but had he thought about the example, or even precedent, that CBS was setting? Here was CBS, arranging a program about press controls, and what does the network do? It agrees to accept government control over the selection of the other guest.

I asked the producer if he would open the program with an explanation to the viewers about how the participants got selected (Morley Safer was going on in my stead). The producer said he would raise the issue at the network. Then, a couple of hours later, he called to say they had canceled the whole show and were instead going to use the time slot to do a straight news program on the Gulf War.

Some of you may wonder why you haven't heard more about the lawsuit before this. It's because, shamefully, Big Media have not only ducked the lawsuit, they have, by and large, failed to report it. For example, *The New York Times*, at this writing, has mentioned it only once, in two paragraphs at the end of a long piece out of Riyadh. Coverage in the rest of the major media has been almost as sparse. I hope this doesn't means what it looks like.

That *Times* story, incidentally, said the press was chafing under the controls and that the military had been making vague promises about relaxing them. But the piece ended by saying that despite such talk, "there was no sign of change here."

How do the large news organizations explain their failure to do more than have meetings with, and send letters to, the Pentagon asking that the rules be softened—especially since the constant response is that the government isn't budging?

Floyd Abrams, a leading First Amendment lawyer who has become an unofficial legal spokesman for the establishment media, told the *New York Law Journal* that the leading news companies may have been reluctant to join the lawsuit because "there is a difficulty in prevailing in a facial challenge to the rules in the early days of the war." Does this mean they'll find their courage only if the war drags on and public opposition grows and then the media will run less risk of being called unpatriotic?

In the same *Law Journal* article, an in-house attorney at the *Times*, George Freeman, said: "We prefer to deal directly with the Pentagon during time of war rather than by what is a more protracted and adversarial way." That sentence speaks volumes about the independence of the press.

In any event, the case is before Leonard B. Sand, a federal judge with a reputation for taking his job seriously. He has already speeded the judicial process. A key date is March 7, which Judge Sand has set for arguments.

The lawsuit, boiled down, says the government's press controls are violative of the Constitution as regards freedom of the press and equal

57

protection of the law. The relief it asks for is a return to the press ground rules of Vietnam, meaning voluntary observance of security rules and freedom of movement and access. The suit is not an antiwar document. Nor do I see it as a hostile act against our political and military leaders.

I see it, instead, as a necessary instrument of leverage which seeks to persuade the government that the suppression of information, for reasons other than national security or protecting the safety of our troops, is a departure from our traditions that will in the end corrode and weaken the public trust that presidents crucially need to govern.

This is no time for the press to cover a desert war by putting its head in the sand.

Chapter Three

Clash of Cultures:
The Press
Versus
the Military

Why don't the military and the press get along?
Is the conflict caused by policy, politics, or
institutional loyalties and antagonisms? Is the
conflict between the military and the press
inevitable? Is their relationship getting worse?

Generals Versus Journalists

Gen. Michael J. Dugan, U.S. Air Force (retired)

There is a good deal of ill feeling among members of the media over how they were treated by the military during the Persian Gulf War. The feeling seems to be mutual. In an interview with David Frost, Gen. Norman Schwarzkopf charged that during the war CNN was "aiding and abetting an enemy." His complaint is reminiscent of Lt. Gen. William T. Sherman's vow that "I will never again command an army in America if we must carry along spies."

Such remarks reflect the long standing—and explainable—tensions in the relationship between the military and media. In free nations, the media shed light on the getting and spending of public treasure (and blood) and question acts of omission and commission by public officials.

The plight of the Kurds and the impact of the media in prompting government action in the U.S. and abroad demonstrates the need for a probing press. I believe Americans appreciate tension between the media and officialdom as an appropriate background in which government institutions work, indeed, work better. The issue is: How much tension? And how can it be better managed?

There are a number of specific issues that arose during the Gulf War—press pools, censorship, live coverage (for each of which "always" or "never" are equally wrong answers)—that should be addressed mutually, now, while the facts are fresh.

Press pools, similar to the recent network arrangement for weekend coverage of the White House, make sense—sometimes. But clearly the degree of control was overdone during the Gulf War. There were, however, some 1,500 news representatives accredited to General Schwarzkopf's headquarters. Now, 1,500 is not an unmanageable number, but it is a number that cries out for management.

Similarly, censorship of stories about specific, sensitive operations, locations, or equipment makes sense—sometimes. Live coverage, the converse of censorship, makes sense when the subject matter is not operationally sensitive. No one wants to watch reruns, even (perhaps especially) in war.

The sources of tension between the military and the media need to be better understood. It seems to me that four—organic, institutional, cultural, and historical—are relevant.

Organic, or fundamental, to the nature of the military and the media is information. Military and media organizations struggle with each other because each has a right and a duty to protect and proclaim certain information. Intelligence information and information on operations are unquestionably the stuff of military secrets, but they are also the makings for great stories of human endeavor, intrigue, and struggle.

Institutionally the military and the media are both "mission oriented" and in public service, yet their missions appear to be antithetical. Military organizations are agents of their governments, subject to all the external constraints that come with a political process, compounded by all the internal restraints associated with a hierarchical bureaucracy. The media organizational structure is slimmer, quicker, and flatter, with a preference for facts and views that promote, if not create, conflict.

Culturally, the military is remote from the mainstream of society, and its members live in a subculture with inherent barriers to external communications. There are different words, different use of the same words, different living conditions, expectations, self-images, and more. The differences are neither good nor bad; they simply exist and, accordingly, must be interpreted by the media to serve a mainstream audience.

Lastly, a bit of history. The story of the Vietnam War is considered to be a "bad" story by senior officers, who blame the media for loss of support at home. But it seems to me that a 10-year war on remote foreign soil, with high losses, inconsistent political leadership and no apparent progress will be a "bad" story every time in a democracy.

Operation Desert Storm, on the other hand, was a "good" story, not for what the media did, but for the facts.

Can the tension between the military and the media be eliminated? No, and there are no simple answers for improving relations. Nevertheless, it would be advantageous for both institutions to find a continuing, independent forum for discussion and for researching ways to better serve the public interest. Both the military and the media view themselves as professions. It would be a useful start if each viewed the other in the same light—and acted accordingly.

The Military Versus the Media

Maj. Gen. Herbert Sparrow, U.S. Army (retired)

In American history, the presence of war correspondents in the battlefield is as old as the nation itself. Isaiah Thomas reported the battle of Lexington in the May 3, 1775, issue of the *Massachusetts Spy*, after having fought with the militia against the British. The Mexican-American War of 1846–47 was reported by newsmen who rode on horseback into battle with Gen. Zachary Taylor. American war correspondents also reported from the battlefield in the American Civil War, the Spanish-American War, and World War I.

American correspondents played a large role in keeping the public informed of the events occurring in World War II. Edward R. Murrow gave Americans regular reports from England before the United States entered the war. Five-hundred and fifty-eight American reporters accompanied the Allied forces on the D-Day invasion of Normandy. A *New York Times* reporter flew in the air force plane that dropped the atomic bomb on Nagasaki in 1945.

Both the Korean and the Vietnam wars were covered extensively by news correspondents. The extent of coverage during the Vietnam War is demonstrated by the fact that at least 53 reporters were killed in Southeast Asia between 1961 and 1975. . . .

Press Access to Combat During World War II

In Europe. The following examples indicate the extent of press coverage in Europe during World War II:

■ *Dieppe Raid*—Six thousand Canadian infantry, British commandos, and American rangers, assisted by 252 ships, conducted a large-scale raid against German coastal fortifications at the port of Dieppe, France, on August 19, 1942. At least four American correspondents accompanied Allied forces on this raid. Since the entire operation was secret, the reporters were kept incommunicado for four days before joining the units to which they had been assigned.

■ *Invasion of North Africa*—American and British troops under the command of Gen. Dwight D. Eisenhower invaded the coast of North Africa at three points on November 8, 1942. The Allied naval force, consisting of 102 ships, landed 35,000 American troops at Casablanca in French Morocco, 23,000 British and 10,000 American troops at Algiers, and 39,000 American troops at the port of Oran in Algeria. Correspondents were with the troops at the landings on the North African coast. *Chicago Tribune* reporter John Hall Thompson jumped into combat with paratroopers near Tebessa, Algeria. Leo Disher of the United Press was aboard an assault ship in the landings at the harbor of Oran and was wounded in the battle.

■ *Bombing of Wilhelmshaven*—The first successful American bombing mission of the war in Europe occurred on February 26, 1943, when 53 bombers attacked Wilhelmshaven, Germany. Six correspondents, including Walter Cronkite, accompanied the American bomber force in this attack.

■ *Invasion of Sicily*—A large amphibious force of 1,375 ships landed 180,000 Allied troops of Gen. George Patton's Seventh Army and British Gen. Bernard Montgomery's Eighth Army on the shores of Sicily on July 10, 1943. Correspondent Jack Belden of *Time* magazine was with the troops at the first landings.

■ *Landings at Anzio*—The Allies attempted to proceed around German lines in Italy by landing a force of 50,000 British and American troops under the command of Maj. Gen. John P. Lucas at Anzio on January 11, 1944. The first wave of Allied troops landed at 2:05 a.m. Associated Press reporter Don Whitehead accompanied the second wave of troops at 2:10 a.m.

■ *Invasion of Normandy*—Under the overall command of General Eisenhower, 150,000 Allied troops, assisted by 2,700 ships and

12,000 planes, invaded Europe on D-Day, June 6, 1944. The invasion force was preceded by paratroopers and glider troops of three airborne divisions that had begun landing shortly after midnight on June 6.

The D-Day landing was well covered by American news reporters. Reporters went in with the first landing forces, and no less than 78 correspondents waded ashore with the first wave of infantry. One reporter did a radio broadcast from one of the landing barges. Some reporters observed the battle on the day of the invasion from troop-carrying planes and bombers while others actually parachuted in with U.S. paratroopers in the early morning hours.

In the Pacific. Press coverage was extensive in the Pacific theater of operations as well, as the following examples show:

■ *Guadalcanal*—Under the command of Gen. Alexander Vandergrift, 19,000 marines of the 1st Marine Division, assisted by 89 ships, invaded Guadalcanal and Tulagi islands in the Solomons on August 7, 1942. Richard Tregaskis of the Independent News Service went ashore with staff officers approximately 45 minutes after the first wave of troops landed on Guadalcanal.

■ *Tarawa*—Under the overall command of Vice Adm. Raymond A. Spruance, 18,000 marines, assisted by at least 33 ships, invaded Tarawa atoll in the Gilbert Islands chain on November 20, 1943. The landings were made under heavy fire from Japanese troops and nearly a third of the marines were hit as they waded to shore. Eight correspondents accompanied the troops. Richard W. Johnston of the Associated Press landed with the assault forces. Robert Sherrod, covering the battle for Time-Life, embarked with the fifth wave of assault troops on the morning of the attack, but found by the time his boat arrived near the beach that no organized waves of troops had landed at the beach after the first wave. Sherrod waded 700 yards to the beach with 15 marines under intense enemy fire after it was discovered that their boat could not be landed.

■ *Invasion of the Philippines*—Gen. Douglas MacArthur returned to the Philippines with an invasion force of four infantry divisions, which landed on the island of Leyte on October 20, 1944. Reporters and camera operators, including William B. Dickinson of the United Press, waded ashore with General MacArthur in the third assault wave and recorded the General's first words: "I have returned."

■ *Iwo Jima*—Under the command of Gen. Harry Schmidt, 30,000 marines invaded the island of Iwo Jima on February 19, 1945. The invasion was witnessed by nearly a hundred American, British, and Australian correspondents. The story of the battle was reported by these correspondents from ships, planes, and the island itself. Keith Wheeler of the *Chicago Times* and Robert Sherrod of Time-Life accompanied the forces landing on the first day. Sherrod found himself in the center of an enemy artillery barrage.

■ *Other Actions in the Pacific Theater*—In Burma, *Time* reporter Jack Belden accompanied Lt. Gen. Joseph Stilwell in his retreat through the jungle. Reporters were with the troops during the stand against the Japanese on Bataan in the Philippines. Stanley Johnston of the *Chicago Tribune* was aboard the aircraft carrier *Lexington* when it was attacked and sunk during the Battle of the Coral Sea. Bob Cromie, also for the *Chicago Tribune*, rode in a bomber in a raid on the Japanese base of Rabaul. *New York Times* correspondent William L. Laurence was present aboard the plane that dropped the atomic bomb on the Japanese city of Nagasaki.

World War II received the greatest press coverage of any military conflict in American history. To cover the action properly, U.S. correspondents flew on bombing missions, went on patrols, and rode destroyers and other naval vessels. Direct radio reports were given from battlefields. By the end of the war, 37 American newsmen had been killed and 112 wounded. In World War II, the United States Office of Censorship, established by President Roosevelt's executive order, did not attempt to censor or restrict the access of the U.S. press to the battlefield. The *Code of Wartime Practices for the American Press*, distributed by the Office of Censorship, concerned itself with what could be printed, *not* how that information could be gathered.

The attitude of the military toward press reporting of the war was expressed by General Eisenhower shortly before the D-Day landings in Normandy:

"I believe that the old saying—'Public opinion wins wars'—is true. Our countries fight best when our people are best informed."

"You will be allowed to report everything possible, consistent, of course, with military security."

"I will never tell you anything false."

The AP's Don Whitehead, who had survived four other beach landings under fire, was given an even more succinct send-off by the commander of an assault unit to which he had been assigned. The officer said: "We are ready to help you .... The people at home won't know what is happening unless you are given information, and I want them to know.... If you're wounded, we'll take care of you. If you're killed we'll bury you."

Access in Korea and Vietnam

The Korean War. Under the overall command of General MacArthur, 26,000 marines of the 1st and 7th Marine Divisions landed behind North Korean lines at Inchon on September 15, 1950. This landing was witnessed by 86 correspondents from five countries, including the United States. The correspondents were briefed thoroughly on the various aspects of the operation. Correspondents went in with the assault forces, including Marguerite Higgins of the *Herald Tribune*, who went in with the fifth wave.

In Korea, as in other wars, U.S. correspondents reported from the front lines. Reporters were with the first U.S. infantry that went into action. By the end of the war 10 or 11 American newsmen had been killed.

The Vietnam War. At its peak in 1967, the Vietnam War involved 540,000 American troops in the fighting. Official U.S. government policy was to provide military transportation for reporters to help them to visit combat and other areas. Correspondents accompanied troops in the field and naval units during exercises and operations. Reporters were more mobile in Vietnam than they had been in World War II and the Korean War and had access to the battlefield by helicopter transport. Television reporters did stories while fighting was going on around them. Fifty correspondents died in Vietnam. The military gave a large press corps wide access to military bases, personnel, and combat zones even during active combat. The Vietnam experience is very comparable to the present situation, where a large press corps wishes to cover overt military activity in timely fashion for television, radio, and print media.

The Military and the Media: A Troubled Embrace

Lt. Gen. Bernard E. Trainor, U.S. Marine Corps (retired)

At first they are polite, respectfully prefacing each question with "sir," but when faced with their own prejudices, the veneer of civility evaporates, hostility surfaces, and the questions give way to a feeding frenzy of accusations. No, these aren't journalists asking the questions. They are young officers and cadets, and I have experienced this phenomenon repeatedly when discussing relations between the military and the media at service academies and professional military schools. It is clear that today's officer corps carries as part of its cultural baggage a loathing for the press.

Indeed, military relations with the press—a term I apply to both print and television media—are probably worse now than at any period in the history of the Republic. I say this recognizing that Vietnam is usually cited as the nadir in military-media relations. But at least during the Vietnam War military men actually experienced what they judged to be unfair treatment at the hands of the Fourth Estate, and the issue was out in the open.

The majority of today's career officers, however, have had no such association with the press. Most of them were children during the war. In the case of those at the academies, some were probably still in diapers when Saigon fell. But all of them suffer this institutional form of post-traumatic shock syndrome. It is a legacy of the war, and it takes root soon after they enter service. Like racism, anti-Semitism, and all forms of bigotry, it is irrational but nonetheless real. The credo of the military seems to have become "duty, honor, country, and hate the media."

Although most officers no longer say the media stabbed them in the back in Vietnam, the military still smarts over the nation's humiliation in Indochina and still blames TV and the print media for loss of public

69

support for the war. Today the hostility manifests itself in complaints that the press will not keep a secret and that it endangers lives by revealing details of sensitive operations. The myth of the media as an unpatriotic, left-wing, antimilitary establishment is thus perpetuated.

Having spent most of my adult life in the military and very little of it as a journalist, I am more qualified to comment on military culture than that of the media. I must admit that in the post-Vietnam years I too was biased against the press. But having had feet in both camps gives me a unique perspective which I now try to share with each, particularly the military.

Did the press stab the military in the back during Vietnam? Hardly. The press initially supported the war, but as casualties mounted and the Johnson administration failed to develop a coherent strategy to bring the war to a satisfactory conclusion, the press became critical. Whether the press influenced public opinion or simply reflected it will be argued for years to come. But it was a misguided policy that was primarily at fault for the debacle, not the media.

The media was, however, guilty of instances of unfair and sensational reporting which veterans of that war still resent. This was particularly true in the latter stages, when the nation was weary of nightly war news and when cub newspaper and television journalists tried to make headlines out of thin gruel. More responsible supervision should have been exercised by editors, but it was not, and many in the military, already frustrated by the war, felt the press as a whole was deliberately trying to humiliate them.

The legacy of the war sharpened the tension which exists between the media and the military, but it is not its cause. The roots of tension are in the nature of the institutions. The military is hierarchical with great inner pride and loyalties. It is the antithesis of a democracy—and must be so if it is to be effective. It is action-oriented and impatient with outside interference. Many things it legitimately does make little sense to civilians who have scant knowledge of military matters. The military wants only to be left alone to carry out its assigned mission.

To the contrary, a free press—one of the great virtues and elemental

70

constituents of a democracy—is an institution wherein concentration of power is viewed as a danger. The press is a watchdog over institutions of power, be they military, political, economic, or social. Its job is to inform the people about the doings of their institutions. By its very nature, the press is skeptical and intrusive. As a result there will always be a divergence of interests between the media and the military. That they are both essential to the well-being of our nation is beyond question, but the problem of minimizing the natural friction between the two is a daunting one.

The volunteer force in a subtle way has contributed to this friction. At the height of the cold war and throughout the Vietnam War, the military was at the forefront of American consciousness. Scarcely a family did not have a son or loved one liable to the draft. The shadow of national service cast itself over the family dinner table and generated in virtually all Americans a real and personal interest in the armed forces. This interest was heightened by the experiences and memories of fathers and older brothers who had fought in World War II and Korea and who maintained a lively interest in soldiering. With the end of the draft and the advent of a volunteer army this awareness disappeared, along with the pertinence of the older generation of warriors. Only the families of those who volunteered for the service kept touch with the modern army.

The military, which for so long had been bound to civil society, drifted away from it. Military bases were few and far between and located in remote areas unseen by much of urban and suburban America. A large percentage of volunteer servicemen married early and settled down to a life where their base and service friends were the focal points of their lives. No longer did uniformed soldiers rush home on three-day passes whenever they could get them. When servicemen did go home, they did so wearing civilian clothes and, given the somewhat more tolerant attitude of the military toward eccentricity in dress and hair style, they were no longer as sharply marked by short haircuts and shiny shoes. Off post they were nearly indistinguishable in appearance from their civilian cohort.

71

To the average civilian, the term military soon came to be equated with the Pentagon, with fearsome intercontinental missiles, and with $600 toilet seats and other manifestations of waste, fraud, and abuse. The flesh and blood association the civilian formerly had with the armed forces atrophied, and he came to regard the military as just another bureaucracy. For its part, the military settled into the relative isolation of self-contained ghettos and lost touch with a changing America. It focused on warlike things and implicitly rejected the amorality of the outside world it was sworn to defend. In an age of selfishness, the professional soldier took pride in his image of his own selflessness. A sense of moral elitism emerged within the armed forces which is apparent today to any civilian who deals with those institutions. The all-volunteer force not only created a highly competent military force, it also created a version of Cromwell's Ironside Army, contemptuous of those with less noble visions. It is no wonder that those who chose the profession of arms looked with suspicion upon those members of the press who pried into their sacred rituals.

Oddly enough I have found striking similarities between my colleagues in both camps. Both are idealistic, bright, totally dedicated to their professions, and technically proficient. They work long hours willingly under arduous conditions, crave recognition, and feel they are underpaid. The strain on family life is equally severe in both professions. But there are notable differences as well. A journalist tends to be creative, while a soldier is more content with traditional approaches. Reporters are independent, while military men are team players. And of course one tends to be liberal and skeptical, the other conservative and accepting.

There is another big difference which bears directly on their interrelationship. The military is hostile toward the journalist, while the journalist is indifferent toward the military. To the journalist, the military is just another huge bureaucracy to report on, no different from Exxon or Congress. But whereas businessmen and politicians try to enlist journalists for their own purposes, the military man tries to avoid them, and when he cannot, he faces the prospect defensively with a mixture of fear, dread, and contempt.

Most of my military brothers in arms would be surprised to know that when asked for an opinion about the military profession, young journalists having no prior association with the military rate career officers highly. They view officers as bright, well-educated, dedicated, and competent, although they wonder why anyone would make the service a career. Their prejudgment of enlisted personnel is far less flattering. Most journalists—mistakenly, of course—have the image of an enlisted man as a disadvantaged, not-too-bright high-school dropout who comes from a broken home and cannot fit into society.

Ask a journalist for his opinion of servicemen after his first reporting assignment on the military, and the view will be radically different. The journalist will lavishly praise the enlisted personnel he met and relate how enthusiastic they were. He will remark how well they knew their jobs. He'll note how proud they were of what they were doing, and how eager they were to explain their duties. Genuine admiration and enthusiasm come through in the reporter's retelling of his encounters. But what of the officers? "The officers?... Oh, they're a bunch of horses' asses."

To understand such a critical assessment of officers, one only has to take a hypothetical, though typical, walk in a journalist's shoes as he goes for his first interview with a senior officer. In this interview, it happens to be a general:

After a seemingly endless round of telephone calls to set up the interview, you arrive—a well-disposed journalist, notebook and tape recorder in hand—at headquarters. You are met by a smiling public affairs officer who signs you in and gets you a pass. You then are led through a series of offices under the baleful stare of staff factotums, while your escort vouches for the legitimacy of your alien presence. At last you arrive at a well-appointed anteroom where everyone speaks in hushed, reverent tones.

After a wait, the door to a better-appointed office opens, and you are ushered in with the announcement, "THE GENERAL will see you now." Not knowing whether to prostrate yourself or simply to genuflect, you enter the sanctum sanctorum vaguely aware of others entering with you, but grateful for their presence. Graciously received by the General, you are invited to sit down THERE, while the General resumes his place behind his imposing desk backed by colorful flags and martial memorabilia. In addition to the General and the public affairs officer, there are several other officers of varied ranks present to whom you are not introduced. All of them take seats at the nod of the General, one of whom places himself facing the General but slightly to your rear, at the outer edge of your peripheral vision.

Following introductory pleasantries, the interview gets underway. You set your tape recorder on the coffee table and open your notebook. This triggers a duplicate reaction on the part of those around you, and an elaborate choreography begins. Your tape recorder is immediately trumped by at least two others, and the General's entourage poises with pencils and yellow legal pads to take note of the proceedings. Throughout the interview, marked by elliptical responses to your questions, you are aware of knowing looks, nods, and shrugs being exchanged around the room. More disconcerting is the series of hand and arm signals being given to the General by the officer sitting to the rear, in the manner of an operatic prompter. You are given your allotted time down to the second, at which time you are escorted out of the office as the General returns to important matters of state.

After turning in your badge and being bidden a good day, you are back out on the street wondering what it was all about. Why all the lackeys? Were they hiding something? Why the signals? Didn't the General know enough about the subject to discuss it without a prompter? Puzzled, you walk away wondering whether your host was a charlatan or a fool.

Obviously the little scenario above is an exaggeration, but those who have been through the process know that it is just barely so.

The attitude of the military is bound to affect that of the press and vice versa. If it is one of mutual suspicion and antagonism, the relationship will never improve, and in the end the American public will be the loser.

There is nothing more refreshing than an open relationship. Senior officers know their business and can talk about it sensibly without a bunch of flacks around. Journalists know that some topics are off-limits in any meeting with the press, and they respect the obligation of a military officer not to disclose information he should not. It is a poor journalist indeed who tries to trap an officer into a disclosure that is legitimately classified. The counter-battery of tape recorders and legions of witnesses are of course intended as protective devices in case a journalist does a hatchet job on the person he is interviewing. This is useless protection, however, because if a reporter is out to paint a deliberately unfair picture of a person or institution, he will do it regardless of recorded safeguards of accuracy. The best protection against the unscrupulous few is not to deal with them.

Each of the services has expended great effort at improving military-media relations. Public affairs officers are trained at Fort Benjamin Harrison, and all major commands have graduates of the school to act as a bridge between the warrior and the scribe. Installations and war colleges sponsor symposia and workshops to improve relations with the media. Special tours of military installations and activities are conducted for the press by the Defense Department and the services, and some components of the Fourth Estate even reciprocate. But these efforts have little effect on military attitudes and make few military converts because most of them end up focusing on the mechanics of the interrelationship rather than its nature. Discussing how best to improve military press pool coverage in the wake of Panama, while a useful exercise, does little to minimize the underlying prejudice between the two institutions, must less eliminate it.

What is frequently overlooked by the military is that the profession of journalism is as upright as that of the military, with pride in its integrity and strict norms of conduct for its members. For example, it is absolutely forbidden at *The New York Times* to secretly tape an interview, by phone or in person, or to mislead a source as to the identity of the reporter. Most newspapers have similar restrictions. As a result there are few instances of yellow journalism today. The journalistic world knows who the unscrupulous are within its ranks and gives them short shrift. An unscrupulous journalist will never last on a reputable paper, and advertisers upon whom a newspaper depends for its existence are not inclined to place ads in papers with a reputation for unfair reporting. This is not to say that journalists will shy from using every legitimate means to dig out a story. The reputation of government agencies, including the military, for overclassifying, for withholding the truth, and for putting a spin on events is well known, and a good reporter will never take things at face value. The tendency of journalists to disbelieve half of what they are told also adds to the military's paranoia.

There is no question, of course, that some journalists go too far in reporting a story, and so do some newspapers. Journalism, besides being a profession, is also a business, and businesses must show profit. This leads to fierce competition. A scoop means sales, sales mean profits, and that is what free enterprise is all about. For a reporter it also means reputation, and if his editors were not pushing him for exclusive stories he would be pushing himself so as to enhance his reputation and maybe win a Pulitzer Prize. Thus a journalist may uncover a story relating to national security which would jeopardize that security if it were made public. This is particularly true if it is on operational matters, the favorite complaint of today's officer corps. In his eagerness to be on the front page, the journalist may disregard the security sensitivity of his story and file it to his newspaper. But that is where editors come in. They are mature people with long years in the business and good judgment on the implications of a story. In truly critical instances an editor will withhold a damaging story.

The record of the American press in this regard is good, despite unsubstantiated claims made by military officers that the press leaks operational information. Let two examples suffice to illustrate the point. Newsrooms knew beforehand of the planned airstrikes on Libya in 1986 and held the news until the raids had taken place so as not to endanger the air crews. Likewise, every Washington newsman knew that Marine Lt. Col. Richard Higgins had held a sensitive job in the office of the Secretary of Defense immediately prior to his United

Nations assignment in Lebanon, where he was kidnapped and later executed. Yet in hopes that his captors would remain ignorant of this possibly compromising information, no mention was made of it in the American press until after it appeared in a Lebanese newspaper.

Whether the press acted responsibly during the December 1989 Panama invasion, when it reported air movement of troops on the night of the operation, is the latest subject of debate. News of the airlift was on television before H-Hour, but nothing was said of a planned airborne assault. Whether anyone in the press knew for certain that an assault was about to take place is in doubt, but if it was known, nothing was disclosed publicly. The air activity was alternately reported as a buildup for military action or part of the war of nerves against the Noriega regime. Our government itself actually contributed to the "leak" with its cute reply to newsmen's questions about the unusual air movements. The government spokesman said they were routine readiness exercises unrelated to Panama, but he withdrew the "unrelated to Panama" part of this statement *prior* to the assault the following day, thus giving away the show.

On the whole the military was satisfied with press coverage of its Panama intervention. Certainly Just Cause received more favorable reporting than the Grenada operation in 1983. However, the one vehicle designed to improve military-media relations during military operations was a failure—the press pool.

The idea of a press pool came about as the result of the exclusion of journalists from the Grenada operation. At the time, the press howled that the people had the right to know what their armed forces were doing and that journalists should not be denied entry to a war zone. The press concluded that they were shut out more to cover up military incompetence than to preserve operational security. They were more convinced of it when stories of that incompetence surfaced. As a result, DoD-sponsored press pools were established to allow selected journalists from the various mediums to represent the press as a whole during future operations. The pool reporters were rotated periodically and were told to be ready on short notice to accompany military units. A list of names was held at the Pentagon for that purpose. They were not to be told beforehand where they were going or what was about to happen.

The system was tested in some peacetime readiness exercises to everybody's satisfaction. But in its first real test, during the 1987–88 operations in the Persian Gulf, reporters complained that they were isolated from the action and kept ignorant of events. Many complained that their military hosts were more interested in brainwashing them than exposing them to the news.

Panama was the second test, and again the pool concept failed. Reporters were flown to Panama but kept at Howard Air Force Base and given briefings during the high points of the operation. When they were finally taken into Panama City, it was to view events and locations of little news value. Meanwhile, journalists not in the pool were streaming into Panama on their own and providing vivid firsthand accounts of the action. Pool reporters cried foul. The military, for their part, complained that the pool journalists made unreasonable demands for transportation and communications facilities and that they were callous of the dangers involved in taking them to scenes of fighting. Nobody was or is happy with the pool arrangement.

The pool concept suffers three fatal flaws. The first is that the military is always going to want to put on its best face in hopes of influencing the reporters it is hosting. When the military is faced with the choice of taking a reporter to the scene of a confused and uncertain firefight or to the location of a success story—well, take a wild guess which the military will choose, regardless of its relative newsworthiness. Second, because the military brings pool reporters to the scene of action, it also feels responsible for transporting them around, and this may not be logistically convenient at times. Third, the military is protective and feels responsible for the safety of any civilians they are sponsoring. Keeping the press pool isolated at an air base in Panama was a genuine reflection of military concern for the reporters' safety. It is only during long campaigns like Vietnam that the protective cloak wears thin, and then usually because journalists find ways of getting out from under the military's wing.

Implicit in the military attitude toward the pool is not only its institutional sense of responsibility, but also its lack of understanding of journalists. If the pool is to work better, the services must recognize that they have no obligation to the pool other than to get them to the scene of the action and brief them on the situation. Beyond that, reporters are on their own. They are creative people who can take care of themselves. Any additional assistance rendered is appreciated but not necessary; it certainly doesn't provide grounds to restrict coverage of the story. Naval operations and in some instances air operations can be an exception because no facilities may be available other than those aboard ships or in a plane. But as the Persian Gulf illustrated, journalists proved to be a resourceful lot by hiring civilian helicopters to overfly the fleet—even at the risk of being shot down.

The press, on the other hand, should be selective in whom they send to war. Pool membership should require a physically fit, versatile journalist who knows something about the military. Few reporters have previous military experience, unfortunately, and few editors can afford the luxury of a military specialist on their payrolls. But the Defense Department would be happy to provide pool members with orientations and primers on military matters. At least then a reporter could learn some military jargon and the difference between a smoke grenade and a fragmentation grenade.

Old-timers long for the days of Ernie Pyle and Drew Middleton, when the military and the press saw events as one, and there was a love bond between the two. In those days the military could do no wrong—but even if it did, a censor saw to it that the public did not find out about it. Those were the days when the nation was on a holy crusade against the evil machinations of Fascism and Nazism. In this desperate struggle, propaganda was more important than truth. Had it been otherwise, many of the World War II heroes we revere today would have been pilloried by the press as butchers and bunglers.

Today's generals have no such friendly mediation. Moral crusades are no longer the order of the day, and unquestioned allegiance to government policy died with our involvement in Vietnam. The government lied once too often to the American people and lost their confidence. Today the press does what Thomas Jefferson envisaged for it when he rated it more important than the army as a defender of democratic principles. It keeps a sharp eye on the military and on the government it serves.

This should not dismay the professional soldier. After all, parents have a right to know what the military is doing to and with their sons and their tax money. If the services act responsibly and honestly, even with mistakes, there is little to fear from the press.

This is the challenge to today's and tomorrow's military leaders. They must work to regain the respect and confidence of the media as their predecessors once had it in the dark days of a long-ago war. The press is not going to go away. Hence, the antimedia attitude that has been fostered in young officers must be exorcised if both the military and the media are to serve well the republic for which they stand.

Rusk to John Scali: Whose Side Are You On?

Bill Monroe

"Whose side are you on, anyway?" An angry secretary of state fired that question at a network correspondent during the Vietnam War.

It's a question as old as journalism, though not always put so bluntly. Wars, hot and cold, tend to bring it out. If American reporters in Baghdad can transmit only what the censors allow, aren't they then serving the purposes of Iraq? If Peter Jennings provides Saddam Hussein an interview platform, is he aiding and comforting the enemy?

In 1968 it was Secretary of State Dean Rusk who put the accusatory question to John Scali: "Whose side are you on, anyway?"

Now 81, Rusk remembered the incident in a recent phone conversation:

"It was at a Friday afternoon backgrounder with Scali and some others. He asked me what I thought was a very loaded question. My question [about whose side he was on] shocked John Scali."

Did the secretary still feel the question was appropriate for journalists today?

"I think it's a question news people should ask themselves occasionally.... There's not going to be any television network if there's not a United States of America."

Here in its nakedness was the thinking that sprang the blunt question. Rusk saw himself as the nation incarnate struggling against Communist aggression. He saw Scali as a reporter loyal only to his network.

Rusk continued in stream-of-consciousness reflections on the related perversities of journalists:

> I've experienced a lot of investigative reporting in my
> life, and I've never run across any that had a positive

81

outcome. It always had a negative outcome. There's never been any example of a writer investigating something positive like the elimination of smallpox in America.

I changed the format of "Meet the Press," by the way. The format used to begin with a statement to the effect that the reporters were not responsible for their questions—the questions were just their way of getting at the answers. I told Lawrence E. Spivak that if he started the program that way, I was going to say that I wasn't responsible for my answers. He said, "You wouldn't do that." I said, "Try me." I notice that, as the program began, they didn't use that line.

John Scali, now 72 and still at ABC, has his own memory of Dean Rusk's ire:

It was the Friday afternoon after the Tet offensive. The Viet Cong had managed bombings and violence in 101 places in South Vietnam—at a time when we were, quote, winning the war, unquote. They had even invaded the U.S. embassy grounds. General Westmoreland came up with the story it was a big, failed offensive— all an American victory. An interesting way of looking at it. The fact that the Viet Cong were able to coordinate that many offensives in that many places meant something significant.

I asked Rusk something like, "Do you think the Tet offensive was a major defeat for the Viet Cong and a victory for us?" He said, "Most certainly," and he repeated the Westmoreland line.

Then I asked him, "Mr. Secretary, weren't you at all dismayed or impressed that they could coordinate all those offensives?"

He went through the whole thing again, repeating the

line about an American victory. He noticed me shaking my head in disbelief, and he burst out with "Whose side are you on, anyway?"

I got angry. I got out of my chair. I was going to hit him in the nose. But two reporters restrained me.

A little later, after I was back at my desk, [State Department spokesman] Bob McCloskey came in and said the secretary wanted to see me. When I went into his office, Rusk said, "John, I'm sorry. It's been kind of a rough period. I want to apologize to you." I accepted his apology.

Scali had a particular right to be angry at Rusk's question. Years earlier he had sat on a major exclusive in order to help the Kennedy administration solve the Cuban missile crisis. A Soviet embassy official had used Scali to convey to the White House a feeler about a possible settlement. Scali passed it on to the State Department and, at State's request, did not put the sensational development on the air. A year and a half later, while the State Department was still denying Scali's requests to go public with it, a U.S. diplomat (Roger Hilsman) revealed it in a book. As a reward for Scali sacrificing the story of a lifetime, a U.S. official had stolen his pants.

Scali's two experiences, first in the Cuban missile crisis and then in the Vietnam War, suggest the ambiguities surrounding a reporter's loyalties. There is, however, an answer to Dean Rusk's question.

A U.S. journalist, like a secretary of state, is on the side of the United States. But not in the same way. A secretary of state reports to the president. Journalists report to the people. The system separating press and government is called democracy.

With their own independent sources of information, the people can judge the president. In fact, they can decide smack in the middle of a war that it's a mistake—and put a stop to it. And they can decide, if they wish, to stay out of a war the president seems to be heading for.

Testimony Before the U.S. Senate Committee on Governmental Affairs

Col. Harry G. Summers, Jr., U.S. Army (retired)

I am most honored to be invited to appear before this committee to testify about a most important matter, the wartime role of the news media. In my 38 years of active military service, including frontline service as an infantry squad leader with the 24th Infantry Division in Korea and as a rifle battalion operations officer with the 1st Infantry Division in the Vietnam War—both divisions, by the way, now serving in the Persian Gulf—it is a subject to which I have given much thought.

As a matter of fact, I was sent to the Army War College in 1979 by Gen. Walter Kerwin, the army vice chief of staff, to do an analysis of the Vietnam War to, among other things, put down the then-prevalent notion that the media lost the war. That study, *On Strategy*, is now used as a student text by the military's war and staff colleges as well as by many civilian colleges and universities. When it was first published in 1982, copies were sent by Rep. Newt Gingrich to all members of the House and Senate.

In the course of my studies I found that most military officers who served in Vietnam hated the news media in general but liked them in the particular. Associated Press reporter Al Chang, for example, spent much time with our infantry battalion in Vietnam, and a friend had high praise for Dan Rather, who accompanied him on patrols in the Central Highlands. As you may know, the late Charlie Mohr of *The New York Times* was awarded a Bronze Star medal for rescuing a wounded marine during the battle for Hue.

And when I was wounded in a jungle ambush, an ambush that killed or wounded almost all the members of our command group, two war reporters traveling with us picked up weapons from dead soldiers and provided security for us until help arrived. We are all prisoners of our experience, and that experience certainly colored my views of the news media.

But more than personal experiences convinced me that blaming the media for the loss of the Vietnam War was wrong. The media, and television in particular, is good at showing the cost of war. But cost of anything only has meaning in relation to value. As that master military theorist Carl von Clausewitz put it over a century and a half ago, it is the value of the political object, the reason for which we are fighting, that determines the sacrifices to be made for it both in magnitude and in duration. And, as he goes on to say, "Once the expenditure of effort exceeds the value of the political object, the object must be renounced. . ."

That's what happened in Vietnam. The political objective was never clarified—as Gen. Douglas Kinnard found, over 70 percent of the generals who fought the war were uncertain of its objectives—and as a result the value was never established. In World War II the objective was national survival, a value so high that we paid over a million casualties in pursuit of it. In Vietnam the objective, and hence the value, was deliberately not established and hence the price eventually was deemed exhorbitant. It was not the news media which reported the price that lost the war, it was the government which, especially in the case of President Lyndon B. Johnson, deliberately failed to establish its value.

Before my retirement from active duty in 1985, I was privileged to serve on a Twentieth Century Fund panel on the military and the media. I commend the findings of that panel, *Battlelines,* to your attention. Edited by Peter Braestrup, a marine combat veteran of the Korean War and *Washington Post* bureau chief in Saigon during the Vietnam War, it provides an excellent historical perspective to the role of the media in wartime. And to that end I have also submitted for the record a copy of my 1986 *Military Review* article on "Western Media and Recent Wars."

Since leaving active military service I have served as senior military correspondent for *U.S. News & World Report,* as a syndicated columnist and, most recently, military analyst for the *Los Angeles Times*, and as a military analyst first for CNN (Cable News Network) and now NBC News.

As a result of that experience, I find the question, "Can the media be trusted?" to be insulting. My colleagues in the media have in the main been as patriotic and as trustworthy as those in the military. In both spheres, however, there are those who did not live up to the standards of their profession. The answer the *Washington Post*'s George Wilson once gave on Vietnam War reporting to a critical Army War College audience was right on the mark. "Look," he said, "we had our Calleys the same as you did!"

Just as the army should not be judged by the aberration of the My Lai massacre's Lt. William Calley, so the media should not be judged by the aberrations of those who violate the rules of journalistic integrity.

I have only two complaints about the current coverage of the Gulf War. Although I have the highest personal regard for CNN's Bernard Shaw, I found it disappointing that he claimed to be "neutral" on the war. I believe strongly that newsmen, like every other American citizen, are bound by the Preamble of the Constitution to "provide for the common defense." And if they choose to abdicate that responsibility, then they have no claim to rights under the First Amendment of that Constitution.

That does not mean they have to be cheerleaders. Like Shaw, they can refuse to be debriefed when leaving enemy territory. They can oppose the war if they choose. They can be critical of how the war is being conducted. But as American citizens they can't be neutral.

Another thing that disturbs me is reporting from behind enemy lines. In World War II that would have been treason. In the Korean War the "reporting" of Australian communist Wilfred Burchett and the *London Daily Worker*'s Alan Winnington was seen as enemy propaganda pure and simple. I thought it revealing that CNN's Peter Arnett chose to justify his reporting from Baghdad by using the example of Harrison Salisbury's reporting from Hanoi during the Vietnam War.

Rumors were that Salisbury lost a Pulitzer Prize for uncritically reporting North Vietnamese propaganda as fact. As Tom Wolfe put it, "It seemed as if the North Vietnamese were playing Mr. Harrison Salisbury of *The New York Times* like an ocarina, as if they were blowing smoke up his pipe and the finger work was just right and the song was coming forth better than they could have played it themselves."

Western reporters in Baghdad are probably not deliberately reporting Iraqi propaganda as fact, but they certainly seem to have succumbed to the Lafcadio Hearn syndrome, the nineteenth century American writer who fell in love with Japan and became more Japanese than the Japanese. Even *The Washington Post* has commented how overly solicitous they seem to have become over the welfare of the Iraqi people. In pursuit of freedom of the press, we have given a psychological warfare advantage to our enemy.

Having said that, however, I think the reporting from the gulf has been excellent. And I also think that pool restrictions on the press there are dumb. They create the erroneous impression that we have something to hide. Reporters ought to have total freedom to see all that we are doing, realizing that transmission might have to be delayed for security reasons.

A general of the army, Douglas MacArthur (who as a major was the army's first "censor" in the opening days of World War I), told his chief of public affairs at the beginning of the Korean War, "Tell the press everything they need to know. And not one thing more."

The Briefers and the Press: Combatants on This Side of the Line

Thomas W. Lippman

In briefings to the press after the U.S. bombing of a Baghdad building that turned out to be occupied by civilians, Marine Brig. Gen. Richard L. Neal and Army Lt. Gen. Thomas Kelly faced the most aggressive and skeptical questioning of the Persian Gulf War.

Increasingly tough questions about what happened led a frustrated Kelly to chastise reporters: "Everything that we're seeing relative to this facility is coming out of a controlled press in Baghdad. So we don't know what all the facts are. We don't have a free press there asking hard questions like you all do here."

But the skeptical questions reflected more than the tensions of the moment or the usual adversarial relationship between reporters and officials. There is a legacy of distrust between the two sides because of a history of war briefings in which the initial version of events turned out to be less than the whole truth.

From Korea to Grenada to the Persian Gulf, modern U.S. history is studded with incidents in which military officers and official spokesmen at the White House, Defense Department, and State Department gave out misleading, incomplete, or false information.

Defects in the System

It also is marked by crucial events, such as the My Lai massacre in Vietnam and the Iran-contra affair, about which government briefers said nothing until reporters found out about them from other sources.

Several briefers from previous administrations said it is rare for official spokesmen to deliberately give out wrong information. But they said there are inherent defects in the briefing system.

88

All said they had never been asked or ordered to lie. But they said the information they gave out was sometimes inaccurate for various reasons, including false reports from the scene, the pressures of time and politics, the briefers' lack of access to the facts, infighting between departments, the natural defensive instinct among officials taking criticism and their desire to put events in the best light, and a need to protect sources of intelligence.

In daily early morning telephone calls, they said, the senior public affairs officers at State, Defense, the White House, and the CIA try to anticipate what questions will be asked at the press briefings. They decide which agency should take the lead in answering the questions and what considerations—the public's right to know, concern for the sensitivities of a friendly country, domestic political implications— have to be weighed.

The lower the rank of the briefer, they said, the less flexibility he or she has to go beyond written "guidance" issued by the State Department and the National Security Council. Often, they said, the public affairs officers will decide not to volunteer information about some subject, but to talk about it if asked.

"Quite often you could tell just by looking at something that you wouldn't announce it," said retired Army Col. Robert L. Burke, former chief of information in Vietnam and at the Pentagon. "Some events had diplomatic problems associated with them, so the State Department would have some control or restriction because of the impact."

If a ground offensive is launched in Kuwait, several former information officials said, the defects of a system in which official briefers control access to information will be magnified, because field commanders in artillery and infantry units often cannot see the full results of their actions and pass only fragmentary data up the line.

It will be "the most lethal ground combat ever," Burke said. "It's going to be an extremely violent, lethal situation in which a lot is going to happen. It will be extremely confusing on the ground and in the air

. . . It will be real tough to cover" unless reporters have direct access to it, as they did in Vietnam, he said.

But allowing reporters to accompany combat missions created a separate set of problems for the official information machine. As Burke well remembers, the differences between what Vietnam reporters saw in the field and what military briefers were saying in Saigon was so great that it undermined the briefers' credibility. By the early 1970s hardly anything they said at the daily briefing, known as the "Five O'Clock Follies," was taken at face value.

There are other well-documented examples:

In Korea, Gen. Douglas A. MacArthur issued reports on the Chinese rout of U.S. troops at Chosin Reservoir that were worded to obscure the facts and salvage his own reputation.

In Vietnam, purported "body counts" of enemy dead, "captured enemy documents" made available by the CIA, and "pacification" reports showing that the war was being won hamlet by hamlet all became targets of reporters' derision. Government accounts of the Tonkin Gulf incident of 1964, which provoked the first U.S. bombing of North Vietnam, turned out to have been less than fully factual.

Inventing Reagan Quotes

Asked in 1983 about reports that the United States was about to send troops into Grenada, White House spokesman Larry Speakes told CBS the idea was "preposterous." Early the next morning, he announced the invasion. Later he said he had misled the press because he had not been told what was happening. After leaving the White House, Speakes wrote a book in which he admitted that he had invented quotations on other occasions he attributed to President Ronald Reagan.

Former *New York Times* and CBS correspondent Bernard Kalb resigned as State Department spokesman after *The Washington Post* revealed the existence of a "disinformation" campaign against Libya that he knew nothing about. If he had not quit then, he said last week, he would have quit a month later when then-Attorney General Edwin

Meese III revealed that the United States had been selling arms to Iran and sending the money to the contra rebels in Nicaragua.

"How many times had I said [at State Department briefings that] America pays no ransom for hostages?" said Kalb, who at the time had been telling reporters that the Reagan administration had no secret dealings with Iran.

After the USS *Vincennes* shot down an unarmed commercial Iranian airliner over the Persian Gulf in July 1988, killing 290 people, Adm. William J. Crowe Jr., then chairman of the Joint Chiefs of Staff, gave a briefing that was inaccurate in several crucial details.

He said the airliner was flying outside designated commercial air corridors and was descending toward the *Vincennes*, and that it failed to identify itself on commercial radio channels—all of which turned out to be untrue or at least open to question.

Crowe, now on the faculty of the University of Oklahoma, did not return telephone calls. Fred Hoffman, a Pentagon briefer at the time of the incident, said Crowe was not being deceitful, he was a victim of a truism of the briefers' trade: The first reports are always wrong.

Because of intense pressure from the media and from within the Reagan administration to get as much information to the public as quickly as possible, Hoffman said, Crowe's briefing was held before he had time to verify the information he was receiving from navy officers in the gulf.

"With the best of intentions, the earliest information often turns out not to be true," Hoffman said.

Some officials "have a tendency to give in" to reporters' demands, Hoffman said, and give out information before it is fully verified. "Then if it turns out to be sour, the same reporters will get up at the briefing later and say, 'But you said, but you said,'" Hoffman said.

Hoffman noted that many of the same reporters who ridiculed "body counts" and other statistics given out in Vietnam are now demanding the same types of statistics from briefers in Saudi Arabia and at the Pentagon who are reluctant to give them because of the Vietnam experience.

"The military information gathering system isn't designed to meet the requirements of the media," said Barry Zorthian, former director of the joint U.S. Public Affairs Office in Vietnam. "It's a compilation from the front, up the line. On the ground, the platoon leader reports at the end of the day in barebones form, company passes it up the line. By the time it gets to headquarters, it's pretty distilled and dry. It serves military purposes. It is not designed to contain the eyewitness observation, the flavor and smell of battle. Therefore, it's almost always unsatisfactory to the media."

Reporters Are Fenced In

That is the reason journalists insist on going into the field to see for themselves, Zorthian said. But military commanders in the Persian Gulf, he said, "in analyzing the mistakes of Vietnam, which they vowed never to repeat, decided unrestricted movement by the press was a mistake."

Several of the former briefers noted that in the Gulf War, the instant worldwide dissemination of information from Baghdad creates pressure to respond quickly and regain the initiative.

When the Iraqis allowed CNN to transmit footage of bodies being carried out of the bombed building in Baghdad, Speakes said, "the American briefers' line wasn't 'Why did we bomb it?' but 'Why did Saddam [Hussein] put women and children in the shelter?' You try to go from defense to the offensive."

The value of what a briefer says, according to Kalb, is a function of how much he or she is allowed to know. Any briefer can give out false information if higher-ranking people keep the facts to themselves.

"You can be an assistant secretary for public affairs at the State Department, as I was," Kalb said, "but if you're out of the loop, you're out of the loop."

Chapter Four

Government Control of Information: Precedents and Parallels

What were the historical roots of the current
tension? Were there precedents for the
Pentagon's restrictions in the Gulf War? How
did previous U.S. administrations handle
information and the press in wartime? What
policies did, and do, other governments follow
in controlling wartime information?

Read Some About It

Arthur Lubow

Ever since organized war reporting began, belligerent nations have been trying to muzzle war correspondents. The stated purpose is always to keep secrets from the enemy. The unstated purpose, when the war, unlike the gulf conflict, goes badly, is to keep secrets from the citizens back home. Although civil libertarians may see a yawning gulf between these two motivations, for a military commander the two overlap. It is easier to prosecute a war if the enemy is befuddled and the home front is bamboozled.

William Howard Russell, the first war correspondent, quickly discovered the dynamic that would govern his profession. Sent to the Crimea in the winter of 1854–55 by *The Times* of London, Russell described the suffering of British troops and the idiocy of their leaders. At Balaclava, he wrote: "The commonest accessories of a hospital are wanting; there is not the least attention paid to decency or cleanliness—the stench is appalling—the fetid air can barely struggle out to taint the atmosphere, save through the chinks in the walls and roofs, and, for all I can observe, these men die without the least effort being made to save them." Lord Raglan, the commanding general, urged *The Times* to suppress Russell's reports on the grounds that they aided the enemy. In fact, the Russians knew how bad conditions were at the front. It was the Britons back home who were in the dark. Once they were enlightened, the Cabinet fell; and at the front Britain belatedly introduced military censorship.

In those days, however, censorship was crude and tentative. The latter half of the nineteenth century was in fact the golden age of the war correspondent. The exploits of these men are legendary. Archibald Forbes sneaked in and out of starving, besieged Paris near the end of the Franco-Prussian War in 1871, to report in the London *Daily News*: "I had brought in, stowed in a wallet on my back, some five pounds of ham. The servants of the place where I stayed put the meat on a dish with a cover over it, and showed it up and down the Rue du Faubourg St. Honoré as a curiosity, charging a sou for lifting the cover." In 1872, pursued by hostile Cossacks across the frigid steppes, J.A. Macgahan rode 400 miles to catch up with the Russian army; and then, finding that the army had advanced, he continued the same distance through what was said to be impassable desert to Khiva. In 1898, witnessing a bloody rebellion against the British Lancers at Omdurman in the Sudan, George W. Steevens wrote for the London *Daily Mail*: "The last dervish stood up and filled his chest; he shouted the name of his God and hurled his spear. Then he stood quite still, waiting. It took him full; he quivered, gave at the knees, and toppled with his head on his arms and his face turned towards the legions of his conquerors." These heroic sagas have long nourished the souls of war correspondents in the way that tales of Sitting Bull comfort the reservation-bound Sioux.

Progress in communications doomed the old-fashioned war correspondent. Because telegraph facilities were scarce and expensive, the early correspondents had relied on the mails; their dispatches were published too late to be of strategic use to the enemy. By the time of the Spanish-American War in 1898, however, the cable was cheap and available. The American authorities installed censors at the telegraph offices where reporters filed (first in Tampa and Key West, later in Cuba) and at the receiving stations in New York. On the battlefield, however, reporters were still perfectly free.

It was the Japanese, in their 1904–05 conflict with Russia, who turned the ratchet of censorship to the squeaking point by introducing what today we call "pooling." Promising Western correspondents a trip to the front, the Japanese authorities kept them bottled up in Tokyo for months. When a handful of reporters were at last selected to go to Manchuria, they were detained under tight escort at a risible distance from the fighting. The Japanese were censoring what reporters could see as well as what they could write. Frederick Palmer covered both the Spanish-American and the Russo-Japanese wars, and he lived to read of the Korean War a half-century later. As an old man he declared that the Russo-Japanese War was the beginning of the end: "It was the start of the secrecy which in the world wars to come barred reporters from the front lines, so that no public should ever know the truth."

For a democracy, total censorship on the Japanese model was thought to be too brutal. An added refinement was required. It arrived with the First World War. Recognizing the need to disseminate helpful news as well as to suppress the unhelpful, upon entering the First World War the U.S. government created a bureau under Colorado publicist George Creel that would not only administer censorship but also supply war news. By the Second World War these functions had evolved distinctly enough for President Roosevelt to create the straightforwardly named Office of Censorship and Office of War Information. As an index of the success of these sister bureaus, one remembers that, thanks to total censorship in Honolulu and misleading official statements in Washington, for a year the United States concealed the extent of the damage at Pearl Harbor. The Japanese knew what their bombers had accomplished. Americans did not. However, correspondents were allowed to accompany the troops, and they witnessed the critical battles, including the landings at Guadalcanal, North Africa, and Normandy.

Unlike the two world wars, the conflict in Korea engulfed the United States without warning. Lacking official guidance, correspondents at the start of the war vividly described the panicked, desperate, under-equipped GIs falling back before the onslaught from the north. Marguerite Higgins of the *New York Herald Tribune* quoted a young lieutenant: "Are you correspondents telling people back home the truth? Are you telling them that out of one platoon of 20 men we have 3 left? Are you telling them that we have nothing to fight with, and that it is an utterly useless war?" General MacArthur's staff branded the reporters traitors and threatened to revoke their credentials, but MacArthur waited six months before imposing formal censorship. By that time most of the reporters actually favored formal censorship over the self-censorship that they had been observing. (One described the procedure as "you-write-what-you-like-and-we'll-shoot-you-if-we-don't-like-it.") Although on paper the code was harsh—no "derogatory comments" about United Nations commanders or troops, and no unauthorized disclosures about the impact of enemy fire, for example—in practice the censors were lenient in letting copy through and lax in punishing infractions.

In Korea, as in the world wars, Washington coupled misinformation to censorship in a flagging effort to control American opinion. Near the end of the war, for instance, in the midst of peace negotiations, an embarrassed White House contradicted accurate accounts that it was about to accede to a divided Korea. As *The New York Times*'s James Reston wrote, "The official art of denying the truth without actually lying is as old as government itself." Censorship and misinformation, both in moderation, were part of the game. The reporters were content, or as content as reporters are temperamentally able to be.

But everything went haywire in Vietnam. That war trampled the delicate pas de deux of the previous half century, in which the government imposed censorship and prettified the truth, while the press tested the censorship and challenged the obfuscations. The peculiar situation of the press in Vietnam stemmed from the unprecedented circumstances of the conflict. It was not a declared war and therefore the president could not impose military censorship. Since the war proceeded largely as a counterinsurgency, it would have been hard in any event to make the face-saving argument that censorship was essential to preserve strategic secrets, rather than to sway opinion back home. With government assistance, reporters in Vietnam traveled easily to the battlefield and, except for minimal restrictions (no identification of casualties until the families had been informed, for instance), described what they saw.

In this first American war of the television era, TV correspondents could record the sorts of images that *The New Yorker*'s Michael Arlen described in one "routine film clip": "Scenes of men moving in to attack, and attacking—scenes, in fact, of men living close to death and killing—with one heart-rending sequence of a young soldier being carried out, his leg apparently smashed, screaming to his comrades, 'It hurts! It hurts!'" Not since the golden age had war correspondents been so free to move.

Without censorship the government was like a man who has lost one arm: it overdeveloped its remaining limb, propaganda. Military prestidigitators in Saigon invented figures to show how well the war was going. Back home, officials from the president on down strong-armed editors and publishers into suppressing and distorting the reports from the field. At Otto Feuerbringers's *Time*, editors privy to the "big picture" from Pentagon brass assiduously rewrote the files provided by their correspondents in Vietnam. At *The New York Times* the new publisher, Arthur Ochs Sulzberger, was summoned in October 1963 to a White House meeting with President Kennedy, who suggested that young David Halberstam had gotten too close to the story in Vietnam and would benefit from a transfer. (Sulzberger declined to transfer him.)

Unable despite these efforts to squelch pessimistic reporting, Washington tried to smother it by inviting dozens of correspondents (Joseph Alsop and Marguerite Higgins were the two most famous) to make quick, escorted tours of the war zone and return with predictions of American victory. What everyone now remembers is the widening credibility gap that eventually swallowed the Johnson administration. But for a time the military's propaganda prevailed. The perception at home was that the war would be won.

However, the policy of letting the reporters see everything and then denying everything they saw ultimately backfired. In this country (and even more in others) the war correspondent has traditionally regarded himself as a loyal auxiliary to his nation's armed forces. In the two world wars American correspondents even wore military uniforms. Although reporters are supposed to be noncombatants, from Richard Harding Davis at Las Guasimas to Charles Mohr at Hue they have carried weapons and joined in assaults. Over the course of the Vietnam War, this partiality to the home team was slowly and painfully eroded. "There gets to be a point when the question is, Whose side are you on?" Dean Rusk told a group of reporters after the Tet offensive. "Now, I'm the secretary of state of the United States and I'm on our side." Even when they favored the American mission of "fighting communism" (and, especially before 1968, most did), American reporters lost their team spirit as they struggled to get their stories heard over the static of misleading bureaucrats. The officials, in turn, grew convinced that the reporters were on "the other side," and blamed the press for souring the American public on the war effort. It was an extreme case of the old dynamic.

To put matters in perspective, consider this incident from the Spanish-American War. Following their triumph at San Juan hill, American troops hunkered down in front of Santiago. They were soaked by torrential rains, raked by Spanish bullets, and racked by tropical fevers. After three days of this, Richard Harding Davis, the most celebrated correspondent of his day, wrote a story for the *New York Herald* that conveyed the desperation, and concluded: "Truthfully, the expedition was prepared in ignorance and conducted in a series of blunders. . . . This is written with the sole purpose that the entire press of the country will force instant action at Washington to relieve the strained situation." When the story appeared, some accused Davis of treason, and the commanding general later said that had he read it in Cuba, he would have arrested and deported Davis immediately. However, between the time that these words were written and published, the Spanish fleet was destroyed, assuring an American victory. There was no need to accuse Davis and his brethren journalists of stabbing their country in the back, of draining America's will to fight. America had won.

Vietnam was a different story—an unprecedented defeat. One lesson in press relations that American authorities took from Vietnam to the current war in the gulf is that the less said, the better. They are providing almost no information, true or false. Instead, they are relying on a censorship that is almost as rigid as the Japanese variety of 1904 –05. Generals prefer to fight with no one watching. For the political leadership, however, a war that lasts more than a few days requires public consent, and the public demands at least some information. The journalists, for their part, are already nostalgic for the good old days of Vietnam, when they could go virtually everywhere and see virtually everything. Both the press and the military are burdened with the memory of Vietnam, but their memories should be longer. Vietnam was an anomaly. In modern war, reporters must be permitted at the front, and they must submit to sensible censorship. Mutual mistrust is part of the shared heritage of soldiers and journalists in time of war. So is mutual accommodation.

Statement Before the U.S. Senate Committee on Governmental Affairs

Barry Zorthian

Mr. Chairman, Members of the Senate Governmental Affairs Committee, I am please to accept your invitation to appear at this hearing for whatever contribution I can make to this examination of the Pentagon's rules governing press access to the Persian Gulf War.

In so doing, let me start with a disclaimer of sorts: simply that I am not here as a government spokesman or a practicing journalist—although I have served in both roles—but rather as someone who will try to draw on his experience to see if I can contribute to better understanding of the issues and can suggest ways in which these might be resolved or at least tempered.

My qualifications for this task include several early years as a working press and radio journalist, 13 years with the Voice of America, many of them serving as chief of the Central News operation, 4 1/2 years as chief spokesman for the U.S. Mission in Saigon, Vietnam, and 12 years with Time Inc. as President of Time-Life Broadcast and later Vice President for Washington. My service also includes four years active duty with the U.S. Marine Corps in World War II and retirement in 1973 as a colonel in the reserve.

Out of all this come some firm convictions as to relations between the government and the media, especially in time of war. I leave to others the discussion of basic issues involving the First Amendment and considerations of national security, except to note that historically, the only censorship acceptable to the American public has been protection of tactical military information which could jeopardize the security of a mission or the lives of personnel. Other comment by the media on broader issues of the war or related policy, critical or otherwise, fair or biased, is not subject to censorship in our open form of society. This point becomes particularly relevant in evaluating the criticism of the media in Vietnam, where violation of military security was not a major issue.

I suggest that regardless of any limitations placed on the First Amendment by national security, it is in the interest of the government, particularly in wartime, for the military to provide as much official information as possible—accurate, candid, timely, complete—as part of its accountability to the public. And it is equally important for the media to provide an independent accounting of these same activities as a check on the military's accuracy and validity. Only in this manner, I believe, can the government expect to develop and maintain the public understanding and support it needs to carry out its policies.

In this process, the military certainly has a legitimate interest in protecting information that affects tactical security. It has a right to prevent interference in the accomplishment of its military mission. And it needs assurance against the transmission, however inadvertent, of critical information through the channels of instantaneous communications available today.

The media has a need for the greatest possible freedom of movement and access and for unimpeded transmission of its findings and observations—all certainly in compliance with security—if it is to fulfill its role as an independent observer and surrogate for the public.

Each side, it seems to me, must recognize and accept fully these needs of the other and both must recognize that the military system of collection of information distilled for bare-bones presentation to the press is not designed to meet the media's desire for personal observation and for detail on the human element. At the same time, the journalist's approach is not a substitute for official evaluation and analysis. The two complement each other and both are necessary to provide the public with the well-rounded basis it should have to form a judgment.

In the gulf today, I believe that the military is performing its part of the task very well, that is, providing an official accounting of operations, with skill and credibility—briefings which incidentally for the first time are being transmitted live to the public without the often criticized intervention of the media; the media is not performing nearly as well in its task of providing an independent accounting, not because it cannot but because it is not permitted to do so by the military.

The current media rules suggest to me that the military has decided that one of the "mistakes" of Vietnam it is determined not to repeat is the unrestricted movement and coverage by the media in that period, which it believes led to a distorted picture of the Vietnam War for the American public. Accordingly, the military has established the current restrictions on the movement and coverage by correspondents to prevent the undisciplined media excesses of the past and wants to project instead a picture of the war which will be controlled and based largely on official sources.

This provides for a tidier and better disciplined coverage than in the past, but I believe the underlying judgment is a mistake. Media coverage by its very nature is undisciplined and there will be little success ultimately in seeking to contain it. The lesson of Vietnam, it seems to me, is a critical need for accurate and credible coverage by both the government and the media, which together present a complete picture for the public; not reliance on the presentation essentially of only one side.

No system will eliminate all controversy, but differences can be held to a minimum and the joint task of informing the public can be achieved, I believe, without acrimony, even though the two elements are and should continue to be adversarial.

To do this, the military must recognize the benefit to the military's credibility in the long run of facilitating unobstructed access and movement for the media within the limits of physical capacity as well as the media's excellent record in Vietnam and elsewhere in observing legitimate security ground rules on a voluntary basis.

For its part, the media must continue to acknowledge and comply in both letter and spirit with the military's legitimate security needs for

103

both protection of tactical military information and for caution in the transmission of information over modern communications facilities. It must also recognize that the large number of correspondents of varying competence seeking to cover military operations presents a physical problem of logistics and potential distraction for the combat commander that must be resolved. And finally, editors and producers at home offices must avoid excessive pressures due to competition and must take responsibility for the caliber and the actions of their representatives in the field and for the final product at home.

With respective understanding of these points, there is no reason the three principal issues of present contention—the escort requirement, the pool system, and the pretransmission review of copy—cannot be resolved in a satisfactory manner. The answer does not lie in setting up the same system that was developed in Vietnam. The gulf is obviously a different situation and requires different procedures. But adherence to the same basic principles is important in resolving these issues. The Sidle Commission report of 1984, which was endorsed as general operating procedure by the Defense Department at the time, points the way to answers: facilitative escorts, not monitors; resort to pools only when they are the "only feasible means" and then for the minimum length of time; and reliance on "voluntary compliance by the media with security guidelines or ground rules established and issued by the military."

It is time to return to these guidelines in both letter and spirit. The present controversy over media coverage can get more intense if and when ground operations begin. The dispute is not necessary and certainly not one the nation needs in the face of all our other major concerns in the gulf and elsewhere. The military and the media have a responsibility to work out satisfactory answers to these issues quickly, so they can get on with the task of jointly, if separately, informing the nation about the war in the gulf. Perhaps that process is underway. Some changes in procedures have been announced in the past week. Let us hope solutions are in sight. The public deserves no less.

Testimony Before the U.S. Senate Committee on Governmental Affairs

Maj. Gen. Winant Sidle, U.S. Army (retired)

Good afternoon. I am Maj. Gen. Winant Sidle, U.S. Army retired. I have had considerable experience with military-media relations starting back in 1949 when I was the PIO of the U.S. Sixth Army in San Francisco. I am an artilleryman, but I also had some 10 assignments to public affairs jobs in between other more normal assignments during my 35 years of service. Some of the more important jobs which involved dealing frequently, often daily, with the press were as deputy public affairs officer of U.S. Army Europe (which included supervising handling the press when the Berlin Wall went up); public affairs assistant to the chairman of the Joint Chiefs of Staff (General Wheeler); special assistant for Vietnam to the assistant secretary of defense, public affairs, and later as director of defense information (media relations) in the same office; chief of information (now called public affairs) in Vietnam (1967–69); chief of information of the army (1969–73); and deputy assistant secretary of defense, public affairs (1974–75). I retired in 1975.

Immediately after the Grenada Operation in 1983, at General Vessey's request I headed a panel of newsmen and public affairs officers that met in 1984 to make recommendations as to how the military should handle the media in future military operations. Our recommendations were approved by both the Joint Chiefs of Staff and the secretary of defense. One of our recommendations was the use of press pools in cases where the military situation precluded full media participation. DoD has used this pool system ever since, including today in Desert Storm.

This pool system has raised many press complaints. I think we should discuss this problem, if it really is one, by talking about

105

military-media relations in general. The truth is that both groups really need each other, but don't seem to fully realize this. The need for press cooperation with the military is obvious. Less obvious but nonetheless real is the need for the military to cooperate with the media to the maximum extent possible.

I say the latter for two reasons. First the military is funded by taxpayer dollars, and the taxpayers have a right to know what the military is doing with a few exceptions. Second, the military should and does want to get credit for the good job they almost always do. The only way for the military to both inform the taxpayers and to get credit for doing a good job is through the news media. True, from time to time the military can make direct, unedited contact with the public through public speeches, live TV and radio appearances, op ed articles and the like, but the main source of military news to the public is via the press.

What does all this mean re Desert Storm? I think it means that both groups should trust each other and be cooperative, not antagonistic. At the same time, both groups must realize each other's problems. For instance, the media would like to be told or see everything important that is going on. That, of course, is not possible since equal in importance to informing the public is the maintenance of adequate information security so that enemy intelligence does not learn anything it doesn't already know via the media and therefore give the enemy an unnecessary advantage. An equally important related restriction is that the media must not publish or air information that would endanger troop safety.

What this boils down to is that the military should give the media all possible information that will not be of real value to the enemy and/ or endanger troop safety.

Has the military been doing this during Desert Storm? It's hard for me to tell from mid-North Carolina, about 6,000 miles away. But I have the impression that perhaps the military has been too restrictive. I also get the clear impression that the media is asking for too much

106

information. This is revealed in televised press conferences where many questions are asked that the military should not answer. One of the most obvious questions is, "When will the ground attack begin?" A stupid question.

Another major factor in the military-media question is the very large number of newsmen on the scene. Some newsmen have phoned me to ask why the pool system has not been terminated per the recommendation of the Sidle Panel. I have answered by pointing out what the panel report also said: "The media were unanimous in requesting that pools be terminated as soon as possible and 'full coverage' allowed. 'Full coverage' appeared to be a relative term and some (media reps) agreed that full coverage might be limited in cases where security, logistics, and the size of an operation created limitations that would not permit any and all bona fide reporters to cover an event." This is certainly the case in Saudi Arabia today.

I have been told that there are over 1,000 newsmen on the scene. That is too many for full coverage, especially when ground combat begins. At the height of the Vietnam War, after Tet in March 1968, we had 648 newsmen accredited. That was the all-time high. However, of this group there were normally fewer than 100 in the field on any given day. During my time in Vietnam, except for the Tet period, we averaged about 400 newsmen accredited, with less than 50 in the field daily. The remainder stayed in Saigon.

As I understand it, the CENTCOM pools are limited to 90 reporters broken down into about 15 groups. Using the Vietnam experience, the poolers should total between 100–150. However, CENTCOM may well have good reasons for the 90 limit.

The fact is that security, safety, and operational considerations preclude absolutely providing the press full coverage. Things would really get messed up if 1,000 reporters were permitted to roam all over the area, either now or in combat.

Going back to the Vietnam example, only 100–150 reporters will find it necessary to go into the field once ground combat begins. The remainder will prefer to remain in Riyadh, Dhahran, and other rear areas to receive, process, and dispatch the news from the field. Also, the one-two person groups representing smaller media (some of these will need to go to the field occasionally), freelancers, and others who can do a better job by remaining near the rear area news centers.

If these assumptions are correct, CENTCOM's current use of pools is a good idea, which should be continued into the start of ground combat and beyond until a sound figure is reached as to how many reporters want or need to go into the field. At that point, CENTCOM could consider dropping the pools, although transportation probably will still have to be pooled.

I don't know the composition of the current pools, but based on the work of my panel, they should be primarily from the same country as the troops being covered. For U.S. troops, they should also represent media that have the most coverage of the U.S public. A standard small pool covering U.S. troops should have representatives from a wire service, a TV network, a news magazine, major newspaper/news syndicate, perhaps a radio network, plus two rotating spaces for smaller news media or the foreign media. As the battle progresses, pools could be switched or modified to fit the action. In any case, the pool system should be very flexible and include all services in coverage.

If and when a ground war begins, I believe that DoD will not have enough qualified personnel available to continue the present security review system with enough speed to satisfy the media. I recommend that the security review system be replaced by a ground rule system similar to that we used with considerable success in Vietnam. The ground rules should be short and simple.

Violations of the ground rules would mean immediate disaccreditation of the reporters concerned and their removal to the rear and perhaps out of country. Editors involved, if any, should be strongly cautioned that a second violation would mean elimination of their agency from covering the war.

With a ground rule system in place, it would be easier for field reports to go quickly back to bureau chiefs in country for consolidation, use, and availability to other media. I fully recognize that this would significantly affect normal press competition, but it would also ensure a greater flow of information to the U.S. public.

One more point about pools. There is no need to keep them in a single group once they arrive at their destination. For example, if they go to a division, they should be briefed and then farmed out to smaller units. Their guides do not have to be PAOs. In Vietnam we made heavy use of assistant operations officers, battalion commanders and even company commanders in some instances. The only rule was that the poolers had to agree to do what their guides told them when troop safety or security was involved, and their guides were to be the judges of when these considerations were involved.

In summary, here's my advice concerning military-media relations in Desert Storm.

To the military: Loosen up a bit. Remember that it is in the military's and the nation's best interests to confirm what you are doing through the eyes of the media. You are doing a good job, but you may not get full credit for it unless you let the media tell your story. Use enough pools to cover the action. Let the newsmen who represent media with the greatest impact have priority on pools. When a pool gets somewhere, break it up for wider coverage. Use ground rules rather than security review, especially after ground combat begins.

To the media: recognize the monstrous problem provided by having too many newsmen on the scene. Major news organizations should hold the number of reporters to the minimum required to do the job. Lesser news organizations must accept the fact that in this situation they cannot receive the same treatment as the larger agencies. Try to send representatives, especially for pool use, who have had combat experience or at least have served in the military. Also, recognize that opinion polls in the United States show great distrust of the media. Cooperation with the military should help close this credibility gap you have created over the past several years.

One line in the Sidle Panel report sums up, I think, the entire problem and its solution. I quote, "The appropriate media role in relation to the government has been summarized aptly as being neither a lap dog nor an attack dog but, rather, a watch dog. Mutual antagonism and distrust are not in the best interests of the media, the military, or the American people.

Thank you.

General Sought to Avoid Past U.S. Mistakes with Media

Richard Pyle

"The most difficult decisions are the ones that involve human life. I agonize over it. I wake up several times at night and my brain is just in turmoil over some of these difficult decisions that I have to make," Gen. H. Norman Schwarzkopf admitted to several journalists in one of his frequent interviews.

"Every waking and sleeping moment, my nightmare is the fact that I will give an order that will cause countless numbers of human beings to lose their lives. I don't want my troops to die. I don't want my troops to be maimed. It's an intensely personal, emotional thing for me. Any decision that you have to make that involves the loss of human life is nothing you do lightly. I agonize over it."

Aides, while accustomed to the candor displayed by their boss in talking with reporters, were dismayed by that particular interview, fearing that it might erode public confidence by leaving a false impression of mental anguish, hardly what the American people were looking for in their Persian Gulf commander. Evidently, Gen. Colin Powell thought so, too, for in a subsequent telephone conversation, the Joint Chiefs of Staff chairman suggested to General Schwarzkopf that he try to avoid being so forthright about personal matters.

General Schwarzkopf, for his part, saw talking with the news media as an essential part of his role as commander-in chief. After all, he had not forgotten Vietnam, when soldiers returning home, himself included, found a country that seemed either to detest the military or care nothing about its sacrifices.

He also had memories of Grenada, where the uproar over the news blackout imposed by Vice Adm. Joseph Metcalf had led eventually to the establishment of the Pentagon's media pool system. In the system, small groups of designated journalists from each medium—the wire services, newspapers, magazines, radio and television—are designated members of rotating pools. If the balloon goes up, those in the pool rotation are flown to the scene of the story. Their written reports, photographs, videotape, and audiotape, after being cleared for security, are sent back via military channels to the Pentagon for distribution to the rest of the news media.

The pools' first major combat test had come during the "Persian Gulf Tanker War" in 1987–88. There it was moderately successful. But in Panama, a year later, it was a fiasco. The pools were flown in hours after the invasion began, but instead of being placed with units in the field, the journalists were confined to a headquarters building where they, like everybody else, were forced to rely on independent television reports to find out what was going on.

General Schwarzkopf, familiar with all this, determined from the start that Operation Desert Shield would not be another Grenada or Panama. He professed to feel strongly that the American people deserved to know the truth, and he scheduled interviews several times a week with journalists, either individually or in small groups. In one interview, on September 13, he defined his views with typically Schwarzkopfian candor:

"Listen," he said, "I ain't no dummy when it comes to dealing with the press. And I fully understand that when you try to stonewall the press, and don't give them anything to do, then before long the press turns ugly, and I would just as soon not have an ugly press. I don't care if they report the truth, I just want them to be correct. Not everything is going to be right. Every time there is something new for the press to look at, I want them to see it, I want them to be out there. I want to create opportunities for them so they are kept informed."

Handling the media was only one of many questions—peripheral, yet crucial—to occupy General Schwarzkopf's time amid the planning of the military operation.

As Operation Desert Shield entered its second month, General Schwarzkopf's officers were grappling not with the enemy, but with the myriad details of providing troop facilities and comforts.

The mail system, for example, was far from perfect, but the sheer volume was overwhelming. At one point 40 tons of mail were backed up at Heathrow Airport outside London because there was not enough space on aircraft flying the gulf to handle it all.

Dan Rather had seen the situation, and the CBS anchorman was convinced that it should be improved. In a radio commentary tacked on to the end of a CBS Evening News broadcast on September 6, he commented:

> Laundry facilities, even rudimentary ones, are non-existent to terrible. The U.S. Army general in charge of this theater, H. Norman "Stormin' Norman" Schwarzkopf, has been quoted as saying, "This isn't important." I hope he has been misquoted, because that is dead wrong and a dangerous thing for a general to think. Especially for infantrymen, who win and lose wars, laundry is important.
>
> Infantrymen, perhaps the general needs to be reminded, walk in filthy, sweat-permeated and salted fatigues that cut and chafe. The troops can't say it, but others can and perhaps should. "Stormin' Norman" needs to storm less, battle less, think and do more. Like, fix the darn mail and get infantrymen in forward positions a way to launder their own fatigues.
>
> And while General "Stormin' Norman" is at it, he can check into foul-ups in hospital and medical supplies. There are a lot of them—most of them appear to be inexcusable—and he can work on getting our best tanks, not our next best, into Saudi Arabia. Dan Rather reporting, with the troops, in Saudi Arabia.

Needless to say, the Rather commentary was not well received at Central Command. Some staff officers laughed at the idea of a TV anchorman lecturing a professional infantry commander—one who had won three Silver Stars and been wounded five times in Vietnam, each time while saving the lives of his men—on how to take care of his troops.

General Schwarzkopf was considerably annoyed by the Rather report but rejected staff suggestions that he invite Mr. Rather for an interview to "set the record straight." Publicly, he fumed over the incident.

"I don't mind getting bad press when we deserve it, but when it's not a correct story, that absolutely drives me up the wall," he said. "Dan Rather's telling me how to do it? From the Intercontinental Hotel in Abu Dhabi, he's gonna let me know how to be an infantryman?"

Five months later, when General Schwarzkopf flew to an airstrip in southern Iraq for a dramatic confrontation with defeated Iraqi commanders, both Mr. Rather and his NBC competitor, Tom Brokaw, happened to be at Dhahran. But only Mr. Brokaw made the trip to Safwan. CBS sources said General Schwarzkopf had intervened personally—to make sure that the CBS correspondent and crew who regularly covered his headquarters in Riyadh were part of the media pool going to cover the meeting in Iraq. Was there a connection? General Schwarzkopf, as far as is known, never said, and his top aides merely shrugged when asked that question. But as one had said, in another context: "The CINC has a photographic memory. He never forgets anything you tell him—unfortunately."

In Bad Company

Gara La Marche

To the Editor:

Tom Wicker observes that the dismissal of a federal court challenge to the Pentagon's Persian Gulf press curbs leaves undisturbed an unprecedented degree of control by the government of "the tone and content of most newspaper, radio, and television reports" about the war ("End of A Great Era," column, April 20). These restrictive press rules, perfected in earlier trial runs in Grenada and Panama, were enforced through strong-arm tactics by United States military officials.

Regrettably, the United States had plenty of company in the censorship business during Operation Desert Storm. Governments worldwide managed the news to maintain or manufacture consensus for their role in the war.

Iraq imposed government escorts on foreign correspondents, and censors screened their reports before transmission. No foreign journalist was permitted to visit Kuwait from the August 2 invasion until after the cease-fire. Saudi Arabia banned or censored all foreign publications, with particular attention to articles about the Palestine Liberation Organization or civilian bombing casualties. The other principal American allies in the region—Egypt, Morocco, and Turkey—backed the United States in the face of substantial popular opposition, moving to disguise the extent of their role and to quash dissent.

Turkish state television, for example, used much of CNN's material on the war, but when the coverage turned to such matters as U.S. strikes at Iraq from Turkish bases or the shortage of gas masks in the country, programming was interrupted for a "commercial break" or scenic waterfall footage. Raids from Turkish air bases were never mentioned in any official statement or on state television or radio.

115

The Egyptian Organization for Human Rights reported that as many as 200 political activists and students were detained. Israel closed nine press offices in the occupied territories and arrested the Palestinian writer and peace activist Sari Nusseibeh on "spying" charges widely believed to be spurious. Fearing mass protests, King Hassan of Morocco ordered sports events canceled and schools closed, and threatened agitators with trials by military tribunals. And the newest U.S. ally, Syria, detained 80 writers and intellectuals for expressing support for Iraq.

Repression in Syria is no surprise. But in Great Britain, the BBC blocked a documentary on the export to Iraq of British-built superguns, on the grounds that the "tone is wrong," and the government detained dozens of Iraqi nationals as prisoners of war and deported others. France banned the distribution, publication, or sale of three publications deemed pro-Iraqi on the grounds they "defend interests that are contrary to France's interests" concerning the war, and expelled one of the editors. The Australian Broadcasting Corporation faced a government inquiry following complaints from Prime Minister Hawke about its war coverage.

Virtually every country with a significant Muslim population, whether or not it was a party to the Gulf War, cracked down on dissent. Antiwar demonstrations were banned in Djibouti and Sri Lanka, and protesters were met with police violence in Nigeria, Pakistan, Indonesia, and the Sudan. Tunisia and Algeria went one step further and expelled foreign reporters who had arrived to cover antiwar protests.

Here in the United States, we will be living for some time to come with the consequences of our wartime retreat from basic First Amendment principles. A few weeks ago, for example, some members of Congress got a letter from the Salvadoran ambassador to the United States, in response to a protest they had lodged about the detention of foreign journalists. The ambassador argued that combat conditions limit freedom of expression—and cited U.S. press policies during the Persian Gulf War in support of his position.

The Filtered War

Caspar Henderson

Iraq

Saddam Hussein went to great lengths to cultivate and manipulate the Western media. Ten days after the invasion of Kuwait, Naji al-Hadithi, described by BBC TV foreign affairs editor John Simpson as "an educated, civilized man," was appointed the director general of the Iraqi Ministry of Information. Al-Hadithi expected war, says Simpson, and knew that "the more Western audiences saw of Baghdad on their television screens, the greater reality it would take in the public mind. It would no longer be a geographical abstraction which could be bombed back to the Stone Age." So he opened Iraq to Western journalists in a way that had not been done in over 20 years.

The Iraqi military, says Simpson, became worried that journalists were acting as spotters for allied bombers when the attacks began. But Simpson thinks the reason they were expelled is that they witnessed the extraordinary accuracy of allied precision weapons, and saw that Iraqi civilian casualties were low. The bombing of the Amira air-raid shelter, however, in which hundreds of civilians died, was an important propaganda victory.

Knocked out by allied bombing, Iraqi TV ceased to broadcast by the third week of the war. Baghdad Radio was reduced to one frequency, while Mother-of-Battles Radio out of Kuwait transmitted for only one week. Baghdad Radio stressed that civilian targets were being hit, but it played down military damage and did not specify locations or the number of people killed. Basra, Iraq's second city, was carpet bombed continually. Iraqi sources were silent on Basra, although the loss of civilian life was thought to be very great; the U.S. military remain taciturn, stressing that Basra was a military town.

Soon after the war began, Iraq expelled all Western journalists except Alfonso Rojo and CNN's Peter Arnett. On February 8 they began to readmit others. John Simpson was not given a visa. In the United States and Britain, the role of Western journalists in Iraq came under scrutiny. The editor of the *Daily Telegraph* said foreigners in Baghdad "can no longer perform the function of a proper journalist— to search for information and present it in context because they are granted selected access and never to military targets." Other "quality" British dailies trusted to their readers' intelligence. Richard Beeston, a correspondent for the *Times* in Iraq, described a method journalists developed for trying to circumvent censorship: they put offensive decoy paragraphs into reports, which would undoubtedly be deleted, in the hope of saving less contentious but revealing passages.

United States

Soon after the Pentagon announced the pool system on January 10, 13 news organizations and prominent journalists said they would file a lawsuit in the federal court charging that Pentagon rules restricting press access were unconstitutional. But the pool system operated throughout the war.

As military briefers were increasingly criticized for being uninformative and withholding information, the Pentagon changed its policy slightly. On February 1, General Schwarzkopf limited televised portions of the briefing to 30 minutes, with time for more detailed questions afterwards. Answers in these off-the-record sessions could not be specifically attributed to the command or its spokesmen.

In the third week of the war the Pentagon banned a video from a camera in a guided missile that showed a terrified Iraqi on a bridge the missile was about to destroy. A cartoon in a U.S. airbase of a giant American superman shielding a terrified hooknosed Arab was censored.

There was at least one documented case of disciplinary action against a soldier. Dick Runels, an airforce maintenance technician, refused to submit his letters to his base commander for approval after *The Voice* in Michigan published a letter of his venting "frustration at a system that has us completely under its control."

The more general question of how the war was covered in the U.S. media also caused controversy at home. According to a figure from Fairness and Accuracy in Reporting (FAIR), a New York media monitoring group, in the run-up to the war the three major U.S. TV networks devoted less than 1 percent of their airtime to organized popular opposition to the Bush administration's gulf policy. Between August 8, 1990, and January 3, 1991, only 29 minutes out of a combined coverage on ABC, NBC, and CBS dealt with organized dissenters. When U.S. forces began bombing Baghdad, the networks seemed to be caught offguard by the vehemence of the antiwar activists who spilled on to the streets. "The peace movement has instantly sprung up," reported ABC's Cokie Roberts on day one of the war.

A survey by a national news organization found that, in early February, over 70 percent of Americans felt that coverage of the war should be subject to more censorship rather than less.

Edward Said lamented the blinkered and compliant attitude of U.S. media towards the crisis. He said there was very little debate about the rapid U.S. military buildup, that nobody really questioned whether the United States ought to be in the gulf, and there was no discussion of the terrible costs to the Arabs of a military strike. "Most of what passes for journalistic and expert commentary has been a repetition of appalling clichés, most of them ignorant, unhistorical, moralistic, self-righteous, and hypocritical. All of them derive, one way or another, from U.S. government foreign policy, which has long considered the Arabs either as terrorists or as mindless stooges to be milked for their money or abundant and inexpensive oil. No one has placed the Iraqi invasion of Kuwait in the context of the Turkish assault on Cyprus, the Israeli devastation of Lebanon, the American invasion of Panama." Former state department spokesman Hodding

Carter argued that ownership of TV networks by certain giant corporations could shape war coverage just as much as Pentagon restrictions.

Great Britain

Censorship of the Falklands War was greater than that of almost any recent conflict involving a Western power, with the possible exception of the U.S. invasion of Panama. Neither the BBC nor ITV chose at the time to alert their audiences to the fact that what they were seeing from the Falklands/Malvinas was entirely controlled by the Ministry of Defense. "Looking back on it," said Sir Nicholas Henderson [of Independent Television News], "I think it would have been better had we, as a practice, regularly put up 'this was censored.' "

In the gulf, both BBC and ITV News drew attention to allied military security considerations affecting their reports, but they did not describe it as censorship. BBC guidelines illustrate the double-think that was at work: "Programmes should make it known in general terms that some information will be held back for (allied) military reasons and that reports out of Iraq are censored." The guidelines further stressed that it must be made plain that the Iraqis restricted Western reporters to approved areas. No mention was made that the allied pool system did the same. Shortly before the war, BBC television rebuffed two approaches by the Saudis, who were nervous over the content of the *Panorama* documentary "Behind Desert Shield." It was broadcast on January 8. However, the BBC denied suggestions that it bowed to political pressure by canceling a planned January 28 broadcast of a *Panorama* program exploring British arms exports to Iraq prior to the invasion of Kuwait. The program was screened after two other programs on the gun had been transmitted.

In the first days of the war censorship struck like measles: satires like "'Allo, 'Allo," "They Never Slept," "Monty Python," and "Carry on up the Khyber" were removed from TV schedules, as was "The Naked and the Dead," a serious World War Two film. Channel 4 canceled a Vietnamese film season, ITV postponed a drama about a disfigured airline pilot, and "Soldier, Soldier," a documentary about the lives of servicemen.

Around 67 pop songs were withdrawn from BBC local radio and some commercial stations for the duration of the war, including such diabolical Iraqi propaganda as "Give Peace a Chance." An historical exhibition at the Victoria and Albert Museum entitled "The March of Death" was canceled. Mathew Hoffman, letters editor of the *Independent*, says that he received many more letters supporting greater censorship of the war news than in favor of greater freedom of information: "It suggests that the urge to censor in wartime is not restricted to the authorities, and that our claim that we wish to print the truth as we find it on behalf of our readers is perhaps a little thinner than we might like to contemplate."

Under-representation rather than censorship of foreign viewpoints was a feature of reporting in Britain. Coverage of Islamic issues and reactions relating to the gulf crisis in the British media was "remarkable for its absence," according to Professor Michael Gilsenan, of Oxford University, and there was "progressively less coverage" as the crisis went on.

When Abbas Shiblack, the Palestinian writer and human rights activist, and others, were detained and threatened with expulsion without rights of public hearing or appeal, many papers protested. Editorials commented that Arab papers were based in London precisely because Britain was a fair society with an open legal system and without censorship.

Saudi Arabia

The invasion of Kuwait was not reported in Saudi Arabia for several days, and the Saudis had to turn to foreign broadcasts. CNN proved very popular. Any footage of Saddam Hussein, pictures of U.S. women soldiers, or mention of Scud attacks on Israel on CNN was, however, immediately cut and replaced by documentaries about the Saudi royal family. Whole pages were ripped out of the *Guardian*,

Newsweek, or *Time* when the Arab coalition was called into doubt. British tabloids and the *Independent* were banned.

France

With its large North African communities and singular foreign policy, French policy on the restriction of information was uneasy. The first images of French Jaguar bombers actually attacking Kuwait were not broadcast until nearly three days after they went into action. On January 16, a peace march in Paris was prevented by order. On January 19, a concert in France by Cheb Khaled, the Algerian Rai singer, was canceled. On January 21, Radio Algiers reported that French police had seized cassettes and videos of the Algerian performer Mazouni singing "Z'dam ya Saddam" ("Forward to It Saddam"). On January 26, three pro-Iraqi magazines published in France, *Al Arab, Ad Dastour,* and *Kol al Arab,* were banned. In the gulf, French crews, without Pentagon pool "privilege," were particularly adventurous in their attempts to get beyond the official story.

Egypt

A lively debate between government-subsidized media led by *Al-Ahram* on the one side, and opposition and independent newspapers, including the unlikely bedfellows of the Marxists *Al-Ahali* and Islamic publications on the other, continued unhindered. The latter opposed Egyptian participation in the coalition and called for an end to the war. TV news strictly followed the government line. Egyptian police and security forces did not permit antiwar demonstrations.

Morocco and Algeria

Farida Moha, Radio France International's Morocco correspondent, stopped working for the network two days after the war began, apparently in protest at French involvement.

Unlike Moroccans and Tunisians, many Algerians watched CNN or French and other European TV channels via satellite. Nevertheless, the Algerian press spoke with unanimity when it condemned Western involvement, reflecting popular opinion shown in massive demonstrations which were virtually ignored by Western media. Its views were significant because, over the last year, it has become one of the freest in the Arab world, although Western journalists (except those permanently accredited) have been excluded from the country.

Israel

Even prior to the war, some polls put at 61 percent the proportion of Israelis who believed that great freedom of the press may harm state security. On the first day of the war a total curfew was imposed on the Palestinian population in the Occupied Territories, and the Israeli Defence Force kept a tight control on Western and Palestinian journalists.

Iran

From the earliest days of the war, Voice and Vision, Iran's tightly controlled broadcasting network, promised in its editorials that it would remain impartial during the conflict. It followed this with a series of attacks on U.S. censorship, and also blamed Iraq for the war. Otherwise, it reported accounts from both sides without comment.

Argentina

"First Platoon," a TV satire on the cowardice and incompetence of the Argentine navy in the gulf, was broadcast on November 16, 1990, but all subsequent episodes were pulled from the schedules.

Turkey

The government confiscated copies of a January issue of *Towards 2000* magazine, following its exposure of defense plans reportedly allowing for up to 300,000 dead. The majority of Turks were against involvement in the war. On January 26, the government banned all strikes, saying the state of war made the ban necessary. In a move perhaps to strengthen their hand in northern Iraq and gain credibility with the West, President Ozal's government hinted that Kurdish, the native language of some 12 million Turkish citizens, might be unbanned.

On January 18, U.S. bombers based at Incirlik, near Adana in southeast Turkey, began bombing missions against Iraq. This followed a vote in favor by the Turkish parliament the previous day, although opinion polls suggested that around 80 percent of Turks were opposed to NATO bases being used for sorties against Iraq. State-run Turkish Radio and Television (TRT) carried a lot of CNN coverage, but abruptly cut reports from Incirlik.

The Arab Press

"The most noticeable feature of Arab press coverage of the Gulf War," said Adel Darwish, who monitored Arab press and media for the *Economist* and the *Independent*, "was its unanimous support for its governments and the lack of debate." The only exception, he adds, was Egypt. The Saudi and Kuwaiti press distorted and rewrote stories syndicated from prestigious British, French, U.S., and Egyptian newspapers. In Iraq there was no attempt to give space to foreign points of view except those of Western peace campaigners.

London-based Arab journalists, according to Darwish, rapidly lost all sense of history and perspective. Writers on Saudi and Kuwaiti papers based in London, which until August 1990 were defending Saddam's killing of Farzad Bazoft, the use of gas on Kurdish civilians, and his threat to "burn half of Israel," penned the most savage attacks against the dictator. Journalists who had attacked their colleagues as "spies and Zionist agents" when they had argued for Bazoft's right to a fair trial, or published investigative reports on Iraq's chemical weapons program, continued to attack the same colleagues, now accusing them of being pro-Saddam because they tried to write balanced reports, reminding readers that gulf rulers were not democratically elected.

Chapter Five

How the Government Policy Worked During Combat

How did the journalists operate under the
restrictions imposed by the military and the
Saudis? Was the press denied the access
necessary to obtain and report information
Americans needed to know, when they
needed to know it?

The Pool

Christopher Hanson

I was a combat pool correspondent, one of the happy few who helped provide America with what Pentagon spokesman Pete Williams called "the best war coverage we've ever had." True, most of us never saw a battle and few of us even saw a dead Iraqi soldier, but at least we got to be part of the big adventure. True, many of our dispatches never made it back to our news organizations, but at least we got to write them. True, military officers controlled our every movement, but that, after all, may be why Williams bestowed his glowing praise, and pool veterans should not take compliments lightly. To help put Williams's tribute in perspective, here is a day-by-day account of what it was like to cover a ground war under the pool system.

February 19—Dhahran International Hotel. Correspondents line up at a U.S. military supply room, hoping to draw the helmets, flak vests, chemical suits, and other gear required to protect them in the field.

"If you can get the gear yourself [that is, from an independent source] you're good to go," says a supply sergeant.

"So it's available independently?" asks a reporter.

"No, only from us." Catch-22.

At the last minute, an army officer announces that the rules have been relaxed: full protective trappings are not required now. Any gear unavailable today will be issued in the field.

February 20— I board a transport plane for the army's Seventh Corps headquarters minus rubber antichemical boots—an essential item in the Desert Storm wardrobe. Upon arrival, we are told by a spokesman, Maj. David Cook, that Seventh Corps is, in fact, *not* prepared to supply missing gear. Antichemical boots are in especially short supply.

128

February 21— With a reporter from *The New York Times* and an AP correspondent, I embark in a Humvee truck on a lurching two-hour journey across the desert. We are headed for the Iraqi border to visit the Second Armored Cavalry Regiment, which we are told will spearhead the most significant American ground assault of the war. The reporters ride in back. In front are two military escorts—Capt. John Koko, 33, and Sgt. Roy Botkins, 29, both reservists from Kentucky. Each carries a loaded M-16 rifle and a box of Cracker Jack. Koko, a fount of wisecracks, is gung-ho about the profession of arms, but contemptuous of his current assignment as a "PAO [public affairs officer] puke." He sings snatches of the army recruiting jingle, "Be all that you can be."

Under canvas later on, Koko discusses his unique approach to public affairs at the front. "My job is rumor control," he says, and then gives his interpretation of that duty: he controls rumors by spreading them himself. It's all part of the continuing effort to relieve boredom. Koko seems especially proud of his part in spreading one rumor: a soldier uses a gas mask pouch as a pillow, but as he shifts position during the night the pressure of his head accidentally triggers an antidote syringe needle in the pouch. It punctures the soldier's neck, killing him instantly.

Koko—who stands about six-foot-four and once served as an army ranger—is now in high gear, regaling us with tales of how he has been patrolling Seventh Corps territory, apprehending reporters who had made their way to the front without permission. He dutifully, if reluctantly, stops Americans, but truly gets a charge out of busting French and especially Italian reporters, because, in his view, neither country is contributing enough to the war effort.

Ironically, news organizations themselves may have done even more than enforcers like Koko to thwart reporters trying to cover the war. The Pentagon, shrewdly enough, had delegated to U.S. news media in Dhahran many decisions on who got pool slots. In early January, the "sacred 16"—*The New York Times, The Washington Post*, Cox, Gannet, *The Wall Street Journal*, and other papers that had kept reporters in Saudi Arabia continuously since late 1990—voted to keep pool slots for themselves. Bitter fights with newcomers resulted. (Eventually, the Defense Department created new pool slots to accommodate some of the newcomers.) All told, reporters seemed to spend more energy fighting each other than fighting pool restrictions.

February 22— At breakfast I seek soldiers' reactions to the latest reports that Iraq has offered to withdraw from Kuwait, raising last-minute talk of a peace settlement. One soldier tells me he would just as soon go ahead with the ground offensive because he has just had his head shaved and doesn't want to be seen back home until it grows out. At that point, Koko comes up and gently rebukes me for talking to troops without a military escort.

Next, we get a lesson in just how well the military's communication system for field reporters actually works. With Koko supervising, we three reporters interview the only woman in camp, a sergeant whose classified intelligence duties make her the female closest to Iraqi lines. She is tough and articulate and it all makes for a nice story. The only problem is that, after I write my piece and send it back to headquarters in a Humvee, it disappears. It never reaches Dhahran, never is issued as a pool report, never gets to my editors. (*The Wall Street Journal*'s John Fialka tells me later that my experience is typical—"Seventh Corps was simply a black hole.")

February 23—Word is that the Second Armored Cavalry does not want reporters along on the ground offensive. But the regimental spokesman, Capt. Bob Dobson, says this restriction applies only to TV crews. He can take one "pencil" and agrees to take me, but only if I agree to his terms—I can go only where Dobson goes and must never venture out by myself. No other escorts are available. Koko and Botkins will be returning to headquarters. Reluctantly, I agree to the terms. The alternative is sitting out the war in the rear. Captain Dobson is now my assignment editor.

February 24— At dawn, the Second Armored Cavalry convoys form up and move out across the misty desert into Iraq. I ride with Dobson, 29, a bright, portly West Pointer with a passion for junk food,

130

who gives me a running commentary on the regiment and its role in the war.

Later, we are ordered to don our chemical-weapons protective suits (I have by now managed to scrounge a pair of the special boots). I then write a story in which soldiers react to the prospect of gas warfare and—almost to a man—urge nuclear retaliation if Iraq uses chemicals. No couriers are available. We have outstripped our lines of communication. The only option for filing stories is the regiment's "E-mail" computer system, which in theory can send articles to headquarters via satellite. But the system is on the blink and remains so for days. My newspaper does not get this dispatch until February 28, when it is far too stale to use.

February 25— A day of massive prisoner-taking and sporadic fighting, including a small engagement just a few hundred yards off to the right of the regimental headquarters column. Dramatic stuff for a newcomer to war, and I write a colorful piece on taking prisoners. Of course, it cannot be filed due to technical difficulties.

At one point, Dobson's public affairs vehicle is bouncing along a rutted track, past a cluster of Iraqis who have just surrendered. They wave and smile. We wave and smile. Then the Humvee hits a huge bump, spilling a good part of its load in front of the Iraqis. It is hard not to feel embarrassed.

The convoy lurches on. I ask Dobson if we can break away from the headquarters detachment and join one of the regiment's squadrons of M-1 tanks and Bradley Fighting Vehicles, which are seeing the real action up ahead. He says he'll try to accommodate me eventually, but can't promise anything. We drive on into the night. At last the convoy halts and circles up. The soldiers dig in as American tank cannons and artillery thunder away nearby. I spend the night sitting up in the Humvee, horrified that the war might be over before I can transmit even one good story.

February 26— A day of excitement, confusion, and frustration. Reports reach headquarters by radio that the regiment's armored squadrons up ahead are engaging Republican Guard tank units. The regiment's assignment, says Dobson, is to locate the main elements of the guard and engage them in battle until heavier U.S. units can move up to finish them off. After pausing during a sandstorm, with 70-mile-per-hour winds, the headquarters column moves off, only to reverse direction and hastily retreat because Iraqi tanks have supposedly been spotted up ahead. Night finds us dug in, watching a light show of explosions and flames along the horizon. The regiment's heavy armor is battling the Republican Guards along a 20-mile front, but from this distance I can make no sense of the action. What could have been my biggest story ever is playing itself out, and I am missing it.

February 27— Dobson gets an update on the battle from the regiment's operations center and gives me a briefing—it seems an entire Republican Guard division has been annihilated. I write a story on the battle. This time, with Dobson's help, I actually manage to file it over the computer hookup, along with all the other hoary dispatches that have stacked up.

Later, with the column having paused to rest up, Dobson and I and a couple of air force liaison officers drive off to inspect the hulk of an Iraqi armored personnel carrier, which has been knocked out by a U.S. aircraft missile. The Iraqi inside the vehicle has been burned beyond recognition. A gunner who sat atop the carrier has been thrown clear but torn nearly in half and horribly mutilated in other ways. I take detailed notes.

"What angle are you planning to use?" asks Dobson. When I make a noncommittal reply, he says, "Here's the angle I would use: There is no glory in war. . . . No one will ever know what happened to these two. Their families will never know. The sand is already covering that [gunner's] body." He shakes his head.

My assignment editor seems to have good news judgment. I take his advice. The problem is that the piece I write is quite graphic, just the sort of story that the Defense Department—with its smart-bomb videos that make combat seem bloodless—has been trying to avoid. Will this dispatch survive the censor's blue pencil?

As things turn out, the dispatch gets through unaltered and no high-ranking meddler comes after me. But this may be because the war is all but over.

A more telling case is probably that of *Los Angeles Times* reporter John Balzar, who was assigned to cover a helicopter aviation brigade in the Eighteenth Army Corps. Before the ground offensive started, his unit was conducting night attacks into Iraq. Apache helicopter pilots allowed Balzar to view infra-red gun-camera footage of one of these raids.

Here is a sample of what he reported shortly before the ground war was launched:

> Through the powerful night-vision gunsights they looked like ghostly sheep, flushed from a pen—Iraqi infantry soldiers bewildered and terrified, jarred from sleep and fleeing their bunkers under a hellstorm of fire.
>
> One by one they were cut down by attackers they couldn't see or understand. Some were literally blown to bits by bursts of 30mm exploding cannon shells. One man dropped, writhed on the ground, and struggled to his feet. Another burst tore him apart. A compatriot twice emerged standing from bursts. As if in pity, the American Army attackers turned and let him live. . . .

This pool report was not censored by the Defense Department, but after it was filed Balzar and the other members of his pool were, in effect, grounded. They were taken to see no combat and spent much of the ground offensive sitting around in a tent.

February 28— My priority today is to interview the soldiers who had fought in Tuesday night's fierce tank battle and to file an afteraction report. But Dobson's priority is to collect Iraqi weapons from the battlefield for the regimental museum. So that, needless to say, is what we do. I take notes as Dobson and three air force liaison officers, with .45s at the ready, clear Iraqi bunkers (no Iraqis are to be seen) and haul off booty. From one bunker the air force men liberate a 26-inch Sanyo color TV set with stereophonic sound.

For much of the day I ride with a young air force captain. He, and not Dobson, now sets my news agenda. At one point, he asks, "Would you like a Pop-Tart?" But he can't find the box. It has fallen off the back off the truck and is lost. The captain is crestfallen. As he drives along, he speaks with a consuming intensity of his fondness of Pop-Tarts, a snack with the flavor of home. Suddenly his eyes bulge. He realizes that he has blundered into a dense field of unexploded cluster bomblets dropped by U.S. planes. Slowly, with great care, he eases the truck through the field. When it's finally evident that he has pulled us through intact, he pauses and says softly, as if to himself, "That really bums me out about the Pop-Tarts."

It's unclear what my lead for today should be—the Sanyo TV or the Pop-Tarts. I lean toward the latter.

March 4— After a journey by helicopter and transport plane, I arrive back at the Dhahran International Hotel. The American Military Police at the front door search my bags far more carefully than they had when I arrived two weeks before. The reason for this thoroughness, explains one MP, is that journalists back from battlefields have been showing up with some interesting souvenirs. He says one member of a CBS crew came in with three Iraqi hand grenades. They turned out to be the trip-wire type, which go off the instant you pull the pin. Other journalists, whom he declined to identify, came in with pistols and antitank weapons, and one had four volatile blasting caps in her pocket. The MP says he has come to question whether the American press corps has very good judgment.

Back in the hotel, I discuss my pool experience with colleagues and conclude that, astonishingly enough, I have had relatively *good* luck with the system. Some reporters covering Seventh Corps got no dispatches back at all. A great many—and this applied to the entire theater of operations—were far from any combat whatsoever; they will be traumatized for years to come not by what they saw of this war, but by what they didn't see.

In the final reckoning, I'm left with this question: Was joining a pool really worth the aggravation? It's a close call, but probably it was

134

in those cases where you actually got to cover some fighting. On the other hand, those passed over for pool slots were not necessarily the losers. Consider *The New Republic*'s Michael Kelly, who was told he would not get a ground combat pool assignment and opted to go on his own. He and a Baltimore *Sun* reporter drove across the desert toward Kuwait City, ahead of the allied forces. Kelly's poignant March 18 account of desperate, surrendering Iraqis, begging reporters to take them into custody, made far better reading than any pool report I saw during the entire war.

Testimony Before the U.S. Senate Committee on Governmental Affairs

Malcolm Browne

My thanks to the committee for its invitation.

By way of introduction, I am a science writer on the staff of *The New York Times*, but I've also spent a considerable part of my career covering military affairs and wars. This began in Korea while I was in the army, which assigned me as a reporter for the military newspaper *Stars and Stripes*. In the years since then I've worked as a correspondent for UPI in Cuba, as the Associated Press Indochina bureau chief in Saigon, as ABC television's Vietnam correspondent, as a freelance writer for magazines and books, and since 1968, as a staff correspondent of *The New York Times*.

Besides the Indochina War, which I covered for a total of eight years, I've covered conflicts in South America, North Africa, and the Indian subcontinent, including the Bengali uprising against Pakistan and the war between Pakistan and India in 1971. My journalistic awards include a 1964 Pulitzer Prize for Vietnam coverage. I have just returned from a month covering the Persian Gulf War for *The New York Times*.

More than 1,000 news correspondents, cameramen, technicians, and administrative staff members are currently in Saudi Arabia and the Persian Gulf, all but a handful of whom are working in the cities of Dhahran and Riyadh. This is by far the largest concentration of journalists assembled to cover any American conflict since World War II.

A group of news representatives this large creates obvious problems, both for the military units they attempt to cover and for the journalists themselves. But these predictable difficulties have, in my view, been severely exacerbated by the rules imposed by American military authorities. These rules have made the Gulf War more difficult to cover than any in my experience, except for the 1971 conflict between India and Pakistan, in which Pakistan, the losing side, imposed censorship amounting to a news blackout.

As I understand it, the ground rules in effect in Saudi Arabia result directly from recommendations made by a commission headed by Maj. Gen. Winant Sidle in 1984. These recommendations included a provision by which the Pentagon can select a small group of journalists as members of combat pools, whose dispatches, photographs, and tapes become the common property of all accredited news organizations. The pools are to be permitted to cover battlefield operations, but under the direct supervision of military escorts and on condition that their products are subject to field censorship.

Media representatives who appeared before the Sidle Commission were unanimous in opposing pools in general, but, according to the commission's report, agreed to cooperate in pooling agreements "if that were necessary for them to obtain early access to an operation."

The latter condition has not been met by the United States military command in Saudi Arabia.

A pooling system has been in effect since the beginning of the gulf crisis. In my opinion, which I believe is shared by most of the correspondents there, this system has resulted in significant impairment of coverage of our armed forces and the war they are fighting.

The following are some of the objections:

First of all, I know of no journalists accredited to the Defense Department who would intentionally jeopardize military security. Moreover, I think that although censorship was neither necessary nor applied in any American conflict since Korea, many correspondents in the gulf willingly accept security reviews of their copy, provided such reviews are conducted solely to prevent military intelligence leaking to the enemy. In fact, the ground rules by which correspondents in Saudi Arabia are bound assure that "material will be examined solely for its conformance to the attached ground rules, not for its potential to express criticism or cause embarrassment."

137

But this condition has not been uniformly respected. On the opening day of the war, which I spent at an airbase from which our F-117A Stealth aircraft were operating, two of us encountered censorship problems. The dispatch I wrote as a member of the pool was reviewed by an escort officer and the unit commander, and was passed for transmission to pool headquarters and publication.

But at about 3 a.m. that night, Frank Bruni of the *Detroit Free Press* (the other newspaper writer in the pool) and I were informed that there had been second thoughts about our articles, in which various changes were requested. As far as I could see no security issues were involved in either story. In mine, one paragraph was deleted and various words changed or deleted in the rest of the text.

In one change, my phrase "fighter-bomber" had been stricken and replaced by the word "fighter." No reason for the change was given, but it seemed to be that the change might have something to do with the air force's efforts to save the B-2 Stealth bomber. If the F-117A were identified in print as a bomber—which it is—I could imagine that critics might assert that the air force had no need for a second Stealth bomber, the B-2.

The dispatch written by Mr. Bruni had been altered in a number of places. In one that I happen to remember, the adjective "giddy" (describing the feelings of a pilot) was changed to "proud."

None of the changes requested by the air force officials seemed substantive to Mr. Bruni and myself, so we agreed to all of them, on the understanding that our copy would be sent quickly. We felt that details of the opening of the war, including the fact that the first shots were 2,000-pound laser-guided bombs dropped precisely on their targets by Stealth fighter-bombers, would be news of considerable importance.

We learned later that morning, however, that our copy had been sent, not to the outer world, but to the 37th Tactical Fighter Wing headquarters at the Tonopah Test Facility in Nevada, which had blocked transmission completely. By the time our stories were ultimately released they were too stale to be of much use to our employers, or the other newspapers entitled to use pool copy—an irony, considering that these dispatches portrayed the opening air force raids as a brilliant success.

The next night, pilots of the Stealth unit revealed to us that they had demolished Iraq's plants and laboratories potentially involved in the production of nuclear weapons. Iraqi nuclear capabilities have been a subject of concern for some months, and this, again, would have been page-one news. We were asked, however, to suppress it on security grounds, and we reluctantly agreed. Less than 12 hours later, however, we learned to our chagrin that AFP, the French news agency, had distributed a story about the raids on Iraq's nuclear facilities, quoting a U.S. Senate source. And that evening, General Schwarzkopf himself announced details of the raids.

As members of the pool, we wondered why we had bothered even to visit the F-117A base, when we could have saved time and a great deal of trouble by simply attending the Washington briefings. It is vitally important for war correspondents to be close to their subject, but in Saudi Arabia, journalists are seldom able to view military developments any closer than they could in Washington.

Col. Bill Mulvey, the commander of the Joint Information Bureau in Dhahran, is a Vietnam veteran doing a heroic job in an unenviable position, caught between a patently unworkable system and the daily complaints of the frustrated newsmen he tries to help. He acknowledged that the system had broken down in our attempted coverage of the Stealth bombers. The failure was not his fault. But this kind of foul-up is inevitable, the system being what it is.

A second and more serious problem than censorship is the lack of access to American fighting men and women, and to front-line areas where the ground war would begin if it takes place.

Journalists who have succeeded in reaching American units in the field know that almost without exception, the soldiers, marines, and officers of these units welcome media attention. They understand that newsmen wish to spend time with them, not to spy on American military intentions, but to see how the troops are getting on in difficult circumstances. Today's correspondents identify ourselves with the soldiers of our generation as strongly as Ernie Pyle did with the soldiers of his.

But certain senior commanders—a couple of division commanders in particular—are apparently loath to have journalists wandering around their commands, even when their men would welcome them. At the time I left Saudi Arabia, only one pool print journalist was covering the entire 101st Airborne Division, for example. I would have to add that because the pool system has failed so miserably, many journalists set out on their own to try to cover American forces in the field, risking arrest and even deportation.

One distinguished writer, John Sack, author of many books on military subjects from the Korean War to the present, had a particularly frustrating experience. During the Vietnam War one of his best read books, *M*, chronicled the experiences of a single infantry company from the time it was formed in the United States, through training, into combat in Vietnam. Mr. Sack intends to write a similar book about a company of the First Infantry Division, that he had lived with at Fort Riley, Kansas, and which he hoped to follow into combat in the Arabian Peninsula. Despite the eagerness of the troops in the company (as well as at least one general officer) to have Mr. Sack rejoin the unit in Saudi Arabia, the pool system, at least up to the time I left Saudi Arabia, made it impossible.

For the month I was in Saudi Arabia I was a pool member, but never once was I able to visit American ground troops, despite my special interest in armor and antiarmor tactics. My sole contact with war on the ground was at Khafji, the Saudi town that was briefly occupied by Iraqi troops and then was retaken. I got there while the fighting was in progress by wangling a place for myself in a Saudi press pool organized on the orders of Gen. Khalid bin Sultan.

I would prefer to believe that the problems newsmen are encountering in covering the Gulf War result solely from mischance, but I'm afraid that the hostility of some senior officers toward the press may be a factor in the difficulties.

Regular readers of the American military press see constant examples of this hostility. For instance, Maj. Gen. Patrick H. Brady, army chief of public affairs until last May and now deputy commanding general of the Sixth Army, wrote in the September issue of *Army* magazine:

> The First Amendment gives the press a constitutional right to publish without prior constraint—not the right to know. The right to know is a sacred right held exclusively by the people, but the people do not have a right to know everything. . . .
>
> Some look on news as just another four-letter word, but I believe it is more useful to look at it as a C-letter word: chaos, confusion, conflict, contradiction, crime, corruption, color, catastrophe. It does not hurt if you add some Ss—sex, sensationalism, state secret—to it. Information must be timely if it is to be news. Being first with the Cs and Ss is the stuff of which news is made.

There have also been suggestions in the military press of a causal relationship in the fact that Grenada, a war from which the press was barred, was an unequivocal victory—probably the only one the United States has won since World War II.

I'm afraid that General Brady's views can only reopen some of the wounds that we all had hoped the years since Vietnam had healed. Fortunately, I believe that most of his uniformed colleagues take a more tolerant view of the news profession.

The paradox is that never since World War II has the American press been as supportive of our armed forces as it is today in the Persian Gulf. So far, the disagreements over matters of fact that so deeply divided the Pentagon from the press in Vietnam have not appeared in the Gulf, largely because American military claims have impressed newsmen as conservative, demonstrable, and reasonable, and because Saddam Hussein is universally regarded as a pariah.

But there are danger signs. If the press-haters in some quarters should prevail in the view that our war in the gulf should be closed against the light of free, honest reporting, a clash is inevitable that would do no American any good.

Thank you.

Out of the Pool

Robert Fisk

One: The Briefing

There is no blood on the floor of the Regency Room at the Hyatt Regency in Riyadh. And although the talk is all of war, there is no hint of pain or fear between the television arc lights and the wood-paneled walls. The ashtrays are regularly emptied. The wall-to-wall carpet is spotless. The flags clustered at one end of the room—American, Saudi, and a curious banner labeled JOINT FORCES with a map of the Arabian Peninsula in yellow protected by palm leaves—might be stage props in a televised drama. Which is, in one sense, what they are.

The style is informal, sanitized, occasionally infused with laughter, as, under the eyes of the world, the allied briefers tell reporters how the war is going. If you watch television at your fireside, you will know the faces well; but attending this extraordinary ritual is probably essential to understand its meaning. Old hands say that Saigon's "Five O'clock Follies" had nothing on this.

It is February, almost a month after the war began. Brig. Gen. Richard Neal, U.S. deputy director of operations, gives the first performance and makes us feel the war is a world away. He is a short man with a chunky face who talks warspeak. "Battlefield preparation" is still going on, as well as "restrikes of strategic targets." There have been 65,000 sorties "to date," and the allies continue "to interdict . . . roads, rail, and bridge systems." He divulges that "three TELs were attacked in Scud-related areas"—a TEL, it transpires, is a transport erector launcher for a missile—and there is much snickering when he suggests that there was an Iraqi technician "trying to check his fuel" moments before an allied bomb exploded beside him.

Six Iraqis have surrendered to U.S. forces. Iraq "continues to

143

disregard the Geneva Convention and also the International Committee of the Red Cross." He places a "high confidence value" on reports that execution squads are roaming behind Iraqi lines to shoot deserters. But what the general really wants to talk about is his pride in the young men bombing Iraq.

"We've got such kids doing the job.... These young kids.... Super equipment.... Unbeatable combination." He speaks of a "combined arms attack" that is "well orchestrated" in a "target-rich environment." He regrets not being able to give us "a good BDA" (bomb-damage assessment). Is the Baghdad airport being used? "I wouldn't buy a ticket on a local airline to go to Baghdad." Much laughter. The general tells us about "a lucrative target" that was "hunkered down."

The speech is packaged, a word that itself appeals to the generals. The Americans now speak, for example, of a "package" when they mean a collection of aircraft participating in a raid. There is, of course, no mention of the suffering of war, least of all reference to civilian casualties (in warspeak, "collateral damage") in Iraq. There is, in fact, no war at all, but rather a husk of words from which all reality has been sucked.

Others talk. Then the floodlights and cameras and tape recorders are switched off for an "off-the-record" briefing at which, in semidarkness, exactly the same performers go on talking, on condition they are referred to as a "U.S. military source." Off the record, a source remarks that "the weather in this part of the world is very difficult to predict. Clouds come one day, rain the next day, the sun will rise the next day. It's very difficult to predict."

Two: The Press Surrenders

A colonel commanding a U.S. air base in the Persian Gulf decided it was time to "honor" the pool reporters who had been attached to his fighter-bomber squadrons since the day the war broke out. He produced for each of them a small American flag that had been carried in the cockpit of one of the very first U.S. jets to bomb Baghdad. "You are warriors, too," he told the journalists as he handed them their flags.

The incident says a lot about the new, cozy, damaging relationship between reporters and the military in the Gulf War. The military preparation for handling this war has been so thorough, and journalists have become so dependent on information dispensed by Western military authorities in Saudi Arabia, that reporters have found themselves trapped.

Journalists are now talking of Iraq as "the enemy," as if they themselves have gone to war—which, in a sense, they have.

When 10 U.S. Navy jets took off from the aircraft carrier USS *Kennedy* at the start of the war, a reporter for the *Philadelphia Inquirer* filed a pool dispatch from the ship, describing how "Thursday morning was one of the moments suspended in time . . . paving the way for a dawn of hope." As Royal Air Force fighter pilots took off from a gulf airstrip several weeks later, a young British reporter told her television audience that "their bravery knows no bounds."

Such language is of the early 1940s, when Hitler's armies were poised to invade England. Journalists in uniforms and helmets are trying to adopt the *gravitas* of Edward R. Murrow. We are being prepared for "the biggest tank battle since World War II" and "the largest amphibious operation since D-Day."

This is as dangerous as it is misleading. When the largest Western armies launch their attack from the Muslim nation containing Islam's two holiest shrines, this is no time to draw parallels with the Second World War. Nor is this the "dawn of hope." It may well be the start of renewed decades of hatred between the West and the Arab world. Yet our reporting does not reflect this.

It is not easy for journalists to cast doubt on the U.S. military claims in the gulf. To do so is to invite almost immediate condemnation and the accusation that we have taken Saddam Hussein's side. In fact, there cannot be a reporter in Saudi Arabia who does not realize that Saddam Hussein is a brutal, wicked dictator who rules through terror. There can be no doubt about the savagery of his army in occupied Kuwait. Reporters who wander off to investigate military affairs in

Saudi Arabia risk, at worst, deportation. The last journalist who did that in Iraq, Farzad Bazoft of the *London Observer*, was hanged.

Yet almost three weeks after the start of the war, journalists have in effect surrendered to Western authorities. They are being forced either to participate in pool reporting under military restrictions—having their reports read and often amended by censors—or to work independently at the risk of having their accreditation taken away.

It should also be said that there are journalists in the pool who are valiantly and successfully filing dispatches that describe the unhappiness as well as the motivation of soldiers at war, the boredom as well as the excitement, the mistakes as well as the efficiency.

But many of their colleagues can claim no such record. Most of the journalists with the military now wear uniforms. They rely on the soldiers around them for advice and protection. They are dependent on the troops and their officers for communications, perhaps for their lives. And there is thus the profound desire to fit in and a frequent absence of critical faculties.

This was painfully illustrated when Iraqi troops captured the abandoned Saudi border town of Khafji. Pool reporters were first kept up to 15 miles from the sighting and—misled by their U.S. military minders—filed stories reporting the allied recapture of the town.

But when the *Independent* traveled to the scene to investigate the story, an NBC television reporter—a member of the military pool—responded with an obscenity and shouted: "You'll prevent us from working. You're not allowed here. Get out. Go back to Dhahran." He then called over a marine public affairs officer, who announced, "You're not allowed to talk to U.S. Marines, and they're not allowed to talk to you."

It was a disturbing moment. By traveling to Khafji, the *Independent* discovered that the Iraqis were still fighting in the town long after allied military spokesmen had claimed that it had been liberated. For the NBC reporter, however, the privileges of the pool and the military rules attached to it were more important than the right of journalists to do their job.

146

Even those who are playing by the rules are having difficulties. When reporters on the carrier USS *Saratoga* quoted the exact words of air force pilots, they found that the captain and other senior officers had deleted all swear words and changed some of the quotations before sending on their dispatches after a delay of 12 hours. On the USS *Kennedy*, pool reporters recorded how fighter-bomber pilots watched pornographic videotapes to help them relax before their mission. This was struck from their report.

But more often, it's the reporters' own omissions that are blatant. At one U.S. air base, a vast banner is suspended inside an aircraft hangar. It depicts Superman holding in his arms a limp, terrified Arab with a hooked nose. The existence of this banner, with its racist overtones, went unreported by the pool journalists at the base.

A pool television crew did record Marine Lt. Col. Dick White when he described what it was like to see Iraqi troops in Kuwait from his plane. "It was like turning on the kitchen light late at night and the cockroaches started scurrying."

This astonishing remark went unquestioned, although there was certainly one question worth asking: What is the New World Order worth when an American officer, after only three weeks of war, compares his Arab enemies to insects?

This is supposed to be a war for freedom, but the Western armies in Saudi Arabia—under the guide of preserving "security"—want to control the flow of information.

There could be no better proof of this than the predicament of the French television-crew members who filmed the Khafji fighting at great risk to their lives, breaking no security guidelines—and then had their tape confiscated because they were not members of the pool.

In reality, the French were merely doing their job. If reporters were trusted to travel independently to the front, as they have done in so many other wars—obeying local military commanders, betraying no secrets, but taking responsibility for their own lives—the whole charade of pools and restrictions could be abandoned.

Generals will always blame the media for their failures, however much we bow to their rules. But the public, whose support for this conflict is partly shaped by what it reads and sees on television, may not forgive the media for its weakness in so humbly accepting those little flags handed out by the colonel.

The Unilaterals

Chris Hedges

On January 18, the day I arrived in Saudi Arabia, I was informed that the U.S. Armed Forces Joint Information Bureau had only one pool slot for *The New York Times*. This meant that I and three other *Times* reporters would have to sit through briefings in Riyadh, work the military for information, and rewrite pool reports that filtered in from the field.

This hardly seemed an auspicious way to cover a war, so the next morning, after receiving permission from R.W. Apple, Jr., who ran our coverage from Dhahran, I climbed into a jeep with several British reporters and headed for the border city of Khafji.

I would never return to work within the system. For two months several colleagues and I bluffed our way through roadblocks, slept in Arab homes, and cajoled ourselves into units. Eventually, following armored battalions in our jeeps through breached minefields to the outskirts of Kuwait City, we raced across the last stretch of open desert and into the capital before it was liberated. Our success was due in part to an understanding by many soldiers and officers of what the role of a free press is in a democracy. These men and women violated orders to allow us to do our job.

In the beginning I drove back from wherever I was to Dhahran to file, but these six-to-eight-hour trips, through half a dozen check-points, began to eat up too much time. In early February, several of us rented jeeps with cellular phones that could make the international calls needed for filing stories. We filled our jeeps with bottled water and food, and began to spend days, and eventually weeks, in the field. I obtained permission from several Saudi families, with whom I spoke in Arabic, to sleep on their floors. Sometimes I stayed with soldiers in the field, sometimes in depressing truck stops. It was lonely, often

149

frustrating work. There were days when, after spending hours lost in the desert, I had little to show for it.

Late one evening, hopelessly lost near the Kuwaiti border, I came upon a long armored column snaking its way north with its lights out. Officers suggested I follow, and I did. After a lengthy drive, we gunned our vehicles up over 12-foot-high sand embankments and parked. I got out to meet a lanky captain and several lieutenants. I had stumbled onto the headquarters of the Sixth Marine Division and the captain made it clear that I was to be handed over to the military police. But while we waited I chatted with the officers, explaining why I had broken the rules and expressing my thoughts about the need for an independent press, even in wartime. The radio crackled. The captain went over to answer it. He returned in a few minutes. "The MPs are on their way," he said. Then, "Get in your jeep," he said slowly, "and haul ass."

I was able to spend several days, with the permission of officers, with units preparing for war. Troops in the field usually received the press warmly. Many had spent months in the desert and welcomed the chance to tell their stories. Most had little affection for the public relations officers.

I spent some time with one infantry battalion and got to know many of its officers and soldiers well. I brought them daily papers when I visited, and later I phoned messages to some of their families. When the battalion was ordered to move up to the Kuwaiti border, the commander painstakingly drew me a map so I could find the new position.

When I showed up one February morning, I was taken to the commander's foxhole.

"The order has come down that there is to be no unescorted press here," he began. My heart sank. "I won't tell you how I personally feel about this," he went on, then paused for a few moments and continued: "As far as I go, you are not here. You must park your car away from the camp. If other officers come in you must keep away, and if you get caught you were here because you were lost and were looking for directions." It was agreed that I would never quote him by name or identify his battalion.

By February the order had gone out that MPs were to detain all members of the press found north of Dhahran and to confiscate their credentials. So while at first we had been able to run roadblocks so long as we wore khaki dress, now more and more cars were being stopped. One soldier gave me a helmet, which helped immensely.

By working outside the pool, we could speak with soldiers without the presence of an escort. This did not always mean that we wrote stories that criticized the military, although people were more likely to speak openly if they thought their conversations were not being monitored.

The fine stories on the Egyptian forces filed by Forrest Sawyer of ABC News and Tony Horwitz of *The Wall Street Journal*, for example, could only have been done by going outside the system. Managed information always has an unreal, stale quality. And while none of us broke scandals or uncovered gross abuses, we were able to present an uncensored picture of life at the front.

It is worth remembering that during the first 24 hours of the fighting in Khafji in February the allied command insisted that only Arab forces were battling the Iraqis. They changed their story after an AP reporter climbed into a U.S. armored personnel carrier and drove into the city, where he witnessed marines engaging Iraqi troops. The United States wanted to build the confidence of the Arab forces, but at the expense of the truth.

I spent time in a 10-acre supply depot and wrote an account of how supply officers barter, beg, and pilfer to get what they need for their men. The article, which I had tried to keep whimsical, failed to amuse a few Marine Corps generals when they read it in the *Times*.

The battalion commander of the two officers I quoted in the piece, a man who knew nothing of my visit, was called in by *his* commanding general and told to keep reporters out of his unit if he wanted to keep his command. Apparently, his superiors had used a computer list to trace the names in the story to his unit.

An unexpected bonus resulting from this article was that the supply officers gave me a desert camouflage uniform and a flak jacket. It was now impossible for anyone who did not question me directly to tell that I was a reporter. Just before I drove away, one of the men reached down and took the blousers off his trousers. "Marines blouse," he said, putting the two elastic bands in my hand.

I ran into trouble, however, a day later. I had just finished reporting a story about how, with the influx of soldiers, Saudi shopkeepers had tripled and quadrupled prices. The price gouging was galling to the troops who, after all, had come as allies. This was the type of story that, although it had no military or strategic significance, would rarely get by a public affairs officer.

On my way back from the shops, I stopped to talk to some officers who ran a field hospital, in the hope that I might be able to write a story about how nurses and doctors whiled away their time waiting for the ground war to begin. But by this time, although I didn't know it, reporters were not just to be turned away from units when they showed up, but arrested. The hospital officials assigned an armed escort to me and I was driven to the headquarters of the Seventh Corps, some 10 miles away.

I was taken to the trailers that made up the press center and turned over to a Captain Miller. A few pool reporters were seated at a picnic table. The captain said I was under detention. When I protested, one of the pool reporters told me to be quiet.

"You can't talk to him like that," he said. "They'll take away your credentials for good."

A captain, armed with an M-16, was placed in the front seat of my car and a lieutenant in a truck in front of me, and I was escorted to King Khaled Military City. At the end of the two-hour trip, I was turned over to a Capt. Archie Davis, who confiscated my Saudi press card. He told me that the rules were for my own good, that he and the other officers were just trying to protect me from the hazards of war. "There are a lot of soldiers out there with pretty itchy trigger fingers," he said.

I was sent back to the Joint Information Bureau in Dhahran, an eight-hour drive, to retrieve the press card from a Maj. William Fellows. "You have an attitude problem," he told me. But he returned the card.

More than a dozen of us, labeled "the unilaterals" by the military press office, had now been detained by military police. We had to decide whether to risk expulsion or abide by the rules. The next day I left without an escort, violating the rules again.

Those of us outside the system were now in a precarious position. We could be arrested for even approaching a unit. In the last weeks before the ground war, I filed stories on the Egyptian and Czechoslovakian contingents and one on a New York National Guard transportation unit known as the Harlem Hell Fighters, a group whose members felt they had been ill treated by the army. Two months earlier they had sent in an official request, which had never been answered, asking that a reporter from a New York newspaper be allowed to visit them.

The ground war was now only days away, and the military police were frequently stopping cars along the road that ran east to west along the Kuwaiti and Iraqi border. By this time, I had my hair cut to military regulations, my jeep marked with the inverted "V" that was on all military vehicles, and a large orange cloth tied to the roof to identify it as part of the allied force. I carried canteens and even a knife, the gift of some marines. I was waved through check points.

By the time the attack was launched, the JIB had issued new regulations: no reporters were allowed to wear military dress, to use cellular phones to file stories, or to mark their vehicles. The new rules came a little late.

The President's "Spin" Patrol

Ann McDaniel and Howard Fineman

It was the worst news of the war. A dozen marines (the actual number turned out to be 11) had been killed in action, the first deaths in what could be a bloody ground campaign. Normally, a staff officer would give the daily briefing, but on this afternoon last week, Gen. Norman Schwarzkopf appeared before the press. He began by showing a spectacular videotape of smart bombs obliterating their targets, and he described the Iraqi losses overnight as "rather sensational." One video showed a truck traveling across a bridge span that was caught in the cross hairs of an American warplane. "And now, in his rear view mirror," the general dryly noted as the bridge blew apart. Only after 23 minutes of superlatives and confident quips did the U.S. commander cryptically announce that the marines had lost "12 KIA." The reporters took the bait. On the evening news shows, the bombs-away video got at least equal billing with the dead marines.

The general's diversionary tactic had been carefully orchestrated. On that morning, like every morning since the war began, White House, Pentagon, State Department, and CIA officials had gathered before dawn to plot the "spin" for the day. Administration officials understand that the United States is engaged in a PR war as well as a real one. Saddam Hussein's strategy, they know, is the same one that worked for Ho Chi Minh in Vietnam: to bleed the U.S. military until the American people give up.

The PR model is a political campaign. Every morning, the administration settles on a "message of the day." For instance, when Iraq broadcast pictures of tortured American POWs, the message was "Saddam will be punished for war crimes." White House spokesman Marlin Fitzwater tests the message at his late-morning briefings. By refusing to allow in cameras, Fitzwater can experiment with his rhetoric and see how it plays with reporters. The message is then fine-tuned for the later State Department and Pentagon briefings, which are on camera and thus more likely to make the evening news.

Bad news: "Talking points" are faxed almost every day to party leaders, business executives, and religious figures friendly to the administration. "Don't forget to mention these points," one memo instructed, "whether it is at a cocktail party or a board meeting." The most effective tools are the videos of high-tech bombs scoring bull's eyes on Iraqi targets. The images left unseen are just as important. The administration has banned cameras from recording the return of body bags to American bases. If bad news must be aired, the usual military briefers—who tend to be anxious, tight-lipped officers—are pushed aside, and the more confident, expansive senior commanders— Schwarzkopf or Joint Chiefs Chairman Colin Powell—step in.

The chief spinner, of course, is President Bush. On a tour of military bases last week, Bush cheered the families of servicemen by predicting victory. "We are on course. We are on schedule," he said. But he also preached sacrifice. Recognizing that a bloody ground war is inevitable, the president wants to prepare Americans for the cost. His rhetoric in the State of the Union address about the "hard work of freedom" was meant to signal the public that dead soldiers would be coming home soon, possibly in large numbers.

Will Americans be willing to pay the price? "When casualties start mounting, that's when congressional support will start sliding," says Rep. Bill Richardson, Democrat from New Mexico. In the Vietnam War, once the body count climbed above 10,000 in 1967, opponents of the war outnumbered supporters. Some poll takers say that Americans will put up with serious casualties—for a time. "As long as the war is definable, achievable, and is seen as reasonably short, support will stand up," says independent pollster Andrew Kohut. Already there are worrisome divisions. While four out of five Americans back Bush's conduct of the war, only one out of two blacks do. With black political leaders arguing that blacks will do a disproportionate amount of dying, the war threatens to become a divisive racial issue. And though the gender gap closed when the war began, support is fragile among women. Bush's macho talk has offended some. "Women aren't interested in sending their sons and husbands to their deaths because Bush feels the need to kick some ass," says a close adviser to Bush, who has warned the chief executive to tone down his bluster.

The message of sacrifice has not played well in the American electorate for more than a decade. Jimmy Carter was pilloried for preaching the politics of less. Ronald Reagan flew high by promising that Americans could have it all, and the consumer society of the 1980s believed him. Indeed, in some ways the war is a diversion from pressing problems at home. Bush's State of the Union was short on domestic initiatives, and Congress is not likely to fill the void. By staying glued to the latest smart-bomb video on CNN, Americans can conveniently forget the country's yawning federal deficit, escalating crime, dropping SAT scores, and deteriorating economy. Only when the images turn to dead GIs will reality set in. For the president's PR machine, the "daily message" could easily get lost in the stark images of combat. The spinmeisters may face a hard choice between showing the true face of war—or opening a credibility gap that could come back to haunt them.

U.S. Lets Some News Filter Through "Blackout"

Howard Kurtz

U.S. officials partially relaxed their "blackout" on news of the ground invasion of Kuwait yesterday less than 12 hours after it was imposed, as some officials conceded the restrictions had gone too far and initial reports showed allied forces faring well.

Although Defense Secretary Richard B. Cheney announced Saturday night that briefings on the war would be suspended for an undetermined period of time, the administration moved quickly yesterday to ensure that positive news filtered through the blackout.

Gen. H. Norman Schwarzkopf, who commands the U.S. gulf forces, convened a morning news conference to announce that the allies were having "dramatic success."

Cheney, who said Saturday he would address no questions about the operation, appeared on CBS's "Face the Nation" to say he was "pleasantly surprised" to report that "the resistance has been light all across the front" and that casualties were "extremely light."

By the afternoon, pool reports from reporters traveling with U.S. forces began arriving again after being held up by officials in Saudi Arabia for at least 10 hours.

Soon only television pictures were lacking, and these too became available from U.S. allies in the war, in a way that had the effect of pushing Arab forces into the combat spotlight.

A British ITN television crew captured dramatic footage of Saudi troops firing into an Iraqi bunker, taking prisoners, tying their hands behind their backs, and carrying off the wounded. ABC's Forrest Sawyer filed reports from an Egyptian unit. And French forces flew reporters by helicopter about three miles inside Iraq, landing them behind French tanks and artillery.

157

Howell Raines, Washington bureau chief of *The New York Times*, said Defense Department officials were using legitimate security concerns "as a means of imposing the blanket management of information of a sort we've never seen in this country. If they've loosened it today, it was because they had good news to report and it was in their interest to report it. What they've put in place is a mechanism to block out bad news and to keep good news in the forefront."

But Army Col. Miguel E. Monteverde, the Pentagon's director of defense information, said officials simply realized that some of the restrictions were impractical.

"It's not just the notion that we're winning the war, so now we can talk about it," he said. "If you have the upper hand, you can afford to be more liberal on things like that.... If things are going well, the risk to the troops is obviously less."

When the ground war began, the Pentagon considered a proposal to block all pool reports for 48 hours, but dropped the idea, Monteverde said. An initial *Washington Post* pool report marked "urgent" was not cleared by military officials for more than 10 hours, and later reports had to be faxed because the normal computer processing was delayed.

Pentagon officials also had ordered that television footage be shipped to Riyadh as well as Dhahran, Saudi Arabia, for clearance by a second layer of censors. Yesterday that requirement was rescinded as well. Monteverde blamed the delays on logistical problems. He said the regular twice-daily military briefings would likely remain suspended for two more days.

The U.S. blackout stood in sharp contrast to the 1944 D-Day invasion of Normandy, when 27 U.S. journalists accompanied Allied forces and filed stories that day. Military historians say blackouts were not used during the Korean War and were briefly imposed only twice during the Vietnam War.

Several news executives refrained from criticizing the military. Andrew J. Glass, Washington bureau chief for Cox Newspapers, said the Pentagon would have been "irresponsible" had it failed to impose a blackout because of CNN's worldwide presence.

Polls show that 80 percent of the public backs military restrictions on the press, a view reinforced in interviews around the country yesterday.

Jack Polk, a car dealer in Austin, Texas, said the news media "have provided inside information to the enemy." Cliff Murphy, a real estate agent in Miami, said "in a military situation, the military should control it." One dissenter was Amanda Wingfield, a University of Texas student, who called the blackout "unbelievable censorship."

Timothy Russert, NBC's Washington bureau chief, said his network had offered to block out the insignia on allied uniforms to avoid disclosing the location of units to the Iraqis.

Far more detailed reporting was permitted during D-Day. The day after the June 6, 1944, invasion, United Press reported: "Some of the first American assault troops storming the French beaches went down under a withering German crossfire. They swarmed ashore over the bodies of their dead until they established a foothold. At one point Nazi machine guns wiped out some of the first troops as soon as the doors of their landing craft swung open."

Do Americans Really Want to Censor War Coverage This Way?

Michael Getler

Along with the Iraqis, the civilian and uniformed leaders of the U.S. military did a pretty good job of mopping up the press in Operation Desert Storm. No one seems to care very much about this except several hundred reporters and editors who know they've been had.

The war, after all, was successful beyond anyone's expectations: an overwhelming American-led victory with amazingly low allied casualties that ended after only 100 hours of ground fighting.

Many people by now probably feel they have a pretty good picture of what happened and may not have noticed or cared much if the news, details, and pictures were a day or two or three late, or if a few things went uncovered, or if the war was over before they found out much. All's well that ends well. Indeed, the polls show a lot of people even think the press did a pretty good job.

But the military, and the civilians who are supposed to control the military, did a better job controlling the press than the press did carrying out its crucial, cranky function in a democracy.

The Pentagon and the U.S. Army Central Command conducted what is probably the most thorough and sophisticated wartime control of American reporters in modern times—what they could see, who they could talk to, where they could go, what they could tell the public, and when they could tell it—a collection of restrictions that in its totality and mindset seems to go beyond World War II, Korea, and Vietnam.

Because it all happened so fast and ended so happily, the implications of the Pentagon's victory over the press may not seem apparent or important. But had the war gone on longer or less well, the chances are that these restrictions would have been used to control and delay

I

even more what the public knew about the fighting. The Pentagon has devised a system that tends to produce "good news"—and the Iraqis turned out to be a "good news" kind of enemy. But if allowed to stand as a model, the Desert Storm system runs the risk of seriously distorting reality for some uncertain time if the next war is a lot tougher.

There were many elements of the Pentagon's plan to control the press. They were there from the start of serious planning by the Defense Department last fall. These include:

Censorship by delay: Perhaps the crucial restriction turned out to be what the Pentagon calls "security review" and what the press called censorship. The issue, as it turned out, was not really censorship. Correspondents told of many instances of foolish military attempts to delete material that had nothing to do with real security—earthy language or embarrassing scenes. Yet there seems to have been relatively little else removed from reporters' copy.

Indeed, this tends to back up the point that news executives repeatedly tried to make to the Pentagon: that reporters will agree to and abide by sensible ground rules about what not to report without the need for field censorship, a system that worked essentially flawlessly in Vietnam. Barry Zorthian, the former U.S. Mission Spokesman in Saigon, has said there were only four or five violations of security—some unintentional—by some 2,000 journalists over a five-year period.

What security review did do, however, is force reporters to turn their stories in to their military minders in the field for review and transmission back to the military press headquarters in Dhahran, Saudi Arabia. Reporters totally lost control over their dispatches, and the military gained the extraordinary power to delay transmissions of news for unspecified amounts of time.

It is impossible to say for sure what happened to every dispatch or what every newspaper or network experienced. But the overwhelming evidence is that virtually all of these dispatches, or "pool" reports, were delayed because of tampering or various other reasons somewhere along the line by the military, at best one day but far more frequently by two or three days. Reporters who had risked their lives, along with soldiers, to ride through minefields and be exposed to Iraqi fire, and who thought they had sent their material on its way to readers or viewers, were almost always disappointed.

There were undoubtedly occasions where public affairs officers tried their best and where bad weather meant that helicopters that might have speeded the movement of stories could not fly. But the fact is the army should not have been in the business of reviewing and transmitting stories and pictures.

"They don't know how to transmit copy just like I don't know how to drive a tank," said the *Post*'s veteran foreign and war correspondent, Ed Cody. Military officers have no incentive to rush back a story that they may not like, or to bug a senior officer to move it faster than a 20-hour "pony express" drive by truck, or to use the electronic means available to them.

The military refused to permit pool reporters accompanying troops to take their own vehicles, usually rented Land Rovers, or suitcase-sized satellite telephones out into the field. The phones could have given reporters direct access to their news desks.

New York Times reporter Phillip Shenon, with U.S. armored forces, told the Associated Press his military hosts took 72 hours to transmit his stories, and that when reporters volunteered to go to a nearby Saudi telephone to file them, "we were given the ludicrous argument that we couldn't leave the base because there was a terrorist threat. They were supposed to help us file our story, but there seemed to be every desire to hinder us in getting the work out," Shenon said.

Contrast these delays with coverage of World War II. On June 7, 1944, within hours of the invasion of France, UPI reported "some of the first American assault troops storming the French beaches went down under a withering German crossfire. . . . They swarmed ashore over the bodies of their dead until they established a foothold. . . . At one point Nazi machine guns wiped out some of the first troops as soon as their landing craft swung open."

162

There is, in my view, zero probability that that kind of accurate, timely, and dramatic reporting would have been allowed to have been transmitted without serious delay by the presslords of Desert Storm.

Fortunately, there were no such scenes to describe this time. But there were also no accounts of the relatively few combat engagements of the war that reached here until the military either wanted them to, or the system got around to moving them, and that usually meant days late—in many cases, not until the war was over. There were few if any pictures transmitted during the fighting of wounded or dead GIs and very few of what must be thousands of dead Iraqis. There were only the fuzziest, delayed accounts of death by friendly fire of U.S. and British ground troops, perhaps understandably, perhaps also to let the bad stuff dissipate before it became public. Pool reporters were kept away from the first significant ground clash at Khafji, while briefers played down the role of U.S. Marines and played up the role of Saudi and Qatari forces.

Death by briefing: The ground war, while it was underway, was described primarily by military briefers in the Pentagon and Saudi Arabia, which is what the Pentagon wanted all along; for them, not the pools or the press, to control the flow of news. The quality of the daily briefings in Riyadh, Saudi Arabia, led to what one reporter described as "death by briefing."

Those televised briefings helped the Pentagon's general press strategy in other ways. Reporters who regularly cover military matters generally know what to ask. A war, however, brings everyone into the briefing room and the briefers know it. So a lot of people get called on who may appear to a television audience to be ill-informed and pushy and that helps feed the view that those at the podium know best about what the public should know.

When the commanding presence of Joint Chiefs Chairman Colin L. Powell or Desert Storm Commander H. Norman Schwarzkopf were added for good measure, the questioners didn't have a chance on the public relations meter.

Until it was clear the enemy was routed, the ground war was

presented in much the same antiseptic way as the air war, in which videotapes of highly accurate smart-bomb strikes were shown to the public while repeated requests by reporters to go on raids or talk to crews of B-52s, which carry huge loads of less accurate bombs, were never acted upon.

Blacking out the ugly parts: As in Grenada and Panama, that first, potentially ugliest look at warfare is what the Pentagon doesn't want anyone to see until it is on its way to doing what it wants to do.

When the ground campaign began, the first thing Secretary of Defense Dick Cheney did publicly was to announce a news blackout, which is known to have annoyed some U.S. generals in the field and which didn't seem to bother the British or French, whose reporters seemed to be getting more real-time information than were the Americans.

The Pentagon then partially relaxed its blackout within 12 hours so that Schwarzkopf could proclaim a "dramatic success" in the early going.

Leakproof pools: The other central element of the Pentagon's press control plan was the "pool" system itself, in which eventually about 150 reporters, cameramen, and technicians out of more than 1,400 in Saudi Arabia at the time, were sent out in small groups with the armed forces to report back to their colleagues and the nation at large.

Contrary to some accounts, the pool system for Desert Storm was not signed onto by news executives of the major media organizations. It was a Defense Department plan, aspects of which drew consistent complaints from news executives in each of its variations.

The pool system originally grew out of a recommendation of the 1984 commission headed by retired general Winant Sidle that was meant to deal with press complaints of exclusion from covering the 1983 invasion of Grenada. Sidle recommended the pool approach to give reporters assured access at the start of conflict, proposing that the pool remain in place "for the minimum time possible" before switching to full press coverage, and that the Pentagon rely on "voluntary compliance" by the press with security guidelines established by the military.

But in the invasion of Panama in 1989, the press pool was still kept away from the start of the conflict, and Desert Storm further violated Sidle's principles both by the crucial demand for field censorship and by keeping the pool system in place throughout the war.

The first published guidelines news executives saw in mid-December provided for something called Phase III, which meant that at some point open—or what the military called "unilateral"—coverage would begin. But Phase III, presumably on orders of Schwarzkopf's Central Command—which seemed to run everything including the civilian defense officials in Washington—was dropped from the final guidelines.

Other aspects of the ground rules, in my view, also showed the Command's determination to place unprecedented restrictions on how the war would be reported.

Early on, Pentagon spokesman Pete Williams allowed that reporters who went to the field on their own and happened to hook up with pools could join that pool. But the final guidelines said "news media personnel who are not members of the official CENTCOM media pools will not be permitted into forward areas. Reporters are strongly discouraged from attempting to link up on their own with combat units. U.S. commanders will maintain extremely tight security throughout the operational area and will exclude from the area of operation all unauthorized individuals."

Reporters had to have escorts with them at all times, and at one point CENTCOM tried to make sure that all interviews were on the record, both measures meant to deny reporters' freedom of movement and to ensure that whoever is interviewed doesn't say anything out of line. The military decided where they could go and who could talk to them—another form of censorship.

There is indeed an unavoidable tension between the military and the press simply because their roles in our society are so different. Yet the fact is that many commanders, field grade officers, and soldiers like having reporters around because they like to have their story told too, their courage and their part of the drama recorded.

The pool system is not without some merit. In a vast operation such as Desert Storm, with massive and swift movements of armor, hundreds of warplanes flying from navy carriers and Saudi air bases, pools can provide a broader picture than we otherwise might get, certainly at the kickoff. But when, as in the case of Desert Storm, the system becomes a method of total control over what gets reported and when, that should be unacceptable for the news media—and untenable as well for the public when the news isn't good.

Some of the best coverage of the war came from those who bucked the pool system. One of those, and one of the newest reporters on the Desert Storm beat, was retired Army Col. David Hackworth, this country's most decorated living veteran.

Writing in *Newsweek*, Hackworth said as a reporter he had more freedom than a commander, "but I was very unhappy with the military's paranoia and their thought police who control the press. Although I managed to go out on my own, we didn't have the freedom of movement to make an independent assessment of what the military is all about. Everything was spoon-fed. We were like animals in a zoo, and the press officers were the zookeepers who threw us a piece of meat occasionally.

"I had more guns pointed at me," Hackworth added, "by Americans and Saudis who were into controlling the press than in all my years of actual combat."

Hackworth also had some critical things to say about the press, some of whom he called "irresponsible and unprepared" and who used the "power of the press for their own little trip."

Indeed, Desert Storm and its aftermath confront the press with many tough questions. Should a newspaper or network decide not to take part in pools anymore to force the Pentagon to change the system? News organizations, by their nature, are competitive, don't work together. Nor should they. So how will they pressure the Department of Defense?

166

How would they have covered Desert Storm without the pool system? This newspaper sent six reporters and a photographer to the war theater, not to mention correspondents in surrounding countries. Will we and other big organizations each send 10 the next time, each with a leased Land Rover and $50,000 satellite phone, and tell them it's okay to drive across a vast, mined desert? And what will smaller papers do?

Who should control the sheer numbers of reporters, cameramen, and technicians that flock to a war zone? Bitter cat fights emerged in Saudi Arabia among organizations trying desperately to land the few places on pools, something military press officers undoubtedly enjoyed watching. Major news organizations with millions of readers and viewers—who invested lots of money in sending as many reporters as possible to the region right from the start and who are rich in military or Arab world specialists—naturally want the spots. But who is to say the reporter from a small paper in Missouri with a guard unit in the war zone cannot go?

There are ways to do it better than Desert Storm.

Ed Cody summed it up succinctly. "Don't just take us along. Leave us alone."

Excerpts from Remarks to the National Press Club

Pete Williams

... In World War II, the most disappointing thing to tell a reporter was probably to say something like, "I'm sorry, the Channel is fogged in. You won't be able to leave for a couple of days." In Vietnam, the most disappointing words a reporter could hear was probably something like, "I'm sorry, but the helicopter left an hour ago." In Operation Desert Storm, it was probably, "Hi, I'm your press escort. I'm here to help you."

If what I read in the newspapers is ... any indicator, then the subject of press pools and escorts is nearly the most frequently written-about item around, with the possible exception of Princess Di and Fergie. Most of the comments made for the press arrangements for the Persian Gulf are not the kind of thing that I will be putting on my resume, so you may probably wonder ... why I would accept this invitation from the National Press Club and come to talk about them. ...

But the reason why I wanted to be with you here today is that I think two myths have grown up in the past two weeks, and they need to be debunked. The first is that the press somehow didn't do a good job in covering Operation Desert Storm, and the second is that reporters didn't have much of a chance to report the war.

Myth No. 1 has best been expressed by writers in your own ranks. This sentiment was expressed perhaps most succinctly by David Gergen writing in *U.S. News and World Report*. He says the American press knocked itself out to cover the war, and then he writes, "And what does the press have to show for this? A big black eye."

Now, I read my job description, Department of Defense Directive 5122.5, and nowhere in it does it say that I am the government's press critic. But none of the criticism that I'm talking about—much of it, indeed, self-criticism from the press itself—gives an accurate picture, I think, of how the press did in covering the Gulf War.

Some of the critics of the press, both those inside and outside journalism, view the relationship between the military and the media as a zero-sum game. If the military credibility is up, then the press credibility must be down. Now it's true, I think, that the military, I'm grateful to say, emerged from all of this with gained credibility, but that's in part true because the press accurately reported what we did—that's how people know what we did. Reporters have asked the tough questions, they've challenged the assumptions, they've exposed the mistakes, and they've held officials accountable. When a public institution passes those tests, then its credibility rises, and when it fails those tests, its credibility drops.

"Euphoria Control"

Another part of the reason for the military's high credibility, I think, is that Secretary Dick Cheney and Gen. Colin Powell made the decision that we would say only what we knew to be true. We were careful not to get out ahead of our successes. We waited for initial field reports to be confirmed. Even in the first few days of the air campaign in January, when the coalition aircraft losses appeared to be very light, we cautioned reporters about saying that it would be easy.

Now, Washington loves to talk about "spin control"—this is the first government operation I can remember that had "euphoria control."

Part of the problem for the press was that many people at home who were watching the story unfold did not understand what goes on in a press briefing. Day after day during the war, there were letters sent to me at the Pentagon saying something like this: "Will you please ask reporters to give their names when they ask questions? And then we can write to their employers and tell them to buzz off."

Now we never did that, of course. Having sat on the other side of the podium, I have always thought that there is no such thing as a bad question. And the ritual of press briefings has its own bizarre etiquette, no doubt about it, but it evolved in the era before live television. And so, what's fair in the briefing room may not seem reasonable or even polite when seen in the living room.

But tough questions are fair game. Plans don't always work the way they are supposed to, and even if they do, it isn't wrong for reporters to ask questions and raise doubt about them in advance. The way to judge the work of the press is to forget about the questions and focus on the stories that are written and broadcast, just as a successful fisherman ought to be judged by the fish he catches and not by the worm he uses. . . .

What public in what other conflict can possibly have been given as much information as the American people in this war? And people responded to that coverage. A *Newsweek* poll found that 59 percent of Americans think better of the news media now than they did before the war. The ABC News-*Washington Post* poll out last weekend shows that by a two-to-one margin, those surveyed thought that the press gained respect. And partly because of the thorough job that the press did, the military gained respect. Thanks to reporters the American people could see what our troops, our commanders, and our weapons were doing.

The *Post*-ABC poll showed that 88 percent of those surveyed thought the military gained respect during the war. Eighty-eight percent. Ten years ago, the military had only half that confidence.

The Second Myth

Richard Harwood, who's the *Washington Post* ombudsman, also said those reporters who long for the good old days of Vietnam should visit the archives. He said they would find no historical precedent for the expensive and detailed Desert Storm coverage. He is referring to the second myth about the Gulf War and the press in it; and that is that reporters didn't have much of a chance to do their jobs because of the press arrangements that we had there.

Last August, after Iraq's invasion of Kuwait, U.S. forces began to arrive a few days after Secretary Cheney's meeting with King Fahd in Saudi Arabia. As the first U.S. Air Force F-15s landed on sovereign Saudi territory, there were no Western reporters in the kingdom of Saudi Arabia. While the Saudi government studied whether to grant visas to journalists, they agreed to accept a pool of U.S. reporters if the U.S. military would get them in. And we did that; we activated the DoD national media pool because at the time there was no other way to get Western reporters into Saudi Arabia.

The pool arrived Monday afternoon, August 13, and continued to act as a pool until August 26. The Saudi government then started to—during the time they were there—issue visas to other reporters, but the news organizations and the Pentagon pool asked that we keep it going until the visa picture cleared up. And so we did.

And starting with those initial 17 who represented AP, UPI, Reuters, CNN, National Public Radio, *Time*, Scripps-Howard, the *Los Angeles Times* and the *Milwaukee Journal*, the number of reporters, editors, photographers, producers, and technicians grew to nearly 800 by December. Except during the first two weeks of the pool, those reporters all filed their stories independently, directly to their own news organizations.

They visited ships at sea. They went to air bases. They talked with marines up north and soldiers training in the desert. They went aboard AWACS (Airborne Warning and Control System) radar warning planes. They quoted generals, who said their forces were ready, and privates, who said they were not. There were stories about helicopter pilots crashing into the sand because they couldn't judge distances in the flat desert light. And reporters described the remarkable speed with which the U.S. military moved so many men and women to the gulf with so much of their equipment.

After the president in mid-November announced a further buildup in U.S. forces to give the coalition a true offensive option, my office began working on the plan that would allow reporters to cover the combat if it came to that, while maintaining operational security necessary to assure tactical surprise and save American lives.

1,400 Journalists Enough?

One of the first concerns of news organizations of the Pentagon press corps was that they didn't have enough staff in the Persian Gulf to cover the hostilities. This was before the numbers reached 800. Since they didn't know how the Saudi government would respond to their request for more visas if combat broke out and since they couldn't predict what kind of restrictions there might be on commercial aircraft in the event of the war, they asked us whether we would be willing to use a military plane to take in a group of journalists who would act as journalistic reinforcements. And we agreed to do so. And in fact a U.S. Air Force C-141 cargo plane left Andrews Air Force Base (Maryland) on January 17, the morning after the bombing began, with 126 news media people on board.

Now the fact that senior military commanders dedicated one of their cargo planes to the job of transporting another 120 or so journalists to Saudi Arabia demonstrated the military's commitment to take reporters to the scene of the action so that they could get the story out to the American people.

In formulating the ground rules and the guidelines for covering hostilities in Operation Desert Storm, we did not do this in a vacuum. We consulted the history books, we looked back at the rules developed in 1942 for World War II. We looked at those handed down by General Eisenhower's chief of staff for the reporters who covered the D-Day landings. We looked at the ground rules established by General MacArthur for the Korean War, and we carefully studied the rules that were drawn up for covering the war in Vietnam.

The rules that finally came out were not intended to prevent journalists from reporting on incidents that might embarrass the military or intended to make military operations look sanitized. Instead, they were intended simply and solely for this reason: to prevent publication of details that could jeopardize a military operation or endanger the lives of U.S. troops.

Now, for example, the sort of things that were in the ground rules, the sort of things that were not to be reported, were details of future

172

operations, for obvious reasons, specific information about troop strengths or troop locations, specific information on missing or downed aircraft or airplanes or ships while search-and-rescue operations were under way, and information on operational weaknesses that could be used against U.S. forces.

I think reporters understood the reasoning behind these ground rules I've just talked about, and of all the aspects of the coverage plan for the war in the Persian Gulf, I think they would agree that they were the least—those rules were the least—controversial.

I think the least understood was the system we had for copy review.

Now reporters covering World War II wrote their stories out in the field and submitted them to a military censor. The censors cut out anything they felt broke the rules and then gave the stories back to be sent on. The decision of the censor, a military person, was final.

No Systematic Censorship

There was no such system of censorship in Operation Desert Storm. There was instead a procedure that allowed us to appeal to news organizations when we thought that material in their stories might violate the ground rules. But unlike a system of censorship, this system in the gulf left the final decision to publish or broadcast in the hands of journalists, not the military.

When the pools were in existence, during the time that they were going, they have been dissolved now, but when they were in existence, 1,351 print pool stories were written. Of those, only five were submitted to our review in the Pentagon, at the final level of review appeal, and we cleared four of them. The fifth involved a story that dealt in considerable detail with the methods of intelligence operations in the field. We called the reporter's editor-in-chief here in town, and he agreed that the story should be changed to protect sensitive intelligence procedures. So I think that aspect of the coverage plan worked well.

Now only the pool stories that were written from reporters—I should say the pool stories written by reporters in the field—were subject to this review that I just talked about, not the live television or radio reports or the thousands of other stories that were written in Dhahran and Riyadh, based on pool reports, military briefings, and original reporting, such as the stories that Eric Schmidt of *The New York Times* did on the air campaign, for example.

As the number of troops in the desert grew, so did the number of reporters to cover them. The U.S. and international press corps, as I said, went from zero on August 2, to 17 on that first pool, to 800 by December, and to nearly 1,400 just before the ground war started.

Most of those reporters, the good ones certainly, wanted to be out where the action was, not standing around the hotel. But with hundreds of fiercely independent reporters seeking to join up with combat units, we concluded that when the combat started, we would have no choice but to rely on pools. Now, frankly, we agonized over this decision, because the part of the job that we dislike the most is setting up pools and keeping them going.

Unilateral or independent reporting worked well all through the fall and early winter. But once the war approached, the number of reporters in Saudi Arabia continued to grow and the competition to get out with the troops was intense. There simply was no fair alternative to pools, especially considering the highly mobile nature of this war, which was prosecuted in a vast desert.

And now that the war is over and General Schwarzkopf has described the plan, it's clear why the press arrangements were not like those in World War II. This was not an operation in which reporters could ride around in jeeps going from one part of the front to another or like Vietnam, where reporters could hop a helicopter to specific points of action.

Media Pools

Before the air phase of the operation began in January, news organizations were afraid, once we told them there would be pools, that we would not get the pools out to see anything. They reminded us of their experience in Panama, where we did get a pool down there and we treated it, while the combat was still going on, to a dissertation on the history of the Panama Canal Zone, not exactly what they had in mind or we had in mind.

So, with that history, they were very concerned that they would never get the pools out to see anything. But as viewers and readers and listeners know, we had the pools in place before the operation started this time. Reporters were on an aircraft carrier in the Red Sea to witness the launching of the first air strikes. They were on board a battleship in the Persian Gulf that launched the first cruise missiles ever used in combat.

They were on the air force bases when the fighter planes and bombers were taking off around the clock. And they were out with several ground units in the desert.

Now, those first days were not without problems. The first stories, once the ground combat started—the ground combat phase of the operation—American units moved very quickly, some of them by air. To cover the conflict, reporters had to be a part of the unit and able to move with it.

Each commander had an assigned number of vehicles for his troops, only so many seats available. And while he could take care of the reporters that he knew were coming, there is no way he could have been expected to keep on absorbing those who would have arrived on their own, unexpectedly, in their own four-wheel-drive vehicles, assuming they could even find the units out west once the war started and once they began to move into Iraq.

Nonetheless, by the time the ground war began, 131 reporters and photographers and technicians were out with the army and marines on the ground. There were reporters out with every division and a few others at the army headquarters, the army corps headquarters in the field.

The pool system allowed us to tell the divisional commanders how many reporters they would be responsible for. And the reporters in those pools, in return, were allowed to stay with the military units they covered, learning as much as they could about the unit's plans and tactics.

Once the ground war started, it wasn't like Vietnam either, with minor skirmishes here and there and a major offensive every now and then. It was, as the world now knows, a setpiece operation with divisions from the army and . . . (marines) moving quickly, supported by air force and navy planes, all of it carefully orchestrated. In this sense, it was like something from a previous war. It was like D-Day. It's useful to remember that in World War II, 461 reporters were signed up at the Supreme Headquarters of the Allied Expeditionary Force to cover D-Day. And of that number, only 27 U.S. reporters actually went ashore with the first wave of forces.

No doubt about it, pools rub reporters the wrong way. But there simply was no way for us to open up a rapidly moving front to reporters roaming the battlefield.

We believe the pool system did three things. It got reporters out to see the action, it guaranteed that Americans at home got reports from the scene of the action, and it allowed the military to accommodate a reasonable number of journalists without overwhelming the units that were fighting the enemy.

Could Have Done Better

Now that the whole operation is just about over and the U.S. troops are starting to come home, it's clearly time to look back. And as I review our own arrangements, there are obviously some things that we could have done much better. And here are some preliminary observations.

We could have a done a better job of helping reporters in the field. Judging from what I've heard from the reporters who went out on pools, those I've heard from so far, we had some outstanding escorts, but we must improve that process. Escort officers should not throw themselves in front of the camera when one of the troops utters a forbidden word, as happens on that piece of ABC news tape from last fall that is shown every time there's a program about the press. I hope the oxide has worn off that tape by now.

We need to teach public affairs personnel how to do their job so that reporters won't feel that their interview subjects are intimidated.

Our first obligation is to get reporters out with the action, so that journalists are eyewitnesses to history. . . . But we must do better at getting the stories back to the press center. Now, some units did very well using computer modems and tactical telephone fax machines. The marines seemed to be best at using the technology of the 1990s to get their stories back.

Others did not do nearly as well. I've heard from reporters who said their stories were delayed for several days, and we need to do better.

But part of the problem was the sheer number of journalists to accommodate. Richard Harwood raised this issue in his column in the *Post* last weekend when he said, "The communication industry, well endowed financially, dispatched far too many people to cover the war." I think that argument deserves some consideration.

When I was a local news director with a mighty one-man Washington bureau, I resisted the occasional urge of the station's management to have our reporter show up every time there was a big event at the White House. I thought he was better used covering the Interior Department.

Now, as somebody who works for the government, I can't decide who goes to the war and who stays home. Maybe it's too much to expect. It's not realistic, perhaps, to expect as competitive an institution as the press to limit its numbers in a war, especially, for example, when local newspapers want to provide coverage to the hometowns where the troops come from. But it is a question worth considering.

Several bureau chiefs told me last fall that in planning for the war coverage, the security of reporters was their concern and not mine. But I don't think that's realistic, because I couldn't ignore that even if I wanted to. It is not morally possible.

Reporters' Safety

We were on the phone to CBS News nearly every day that Bob Simon was missing—and thank God that his crew is safe and sound, he and his crew. And when a group of U.S. journalists was captured in Iraq after the cease-fire, after the temporary suspension of offensive operations, four news industry executives wrote to the president saying that no U.S. forces should withdraw from Iraq until the issue of the journalists was resolved.

The issue was raised by the U.S. government with the Iraqi representative in Washington, with its ambassador at the United Nations, with an intermediary in the Soviet government, with the International Red Cross, and at two meetings between the U.S. and Iraqi military officials in the gulf.

Everyone in this room is relieved that they are free, but we must drop the pretense that the safety of journalists is not the government's concern.

Now, there are undoubtedly more lessons to be learned from the journalists who covered the war themselves. I've heard from a few of them already, and this week I'm sending a letter to every reporter who took part in the pool, asking for every reporter's criticisms, observations, and suggestions. And I will soon arrange to meet with the bureau chiefs of Washington news organizations to continue the discussions that we've been having since last fall.

Whatever else the press arrangements in the Persian Gulf may have been, they were a good-faith effort on the part of the military (to get) reporters on the scene. They were a good faith effort to get as many reporters as possible out with the troops during a highly mobile, modern ground war, and they were a good-faith effort to allow as much freedom in reporting as possible while still preventing the enemy from knowing what we were up to. This was, after all, an enemy that had virtually as much access to American news reporting as people here at home had.

From what we've been able to learn so far, Iraqi military commanders did not have a clue to which coalition forces were out there, where they were or what they were up to. They appear to have been caught totally off guard by the quick move of the XVIIIth Airborne Corps west of Kuwait deep into Iraq. And for the sake of the operation and the lives of those American, British, and French troops, we could not afford to let the enemy learn that.

In last week's issue of *Newsweek* magazine, Jonathan Alter, I think, misses the point of all this. He says, "With its quick win, the Pentagon will surely try to repeat its press policy next time." Well, I don't know if that's true or not. If next time means that we're once again in Saudi Arabia and we're once again facing Iraq in occupied Kuwait with 1,400 journalists, maybe. But the point is that these press arrangements were dictated by the nature of this military operation and the number of reporters on the scene. The next military operation will undoubtedly be different.

I think the point was better understood by Arthur Lubow writing in *The New Republic*. He said this: "In modern war, reporters must be permitted at the front and they must submit to reasonable censorship. The critical point," he said, "is mutual mistrust is part of a shared heritage of soldiers and journalists in times of war, and so is mutual accommodation." And it is to mutual accommodation that I renew my pledge to you today.

Thank you.

Q-and-A Excerpts

Q. In view of the military's close-out of reporters in Grenada, Panama, and the gulf, would you not agree that the historic role of the war correspondent is finished for American journalism?

A. Well, I wouldn't argue that there was a close-out of reporters in the gulf, especially when you have 131 reporters who are out with ground units when the war was going on and another number—I'm not sure of the number, 15 or 20 or 30 or so—who were out on ships at the time or with medical units or on the air force bases, many more reporters, it needs to be noted, than were—as I said during the text of the remarks—in with the initial landing force in D-Day.

I think the thing that is hard to get clear about this operation is that for a long time all the U.S. forces were doing was sitting around waiting for the war to start. I mean, people keep—I got a letter the other day from someone who said that in early December he had trouble getting out with a unit and what if that—what if he'd had that trouble during the Vietnam War.

Well, the unit he wanted to get out with was not in a war. It wasn't doing anything. It was sitting there waiting. I think that is one of the big frustrations from this operation. We put the forces over there, and they sort of sat there for a long time and didn't do much except move around and do desert training. And there came a point where those stories were monotonous for readers and viewers and certainly for reporters.

At the same time, there were units, those that were close in like the 101st Airborne (Division), for example, that were close to Dhahran, that got to a point where 10, 15, 20 reporters, new ones coming everyday. And the commander said, "I need to get on, I need to do some other things, and I keep having to host reporters."

The ground war lasted only four days. The ground war, I think, was well covered. So, no, I certainly wouldn't argue that the role of the war correspondent is dead. I think we did a great job getting reporters out with units when the war was actually going on.

Q. Can you talk a bit about the misinformation campaign practice in the war, such as conducting highly publicized marine exercises to make Iraq think the attack would come from the sea?

A. Well, I'm unaware of any misinformation campaign. . . . I can pledge to you that I was part of no misinformation campaign.

Amphibious Exercises

Now, specifically about the big marine amphibious exercise, there were several marine amphibious exercises. The first one was in a

Persian Gulf country which did not want to flog the fact that it allowed a U.S. military exercise. And so, because that's what our host said we should do, we kept our promise that we would not—they didn't want to allow reporters in to cover it, basically. And we got beat up on that a lot. Reporters said, "Hey, how come we can't go cover this exercise?" And it was—it's something we couldn't permit.

The point is, reporters wanted to cover that exercise. We were not trying to flack it. Now, as the exercise moved further up the coast and closer to Kuwait, again, reporters wanted to cover that exercise. And it was in Saudi Arabia, and there were obviously U.S. military forces there, so it was something that they could cover.

The point is we didn't have to flog it; reporters wanted to do that. I won't go into exhaustive detail about the bizarre telephone conversation I had on Saturday with some of the larger egos in the journalistic community who wanted to say, "You know, he's got a better stand-up location than I do." So that's also part of my job. But we were not trying to emphasize the military—the amphibious exercises. Even if we wanted to do that, we didn't have to.

Q. Were there any discussions about bombing the hotel in Baghdad that was an Iraqi military command, even though journalists were there?

A. The—what we discovered in our intelligence operations was that there were points in Baghdad; there were buildings under which there were critical fiber optic—they call them—the intelligence analysts call them "nodes"; intersections of fiber-optic cables where several cables came together and were switched. Not a big, elaborate thing; fiber-optic stuff is pretty small these days, but, nonetheless, they were critical switch points. If you could hit the nodes, if you could hit these busy intersections of fiber-optic cables, you could do a lot to break down communications, command and control communications during the war.

One of these nodes was under the Al-Rashid Hotel. But it was a hotel. And one of the things that we worked very hard on in the war was not to target civilian targets. A hotel is clearly a civilian target.

The fact that there were Western reporters in that hotel only further persuaded us of the wisdom of our decision not to hit a hotel that had not only Western journalists, but foreign diplomats and lots of other civilians there.

No Live Crew

Q. How do you feel about Walter Cronkite's proposal of no live telecast from the battlefield? Can it work in this period of media saturation?

A. . . . Mr. Cronkite's suggestion is that there's too much emphasis on instant reporting, that there's no reason why a report can't be delayed for 24 or 48 hours. That's easy for him to say now. . . . as a former broadcaster, I have a hard time discriminating against, to say it's OK for a wire service story to go, but that television story, we're going to have to hold that. That would be a very tough cut for a government spokesdude like me to say. I think that would be a hard sell.

Technology limits this to some extent. Now Bob McKeown and Forrest Sawyer did join up with some Saudi units and in some Egyptian units and followed with them as they went into Kuwait, and they were able to stop at various points and set up their gear, but it's still a cumbersome thing. Fred Friendly once described television journalism as like trying to write with a 1,000-pound pencil. Now maybe the pencil is down to 950 pounds, I don't know, but it's still a pretty awkward thing.

I think it would be very, very hard for the government to tell television folks that they can't report; there has to be a 48- or 24-hour embargo on what they do, but not on the rest of the media.

Keeping Cool

Q. Was it official Pentagon policy never to show ire or anger . . . to press cross-examination at the daily war briefings, or did you never get mad?

182

A. . . . Well, a lot of the briefings were done by some people who were not public-affairs-trained people. They were operators, they had real jobs, and they were drafted, as it were, the only draftees I think, of the entire operation, to help us with the briefings. I am talking about General Neal over in Riyadh and the ones that I worked with in the Pentagon, Capt. Dave Herrington, Adm. Mike McConnell from the intelligence side and the very famous, and now deservedly so, Lt. Gen. Tom Kelly, who was the director of operations for the Joint Staff. He was the top—in the military, the operators are the guys who run the war.

There's operations, there's logistics, there's intelligence, there's planning, but when the thing actually happens, when, as they say in the military, the balloon goes up, then it's Tom Kelly in the gondola— I'm taking this metaphor too far I sense, but anyway he is the head operator, and he is the one who did our briefings.

I did actually get a lot of mail from people who said, "Why don't you tell those guys to button their lips?" But I think that General Kelly legitimately felt and said so at the end of the briefings, there's no such thing as a bad question. We—I understand the frustration of reporters, especially during the air war. I mean, it was a hard thing to cover the air war, because you could cover the planes taking off and you could cover the planes landing, but you couldn't cover the most interesting part, which is the part in between because it was happening somewhere else. In fact, it was happening in Iraq or in occupied Kuwait. There were no reporters that I know of in occupied Kuwait during the war, at least those that could get their stories out, and there were lots of restrictions on what you could say from Iraq.

So it was a frustrating thing to cover the war during those days. And reporters were frustrated. They always want to know more. The good reporters want to know most of all. So it was not a difficult thing to keep our cool, no.

Q. You say there was no censorship. Why then were returning fliers called "proud" at military censor's demand, rather than the reporters chosen word of "giddy?"

A. Well, again, I mean, I think that was—there was some of that happy to glad stuff, and it's indefensible. It is overzealousness on the part of some of those people who performed their jobs early. When we heard about that stuff, we asked them not to do that, but that the ground—I said, "Show me in the ground rules where it says you can't describe somebody as giddy."

It's not there, it was clearly beyond the scope of the ground rules, and it was just excessive zeal on their part, and it's indefensible.

Q. If you only wanted to keep reporters from publishing information that would harm operations and not sanitize coverage, why did the military routinely keep pictures of American injured from being published, and why were reporters denied access to field hospitals?

A. I know of several cases where reporters were present in field hospitals. There was no rule that said you couldn't photograph injured military personnel. All we said is you have—you should get the permission of the injured.

I guess the—my—thought behind it was if there's a car accident right now at 14th and G and we all go off to the hospital with our betacams to go cover that accident, the hospital isn't going to let you go right in and start shooting tape. You have to have permission from the hospital, you have to have permission from the injured.

I don't know that soldiers in combat surrender those sort of fundamental rights. But there was no rule that said you couldn't. Indeed, I saw many such pictures.

How Many?

Q. Several questions on this issue. Throughout the war, we were told there were 540,000 Iraqi soldiers in the Kuwait theater. If 60,000 were captured and 120,000 killed, that leaves 360,000 unaccounted for. Newsweek now says there were only 250,000 Iraqi soldiers in the Kuwaiti theater. Were half of the original 540,000 withdrawn, killed by bombing, or never there in the first place?

A. Well, I don't know the answer to the question. I suspect there's no one right now who knows the answer to the question. But let me just say a word about how one tracks this sort of thing. This gets into what the intel guys like to call sources and methods, which is, you've got your sources, and military intelligence people have their sources, and as we've learned during this banquet, reporters are not always interested in exposing their sources, and neither are intelligence people.

So without getting into that sort of level of detail, I guess you could say that the way you know how many military forces are there is to sort of try to look, and you can't count individual soldiers. You can't count hats or noses or boots and divide by two. You try to get some idea of, as you study a nation's military, of how it's set up. How many people, in general, are there in a regular Iraqi army division? What's their general field practice? When they deploy a division, how many tanks are in an Iraqi armored division, in general? How many in a brigade? How many in a battalion? And you try to find out where those units are, and you use other sources of information to triangulate the information you have about an individual unit and then you begin to make estimates, and then you try to corroborate those estimates using other sources at your disposal.

You don't take a roll call. You can't count individuals. You have to get the best estimate that you have, based on their sort of unit structure. I'm trying to think of an example, and I'm trying to come up with one that doesn't sound hokey. But if you know how many people are on the average roster of a professional football team and you hear that there are three teams' worth of people going to come for dinner, I mean, you'd have some idea how many places to set. Basically, that's the process that you use.

Now, once the ground war—once the air war started, we had some trouble counting that sort of stuff because they took cover. That's No. 1. No. 2, we know now—and we're only beginning to understand, we're only beginning to get a clear picture of this—that there were massive desertions from those units.

Once the air war started, some people were killed, they were either buried on the spot, or in many cases, their bodies were withdrawn from the battlefield. It's hard for us to know how many of those there were.

The second thing is there were simply massive desertions; units moved, and by the time they stopped at their new place, everybody wasn't there. There were desertions on the spot, and we're only now, I think, beginning to understand how big those desertions were, the order of magnitude of some of them. And not just in the front-line units, the infantry units that were down on the southern border of Kuwait that it shared with Saudi Arabia. So you can't just perform that mathematical calculation and say, "Aha, that's how many Iraqis must have died in the war." We're only now beginning to get a picture of how many deserted, and it's going to be a while before we have that sorted out.

Q. So do you think your original estimate was correct?

A. Yes, I think the original estimate—our intelligence people think the original estimate that they made when the air war started on January 16 was the best estimate they could get. I think they're pretty confident that there were somewhere in the neighborhood of 540,000 forces in Kuwait and the areas of Iraq immediately surrounding Kuwait. How many were there when the ground war started, I don't think we have a firm handle on yet.

Peter Arnett's Baghdad

Q. What do you think of Peter Arnett's reporting?

A. Well, I have no trouble with Peter Arnett's reporting. I think that, and felt all along—I did not criticize Peter Arnett's reporting during the war. I certainly am not going to now—No. 1, in part, because as I said before, I'm not the government press critic. But the other thing is we all understand the sort of restrictions that reporters in Iraq were under, and I think the immense value was obvious even during the war. As reporters would leave and go to Amman, then they would begin to write stories—the first, I think, were British reporters who went back and then began to write stories for the *Times* of London and so forth—on what they felt was really going on. And as reporters have come out of Baghdad, we begin to see the information that they gathered during the war. If they hadn't been there during the war, they wouldn't know what they're able to report now.

Q. Why should organizations cooperate with a pool when McKeown and Sawyer violated the rules, got away with it, and were even applauded for their enterprise? It seems the rules apply to all but the networks, or did you cave in to Dan Rather, Jennings, and the companies?

A. Yes, of course, we did—that's what I always want to say in the briefings. No, no, of course, we didn't cave in to anybody. The thing about Bob McKeown and Forrest Sawyer is that they were with—they asked permission to join up with—a Saudi or Egyptian unit. The problem we had is that there were a huge number of reporters wanting to join up with U.S. units.

Now there were television crews with U.S. military units, with the marines and with the army. I can't remember how many crews there were, but there was a television crew on the average of just about every division or so, one-to-two divisions' worth. So there were lots of television people out with the Army VIIth Corps, XVIIIth Airborne Corps, Marine 1st and 2nd divisions—or 1st and 2nd Marine Expeditionary brigades.

They were there with them. They did not take with them the portable satellite up-links for a couple of reasons. The army moved so quickly that there was never time to set that stuff up. One unit was moving 47 out of 50 hours, on the move, so it's hard to do that. Some of the other units were moving more slowly, let me just put it that way.

Future of Pools

Q. Given the restrictions of the pool reporting system and the degree to which information was held back, is there really any reason the media should go along with the pool system in the future?

A. Well, one can't say that every military operation is going to demand a pool. But let's say that you get into another situation where there's a huge number of reporters who want to go out in the field. The military commanders come to us.

If you're (Maj. Gen.) Barry McCaffrey, who is the commander of the 24th Infantry Division and you called him up on the phone and say, "Barry, could you take 150 reporters?" There is simply no way that can happen. He is going to say, "I can't do that, I can't take 150."

So then you start saying, "Well, what's a reasonable number?" And you have to try to get down to that. If you get down to that and there's more that want to go than you can possibly accommodate—Barry McCaffrey's unit was moving quickly, you could not have 200 or 300 guys following the 24th Infantry Division in rented jeeps. It simply would not be possible.

You know, I don't mean to be ludicrous, I don't mean to be—I'm not trying to make a straw man here, but there were people who said, "Why can't we follow the military in our jeeps?" A good and fair question, but some of these units moved so quickly, especially airborne units, that wasn't practical, so you have to limit the numbers. Once you start limiting the numbers, then you can either go unilateral or pool, but you're still going to have to have some kind of limitations.

I think you have to separate out here. Everybody hates pooling because it isn't competitive; I'm not just filing to my boss at *USA Today*, but I'm filing to everybody else. That is one thing that bugs reporters.

OK, we can look at that in the future. Should we have pools or should we stay unilateral? But there's a separate question, that is: When you have more reporters that can go out to the battlefield—that want to go out—than you can possibly accommodate in a modern kind of war, you have to have some limitations. Why should reporters sign on to those limitations? Because it gets them out with the units.

Q. There was a massive breakdown in the transmission of copy from reporters with troops with the advancing ground forces. What happened, why did the copy foul up at JIB (Joint Information Bureau), and was anyone punished for this mistake?

A. As I said in the text, it varied. I think the marines in general did

188

pretty well. They had computer modems, M-mail systems, they had tactical fax machines. They did better.

The army had more difficulty. They were moving. They said, "All right, let's use ground couriers." That was clearly too slow, so they said, "All right, let's switch to air couriers." And they switched to air couriers the day that the weather was so bad that not a single helicopter was flying. No helicopters flew, not only the ones carrying our pool reports, but also the ones carrying troops and carrying logistical supplies. There were no helicopters flying; it was too dangerous. So we said, "All right, let's get back to the ground thing again." We go to the ground system. The helicopters start flying again.

I don't know, I'm not aware of copy piling up for days at the Joint Information Bureau in Dhahran. I don't know of any instances of that. I think the problems were out west with the forces that went deep into Iraq. The stuff moved out at sort of Civil War-era speeds, and we clearly have to do better.

Q. Since the cease-fire in the Persian Gulf has not been formalized, are the guidelines, particularly the press pool rules, still in effect?

A. The overall—there are no press pools, No. 1. The press pools were disbanded, I think, the Saturday after the ground war stopped or the Friday perhaps. The president announced the suspension of hostilities on a Wednesday evening, and I think we stood the pools down within a day or so. The general ground rules and guidelines, however, on "don't report future military actions" and all that stuff are still in effect.

The Trouble Over Dover

Q. What was the rationale behind closing Dover (Delaware) Air (Force) Base to journalists, and how did this restriction fit into the stated reasons for censorship?

A. Well, it had nothing to do with the reasons that I've talked about earlier for the ground rules and the guidelines, which were, again, only to preserve operational security or safeguard the lives of the troops.

189

Dover is a different case. Dover is a transit point. Dover is a morgue. It's a place where forensic pathologists work. For example, . . . the remains of Americans missing in action that were turned over to the United States by the government of Iraq have been sent to Dover for positive identification. That's one of the things that Dover does.

The decision we made was that families of those who were killed in action should decide where the services are. Now naturally they are going to want those as close to home as possible. There is no reason they should have to pack up and go to Dover to get the service. If they want it to be at home, if they're a soldier, say with the 24th Infantry, they may want it to be at Fort Stewart. And the unit, Fort Stewart, may want to have a ceremony. That's perfectly appropriate. If the family wants it there, if the unit wants it there, that's where it ought to be.

There really wasn't anything happening at Dover other than the caskets being unloaded and shipped on, and that wasn't the only place it happened. For example, it may well have been that body bags could have come from Saudi Arabia and gone through Frankfurt or gone through somewhere else on their way to Dover. So there is nothing special about Dover.

Q. But Dover is part of the war, part of what is covered by reporters in a war.

A. Granted, so is Frankfurt, and so is the initial point where the body bags are loaded onto the airplane at the first point. The argument that reporters used in the court challenge was that they wanted to be able to cover the services at Dover. There weren't any services at Dover.

The other part of it is, put yourself in the position of a mother, a father, a husband, a wife of someone who has been killed in action and you know that your son, your husband, and indeed in this operation your wife, your mother has been killed in action and is coming back to your hometown, to Casper, Wyoming. And you're sitting there and you're watching the news and you see a body bag being shipped off the airplane and sent onto another airplane. Well, is that your son, or is that your husband, is that your daughter or not? I think that's a lot of anxiety for families.

There is an idea somehow that we're trying to sort of pretend like people don't get killed in a war and that we do that by not allowing coverage at Dover, which, of course, is ludicrous because there are reporters covering the fact that—I mean I think of the stories in Saudi Arabia, in the case where the Scud missile attacked the barracks where reporters were present and they showed the bodies being pulled out of that barracks. Now if we were sensitive, if we wanted to pretend like people weren't killed in a military operation, we would have started there. We wouldn't have waited until they got to Dover, and we didn't obviously.

Q. President Bush has told the Iraqis to stop using combat helicopters. If they don't heed the warning, what happens?

A. I think we have a couple of concerns. The agreement that General Schwarzkopf worked out in the desert with the Iraqi military, who met in that tent out there up by Safwan, was that they wanted to be able to use helicopters because they said the air war had blown out bridges and roads, and it made it hard for them to move things around. As they said, "We would like to be able to use our helicopters because we need the transportation help."

Quite another matter to use those helicopters for offensive military operations, whether against their own people or whatever else. We still have U.S. forces in southern Iraq in the area of Iraq which we control. We still have to be concerned about the security of those forces. And when helicopters that can shoot start flying, that's a subject of concern to us.

Another point is we're concerned about overall stability in the region. We want to see peace returned to that area. And the use of helicopters in an offensive military way is totally opposite of what we want to see happen there. So that is a subject of concern to us. What precise action we'll take is something that will have to be decided by the secretary and the president, General Powell, and I don't know that there's an answer yet. . . .

Thank you all very much.

Chapter Six

What We Missed

Was anything revealed after the war that might indicate that the press was denied access to important information that it should have had during the crisis and war?

An Unknown Casualty

Tom Wicker

With the Persian Gulf War over and won, the air force has chosen to disclose a fact that few television viewers or newspaper readers could have suspected while the fighting was going on. The famous "smart bombs" made up only 7 percent of all the U.S. explosives dropped on Iraq and Kuwait.

In fact, despite all those TV scenes of precision-guided bombs going down the chimneys or in the doors of Iraqi targets, 70 percent of the 88,500 tons of bombs dropped on Iraq and Kuwait in 43 days of war missed their targets. This is not a condemnation of the air force, which did an outstanding combat job and voluntarily made these facts public—*after* the war. It *is* a damning commentary on the controlled information policy exercised by the Pentagon *during* the war. And it's no compliment to the American press or public, both of which too tamely accepted military censorship.

The point is not that military officials lied; they said the war was being won, and it was. It is not even that they impermissibly distorted the facts—smart bombs were about 90 percent successful—though the nation was *not* told that 81,950 tons of unguided bombs had an accuracy rating of only about 25 percent. Of these, 62,137 tons missed their targets.

The real and dangerous point is that the Bush administration and the military were so successful in controlling information about the war that they were able to tell the public just about what they wanted the public to know. Perhaps worse: press and public largely acquiesced in this disclosure of only selected information.

Suppose the military *had* been lying. Suppose the briefers *had* been radically distorting the facts. Suppose in the next war, and all the talk about *Pax Americana* presupposes one—Pentagon and military officials are not so circumspect as Generals Schwarzkopf and Powell and

Secretary Cheney usually were this time? If information can be controlled at all, without public reaction or sufficient press protest, it can be controlled to any particular purpose the controllers may desire.

Since the fighting ended, we have learned—for another example—that the vaunted Patriot antimissile missiles were destroying Scud missiles as claimed, but not Scud warheads. The catastrophic damage said to have been inflicted on Kuwait by Iraqi invaders has been downgraded, both as to its extent and the cost of restoration. While there's no doubt that the occupation was bestial, it's no longer clear that Iraqis actually threw babies out of their incubators, as was alleged during the war.

There's nothing new in wartime about exaggerated claims of success or inflammatory charges of enemy atrocities. The need to keep the home fires burning is obvious, and since the days of Alexander the Great it's been acknowledged that the first casualty of war is truth.

Nor is there anything new in the military trying to control information. Censorship of reporters' stories was imposed in World War II. Though there was no censorship in Vietnam, reporters were given guidelines as to what could not be reported, and briefers—in Saigon and in the field—habitually put the best face on things.

In the Gulf War, however, though it was clearly a less challenging episode than World War II and Vietnam, the military went further than ever in order to control information. Not only did stories have to be cleared before publication or airing, reporters and cameras were limited in their movements and inadequate "pool" coverage was the rule. Even troop interviews were monitored and sometimes forbidden. Ernie Pyle, the famous World War II correspondent, could not have done his work with his movements so limited.

Polls showed that the American public by a wide margin approved this drastic information control. One reason may have been demonstrated public dislike for the press; another probably was that so much information seemed to come through on television, and so many events were shown as they happened, that many Americans watching at home did not realize that they were seeing only what their government and military permitted them to see—not including the bodies of dead Americans or "collateral damage" in Iraqi cities.

Nor did press and television, to their discredit, protest as effectively as they should have, or always make it as clear as they could have, that much of what they conveyed—like the can't miss version of air force bombings—was not only controlled by the military but prettified for home consumption. Thus was the First Amendment badly wounded in Desert Storm—though war-giddy Americans seemed not to know about or mourn this national casualty.

U.S. Bombs Missed 70 Percent of the Time

Barton Gellman

Precision-guided bombs, the icon of Pentagon briefings and the military's preferred image of the Persian Gulf War, made up barely 7 percent of the U.S. tonnage dropped on Iraqi targets, Air Force Gen. Merrill A. McPeak disclosed yesterday.

McPeak's remarks, coupled with new details on the accuracy of unguided bombs from a senior Pentagon official, added up to this startling picture of the air war: of 88,500 tons of bombs dropped on Iraq and occupied Kuwait, 70 percent missed their targets.

The air force chief of staff did not call yesterday's briefing to talk about the misses. With budget season in full swing and the Pentagon's five-year restructuring now uppermost in his mind, McPeak made his first major postwar appearance "to tell an American success story" and claim the lion's share of credit for the rout of Iraqi forces in Kuwait.

Though careful to note that "all the services made a very important contribution" and to pay homage to the ground and sea campaigns, McPeak added, "My private conviction is that this is the first time in history that a field army has been defeated by air power."

Few independent analysts doubt that Iraq's collapse after 43 days of war was due in large part to the most intense aerial bombardment in history. McPeak laid out the air campaign in new detail, with so relentless an emphasis on success that his list of lessons learned in the war suggested the air force had known them all beforehand.

Among his most notable disclosures, however, was that laser-guided "smart" weapons, so indispensable to the military and political strategies of the air war, accounted for only 6,520 of 88,500 tons of destructive force that U.S. planes dropped on Iraq and occupied Kuwait. McPeak said they hit their intended targets about 90 percent of the time.

A senior Pentagon official said the 81,980 tons of "dumb," or

197

unguided , bombs had an accuracy of only about 25 percent. McPeak declined to specify the success rate of unguided bombs, but conceded after the briefing that they were "much less" accurate than their laser-guided counterparts.

Because far more unguided bombs were dropped than guided ones, and because the unguided bombs were far less accurate, the portrait that emerged yesterday contrasted sharply with the high-tech, never-miss image that the Pentagon carefully cultivated during the war.

Calculations based on the information provided by McPeak and the senior official suggested that 26,363 tons of bombs hit targets, and 62,137 tons missed.

In some ways, military analysts said, that bottom-line figure is misleading. Unguided bombs have been missing targets for as long as planes have been dropping them, and if anything was new about the Gulf War it was the quantity of precision bombs used.

McPeak said Iraq absorbed half again as many precision bombs in 43 days as Vietnam did in 8 years of war.

But equally misleading, analysts said, is the unfailing exactness portrayed in every gun camera videotape released publicly by military authorities.

Senior officers have said they viewed extensive footage of bombs that missed targets or hit targets selected in error, such as the civilian building across the street from the Iraqi Interior Ministry, but the Pentagon has released none of the footage. McPeak brought new videotape to yesterday's briefing and once again every bomb struck where it was aimed.

McPeak took pains to praise not only the combat weapons and air crews but the logisticians and transporters who helped move an enormous expeditionary force to the gulf.

He compared the effort to a Berlin airlift every six weeks and said it was the equivalent of moving every resident of Oklahoma City with their vehicles, food, and household goods.

"This was certainly the largest airlift in history," he said. "We moved an army halfway around the world and set it up from scratch."

It did not appear to be entirely coincidental that the air force also chose yesterday to release a 22-page "perspective" paper making the case for the C-17, the next generation transport plane on the Pentagon's shopping list.

Growing cost estimates have given some members of Congress qualms about the plane, but it is a top-priority acquisition for the army and air force.

In a week when senior Pentagon officials began raising questions about the combat-readiness of the army national guard, McPeak also singled out the performance of guard and reserve combat pilots from New York, South Carolina, and Louisiana. He said it is easier to maintain combat readiness among air force reserves because many of the combat pilots also fly as civilians.

McPeak defended the decision of allied air forces to descend upon an Iraqi convoy fleeing Kuwait City in the final days of the war on a northern artery that became known as the Highway of Death. Scores of Iraqis were killed there and hundreds of vehicles destroyed in the panicky retreat toward the Iraqi border.

"When enemy armies are defeated, they retreat, often in disorder, and we have what is known in the business as the exploitation phase," McPeak said. "It's during that phase that the true fruits of victory are achieved from combat."

McPeak said a general's obligation is to his troops, and that "often causes us to do very brutal things. That's the nature of war."

The air campaign against Iraq was designed in four phases, he said, with the first three intended to last 30 days and set the stage for the ground war.

Allied commanders changed the plan—McPeak likened the process to a quarterback calling audibles—because the weather was the worst ever recorded in the gulf, the "great Scud chase" took up more resources than expected, and Gen. H. Norman Schwarzkopf, commander of the allied forces, wanted to merge the three phases. Schwarzkopf launched the ground war nine days later than planned.

U.S. Relied on Foreign-Made Parts for Weapons

Stuart Auerbach

When allied officers urgently needed special battery packs to power their command and control computers during the Persian Gulf conflict, the U.S. government had to send to Paris and Tokyo to get them.

Similarly, when Teledyne Corporation needed transistors to meet a rush order for one of the most critical items in Operation Desert Storm—the transponder that beams electronic signals so allied aircraft could tell friend from foe—French diplomats cooperated to get speedy delivery.

And when American manufacturers ran short of critical parts for video display terminals needed to analyze real-time intelligence data from reconnaissance planes, the U.S. government went to the Japanese Embassy here for help.

With the globalization of high-technology industries, U.S. troops in combat in the Persian Gulf found themselves dependent for the first time on foreign countries for the tiny semiconductor chips, transistors, and other electronic parts essential to their advanced weapons.

The weapons are manufactured in the United States, but frequently they rely on foreign-made parts. Deep stockpiles of foreign components, such as the semiconductors in the computer that aims and fires the main gun of the army's Abrams tank, are not maintained in the U.S. arsenal. There are simply too many parts to do that. Increasing inventories would add to the defense budget at a time of heavy pressure to reduce spending.

While the issue of the Pentagon's dependence on foreign suppliers was debated before the Gulf War, it came into sharp focus during the conflict when the Bush administration had to seek help from foreign governments in several cases to get parts needed by American manufacturers.

Foreign manufacturers often were reluctant to put the Pentagon's purchase orders ahead of their regular customers' without prompting from their governments, according to officials at embassies here and at the Commerce Department. But there was no case of a foreign manufacturer refusing to supply parts for political reasons, officials said.

On nearly 30 occasions, the Bush administration needed help from foreign governments to get delivery of crucial parts for the war effort.

Despite full cooperation from foreign governments, administration officials said the degree of foreign reliance complicated the smooth flow of supplies and renewed fears that U.S. military readiness may be compromised by shortages in this area.

These fears were expressed most vividly in a 1988 report by the Defense Science Board, a top Pentagon advisory panel, which found the U.S. military "dangerously dependent" on foreign supplies. The conclusion was echoed last May by Congress's Office of Technology Assessment and in January by the General Accounting Office, the watchdog agency of Congress.

"If the foreign governments were neutral or were not disposed to help us out, we could have run into some real problems," a senior administration official said. "We were sweating bullets over it and the military was sweating bullets, too."

His view was repeated by former Commerce Department trade official Clyde Prestowitz, who was member of the Defense Science Board and now runs a Washington think tank, the Economic Strategy Institute.

"I think we are much more vulnerable than we understand," Prestowitz said. "In this case the allies were supportive. But you can see the potential for damage when they are not supportive."

Former Deputy Undersecretary of Defense Stephen D. Bryen said when the federal government seeks the help of foreign governments to get rush orders of electronic supplies, the United States reveals weaknesses in its defense production "to outsiders who may not share our security concerns."

An official of the Japanese Embassy here noted that the cooperation his government provided the U.S. military in weapons procurement runs contrary to the strong strain of pacifism in Japanese society.

Despite what the Japanese diplomat described as a gray area regarding Japanese laws against exporting weapons, he said his country's help "verified that we are a very reliable source" for the U.S. defense industry.

Foreign Ministry spokesman Taizo Watanabe said there remains "a strong abhorrence" in Japanese public opinion against exporting arms.

But he added during an interview here with reporters and editors of *The Washington Post* that opposition lessens when Japanese are told the parts are for general civilian use as well, and it is Americans, not Japanese, who put them in weapons systems. Even with that explanation, Watanabe acknowledged, the sale of Japanese parts for U.S. weapons "still meets some psychological resistance."

The Defense Science Board report listed four tactical missiles that were used in Operation Desert Storm as the "most visible examples" of sophisticated weapons that depend on foreign-made parts. These include air-to-air Sparrow and Sidewinder missiles used in aerial dogfights, ground-based Tow antitank missiles, and air-to-ground Maverick missiles.

"It is these 'consumables' which would be in greatest demand in a conventional war and are most at risk, because of the dependence on foreign sources," the Defense Science Board report said, although there were no indications that any of the special orders involved those missiles.

The guidance system of the Sparrow, for instance, contains circuits from Japan, a critical semiconductor from Thailand, and other parts from Germany.

Commerce Undersecretary Dennis Kloske, who was in charge of making sure American industry was mobilized to supply the fighting forces in the Persian Gulf, said "one area of U.S. vulnerability" comes from the U.S. electronics industry, which has trouble gearing up to meet the increased needs of military at war because so many of the vital components for computers and other products come from overseas suppliers.

For example, he said, for the Persian Gulf War, defense contractors required semiconductors, video display terminals, and other computer equipment from Japan; electronic components from Japan and France for measuring and calibrating equipment made here; and radio gear and avionics from Britain.

"What this points out is the U.S. defense mobilization base has become global," said Kloske, who as a Defense Department aide from 1987 to 1989 drew up the defense mobilization plan.

He said this requires greater stockpiling, especially of critical electronic components that only are available from foreign suppliers.

But former Commerce Undersecretary Lionel Olmer, who was a member of the Defense Science Board, said its studies showed that Defense Department procurement officials often had little idea what parts in U.S. weapons came from overseas. Such parts most often were small but critical components that were bought by the contractors and subcontractors. The GAO study seconded that view.

Further, Olmer said, it would be too expensive to begin stockpiling of the foreign-made parts used in weapon systems.

Drawing on his Pentagon experience, Kloske added the military generally opposes stockpiling parts of ammunition, preferring to use money to buy weapons systems.

But Jerry Sullivan, a former deputy undersecretary of defense who now acts as a consultant and teacher at the University of Maryland, said a Pentagon study showed the value of foreign-made components in the missile systems is small enough that the Pentagon could stockpile the parts if it were deemed worthwhile.

U.S. Scrambled to Shape View of Highway of Death

Steve Coll and William Branigin

The U.S. Navy's Silverfox bombing squadron swooped beneath low clouds north of Kuwait City in the early hours of February 26 and suddenly found itself overlooking an attack pilot's dreamscape— more than 1,500 Iraqi tanks, armored vehicles, jeeps, water and fuel tankers, ambulances, tractor-trailers, and passenger cars clogged in a traffic jam on a six-lane highway headed north.

Fire and shrapnel exploded on the highway as bombs fell from the Silverfox squadron's A-6E and other attack planes. Navy, air force, and marine pilots trapped the long convoy by disabling vehicles at its front and rear, then pummelled the traffic jam for hours. Scores of Iraqis were blown apart or incinerated in their vehicles. The victims were "basically just sitting ducks," said Cmdr. Frank Sweigart, the squadron leader, when interviewed later that day by reporters.

The highway north of Kuwait City became the most vivid scene of destruction in the six-week Persian Gulf War, its images of wreckage and death contrasting sharply with emotionally remote "smart bomb" videotapes and television pool reports filmed from the rear of the desert battlefield.

Yet the way the highway bombing unfolded—its ferocity, timing, and public presentation by senior U.S. military officers—also constitutes one of the war's most complex and ambiguous episodes.

The bombing demonstrated one grim irony of the brief ground phase of the conflict: that a war undertaken to drive Iraqi forces from Kuwait ended with some Iraqi troops desperately trying to leave the emirate while U.S. forces held them in place and destroyed them.

U.S. military officers said their main purpose in pounding fleeing Iraqi troops was to protect allied forces elsewhere on the battlefield by cutting off potential reinforcements for Iraqi Republican Guard divisions north and west of Kuwait. In retrospect, some officers say the doomed Iraqis crowded on the highway—many of whom had loaded their vehicles with loot stolen from Kuwait—probably wanted to go home to Baghdad, not reinforce the Republican Guard. But there was no way to know this in the heat of battle, they added.

While the bombing was an act of war ordered by allied field commanders seeking to protect their troops on a dangerous battle-field, it also was the focus of a public relations campaign managed by the U.S. Central Command in Riyadh, Saudi Arabia—a campaign designed to shape perceptions of the war's last and most violent phase, which culminated in the near-total destruction of Iraq's army in Kuwait and southern Iraq.

To the northeast of here, more than 400 charred vehicles and dozens of bodies mark the 50-mile stretch where another fleeing Iraqi convoy was destroyed along a second road that connects the Kuwaiti town of Jahra to Iraq.

But the "highway of death," as the road near Mutlaa has come to be known, may be something of a misnomer. It is now apparent that more Iraqis fled their vehicles and were taken prisoner than were killed by U.S. bombing of the highway. There still are no reliable figures on precisely how many people were killed in the convoy, but reporters who visited the scene as bodies were being collected say the most they saw at any one place was 40, and they estimated that a total of 200 to 300 Iraqis may have died at the scene.

The following reconstruction is drawn from interviews with Kuwaiti witnesses, U.S. field commanders and soldiers in Kuwait, officers with the U.S. Central Command in Saudi Arabia, and pool reports of interviews with U.S. pilots conducted at the time of the bombing.

Feverish, Fatal Flight

Huddled in their homes beside the highway leading from Kuwait City to Iraq, Kuwaitis who had suffered through more than six months of brutal occupation listened with amazement to the chaotic sounds of a panicked Iraqi army on the move. In the black of night, tanks and armored vehicles rumbled, car and truck horns blew, voices cursed in Arabic, and every so often there was the crunch of a traffic collision, then more curses and blowing horns.

It was Monday night, February 25, less than 48 hours into a ground offensive the Kuwaitis hoped would liberate their besieged country. Ever since the ground war began, there had been signs that Iraqi troops were preparing to leave Kuwait. Sunday, for example, they had been seen loading television sets and other booty into stolen cars and trucks. Now the flight was feverish, "as if they were racing to get to Iraq," recalled Manawar Said, a Kuwaiti Education Ministry employee who lived by the highway.

Near midnight came the first thunder of bombs. Iraqis on the highway redoubled their panicked flight, only to exacerbate the traffic jam. Vehicles poured into the southbound lanes to head north and collided with one another. Hundreds of Iraqis jumped from their cars and trucks and ran off into the night, desperate for a place to hide. Some crouched in a nearby cemetery. Many sought refuge in empty houses.

By morning, the highway was a mangled scene of destruction and death. Planes from the aircraft carrier USS *Ranger* buzzed the convoy again and again, dropping cluster bombs and whatever other munitions they could hurriedly load onto their attack planes. Marine F/A-18 jets unleashed 500-pound bombs on the stranded vehicles. Air Force F-16A fighter-bombers raced north from bases in Saudi Arabia. There were so many planes striking the convoy, pilots said, that the "killing box" had to be divided in half by air traffic controllers to avoid mid-air collisions.

U.S. pilots, and Kuwaiti civilians who witnessed the attack, were struck by the scale of its destruction. A few felt pity for the Iraqi victims or expressed mixed feelings about the one-sidedness of the bombing. But most said they thought the Iraqis were getting only what they deserved.

"I think we're past the point of just letting him get in his tanks and drive them back into Iraq and say, 'I'm sorry,'" U.S. Air Force Lt. Col. George Patrick told a media pool reporter that Tuesday as he rested between missions against the convoy. "I feel fairly punitive about it."

Navy pilot Sweigart, speaking to a reporter on the *Ranger* as he reloaded between attacks on the highway, said, "One side of me says, 'That's right, it's like shooting ducks in a pond.' Does that make me uncomfortable? Not necessarily. Except there is a side of me that says, 'What are they dying for? For a madman's cause? And is that fair?' Well, we're at war; it's the tragedy of war, but we do our jobs."

Kuwaiti civilians living near the highway where Sweigart's bombs exploded felt none of the pilot's ambivalence. "These people who left Kuwait at the last moment were the security forces of Iraq, the people who really controlled the city," said Kamel Awadi, a Kuwaiti marketing executive who listened to the bombing from a two-story house near the tail end of the trapped convoy. "They were the most brutal, the most vicious people in Kuwait. . . . We have no pity on them because they had no pity on anybody."

Shaping World Perceptions

That Tuesday morning, while bombs exploded on the highway, senior U.S. military officers stationed far away at command headquarters in Riyadh wrestled with an unexpected problem: how to counter Iraq's surprise claim that the troops attempting to flee north from Kuwait were part of an orderly withdrawal from the emirate designed to comply with United Nations resolutions.

As the Iraqi vehicles rumbled and collided in the darkness that Monday night and early Tuesday morning, Baghdad radio announced that Iraq's government had ordered all of its troops to withdraw from Kuwait, ending months of defiant occupation.

Baghdad's pullout order posed several problems for the U.S.-led military coalition. Continued allied attacks raised the specter of a one-sided slaughter of retreating Iraqi troops, possibly complicating U.S.

political problems in the Arab world. Perhaps more importantly, a successful Iraqi withdrawal from Kuwait would deprive the allies of the chance to humiliate Iraqi President Saddam Hussein, destroy the remnants of his army, and prevent him from posing a continued military threat in the region.

By Tuesday morning, with allied ground forces rolling into Kuwait and across southern Iraq, the total defeat of Iraq's military had become a clear but generally unstated U.S. war aim. The aim was politically sensitive because the United Nations resolutions under which the war was organized did not go beyond the liberation of Kuwait.

As the bombing proceeded Tuesday, the United States responded to the Baghdad radio announcement by playing down evidence that Iraqi troops were actually leaving Kuwait, emphasizing that Iraqi forces had to abandon their weapons and armor to avoid allied firepower, and later arguing that Iraqi troop movements out of Kuwait were not a voluntary pullout but a retreat under fire.

At the same time, U.S. forces rapidly pressed a planned flanking maneuver into southern Iraq and northern Kuwait to block enemy troop movements to the north and west. The bombing of the highway was seen by commanders in the field as a part of this tactical maneuver. "We moved on them so fast they didn't have time to reinforce over there [to the north and west] or exercise their own counterattack," said Col. Bill Steed, chief of operations for the Marine Corps in Saudi Arabia, in an interview last week.

While Steed and other field commanders were calling in massive air strikes on Iraqi convoys moving out of Kuwait City on Tuesday morning, U.S. military briefers in Riyadh offered a carefully drawn, and in some respects inaccurate, picture of the fast-changing battlefield.

At 7 a.m. Tuesday, five hours after Baghdad's withdrawal announcement, a U.S. military officer emerged from the war room of U.S. Central Command headquarters to brief dozens of reporters on overnight developments. The officer, who cannot be identified under Pentagon rules, was peppered with questions about whether Iraqi troops were leaving Kuwait.

The officer said the U.S. command did not "have any real evidence of any withdrawal at this time. There are vehicles on the road, just as we've implied throughout the campaign . . . There are still not any indications of a significant amount of movement in any direction, north or south."

Asked about reports that U.S. pilots were hammering retreating troops near Kuwait City, the officer acknowledged that the air campaign was being pressed with full force, but he repeated, "There's no significant Iraqi movements to the north."

In fact, most Iraqi troops in and around Kuwait City began to flee toward the Euphrates River on Monday night, according to Kuwaiti witnesses. U.S. military sources in Riyadh said the officer who gave the briefing believed his characterization was accurate because it was not clear as he spoke whether the Iraqis being bombed on the highway were going home to the north or heading west to reinforce the Republican Guard.

By noon Tuesday, interviews with U.S. attack pilots conducted by media pool reporters that morning and circulated on news wire services had undermined the briefer's portrait of Iraqi movements. Pilots flying bombing missions over the highway indicated that a large-scale Iraqi retreat from Kuwait was underway, and one pilot told a pool reporter that bombing the retreating Iraqis was like "shooting fish in a barrel."

As the day wore on, senior officers with the U.S. Central Command in Riyadh became worried about what they saw as a growing public perception that Iraq's forces were leaving Kuwait voluntarily and that U.S. pilots were bombing them mercilessly, according to U.S. military sources. Relaying these worries to the Pentagon as they prepared for Tuesday's scheduled televised news briefing, senior officers agreed that U.S. spokesmen needed to use forceful language to portray Iraq's claimed "withdrawal" as a fighting retreat made necessary by heavy allied military pressure.

That strategy became evident in Saudi Arabia at 4:45 p.m. Tuesday (8:45 a.m. in Washington) when President Bush stepped in to the

White House Rose Garden to make a brief and hastily arranged televised statement saying the war would continue despite Baghdad's withdrawal announcement, that Iraq could not be trusted , that Iraqi troops were retreating under pressure, not voluntarily withdrawing, and that Saddam Hussein was attempting to achieve a political victory from a military rout. Bush vowed that the Iraqi president would not be permitted such a propaganda victory.

The president's statement was followed quickly by a televised military briefing from Saudi Arabia, which had been postponed earlier, apparently to accommodate the White House announcement. At the Saudi briefing, Brig. Gen. Richard Neal emphasized that Iraqi forces were not withdrawing, but were being pushed from the battle field.

"Saddam Hussein has described what is occurring as a withdrawal," Neal said. "By definition, a withdrawal is when you pull your forces back, not under pressure by the attacking forces. Retreat is when you're required to pull your forces back as required by the action of the attacking forces. The Iraqi army is in full retreat."

In fact, however, tens of thousands of Iraqi soldiers in and around Kuwait City had begun to pull away more than 36 hours before allied forces reached the capital.

While the Iraqi troops may have pulled out because they were battered by allied bombing and fearful of a ground attack, they did not move out under any immediate pressure from allied tanks and infantry, which still were miles from Kuwait City.

The U.S. Army's Tiger Brigade did attack the paralyzed Iraqi convoy on the road from Kuwait City on Tuesday afternoon, but only after hours of relentless air strikes had pinned down the fleeing Iraqi vehicles. Units of the 2nd Marine Division also reached the road from Kuwait on Tuesday and began striking it with artillery and tanks. Capturing the highway intersection controlling entrance to Kuwait City was a primary objective "from day one," said Lt. Gen. Walter Boomer, the Marine commander in Operation Desert Storm.

Souvenirs of Destruction

These days, the "highway of death" is Kuwait's main tourist attraction. Kuwaitis in traditional robes and headdresses tote video cameras up and down the highway to record the devastation. U.S., British, and Arab coalition soldiers tour the mayhem and take snapshots of each other alongside junked tanks, armored personnel carriers, and other vehicles.

Hand grenades still in plastic wrappers lie strewn on the ground alongside a school bus packed with ammunition boxes and pencils and other school supplies. Other loot included children's story books, bags of flour and rice, suitcases stuffed with clothes, new athletic shoes, women's high heels, and a dirty white wedding dress that someone had tied to the doors of a military ambulance.

Several groups of U.S. and British soldiers on a recent day were trying to remove Iraqi tanks and armored personnel carriers for their units' museums, and some Kuwaitis were trying to recover civilian cars and vans that they claimed had been stolen from them by the Iraqis.

U.S. soldiers cleaning up the damage said they were satisfied justice had been done on the highway. "It was like a robbery," said Staff Sgt. Casey Carson of the Tiger Brigade. "It was like we were the police force and these guys got caught trying to burglarize a house."

Asked what he thought about the destruction all about him, Marine Lt. Roy Blizzard replied: "The thing that really bothered me was that in every truck you could see a bag of loot. . . . They made us come here and do it. They should have listened to the president and left."

211

Army Is Blaming Patriot's Computer for Failure to Stop the Dhahran Scud

Eric Schmitt

The Iraqi missile that slammed into an American military barracks in Saudi Arabia during the Persian Gulf War, killing 28 people, penetrated air defenses because a computer failure shut down the American missile system designed to counter it, two army investigations have concluded.

The Iraqi Scud missile hit the barracks in Al Khobar near Dhahran on February 25, causing the war's single worst casualty toll for Americans. The allied Central Command said the next day that no Patriot missile had been fired to intercept the Scud, adding that the Scud had broken into pieces as it descended and was not identified as a threat by the Patriot radar system.

But further investigations determined that the Scud was intact when it hit the barracks and was not detected because the Patriot's radar system was rendered inoperable by the computer failure.

"The radar system never saw the incoming missile," said Col. Bruce Garnett, who conducted one of the investigations. He recently retired as the Patriot project manager at the army's Missile Command in Huntsville, Alabama.

Support from Separate Study

The 11th Air Defense Artillery Brigade at Fort Bliss, Texas, which operated all 20 Patriot batteries in Saudi Arabia, prepared a separate report that reached the same conclusions, an officer familiar with the inquiry said.

Army experts said in interviews that they knew within days that the Scud was intact when it hit, and that a technical flaw in the radar system was probably to blame.

212

The problem was identified and corrected in all the Patriot batteries within weeks of the attack, officials said.

The army investigations raise questions why the Pentagon and Central Command perpetuated the explanation that the Scud broke up.

The Central Command officials denied that they were aware of the army's initial findings of computer malfunction. "It was not something we had at all," said Lt. Col. Michael Gallagher, who was a Central Command spokesman in Riyadh.

During the war, American military officers were reluctant to discuss any weapon failings. But even after the cease-fire, many officers were averse to say anything that might tarnish the one-sided allied victory over Baghdad's forces.

The senior army official familiar with the investigations said the service would not comment on the inquiries until top-level service officials had reviewed the conclusions.

Family members of some of the victims of the Dhahran attack have tried to get more information from the army but say the Pentagon has refused to release any details.

Rita Bongiorni of Hickory, Pennsylvania, whose 20-year-old son, Joseph, was killed in the attack, said she had written the secretary of the army, Michael P.W. Stone, for an explanation, but had received only a form letter saying a comrade was at her son's side when he died.

When Mrs. Bongiorni requested a detailed autopsy report, she said the cause of death was listed simply as "Scud attack."

"I just want to know the truth, and I'm not sure we'll ever know," Mrs. Bongiorni said in a telephone interview. "I don't feel the army's been up front with us."

The performance of the Patriot system, hailed as one of the high-technology success stories of the war, has since undergone some re-evaluation.

Some scientists recently asserted that use of the Patriot in Israel and Saudi Arabia might actually have increased the amount of explosive debris scattered over the landscape, as Patriot as well as Scud warheads fell to earth.

Nevertheless, the weapon succeeded in intercepting virtually all of the Iraqi Scuds fired toward cities or military installations during the war, and several countries are rushing to buy Patriots at a cost of about $1 million each. The sales could yield billions of dollars in new orders for its manufacturer, Raytheon.

Since the beginning of the air war on January 17, Raytheon's stock has increased in value to $81.88 a share from $68.50.

A spokesman for Raytheon, Larry McCracken, declined to comment until the army makes public the inquiry findings.

The Patriot's performance is also an issue in the debate over the Pentagon's proposals for a missile defense system commonly known as "Star Wars." Backers of the program point to the Patriot's success to bolster their argument for greater spending on research and development of ballistic missile defenses.

The Patriot works by locking its ground radar on an incoming missile and relaying the signals to a computer at a control station that tracks the target's speed, trajectory, and predicted course.

Using a series of complex, split-second computations, the computer calculates when to launch its missiles and, in the case of Scuds, fires two Patriots—each with a 200-pound conventional warhead traveling at 2,000 miles an hour—at each Scud. The Scuds travel at more than 4,000 miles per hour.

Two Patriot Batteries in Area

In Dhahran, the night of the fatal attack, there were two Patriot batteries—Alpha and Bravo batteries of the Second Battalion, Seventh Air Defense Artillery Regiment—whose protective reach extended well beyond the American military barracks in nearby Al Khobar, army investigators said.

Four hours before the Scud firing, Bravo battery was shut down for routine maintenance on its radar system, a senior officer in the 11th Air Defense unit said.

The remaining battery was thought to provide adequate protection, but multiple computer problems, including four days of continuous operation, combined to cause a shutdown just a few minutes before the Scud attack, the officer said. As the Scud streaked toward the Persian Gulf city, Patriot batteries north of Dhahran detected the incoming missile on their radars but assumed that Alpha battery in Dhahran would attack, said Colonel Garnett, the former Patriot program director.

No Patriots were fired, army investigators said, and the Scud crashed into the barracks, killing 28 people and wounding 97 others.

Focus on Computer Software

Army investigators quickly ruled out operator error or problems with the launchers and focused on the complex computer software program, made by Raytheon, that translated signals from the functioning radar to aim and fire the Patriots.

Colonel Garnett and other senior army officials familiar with the investigations said an unforseen combination of "dozens" of variables—including the Scud's speed, altitude, and trajectory—had caused the radar system's failure.

Colonel Garnett described the case as "an anomaly that never showed up in thousands of hours of testing." His comments were first published in a recent edition of *The Army Times*, a weekly publication.

Col. Joseph Garrett, a commander of the 11th Air Defense Unit, refused to comment on his inquiry, which has been forwarded to Lt. Gen. John J. Yeosock, commander of army forces in Saudi Arabia during the war.

Although investigators determined within 72 hours that a technical problem had caused the failure, Colonel Garnett said it took "several weeks" to pinpoint the precise error "buried deep" in computer tapes made of the engagement on the radar system's high-speed, digital data recorder.

He and other investigators refused to provide more details of the problem, citing the classified nature of the system. Once identified, though, the problem was easy to fix, army investigators said, and software was replaced in all 20 batteries in the war zone.

Colonel Garnett said the army upgraded the Patriot's software program three times during the fighting. The fine-tuning improved the system's ability to shoot down Scuds at higher altitudes—lessening the chances that explosive debris would fall on friendly cities—and to discriminate between the explosive warhead and other parts that broke off during an attack.

U.S. Military Faces Probe on Performance

Frank A. Aukofer

Government inspection and audit agencies are conducting 88 separate investigations of U.S. military operations and equipment used in the war against Iraq, according to documents obtained by *The Milwaukee Journal.*

As the investigations are completed, they are expected to fuel the ongoing debate over whether American military leaders painted too rosy a picture during the Persian Gulf War about the performance of high-technology aircraft and weapons systems.

The investigations, only a few of which have been completed, cover everything from intelligence and the performance of weapons systems to the impact of the employment of women in Operation Desert Storm.

About half of the investigations are being conducted by the General Accounting Office (GAO), the watchdog agency of Congress. Others are being carried out by inspectors general and audit offices in the Pentagon and the military services.

Among other things, government investigators are looking into the performance of the army's Apache attack helicopter, wear and tear on the C-5, C-141, and C-130 cargo aircraft; the operations of marine and navy weapons systems; how American and allied troops trained for Desert Storm; the performance of the Bradley Fighting Vehicle and the M1-A1 tank; and how Defense Department personnel performed in maintaining and repairing critical equipment.

Other areas under scrutiny include ammunition supply systems and management; field rations; the performance of commercial airliners in the Civil Reserve Air Fleet (CRAF); performance and costs of the military airlift and sealift commands; the mobilization of reserve forces; the readiness of hospitals and medical teams, including

Veterans Administration hospitals in the United States; minesweeper operations; and even whether the government was overcharged by shippers.

Of the 88 investigations, 41 are being carried out by the GAO and the others are being conducted by the military services and the Pentagon. The GAO had three investigative teams in the Persian Gulf before, during, and after the war, starting last December 30 and continuing through last April 17.

Some of the criticisms of the military's public descriptions of the war surfaced recently at a joint hearing by two House Armed Services subcommittees. The subcommittees were seeking information about how America's high-tech weapons worked in the war.

One of the witnesses, Pierre M. Sprey, a former Pentagon systems analyst and a prominent member of the military reform movement, told the subcommittees that most of the highly touted weapons had not worked as well as advertised.

"The country has been poorly served by the shamelessly doctored statistics and the hand-selected video clips of isolated successes that were pumped out to the media during the war in order to influence postwar budget decisions," Sprey told the subcommittees.

He urged members of the House Armed Services Committee to take active measures to make certain that insights from the Desert Storm combat information were preserved and not distorted, censored, or buried by advocates of particular weapons systems.

Later, the Armed Services Committee chairman, Rep. Les Aspin (D-Wis.), citing Sprey's and other conflicting testimony, called on President Bush to appoint a civilian-led commission to study the lessons of the Gulf War.

He pointed out the discrepancy between the testimony by Sprey, who said the war's outcome would have been the same even if the United States had exchanged equipment with Iraq, and William Perry, a former undersecretary of defense, who said that what defeated Iraq was America's technological edge in weapons. The technology had a multiplier effect and expanded the capabilities of U.S. forces, Perry argued.

Sprey's point was that the high-tech weapons were far less important than the training and tactics of allied troops against an enemy that was demoralized by the actions of Iraqi President Saddam Hussein.

"Who is right?" Aspin said. "Perry? Sprey? Both? Neither? Our military is going to shrink. We're going to need force multipliers even against less sophisticated adversaries when they outnumber us. Sorting this out is where a major review by a presidential commission could be vital to our national defense."

Letter Sent to Bush

In a letter to Bush last week, Aspin said an independent commission could be structured along the lines of a survey of allied bombing carried out by the United States after World War II. He said the commission could first issue a classified report to the president and Congress, then tell the public what it had found. If it is headed by reputable citizens with a talented staff, the findings will have credibility with Congress and the American people, he said.

"[The commission] should analyze the ingredients of our military success in the gulf, including the contribution of specific military strategies, tactics, weapons, and support capabilities," Aspin told Bush.

"Second, it should identify any weak spots in our preparations, planning, and performance. Third, it should examine the likely relevance of the Persian Gulf experience to other conflicts to help ensure that we do not overgeneralize from the specific circumstance of this war."

Should Bush establish the commission Aspin suggests, it would have access to the results of the 88 Desert Storm investigations now under way.

About 80 to 85 percent of the GAO's investigations are carried out at the request of congressional committees and individual members of Congress. Others are done on the agency's own initiative or are required.

The GAO has a staff of about 5,100, the vast majority of them investigators and auditors. About 3,000 are based in Washington and the others work in 14 field offices.

The Performance
of the Press

Chapter Seven

Washington and Saudi Arabia: How Good Was the Press?

How well qualified were the reporters to cover the Gulf War? How good was the coverage they provided? Was the press sufficiently independent from the government, or was it "co-opted" by the military? Did reporters put speed, volume, and their bylines ahead of quality and insight?

The Instant Replay War

Robert Lichter

The Persian Gulf crisis triggered more network news stories in a shorter period of time than any event in television's history. From Iraq's invasion of Kuwait on August 2 through the allied cease-fire on February 27, ABC, CBS, and NBC broadcast 4,383 gulf-related stories on their evening newscasts, with a total airtime of 126 hours 29 minutes. Thus, the three major networks together averaged about 20 gulf stories lasting 36 minutes per night over a seven-month period. By comparison, the 1988 presidential campaign yielded only 2,301 news stories over 22 months.

Coverage of the war itself produced 1,733 stories lasting 53 hours 33 minutes during 42 evenings of scheduled newscasts, not including the many special broadcasts at other times. War coverage averaged 14 stories lasting 25 minutes per network per night, more than the entire normal network evening newscast. (Many wartime broadcasts were expanded to an hour.) The leading news topic was the air war (339 stories), followed closely by reports about ground action (303 stories). Other major topics included discussions of allied war strategy (205 stories), diplomatic efforts to end the war (189 stories), and the war's effect on Israel and the Palestinians (173 stories). The following is a summary of coverage for each week of the war.

Week One: January 17–23. The outbreak of war preempted the evening newscasts on January 16 and set off an unprecedented 42 continuous hours of war news. During the first week's scheduled evening newscasts alone, the networks broadcast 337 war-related stories lasting more than 11 hours. Most of the coverage focused on the start of the air campaign (120 stories) and on Israel's role in the war following Iraq's Scud attacks (72 stories).

Week Two: January 24–30. The coverage remained heavy (320

224

stories), but the focus became more varied. Leading topics were the air war (56 stories), civilian damage within both Iraq and Israel (33), and the oil spill in the Persian Gulf (26).

Week Three: January 3–February 6. As war news became more routine, network coverage dropped to 235 stories. The ground fighting in Khafji generated the most attention (42 stories).

Week Four: February 7–13. The Baghdad bunker bombing on February 13 helped to make civilian casualties the top news topic of the week, with 44 stories out of a total of 221.

Week Five: February 14–20. Iraq's offer to withdraw from Kuwait, coupled with mediation efforts by the Soviet Union, made diplomacy the week's leading topic, with 71 stories. The focus of air war stories became battlefield preparation; 39 stories were devoted to war strategy.

Week Six: February 21–27. The war's final week was also its most intensively covered—353 stories, an average of nearly 17 per network broadcast. The week began with furious attention to diplomacy (85 stories), followed by 131 stories on the hundred-hour ground war that began February 24.

War Sources

Military spokesmen and troops were by far the most frequent sources on TV news. Their 1,653 comments accounted for two out of every five American sources. More than 40 percent of the military sources (713) were the enlisted men and women and junior officers who presented a grunt's-eye view of the conflict. Another 360 statements came from senior officers in the field or at the Pentagon. The remainder were references to unidentified "Pentagon sources." Among the services, marines were quoted the most often. Their 306 appearances outranked the army's 262, despite frequent sound bites from army generals Powell (36) and Schwarzkopf (80). Air force personnel were quoted only 159 times, and the navy's only 75 times.

The Bush administration was the source of another 797 statements, including 183 from President Bush and 62 from Secretary of Defense Cheney.

Among foreign sources, Iraqis were quoted most frequently, more than all of the United States' coalition partners combined (495 to 447 citations). Saddam Hussein was quoted 68 times, making him the third most frequently cited individual source, after Bush and Schwarzkopf. In contrast to the 495 quotes from Iraqi sources, television viewers heard from only 302 Israeli, 112 Kuwaiti, and 79 Saudi sources.

Rating the Combatants

Despite his visibility, TV news coverage of Saddam was highly negative. Only one out of eight sources who evaluated the Iraqi president provided words of praise, and those sources were predominantly his fellow Iraqis or Jordanians. For example, a Jordanian woman told CBS that, "Saddam Hussein is good . . . I love Saddam Hussein." George Bush received a slight majority of positive comments (56 percent), with most of his support coming from Americans. More than 90 percent of U.S. sources had praise for Bush, while three out of four foreign sources criticized him. Much of the criticism of Bush was voiced by Iraqis, such as a government official who charged, "Bush is like Hitler and is a war criminal."

Israel's decision not to respond to Iraq's Scud attacks earned it praise from three out of four TV news sources, the most positive profile among the Gulf War players. The Soviet Union, in the spotlight for its mediation efforts, received evenly balanced evaluations. The worst press of the conflict went to the Germans and the Japanese. They received unanimously negative evaluations for allegedly failing to support the coalition.

Surprisingly, the U.S. government fared little better than its Iraqi counterpart in the sound bite battle. Nearly three out of five sources (59 percent) criticized U.S. government policies during the war.

Evaluations of the United States centered on the bombing campaign and the civilian damage it was causing in Iraq. More than a third of all evaluations of U.S. policy focused on those two categories, and 68 percent of those statements were critical. After the Iraqi bunker bombing, one Jordanian stated, "the U.S. people running this war are either liars or very stupid people. They may have smart bombs, but they don't have very smart minds." Iraqi policy received even greater criticism—63 percent negative comments from sources. The Iraqis were most often criticized for their Scud attacks on Israeli cities, the release of oil into the Persian Gulf, and alleged atrocities in Kuwait.

Rating the Warriors

The performance of the American military in the Gulf War yielded almost universally good press: 95 percent of the more than 300 sources who discussed this area praised the military's effectiveness in the war. CBS's Dan Rather summarized the first full day of the war: "In sports page language—this is not a sport, it's war—but, so far, it's a blowout."

As the workhorse for much of the air war, the air force received the largest dose of praise (83 positive and only 2 negative evaluations). The marine corps, which acquired the media spotlight during the ground war as the army vanished into the western Saudi desert, received unanimously positive ratings. Among weapons systems, the Patriot missile was the media darling, with 91 percent positive ratings. One U.S. serviceman called the Patriot "the king of air defense artillery right now, not only for the United States, but probably in all the free world."

The Iraqi military also got fairly good ratings early on, but its reputation slid as the weeks passed. Four days into the war, a U.S. military briefer stated that the Iraqis possessed "some of the most formidable air defenses ever encountered." During the first week of the war, more than three out of five such estimations of Iraqi strength (61 percent) were positive. By the final week of the war, Iraq's military power had become the butt of jokes. "That an entire battalion would surrender to a bunch of helicopters," NBC military analyst James Dunnigan noted wryly, "certainly writes a new chapter in military history."

Rating the War

The debate over the Gulf War began not in January, but in November, with George Bush's decision to deploy additional forces to the gulf. Among sources who debated the merits of using force during the next four months, more than half (55 percent) gave antiwar opinions. During the war itself, 57 percent of sources voiced opposition. Early coverage was critical of the war option; even Ronald Reagan's former Navy Secretary James Webb was among those opposed to war: "The President's error in sending so many troops should not be compounded by a further error of using them. . . . " Only in December, with congressional hearings virtually over and most of the organized protests still a month away, did a majority of sources (82 percent) support armed intervention, although discussion of this issue was light.

In January, the debate moved into high gear, with the congressional vote on the use of force and reaction to the start of the war. The high level of debate in January also saw the lowest level of support for the war, as 61 percent of sources came out against the use of force. Said one U.S. marine's mother: "I don't believe in war. I don't feel like sacrificing my son for oil." Even as the war ended victoriously in February, the level of support among sources remained below 50 percent for the month.

The predominance of antiwar voices was also reflected in television coverage of demonstrations. During the war, the networks broadcast 54 stories on antiwar demonstrations or protests, nearly double the number of stories (28) that focused on pro-war demonstrations. By contrast, a Times Mirror poll (released on January 31) found that three times as many Americans had attended pro-war rallies as antiwar rallies.

Although the networks showed more critics than supporters of the war, they described the public as generally supportive. When discussing public opinion, 84 percent of reporters stated that the public was backing the war. The remainder argued that the public was divided or stressed those groups that remained opposed to the war.

Images of War

The most frequently televised images of the Gulf War were not of combat or military casualties, but of damage and injuries inflicted on civilians. We coded 1,217 individual camera shots of nonmilitary damage, nearly 30 such visuals per night. Nearly half (48 percent) of these shots showed damage to civilian areas inside Iraq. Under a quarter (23 percent) focused on images of destruction in Israel, and one in eight (13 percent) depicted the Persian Gulf oil spill. These pictures were far from antiseptic; 223 (or 18 percent) depicted human casualties, mostly from Iraq (151) and Israel (66).

Combat visuals also appeared frequently on the nightly news. The brevity of the ground war insured that most visual images depicted airborne combat. The networks featured 594 pictures of the air war, mostly camera shots from allied planes, or Patriot missile launches over Israel or Saudi Arabia. Ironically, the number of air combat visuals virtually equalled the number of images of Iraqi civilian damage (590). Images of ground combat, mostly from the last days of the war, totaled 404 shots—just over a third of all combat visuals.

Despite the paucity of allied casualties in the war, a large proportion of the military casualties shown on the networks were U.S. or coalition troops. Of the 130 shots of dead or wounded servicemen, more than two-thirds (91) were allied casualties; Iraqi troops accounted for the remaining 39. The Iraqis were more often depicted as prisoners; 182 of the 258 visuals of POWs were of captured Iraqi soldiers. Overall, shots of Iraqi military damage (casualties and wreckage such as burning tanks) outnumbered shots of allied military damage by 387 to 281.

229

The ABC Difference

Although coverage by CBS and NBC was similar on most of our measures, ABC produced a distinctively antiwar profile. This reflects both the distribution of opinion and the selection of subject matter in ABC's war coverage. In the opinion debate, ABC proved more likely to air criticisms of U.S. policy and leadership than did CBS or NBC. Fewer than half of ABC's sources (44 percent) provided positive evaluations of President Bush. In contrast, 58 percent of NBC sources and 63 percent of CBS sources praised Bush. Similarly, three out of four evaluations of U.S. policy on ABC were negative. For example, Peter Jennings talked to the Iraqi Ambassador to the United Nations, who protested that the U.S. was "carpet bombing all cities and towns, killing children and ladies and elderlies and even sick people in hospitals." At the other networks, the policy debate was about evenly balanced—48 percent of sources on CBS and 50 percent on NBC supported U.S. gulf policies. Sources on ABC were also less likely to praise Israel than were those on the other networks (60 percent versus 79 percent combined positive ratings). Finally, opinion on the war itself was balanced on the other networks but nearly two to one negative on ABC.

We found similar gaps in the selection of topics, sources, and pictures. ABC aired half again as many stories on civilian damage as did either of its rivals. ABC quoted Iraqi sources half again as frequently as CBS and NBC but cited fewer Israeli sources and showed fewer visuals of damage to Israel from Scud attacks. Finally, ABC broadcast the most stories (20) on antiwar demonstrations.

230

Talking Back to the Tube

Richard Valeriani

In 1982, I covered the Falkland Islands War from the "trenches" in downtown Buenos Aires. The Argentine military wouldn't let reporters go to the islands and the British military imposed severe restrictions, too.

The tight British control was much admired in the Pentagon, where many of the officers who had held junior- or middle-level rank in Vietnam were now top brass. Many still blamed the news media for the outcome in Vietnam.

A year later, during the invasion of Grenada, those officers went the British one better. They simply excluded the media, including me, for the first three days. This time, I was forced to cover the war from the "trenches" of Barbados.

After Grenada, the press and the Pentagon agreed on guidelines for coverage of such events in the future, but those guidelines were circumvented during the military operations against Panama.

When President Bush and the Pentagon proclaimed that this war would not be another Vietnam, they were right on the money as far as the media were concerned. There would be no unlimited coverage as there had been in Vietnam. In the wryly trenchant words of *New York Times* media writer Walter Goodman, "The Pentagon won ground superiority over the press before it achieved air superiority over the Iraqis."

In an effort to highlight the journalistic issues that have emerged in the first six months of the gulf crisis, in late January I spoke with a number of people with special insight into the coverage. (Jesse Jackson, David Gergen, and Hodding Carter III made their comments at the Alfred I. duPont-Columbia University forum on January 29, 1991.)

231

Reuven Frank

All this "liveness" is bullshit! There isn't anything happening live except for some Scud attacks. What we're getting "live" is briefings about events that are from 12 to 48 hours old. And reporters talking to each other "live."

Reuven Frank is a former president of NBC News.

William Broyles, Jr.

The war has become a television show, which I expected, but in a very bloodless and distant kind of way. You get an occasional Scud missile attack, which, as terrifying as they are, don't seem that much more frightening than your typical eleven o'clock news on a local TV station. The sense of war as the massing of the means of death and destruction and its application against an enemy is, I think, completely lacking.

I think the only way we'll ever get Iraq out of Kuwait is if Americans and other people with boots on go in and do it, which is a very different kind of war than looking down sights with these video bombers. And when that happens, I think the coverage will be crucial.

Much of the crucial feedback in Vietnam wasn't coming back up the army chain of command. It was coming from reporters. My Lai was detected by reporters. The malfunction of the M-16 under general conditions, which was of considerable interest to the war effort and to the troops, came about because of the reporting, not because Colt Arms Manufacturing or the Pentagon itself was reporting it.

Ultimately, what was important about the Vietnam War was the state of mind and the strategy of the North Vietnamese and their determination to outlast us no matter what their casualties. I think the nature of their determination was something that American intelligence and the press never did capture.

William Broyles, Jr., a decorated Vietnam marine veteran, is a former

232

*editor-in-chief of*Newsweek *and cocreator of ABC television dramas "China Beach" and "Under Cover."*

Phil Donahue

We've got a press very, very conditioned to be popular and not to rock the boat in an age when we have fewer and fewer people going it alone and larger and larger press establishments more and more likely to buckle under the pressure.

And if you're a media person, how can you possibly not support Peter Arnett's presence in Iraq? Are his reports going to be homogenized? Certainly! But we know that. Celebrate his presence there. Hope he doesn't get killed. Divide everything he says by 10, but keep him there.

Phil Donahue is a syndicated talk show host.

David Halberstam

I believe the networks are essentially isolationist. The only time you get foreign coverage is, in effect, when you have ferocious film or when something happens to Americans at point-blank range.

The classic example of that is the networks' overcoverage of the Iran hostage crisis and the almost absolute failure to cover what I consider geopolitically a more important story—the Iran-Iraq War.

When you have that kind of imbalance, it really skews the nation's capacity to have a serious agenda, because you respond to the pseudo-event or the televised event rather than the event that will affect you in the long run.

David Halberstam won a Pulitzer Prize for his reporting from Vietnam in 1964 for The New York Times; *he is the author, most recently of* The Next Century.

Liz Trotta

The experts are doing the job that the correspondents should be doing. It's just one more person chipping away at what the correspondents classically have been able to do! Expertise should be the province of someone who has been in the area a long time, who probably speaks the language, maybe has even been in jail a few times, but knows the terrain.

It's another example of television news ceding its responsibility. They don't have any smart people around any more.

Liz Trotta, a veteran war correspondent for both NBC and CBS News, is the author of the forthcoming Fighting for Air: In the Trenches with Television News.

Peter Braestrup

We're in a period of culture shock. A new generation of journalists is learning about war and they're learning about the military. They're all bright enough, they're all energetic enough, but this is like landing on Mars. Their use of military terminology is always wrong: they don't know the difference between a brigade and a battalion, between a machine gun and an automatic rifle.

We've had five-and-a-half months to get people out there and to learn it, but a lot of them just didn't. They're ahistorical; they can't remember any precedents for anything. They keep discovering the world anew. They either concentrate on high-tech stories or on what an ABC producer described to me as "boo-hoo journalism," that is, asking, How do you feel? not What do you know? They're looking for that little emotional spurt. They don't know what the wider vignette means. They're yuppies in the desert.

The military are learning, too, with some of the stupid censorship things they're doing. A lot of the military are living a myth—that TV news had a decisive effect of public support for the war in Vietnam.

234

Professor John Mueller, of the University of Rochester, wrote a classic book, *War, Presidents and Public Opinion,* which examined the public opinion polls for Korea and Vietnam. In Korea, you had censorship and no TV. In Vietnam, you had less censorship and TV. Public support for each war fell at roughly the same rate among the same groups.

People don't need television to impress upon them the realities of war. It's a self-serving, self-aggrandizing myth the television people promote: unless we're there, the American people don't really know what's going on. Of course, the military think that's true. They hate TV or fear it. The media and the military play into each other's hands.

Peter Braestrup, who covered Vietnam for The New York Times *and was Saigon bureau chief for* The Washington Post, *is director of communications and senior editor at the Library of Congress.*

Scott Armstrong

The biggest quandary for the U.S. military during the '70s and '80s was how to project force into the Middle East. There was an obvious need, given oil, given unrest, and given the Soviet Union's interest in the region. The United States wanted to be able to fight a war there with equipment up to NATO standards. So the military installed the Command, Control, Communications, and Intelligence [C^3I] infrastructure in Saudi Arabia; it's an air-defense and targeting system that fuses information into one computer display. The Saudis bought the argument and paid for the equipment. The problem was the Saudis wanted to minimize the number of Americans to go with it. It was a "freeze-dried" package; in case of war just add troops and water.

How did the press miss a $50-billion-dollar deal? It was sufficiently arcane; it was not planned and administered in Washington, but in Florida; and it was not connected to inter-service rivalry. It was an air force program that the air force kept to itself.

Without this understanding it is impossible to explain how 600,000 people were so rapidly deployed. And it's impossible to appreciate how entangled we are with the Saudis. Without this Saudi infrastructure the American war machine is an uncoordinated mass of independent appendages. Without us, the Saudis can't run this system, without the American contractors who put it in and so forth. That is offensive in the world of Islam: the infidel has become the eyes and ears of the protector of Mecca and Medina.

After the war this infrastructure will be the linchpin for our version of the regional security coalition. The real "new world order" is going to have to require some American presence—a presence that is corrosive to the coalition.

The fact that these arrangements were made without the press knowing about it is startling enough. But to think that the press can pay attention to the postwar solution without paying attention to this is nonsensical.

Scott Armstrong, a former Washington Post *reporter and the founder of the National Security Archives, is a visiting scholar of international journalism at American University's School of Communication. His comments expand on reporting he did for an article in* The Washington Post *on November 1, 1981.*

Ralph Nader

The peace march in Washington [on January 26, 1991] was probably the biggest citizen demonstration ever in Washington in winter. CBS gives them a four-second—that may be an exaggeration—scan while someone is saying, "Meanwhile, there were protests on both coasts today." They didn't interview anybody.

Now if these marchers, instead of doing it peacefully, started a small riot in downtown Washington, they would have gotten more than four seconds. So what the media are really saying is, If you break the law, block traffic, take over buildings, and so on, we'll give you coverage.

Then there's the senior member of Congress, Henry Gonzalez, the chairman of the House Banking Committee, who has put in a resolution to impeach Bush on the war issue; he's virtually shut out [of the news].

This is a senior member of Congress, a leader of the Hispanic community, and he isn't even viewed as a curiosity. The media have gone to the point where they don't even cover the bizarre if the bizarre reflects a dissenting ideology.

Ralph Nader, consumer advocate, is the author of several books about corporate America.

David Gergen

I worked in the Reagan White House, and I can tell you that television had an enormous impact on our policy in Lebanon. We withdrew those marines from Lebanon in part because of television. We asked the Israelis to stop bombing in part because of the television pictures that were coming back from Beirut.

In this particular crisis, though, television has had precious little impact so far on the course of American foreign policy. What has been said and done has been decided upon by our executive branch, by the White House, by the military—without much regard to what television thinks or is saying or doing.

In effect, in this crisis television is serving as an international party line, in which we have all sorts of players who can talk to each other. There's a great deal of interaction going on through television, but it is not an independent force in the crisis.

Another point has struck me about this crisis: we see here the greatest diversity of voices on television, including C-SPAN and public television, telling us what's going on. The moments that bring us together as a people—the common understanding we have about the war, the common images we have of what's happening in this war—are increasingly the releases of the government.

237

So that I would argue that in a crisis what we're learning is that the more television voices there are, the more power the government has. And I think that's something to bear in mind here.

I have spent a lot of time in government and worried a lot about restoring the power of the presidency. But at the same time, today, perhaps because of a different perspective, I have growing concerns about the balance that exists between our institutions. We got into this war, frankly, without having a vigorous national debate in the country. We essentially committed ourselves, and then we had the debate. What that suggests to me is that we in journalism have even a higher responsibility to provide robust debate before the fact, as policy is being formulated, to give the public a better understanding going in.

David Gergen, the first director of communications in the Reagan administration, is editor-at-large for U.S. News & World Report *and a political analyst for television and radio.*

Jesse Jackson

We have this [closed] circle of experts. Since [the invasion of Kuwait on] August 2, I have talked with Saddam Hussein for 6 hours, two hours on tape. Longer than any American. I met with Tariq Aziz for almost 10 hours. I took the first group of journalists into Kuwait, negotiated for the release of hostages.

And when we got back, there was not one serious interview by a network. A categorical rejection. Now why is there no interest in what we saw, observed, and got on tape?

The Reverend Jesse Jackson, a former Democratic candidate for president, is Shadow Senator from Washington, D.C., and host of the syndicated "Jesse Jackson Show."

Hodding Carter III

Government is going to complain about anything which falls outside the official line. The media should simply ignore it. When Marlin Fitzwater says, "I don't know why you're so intent on proving massive failures of some kind," as he did, put it down as inevitable. When there's grousing about coverage of the antiwar demonstrators—which, I would note, was almost nonexistent—congratulate yourselves in the media on doing your jobs. When we keep antiwar advocacy ads off of local stations, be ashamed. When there is outrage that Saddam Hussein is given air time or that censored pictures are shown of civilian destruction in Iraq, remind yourself of what the alternative is, which is a society and a media like Iraq's.

We are now doing what I think is essentially phony coverage. What can we be doing? Well, let's start at the top, and I mean that literally. The pro forma objections of the network news divisions to the press rules are of limited interest to this White House. (The muscular objections of the corporations that own these network news divisions would be more interesting to this White House. I would suggest, however, without much fear of contradiction, that there's no more taste for sustained real coverage of this war in the major corporate headquarters than there is in the White House.) Right now we ought to realize that, as reporters, the first ground rule is to do your business and not abide by rules that you don't accept, and to take the consequences. That means getting out and seeing what you can do until you're stopped. It means actually behaving like a reporter instead of like someone who gets his information only from feedings, from briefings. Test the limits. Don't roll over. Keep trying.

Hodding Carter III, who was the State Department spokesman for the Carter administration during the Iran hostage crisis, is president of Main Street, a television production company.

The Media Impact on Foreign Policy

Joseph Fromm, Murray Gart, Thomas L. Hughes, Peter Rodman, and Lester Tanger

A group of five members gathered at the Cosmos Club [in Washington, D. C.] for a roundtable discussion on the media and foreign policy, then updated their remarks through late February [1991]. The participants included:

Joseph Fromm, chairman of the U.S. committee of the International Institute for Strategic Studies and former assistant editor of U.S. News & World Report.

Murray Gart, former editor of The Washington Star *and chief of correspondents for Time-Life Inc.*

Thomas L. Hughes, chairman of the Carnegie Endowment for International Peace and former assistant secretary of state.

Peter Rodman, senior fellow at Johns Hopkins University's Foreign Policy Institute and a former member of Henry Kissinger's National Security Council staff.

Lester Tanzer, moderator of the discussion, editor of Cosmos *and former managing editor of* U.S. News & World Report.

Tanzer: The war in the Persian Gulf has revived the great debate that started with the Vietnam War over the role and impact of the media on foreign policy. Do the media, as critics claim, impede the conduct of foreign policy?

Fromm: The media had less impact on the Gulf War than if it went poorly or had gone on longer. It was an exceptional if not unique event, but the Gulf War still raised many of the fundamental issues involving the relationship between the media and the government, not just in the conduct of war but in the conduct of foreign policy generally.

Hughes: The gulf crisis is probably the single most dramatic example we've ever had of a whole set of intersecting issues, involving the public, the president, and the conduct of military and foreign policy, with electronically imposed deadlines with all the consequences for everybody's behavior and commentary. Included were hundreds of thousands of troops, deployed to a very strange place, many of them interviewable, with their parents and children and grandparents also interviewable on an around-the-clock basis by TV networks, instantaneously broadcasting around the world.

All of these elements were conspicuous in the prehostility months of 1990. Some of them, of course, were suppressed by the blackout of news coverage at the height of the land war. But all will reemerge with the diplomatic and political collisions as the peace process gets underway.

Fromm: As I see it, the saturation coverage—coverage in real-time of the first truly televised war—involved the American public emotionally in the conflict on an unprecedented scale. But I don't think the media had as much effect on the strategy or conduct of the war as on the administration's public information policy.

Rodman: Everyone on the American side, civilian and military, I suspect, must have been constantly concerned about public and international perceptions as the media might shape them. They are probably all relieved that things worked out well—that negative perceptions never turned into major political problems that affected events.

One potential problem, for example, was civilian casualties in Iraq. But the administration survived even the tragedy of the bombing of the air raid shelter/bunker, partly because it had gained credibility in the very first days of the war from the media's independent confirmation of how precisely targeted the bombing was.

Gart: It seems to me that the media were managed in a way that minimized the opposition of the press, which didn't stray very far from the official line of what was happening. In fact, the media was used, unknowingly, to help the military convince the Iraqis that it planned big amphibious landings, which tied up many Iraqi troops. The press didn't raise much objection to being used that way. And, in general, the official line from the White House and Pentagon prevailed with virtually no criticism—perhaps because the war was so short and casualties relatively few.

Fromm: I'd enter one caveat, namely the role of the media, especially television, in Baghdad, where they operated under the control of Saddam Hussein. He was effective, for a brief time, in using CNN and then the other networks to transmit pictures of civilian casualties to support his claim that the United States and its allies were waging an indiscriminate bombing campaign against civilians. Reporters' movements were limited and controlled. Not until journalists left Iraq did some report that bombings were concentrated on military targets and that the Iraqis were trying to protect their military equipment by placing them in residential areas or other civilian sites.

Did the networks give aid and comfort to the enemy by televising only what the Iraqis wanted them to see and perhaps helping Saddam arouse antiwar and anti-American sentiment? This controversy will continue long after the end of the Gulf War, raising in new form the basic question of whether democracies in the TV age must operate at a disadvantage in the conduct of war.

Instantaneous Communication

Gart: We saw spectacular progress in the technology of electronic journalism, but the coverage frequently failed to distinguish between what could be filmed and what mattered. Even so, the dimensions of TV reporting grew exponentially, so that it will probably have major impact in the future on waging war and implementing foreign policy.

Before full-scale war broke out, the media were having quite an impact. We saw presidents or their top advisers announce policy or other decisions over television, with the enemy or other participants watching and reacting quickly. The fact that leaders can speak across international borders and reactions can be instantaneous makes for quite a difference in the development of foreign policy.

Fromm: This extra-governmental role of television has caused a kind of high-speed action-reaction in foreign policy that is one of the most important developments in recent years. People want things resolved quickly. It makes patient kinds of diplomacy much more difficult.

Rodman: Instantaneous communication among governments is not necessarily a good thing. Maybe I'm old-fashioned, but there's something to be said for governments reacting in a considered way to things that happen, being given a little time to think about their response. I also happen to believe in a certain degree of confidentiality, which is a way of sometimes making wiser decisions and accommodations possible. But this is the modern age and is something that can't be undone.

Hughes: All this raises in a very acute form the question of whether it's possible—even in the most central issues of peace and war—to conduct delicate military and diplomatic assignments when executive prerogatives have eroded this much.

Tanzer: With what danger?

Hughes: With the danger that you can't have a sustainable policy, with the danger that spokesmen are enticed into inconsistent statements directed to different audiences, with the danger that the president says one thing one minute and the soldier on the screen or the senator or the allied official the very next minute expressing disagreement.

Fromm: Another aspect that is important is the use of TV by an adversary, say, Saddam Hussein, to humanize the enemy. Or in the effort of terrorist leaders, in the Iran hostage crisis when mobs demonstrated in Teheran for the peak television news hours, to raise worries about the safety of the hostages. Does TV by its dramatizing the plight of the hostages enhance the security of the hostages, or does it make it more difficult for a president to contemplate the use of force in dealing with terrorists?

Actually, President Bush handled the hostage situation adroitly in the early phases of the Iraq crisis. He didn't involve himself with the hostage families and contribute to the drama on television or to making the hostages the central issue. Bush did not let his hands be tied by hostages as Jimmy Carter did. He swore to put the national interest above the hostages, if necessary. And Saddam Hussein eventually freed the hostages.

Tanzer: U.S. casualties in the Gulf War were remarkably light, but in general do pictures on TV of casualties and suffering make it difficult for a president to go to war, to use military force?

Hughes: Very much so, and to sustain a war once it has begun. And they make policy controversial from day one. They affect the ability to conduct or at least hold at bay for a reasonable period of time decisions on potentially controversial policies.

Tanzer: If we look at the role of the media in wars, is it possible to undertake major military actions without censorship?

Rodman: Government always tries to put restrictions on coverage during war. This becomes an issue in itself, an issue of debate and controversy that further complicates things for the government. I don't know if the media in this day and age understand that in conditions of genuine war a certain degree of censorship is inescapable and that new rules apply. But our media have grown up over the years not accustomed to any such restraint.

Gart: Clashes between the press and the military are inevitable in the early stages of every conflict. They were necessary to establish this war's boundaries between sensible military security restrictions and the public's need to know what was happening. Excesses on both sides of the argument, however regrettable, were to be expected.

In the Grenada landing, the military went out of its way to exclude the press almost as if the military simply wasn't willing to let the public in on what was going on. I think it was a mistake. The press can be contained in ways so that it must conduct itself in a disciplined manner. If cameras are not taken to the places where things can be seen, it's very difficult for the camera to report.

Hughes: Hostilities, once they have broken out, are one thing. In that case, greater restraint by reporters and workable pressures by the government can be employed. But a nonhostile situation is something

244

else again. We never really experienced anything like the six-month run-up to the UN's January 15 deadline for Iraq. There's something other-worldly about a TV hero or heroine smilingly addressing the national security adviser and saying, "Do you know something that I don't know?" or "Is something going on behind the scenes we're unaware of?" Of course, one hopes there is—there should be.

An Adversarial Relationship

Fromm: That raises the broader question of the media-government relationship in the field of foreign policy. It seems to me that a great change has taken place, not just in the last few years but over a longer span, that the media-government relationship has become essentially an adversarial one. If one goes back to World War II or Korea, the relationship was fairly congenial and cooperative. That's all changed. Now there's this very acute adversarial relationship which stems from Vietnam, Watergate, and the breakdown of trust, as well as the breakdown of the foreign-policy consensus. The government has lost its mystique, and the press is prepared to challenge the government on its conduct of foreign policy.

Tanzer: The adversarial relationship obviously complicates the conduct of foreign policy, but is it good or bad for the country?

Gart: It's good for the country. Foreign policy, in my view, is public policy. And public policy, it seems to me, has to be debated publicly, formulated publicly, and probably has to be subjected to the same kind of scrutiny by the press as domestic affairs.

Rodman: Actually, I think that over our history, periods of warmth between press and government are unusual. In a lot of our history, there has been a pretty raucous press. It's a fact of life. The issues are important enough, so how can you justify not having the most vigorous debate?

However, there is another related issue, beyond the Gulf War. There is a cultural element to the adversarial relationship. I saw some in the press who seem to be ready to take up where they left off in

245

Indochina. Stories that highlight the dangers of casualties, that highlight the human interest in a way that's almost calculated to raise the pain level when people are killed; stories that focus on military snafus, or why shouldn't the government be more willing to do this or that. I'm not sure the press has to be the opponent or make itself an arm of the antiwar movement, as some did during the Vietnam War.

Tanzer: Is it a thirst for confrontation with the government that drives the media as much as a thirst for the dramatic, such as people waving antiwar signs or staging demonstrations?

Rodman: I'm not sure whether TV, in highlighting the antiwar movement and maybe giving them more attention than they deserve, is displaying a political bias or is just after a dramatic story.

Tanzer: In talking about the impact of the media, we seem to be referring almost exclusively to television. Why is that?

Hughes: There is something peculiar and special about TV as compared to print journalism. Traditionally, print was a medium of choice for a volitional audience. The audience chose what it wished to read. It chose whether it wished to read the newspaper in the first place. It chose whether it wished to read this particular column. It could skipread. It was not a captive audience.

Television produces a captive audience, an audience that's addicted to TV for one reason or another, whether it's a sports program coming up or the soap opera beforehand. In peacetime, a lot of people out there are watching television who normally are not interested in foreign affairs, who normally would not opt to see a foreign affairs program. These people have a very limited attention span. They are fed rapid-fire, hot, intense foreign coverage. What comes through to them is hostility. They see a world out there that's very different from theirs, that's culturally so distant that the connections can't be made. Foreigners seem to be anti-American, and not just those we are fighting. TV presents one disaster after another. That is bound to have a really important conditioning effect on the viewing audience.

Fromm: In the past, the bulk of people had very little interest in, or knowledge of, foreign affairs. Now foreign policy and foreign affairs

246

have been democratized, so everyone is aware of what is going on. But it's a kind of involvement of ignorance. The viewer has a very superficial knowledge of foreign affairs, but not the depth if he or she had read *The New York Times* or a number of other publications. They may have views, but are the views based on serious knowledge or on this extremely superficial and theatrical presentation?

Rodman: I'm worried that television is, in a sense, less responsible than print journalism, at least at the major newspapers, in separating reporting from commentary. There are newspaper correspondents who are tendentious. But I see tendentious pieces much more often on TV. With a lot more individuals in TV who want to make their careers by being hard-hitting, television just may not be adaptable to self-enforcing standards.

Fromm: Part of it is that television is a mixture of journalism and show business—perhaps more show business than journalism—and therefore it has to keep winning and keeping an audience.

Hughes: Having sounded a little negative about our national newscasters, let me say that I think most of them, if you pressed them on the point, would confess to feeling a certain amount of *noblesse oblige*. They know that they're powerful. They know they're addressing audiences of millions every night.

Incidentally, that national network role may soon break down with new technological advances. Pretty soon, local TV stations are going to be able to pick, for economic reasons, a minute of national coverage, if they wish, and save money by using local commentators to cover world affairs. We are already familiar with the splintering of government. You can imagine the splintering of the television newscasting industry in favor of centripetal news reporting. We may find 5 or 10 years from now we have even less of a universal, generally accepted data base in this country on foreign policy questions that we do now.

Gart: It would be a mistake to generalize totally about television. TV has been developing the ability in recent years to deal with complex issues. That's exemplified every night in the "MacNeil/

Lehrer Report," where people are assembled who know what they're talking about. Each of the networks has tried in its own way, even beyond the Sunday ghetto of "Meet the Press," "Face the Nation," "The David Brinkley Show."

The Media's Growing Influence

Tanzer: Have the media been getting more influential in foreign policy in recent years?

Gart: A good deal more. Public officials, thanks to television and print, are put to a much greater test in formulating and conducting foreign policy. You'll recall some months ago that we were informed that seven out of eight past secretaries of defense and two former chairmen of the joint chiefs had views at variance with President Bush's stated Iraq policies. The media force the president to take those views into account. I'm not sure that's all bad. It seems to me that providing that kind of input into the development of policy is probably better than relying on a small group of advisers to formulate policy.

We all remember when the White House in the Reagan administration sent a group off to Teheran with missiles and Bibles to do business in secrecy on the hostages held by Iran. We'd have been pretty well-served at the time if some smart reporter picked up a whiff of that and got into print or on the air.

Rodman: I have to disagree because I'm not sure I like the idea that the media should be one of the determiners of policy or that their job is to sabotage policies even if the policies are stupid. It really isn't their function. At the same time, I'm willing to absolve the media of responsibility for a lot of what they are, in fact, literally being the media of communication for. The Congress, for example. If we have opposition to present policy, it's because members of Congress are opposed, or former officials are opposed. So the media report this. Certainly, the Congress uses the media, certainly the Congress has the advantage of television now and can make a more dramatic impact than formerly.

248

Gart: I would agree that the press should not be involved in the formulation of policy. The proper role, reporting from abroad, is to bring reality home, so that policymakers and others who are engaged in the debates over foreign policy have an opportunity to deal with that reality.

Hughes: Policymakers are certainly more influenced by television than they used to be. The role of television inside the White House, inside the State Department, inside the Pentagon has grown ever since the days when Lyndon Johnson sat there transfixed, watching three television sets. Those were the simple days when all you had to worry about was what was going to be the lead on the evening network news. Now you worry about a new headline every hour for CNN—Cable News Network—which demands from the government at least one new story every hour. They don't want to run at ten o'clock what they ran at nine. So the government is increasingly tied up to a television schedule. And the penalties for political leaders not participating in this game are severe, penalties in terms of competition with other political leaders for coverage. We are increasingly a media-driven society, and the government is increasingly media-driven as well. Someone must "occupy the field"; if not you, your opposition.

Tanzer: Hasn't TV concentrated foreign-policy-making more sharply than ever in the White House because of this demand for instant reaction?

Hughes: In part, yes, but at the same time television is a tremendous equalizer. I'm not speaking only of equal time, which is also an interesting story because there are only two sides to a story on television, never three or four or five. Equal time is satisfied if you have two sides. But TV is also a tremendous equalizer in the sense that it equalizes the president and the bowler in Akron! It equalizes the president and the call-in voice from nowhere.

Tanzer: Are the State Department and other agencies less of a factor when the White House has to make a decision quickly?

Hughes: Yes, of course. And another phenomenon of the gulf crisis was the hapless role of Congress, which in a way gave the president

249

more of a role than he might otherwise have had. Normally the Congress is equally involved. Things changed somewhat once fighting began, but I sensed a real strain on the part of the Congress before hostilities started because they didn't know which way events were going to come out. They'd profoundly prefer to be on the right side when it's all over. From August through December, this freed the media to take up the congressional role, which it did with a vengeance. The lawmakers worried about choosing the wrong side in retrospect and paying political penalties later on. By contrast, the media are totally penalty-free.

Tanzer: Free to do what?

Hughes: Say anything, make all the arguments.

Fromm: In other words, the media are running, in effect, the permanent congressional hearing.

Hughes: All the time.

Fromm: And they pick the players. They pick who will be the advocate of the administration's foreign policy, who will be the critics.

Rodman: Even how to wage a war. There was enormous speculation in newspapers, magazines, on television, on how the war would or should be fought, our tactics, often with retired military officers as consultants.

Tanzer: Some scholars have said that TV exerts its greatest influence by helping shape the foreign-policy agenda, that is, not so much telling people what to think as what to think *about*.

Fromm: It seems to me that TV shapes the agenda in a broader sense. Take the Ethiopian famine. It had been going on for years. Television discovered it, and it moved near the top of the foreign policy agenda. I think this is true for South Africa as well. The violence in South Africa, when it was televised every night, got to be a major preoccupation in the foreign policy establishment. When South African authorities managed to get rid of the cameras, there was less of a priority put on South African policy. In that sense, TV can set the agenda—if it lights on something and brings it into people's homes, the government has to pay attention to it.

TV's Impact Abroad

Rodman: Let me shift to a different aspect of the same problem. Eastern Europe is a place where television had a historic impact. In one example, Timisoara, where the uprising began in Romania, was an area where people could pick up Hungarian television. East Germans could watch West German television. Radio Free Europe and Radio Liberty, cumulatively over years, turned out to have enormous impact. Events in China had their reverberations in Eastern Europe, maybe gave people there, dissidents, a certain sense that there was something going on, the vulnerability of Communism. The people of the Communist world who had always been cut off from access were affected deeply by the outside information that did get to them via outside media.

Fromm: On Tienanmen Square: If it hadn't happened that the Chinese had invited television in for the Gorbachev visit, and television was there, I wonder if the massacre would have had any significant impact here? Certainly not on the scale it did.

Gart: The reverse is also true. When the Israelis succeed in barring television from the West Bank and Gaza, coverage falls off. And the inattention grows even if killings and violence do not subside.

Hughes: In Eastern Europe, 1989–90, certainly television producers regarded that as a story that, in their terminology, would build. West German television was filming the escape of East Germans from Hungary, over the borders, and beaming it back every day into East Germany. You'd have to say that this was terrific television—a building story over a period of months, playing a wonderfully enhancing role until the Berlin Wall came down.

Fromm: Another example of television "being there" and affecting events was in Manila in the last days of Marcos. Sen. Richard Lugar of Indiana makes the point that television turned American foreign policy around because they were taking pictures of these crowds stopping Marcos's tanks and of what Marcos was doing. And

251

Lugar, who was out there at the time, said that the impact of the media was decisive in turning the Reagan administration around in withdrawing its support of Marcos.

Gart: That wasn't the intent of television. The intent of the coverage was to bring home the reality of what was happening, not to formulate policy.

Hughes: Let's not get carried away with the nonideological role of the press or the absence of any policy intentions. We're pleased that television played a role in producing the result it did. Still, there were some people in the press who were very pleased with developments in the Philippines and were glad to enhance them photographically and every other way. They were not disinterested in the outcome.

Tanzer: It is often said that the government-press relationship is a two-way street and that the government tries to use the press to shape public opinion. Can we expand on that?

Rodman: The media are independent, and the government does not control them. From my perspective, the government struggles to get its case before the people through the media, which can sometimes choose not to present the government's case much at all. President Reagan once wanted to give a national television address on Central America before an important congressional vote, but the three networks decided they were not going to make time available. So the president can make a major speech on a subject and get maybe two sentences on the networks. How these things are covered is totally dependent on how the newspapers or the networks choose to present what the president says.

Now presidents, if they are clever, can to some degree control perceptions and images. But on substance, it's much harder to do.

Hughes: Clever managers will try to create photo opportunities for the presidents and for foreign policymakers. In the case of someone like Mike Deaver, you get "Masterpiece Theatre." In a way, this is a distortion of the foreign policy process. It goes to the question of how filmable something is. TV goes where the camera goes. Summits are filmable. Presidents are filmable. War and soldiers and violence are filmable. Sometimes disease and starvation are filmable. But economics is not very filmable. Anonymous sources are not very filmable. Process is not very filmable. Several important aspects of what a total foreign policy would look like are cheated by the camera.

Tanzer: What are the implications?

Hughes: You've got a built-in distortion. A kind of favorable tilt in coverage toward things that are filmable and obvious lack of interest in those that are not. Last year, people said that economics was coming to the forefront of foreign policy. Economics means a great deal of anonymity—nongovernmental decisions made by nonstate actors. How are you going to film that?

Fromm: To illustrate the point, consider the Uruguay Round of GATT negotiations. You may have read about it in your newspapers, but how often did you see it on TV? Yet it may have greater long-term impact than the Mideast crisis. It will have profound impact on prosperity for the United States, yet the gulf crisis is filmable, GATT is not.

The Question of Leaks

Tanzer: Let's turn to the question of "leaks," which seems to plague all presidents. Have things gotten worse in recent years?

Rodman: I'm impressed by how well the Bush administration has kept a lot of its policy discussions secret. Let me make my own position clear on leaks. I believe that a certain confidentiality is justified and necessary. I think the government has a right to conduct its deliberations, its exchanges with other governments, in secret. I think accommodation among governments is sometimes more easily achieved if not every step is public. So I believe in the government's right to try to keep diplomatic and military secrets. Now the press is always going to be trying to find out everything and not show any particular restraint. That's a fact of life.

Tanzer: What makes people leak?

Hughes: Often, just the sheer joy of it.

253

Rodman: Sometimes there's a purpose to it, but often not, as Tom suggests. There are varieties of motives, not all admirable. Some of it is political warfare, bureaucratic warfare. Trying to influence the debate or trying to influence the president. If a particular agency loses a policy decision, it will try to conduct guerrilla warfare against it. Somebody who disagrees with a decision may leak it in order to generate congressional pressures. Some of the leaking comes from people who don't want to admit that they don't know something and are egged on to show they are knowledgeable.. Since a lot of the leaking is warfare against the president's ability to make his own policy, I think he has a right to protect the integrity of the process. Internal discipline by the administration is a reasonable objective.

Hughes: In the Kennedy, Johnson, and Nixon administrations, which I served, all three presidents lived in an atmosphere of desperation about leaks. Part of this was just the frustration over the gradual decline of presidential authority and the growth of bureaucracies whom the presidents suspected of sharing information with Congress and the press. Whatever the facts, there was a real fixation on leaks. In all three administrations there were temptations toward classifying and overclassifying information. All dabbled with covert operations in part as a way of keeping the public in the dark.

Fromm: As a matter of fact, there is a lot of confusion in government as to the responsibility of the media. The government does have a right and responsibility to impose discipline on its own ranks, but they can't count on the press doing the job for them by rejecting leaks.

Tanzer: Have the dangers to national security caused by leaks been exaggerated?

Gart: Yes. Most of the things that I've known that have been "secrets" haven't been secrets at all. Secrecy has a validity at a given moment in time. And secrets disappear. They lose their basic character very quickly. They are very perishable. I think the press, though, has to be responsible about what it does about leaks. There are leaks that are irresponsible, dispensed by irresponsible people. The press

254

makes a serious mistake by rushing to print or on the air without checking if the information makes any sense.

Fromm: Or what the motive is of the leaker.

Rodman: The motive may be the most interesting story, but that is part of the story that rarely gets told.

Gart: With the massive flow of information we have, there are bound to be things that get out one way or another. But whether they are damaging is really open to question.

Rodman: I suspect there is a lot of stuff leaking out of possible military actions that is totally irresponsible, some of it speculation. With many leaks, lives may not be at stake, but policymaking may suffer. I think there were a lot of leaks of covert operations that did harm because they embarrassed other governments and make it harder to get them to cooperate with us because they are not sure how secure their information will be.

You may be interested in an experience we had on the bombing of Libya in April 1986. This was rumored and leaked about for a week before it happened. There was much leaking, a lot of it accurate, about what might happen and when, some of it not accurate. I was in the White House then and was very worried about the loss of strategic surprise from all this leaking. But it went on and on, and we actually postponed the strike for a couple of days for some other reasons. It occurred to me that this was actually a brilliant strategy because Khaddafi was saturated with information and the Libyans tried to maintain a high state of alert for 10 days. It ended up being a great deception strategy because there was an excess of information, and they never did know the exact time.

Trained Seals and Sitting Ducks

Lewis H. Lapham

Journalism consists in buying white paper at two cents a pound and selling it at ten cents a pound—Charles A. Dana

Between the two campaigns waged by the American military command last winter in the Arabian desert—one against the Iraqi army and the other against the American media—it's hard to know which resulted in the more brilliant victory. Both campaigns made use of similar tactics (superior logistics, deception, control of the systems of communication), and both were directed at enemies so pitiably weak that their defeat was a foregone conclusion.

The bombardment of Baghdad began on January 17, and within a matter of hours the newspaper and television correspondents abandoned any claim or pretension to the power of independent thought. It was as if they had instantly enlisted in the ranks of an elite regiment, sworn to protect and defend whatever they were told to protect and defend by the generals who presented them with their morning film clips and their three or four paragraphs of yesterday's news.

By the end of the first week I no longer could bear to watch the televised briefings from Washington and Riyadh. The journalists admitted to the presence of authority were so obviously afraid of giving offense that they reminded me of prisoners of war. The parallel image appeared on cue five weeks later when what was left of the Iraqi army stumbled across the desert waving the white rags of surrender.

The Iraqi troops at least had suffered the admonitions of gunfire. The American media surrendered to a barrage of propaganda before the first F-16 fired its first round at an Iraqi military target. The Pentagon's invitation to the war carried with it a number of conditions—no reporters allowed on the battlefield except under strict supervision, and then only in small task forces designated as "press pools"; all dispatches submitted to the military censors for prior review; no unauthorized conversations with the allied troops; any violation of the rules punishable by expulsion from the theater in the sand.

The media accepted the conditions with scarcely a murmur of protest or complaint. Who could afford to decline even so ungracious an invitation? The promise of blood brings with it the gift of headlines, audiences, single-copy sales, Nielsen ratings, Pulitzer Prizes, and a swelling of the media's self-esteem. A television network on assignment to a war imagines itself outfitted with the trappings of immortality. The pictures, for once, mean something, and everybody has something important to say.

On the fourth day of the bombing Dan Rather confirmed the Pentagon's contemptuous opinion of a media cheaply bought for a rating point and a flag. He appeared on a CBS News broadcast with Connie Chung, and after reading the day's bulletin, he said, "Connie, I'm told that this program is being seen [by the troops] in Saudi Arabia. . . . And I know you would join me in giving our young men and women out there a salute." Rather then turned to the camera and raised his right hand to his forehead in a slightly awkward but unmistakably earnest military salute.

The salute established the tone of the media's grateful attendance at what everybody was pleased to call a war. Had anybody been concerned with the accurate use of words, the destruction of Iraq and the slaughter of an unknown number of Iraqis—maybe 50,000, maybe 150,000—might have been more precisely described as a police raid, as the violent suppression of a mob, as an exemplary lesson in the uses of major-league terrorism. Although the Iraqi army had been much advertised as a synonym for evil (as cruel as it was "battle-hardened," possessed of demonic weapons and a fanatic's wish for death, etc.), it proved, within a matter of hours, to consist of half-starved recruits, as scared as they were poorly armed, only too glad to give up their weapons for a cup of rainwater.

But the American media, like the American military commanders, weren't interested in the accuracy of words. They were interested in the accuracy of bombs, and by whatever name one wanted to call the Pentagon's trade show in the Persian Gulf, it undoubtedly was made for television. The parade of images combined the thrill of explosions with the wonder of technology. Who had ever seen—live and in color—such splendid displays of artillery fire? Who could fail to marvel at the sight of doomed buildings framed in the glass eye of an incoming missile? Who had ever seen the light of the Last Judgment coursing through a biblical sky?

Most of the American correspondents in Saudi Arabia experienced the war at more or less the same remove as the television audience in Omaha or Culver City. They saw little or nothing of the battlefield, which was classified top secret and declared off-limits to the American public on whose behalf the war presumably was being waged. The military command provided the media with government-issue images roughly equivalent to the publicity stills handed around to gossip columnists on location with a Hollywood film company. Every now and then the government press agents arranged brief interviews with members of the cast—a pilot who could be relied upon to say hello to all the wonderful folks who made the plane and the ordnance, a nurse who missed her six-month-old son in Georgia, an infantry sergeant (preferably black) who had discovered that nothing was more precious than freedom. But even this kind of good news was subject to official suspicion. A reporter who said of some pilots that the excitement upon returning from a mission had made them "giddy" found the word changed to "proud."

The Pentagon produced and directed the war as a television miniseries based loosely on Richard Wagner's *Götterdämmerung*, with a script that borrowed elements of "Monday Night Football," "The A Team," and "Revenge of the Nerds." The synchronization with prime-time entertainment was particularly striking on Super Bowl Sunday. ABC News intercut its coverage of the game in progress in Tampa with news of the bombing in progress in the Middle East, and the transitions seemed entirely in keeping with the spirit of both events. The newscasters were indistinguishable from the sportscasters, all of them drawing diagrams in chalk and talking in similar voices about the flight of a forward pass or the flare of a Patriot missile. The football players knelt to pray for a field goal, and the Disneyland halftime singers performed the rites of purification meant to sanctify the killing in the desert.

The televised images defined the war as a game, and the military command in Riyadh was careful to approve only those bits and pieces of film that sustained the illusion of a playing field (safe, bloodless, and abstract) on which American soldier-athletes performed feats of matchless daring and skill.

Like the sportscasters in the glass booth on the 50-yard line, the newscasters standing in front of the palm tree or the minaret understood themselves to be guests of the management. Just as it never would occur to Frank Gifford to question the procedures of the National Football League, so also it never occurred to Tom Brokaw to question the ground rules of the war. When an NBC correspondent in Israel made the mistake of talking to New York about an Iraqi missile falling on Tel Aviv without first submitting his news to the local censors, the Israeli government punished his impudence by shutting down the network's up-link to the satellite. The embargo remained in force until Brokaw, at the opening of "NBC Nightly News," apologized to Israel for the network's tactlessness.

Between representatives of competing news organizations the protocol was seldom so polite. The arguments were about access—who got to see whom, when, why, and for how long—and the correspondents were apt to be as jealous of their small privileges as the hangers-on attached to the entourage of Vanilla Ice. When Robert Fisk, a reporter for the British paper *The Independent*, arrived at the scene of the fighting for the town of Khafji, he was confronted by an NBC television reporter—a licensed member of the day's press pool—who resented the intrusion. "You asshole," the television correspondent said. "You'll prevent us from working. You're not allowed here. Get out. Go back to Dhahran." The outraged nuncio from NBC summoned an American marine public affairs officer, who said to Fisk, "You're not allowed to talk to U.S. Marines, and they're not allowed to talk to you."

Even under the best of circumstances, however, print was no match for television. The pictures shaped the way the story was told in the papers, the newsmagazines, and the smaller journals of dissenting opinion. Although a fair number of writers (politicians as well as scholars and plain citizens) took issue with the Bush administration's conduct of the war, their objections couldn't stand up to the heavy-caliber imagery delivered from Saudi Arabia in sorties as effective as the ones flown by the tactical fighter squadrons. *Time* and *Newsweek* followed the pictures with an assault of sententious rhetoric—"The greatest feat of arms since World War II . . . Like Hannibal at Cannae or Napoleon on a very good day."

At the end as in the beginning, the bulk of the writing about the events in the Persian Gulf was distinguished by its historical careless-ness and its grotesque hyperbole. The record strongly suggests that the Bush administration resolved to go to war as early as last August, almost as soon as Saddam Hussein made the mistake of invading Kuwait. If the war could be quickly and easily won, then the administration might gain a number of extremely desirable ends, among them the control of the international oil price, a revivification of the American military budget, a diversion of public attention from the sorrows of the domestic economy, a further degradation of what passes for the nation's political opposition, a cure for the mood of pessimism that supposedly had been undermining Washington's claims to world empire.

But none of these happy events could be brought to pass unless a credulous and jingoistic press could convince the American people that Hussein was a villain as monstrous as Adolf Hitler, that his army was all but invincible, that the fate of nations (not to mention the destiny of mankind) trembled in the balance of decision. It wouldn't do any good to send the grand armada to the Persian Gulf if the American people thought that the heavy guns were being wheeled into line to blow away a small-time thug.

260

The trick was to make the sitting duck look like the 6,000-pound gorilla. Much later in the proceedings Lt. Gen. Thomas Kelly could afford to say, amidst applause and self-satisfied laughter at the daily press briefing at the Pentagon, that, yes, sending B-52s to carpet bomb a single Iraqi Scud site was, come to think of it, "a delightful way to kill a fly." But in the beginning the generals were a good deal more careful about the work of disinformation. By October, Washington was besieged with ominous reports—about Hussein's chemical and biological weapons, about the price of oil rising to $50 or $100 a barrel, about the nuclear fire likely to consume the orchards of Israel, about the many thousands of body bags being sent to Saudi Arabia to collect the American dead. All the reports derived from government sources, and all of them proved to be grossly exaggerated.

The advantage of hindsight suggests that President Bush and his advisers chose Saddam Hussein as a target of opportunity precisely because they knew that his threats were mostly bluster and his army more bluntly described as a gang of thieves. The media never subjected the administration's statements to cross-examination, in large part because the administration so deftly promoted the fiction of a "liberal press" bent on the spiteful negation of America's most cherished truths. The major American media are about as liberal as Ronald Reagan or the late John Wayne, but in the popular mind they enjoy a reputation (undeserved but persistent) for radicalism, sedition, and dissent. The administration well understood that the media couldn't afford to offend the profoundly conservative sympathies of their prime-time audience, and so it knew that it could rely on the media's complicity in almost any deception dressed up in patriotic costume. But for the purposes of the autumn sales campaign it was necessary to cast the media as an antagonist as un-American as Saddam Hussein. If even the well-known "liberal press" could be brought into camp, then clearly the administration's cause was just.

The media loved the story lines (especially the ones about their own dread magnificence), and by Christmas every network and every magazine of respectable size had designed for itself some kind of red, white, and blue emblem proclaiming its ceaseless vigilance and its readiness for war. When the steel rain at last began to fall during the second week of January, most of the national voices raised in opposition to the war had been, as the Pentagon spokesmen liked to say, "attrited." Through the five weeks of the aerial bombardment and the four days of the ground assault the version of the public discourse presented in the media turned increasingly callow. *Time* and *Newsweek* published posters of the weapons deployed in the Persian Gulf, and the newspapers gave over the majority of their editorial-page space to columnists gloating about the joy of kicking ass and kicking butt. Andy Rooney on "60 Minutes" struck what had become the media's preferred note of smug self-congratulation. "This war in the gulf," he said, "has been, by all odds, the best war in modern history. Not only for America but for the whole world, including Iraq probably. It was short and the objectives of victory were honorable. In spite of all the placards, the blood was not for oil. It was for freedom. We did the right thing."

The return of the nation's mercenary army was staged as a homecoming weekend for a college football team, and the troops arriving in Georgia and California found themselves proclaimed, in the words of *Life* magazine, "Heroes All." Many of them had spent several uncomfortable months camping in the desert, but few of them had taken part in any fighting. The number of American casualties (125 dead in action, 23 of them killed by "friendly fire") once again posed the question of whether America had gone to a war or to a war game played with live ammunition. But it was a question that few people cared to ask or answer.

Maybe the question is irrelevant. In the postmodern world maybe war will come to be understood as a performing art, made for television and promoted as spectacle. Maybe, as the producers of the charades on MTV would have it, Madonna is Marilyn Monroe, true love is a perfume bottle, and George Bush is Winston Churchill.

Certainly the administration succeeded in accomplishing what seemed to be its primary objectives. The cost of oil went down, and the prices on the New York Stock Exchange (among them the prices paid for Time Warner, the Washington Post Company, CNN, and The New York Times) went up. The country welcomed the easy victories in Kuwait and Iraq with band music, ticker-tape parades, and speeches to the effect that once again it was good to be American.

Still, I find it hard to believe that the American people feel quite as triumphant as they have been made to appear in the newsmagazines. The cheering rings a little hollow, as if too many people in the crowd were shouting down the intimation of their own mortality. The elation seemed more like a feeling of relief—relief that so few Americans were killed and that almost everybody, this time at least, got home safely.

Maybe the war in the desert was a brilliant success when measured by the cynical criteria of realpolitik, but realpolitik is by definition a deadly and autocratic means of gaining a not very noble end. The means might be necessary, but they are seldom admirable and almost never a cause for joyous thanksgiving. If we celebrate a policy rooted in violence, intrigue, coercion, and fear, then how do we hold to our higher hopes and aspirations? We debase our own best principles if we believe the gaudy lies and congratulate ourselves for killing an unknown number of people whom we care neither to know nor to count. How do we tell the difference between our victories and our defeats unless we insist that our media make the effort of asking questions other than the ones that flatter the vanity of the commanding general? Like the seal balancing the red, white, and blue ball on the end of its faithful nose, a servile press is a circus act, as loudly and laughingly cheered by a military dictatorship as by a democratic republic.

263

The Gulf Between the Media and the Military

Henry Allen

The Persian Gulf press briefings are making reporters look like fools, nit-pickers, and egomaniacs; like dilettantes who have spent exactly none of their lives on the end of a gun or even a shovel; dinner party commandos, slouching inquisitors, collegiate spitball artists; people who have never been in a fistfight much less combat; a whining, self-righteous, upper-middle-class mob jostling for whatever tiny flakes of fame may settle on their shoulders like some sort of Pulitzer Prize dandruff.

They ask the same questions over and over. In their frustration, they ask questions that no one could answer; that anyone could answer; that no one should answer if they could answer. They complain about getting no answers, they complain about the answers they get. They are angry that the military won't let them go anywhere, the way they could in Vietnam. They talk about war as if it were a matter of feelings to be hashed out with a psychotherapist, or a matter of ethics to be discussed in a philosophy seminar. A lot of them seem to care more about Iraqi deaths than American deaths, and after the big oil spill in the gulf, they seemed to care more about animals than people—a greasy cormorant staggered around on CNN until it seemed like a network logo, along the lines of the NBC peacock.

They don't always seem to understand that the war is real.

They don't seem to understand the military either. Meanwhile, the military seems to have their number, perfectly. Media and military cultures are clashing, the media are getting hurt, and it's all happening on television, live from Riyadh and the Pentagon.

It is a silly spectacle.

It is so silly that 80 percent of Americans say they approve of all the military restrictions on the reporting of the war, and 60 percent think there should be more. When a *Washington Post*-ABC News poll

264

asked if we should bomb a Baghdad command and control center in a hotel where American reporters are staying, 62 percent said we should give a warning and then bomb even if the reporters are still there, and 5 percent said we should bomb with no warning.

Yesterday the *Los Angeles Times* quoted John Balzar, one of its correspondents in Saudi Arabia: "I was a sergeant in Vietnam and now I am a journalist here. In both wars, I feel like I'm in the wrong place at the wrong time, and I am going to go home and have people throw rocks at me."

It is so silly that "Saturday Night Live" recently went after the media with the same wise-guy irony it might have used on the military back in the '70s.

An actor playing a briefing officer says: "I am happy to take any questions you might have with the understanding that there are certain sensitive areas that I'm just not going to get into, particularly information that may be useful to the enemy."

A reporter asks: "I understand there are passwords our troops on the front lines use. Could you give us some examples of those?"

And so on, the point being that the reporters are either fools or traitors.

The point could just as well have been media self-righteousness, or their obsession with contradictions and ironies.

After a marine reconnaissance team was trapped near Khafji, a reporter asked Air Force Gen. Pat Stevens IV: "You said recently our communications were 'superb,' but the marine recon team was taken by surprise. How then can you call our communications 'superb'?"

In a briefing after U.S. planes bombed a building where civilians were hiding, one reporter adopted the Mike Wallace autograph-model tone of astonished innocence: "Are you saying then that you're not watching these buildings that you're going to target 24 hours a day?"

One reporter asked if we had put a limit on the number of Iraqi casualties we will inflict. Then there was the young woman with the National Public Radio accent, that elegant confection of crispness and offhandedness that you hear on "All Things Considered." After the big oil spill, she wanted to know if Gen. Norman Schwarzkopf had been aware before the war began of the damage such a spill could do, and if so, had such a possibility entered his moral reasoning when he was deciding whether to start the war.

Why is this happening? Why do the reporters at the briefings seem to be on one side and the briefers on the other? And why do so many people cringe and hoot at the reporters, and admire the briefers?

Oil and water, dogs and cats, Hatfields and McCoys.

In "Battle Lines: Report of the Twentieth Century Fund Task Force on the Military and the Media," Peter Braestrup, a former marine and journalist, cites studies indicating that military values "are closer to those of Middle America than to those of the more permissive members of the media . . . Not surprisingly, given the media's focus on conflict, deviance, and melodrama, most senior military men do not see the media as allies of civic peace and virtue . . . There is no counterpart in journalism to 'duty, honor, country,' or to the military leader's ultimate responsibility for life and death and the nation's security."

The military demands team play. Journalists fight not only with the people they cover but with each other.

The military is hierarchical. Reporters have no rank.

The military values loyalty and confidence in superiors. The press values objectivity and skepticism.

At a Senate hearing yesterday, former CBS anchor and war correspondent Walter Cronkite said the military "has the responsibility of giving all the information it possibly can to the press and the press has every right, to the point of insolence, to demand this."

Sen. John Heinz (R-Pa.) went to the point of insolence himself when he cited a long list of media woesayings about the military before the war started, and a long list of successes since, concluding: "Any advice for your colleagues?"

"No," Cronkite said.

The military is average guys who take pride in their anonymity. The big-time press is high-achievers struggling for the brief candle that passes for stardom in the media. (What's the last time you thought about Dorothy Kilgallen? Westbrook Pegler? Chet Huntley?)

When the military makes a mistake in combat, its own people die. When the press makes a mistake, it runs a correction.

For 20 years, they've been getting further apart, each heading in its own direction, proud of becoming an island of virtue, unto itself.

But why do the reporters look so bad? What's hard for viewers to understand is that they are merely doing the poking, nagging, whining, demanding, posturing, and hustling that are the standard tricks of the reporting trade—people don't have to tell them anything, after all, so they have to worm it out of them. And there are many reporters there who have never covered the military before. It's an ugly business, and in the Persian Gulf they do it on television, and they do it with the tone of antagonism, paranoia, and moral superiority that arose two decades ago in response to the lies and failures of Vietnam and Watergate.

There is a lot of history here.

Back in the '70s, reporters were heroes of sorts—one bumper sticker even said "And Thank God for *The Washington Post.*"

Government officials and military officers were the villains.

In the years since, the press has changed very little, and the military has changed a lot.

Besides polishing its public relations techniques with courses at Fort Benjamin Harrison, the military seems to have studied the master, Ronald Reagan, and the way he buffaloed the press with his nice-guy rope-a-doping—rope-a-dope, you recall, being how Muhammad Ali let George Foreman punch himself into exhaustion.

In the Persian Gulf briefings, the military briefers adopt the Reagan/Ali style, taking punch after punch, looking humble, cocking their heads, being polite, and playing the tarbaby. They don't let the reporters get to them. They confess errors—deaths by friendly fire, bombs that missed. Like the Viet Cong, they only fight when they know they'll win. They come on like the silent majority in desert fatigues, while the reporters come on like Ivy League Puritans, pointing bony fingers and working themselves into rages.

267

Why, the reporters demand, can't they drive north and interview whatever troops they want? Why can't they talk to fighter pilots? Why are they restricted to pools? Why are so few journalists going to be allowed to cover the ground war?

This is not Vietnam, where combat was only a helicopter ride away—although it's interesting to note that one study says in Vietnam no more than about 40 reporters were ever out where the bullets were flying, except during the Tet Offensive of 1968 when the number might have gone to 70 or 80. Access to the siege of the marines at Khe Sanh was limited to 10 or 12 reporters.

In Saudi Arabia, the military is keeping journalists on a short leash, but no shorter, probably, than it would keep them on in peacetime if they were doing stories at Fort Hood or Camp Pendleton. Corporations, professional football teams, police stations, and political conventions keep a close eye on journalists too. And no journalist would expect to get very far with businessmen and politicians by being as quarrelsome and ignorant as some of the journalists covering this war.

The parallel between other institutions and the military doesn't go very far, though. The military is a separate culture that is difficult to explain to anyone who hasn't been in it. As Bernard Trainor, a retired marine lieutenant general writes: "Whereas businessmen and politicians try to enlist journalists for their own purposes, the military man tries to avoid them, and when he cannot, he faces the prospect defensively with a mixture of fear, dread, and contempt."

Trainor covered military affairs for *The New York Times* after he retired. He has seen the military-media war from both sides. Last December in *Parameters*, an Army War College magazine, he wrote: "Today's officer corps carries as part of its cultural baggage a loathing for the press . . . Like racism, anti-Semitism, and all forms of bigotry, it is irrational but nonetheless real. The credo of the military seems to have become 'duty, honor, country, and hate the media.'"

With the end of the draft, Trainor says, the military "settled into the relative isolation of self-contained ghettos and lost touch with a changing America. It focused on warlike things and implicitly rejected the amorality of the outside world it was sworn to defend. In an age of selfishness, the professional soldier took pride in his image of his own selflessness. A sense of moral elitism emerged within the armed forces."

Hate! Scores to settle! As Secretary of Defense Dick Cheney recently told the U.S. Chamber of Commerce, "You might never know from all the stories we saw in recent years about $600 toilet seats that our defense industry was capable of producing effective systems and weapons to support our men and women in uniform." He went on about "doom and gloom reporting," and cited a 10-year-old story in the *Boston Globe* attacking the Tomahawk missile, even giving the exact date—November 22, 1981.

The media have pulled away from mainstream America too.

Once, reporters were part of whatever team they covered, in a vague and unreliable way. They cut deals, they protected their favorites. But after Vietnam and Watergate, they declared a sort of ethical independence and came to think of themselves as inhabiting a neutral territory of objectivity and value-free analysis. (It should be pointed out that objectivity is not an attitude that goes down well when there's an enemy shooting at American troops—hence the antagonism directed at Peter Arnett, the CNN reporter covering the war from Baghdad.)

Anyway, things changed in the '70s. Suddenly, the media had prestige. Instead of drawing their staffs from high-school graduates, failed novelists, and the occasional aristocrat looking to get his hands smudged, big-time media were getting résumés from people who had grown up in the class segregation of upscale suburbs, day-school products who had never been in places where you don't let your mouth write checks that your butt can't cash, had never been yelled at with the professional finesse of a drill sergeant, a construction boss, or a shop teacher. The most important experience in their life had been college. During the summers, they had internships, not jobs. A lot more of them were women. After the draft ended, virtually none of them even knew anyone who had been in the military, much less served themselves. They were part of what sociologists called the new class, the governing class, the professional class. They were a long way from most Americans.

The military came closer.

An army infantry battalion commander in Saudi Arabia recently told his troops what kind of people they all are. "Like I told you before, this is not the Izod, Polo-shirt, Weejuns loafers crowd. Not a whole lot of kids here whose dads are anesthesiologists or justices of the Supreme Court. We're the poor, white, middle class, and the poor, black kids from the block and the Hispanics from the barrio. We're just as good as the . . . rest, because the honest thing is, that's who I want to go to war with, people like you."

Not people like the media.

But the military can't go to war without the media, either.

And oh, how the military wants to be honored, to have its deeds recorded for history. And how good journalists are at doing it, if their audiences and editors want to hear it. Both sides, in fact, like to sit around telling stories about their adventures, giving it all a mythological glow. Both feel they are underpaid and undervalued. Both feel they are sacrificing for a greater good. And in wars, journalists for once share a little of the risk with the people they are covering—in most peacetime stories, a story about an election or a stock speculator, say, this would be called a conflict of interest. Secretly, you suspect, the military admires the media's soldier-of-fortune independence, and the media admire the orderliness and blood-and-dirt courage of the military.

They're so close, you say. There's no reason they can't work together. And then you turn on the TV and watch the press briefings.

"General," a reporter drawls, "I wonder if you could dwell for a moment on the apparent contradiction between . . ."

Another Front

Michael Massing

The war may be over, but the battle over press access rages. In a U.S. District Court in New York City, an eclectic group of news organizations, including *The Nation, Harper's,* and *The Village Voice*, is pressing a suit against the Defense Department, charging it with imposing unconstitutional restrictions during the gulf conflict.

In the current climate, the outcome of any contest between *The Nation* and the nation would seem foreordained. Yet the effort certainly seems worthwhile: if Dick Cheney and Colin Powell go unchallenged now, there's no telling what they or their successors might attempt in the future.

Looking back at the gulf conflict, though, it seems clear that access was not really the issue. Yes, the pools, the escorts, the clearance procedures were all terribly burdensome, but greater openness would not necessarily have produced better coverage.

Consider, for instance, the case of *New York Times* reporter Malcolm W. Browne. A veteran war correspondent, Browne was highly critical of the Pentagon's restrictions. "Each pool member," he declared in an article in the *Times Magazine*, "is an unpaid employee of the Department of Defense, on whose behalf he or she prepares the news of the war for the outer world." To illustrate the point, Browne recounted his own experience as part of a pool taken to interview F-117A pilots returning from bombing raids over Iraq. In one dispatch, Browne's description of the F-117A as a "fighter-bomber" was changed to "fighter"; in another, a colleague's characterization of the pilots as "giddy" was changed to "proud." Browne was also kept from filing a story about the bombing of Iraq's nuclear weapons development plants, only to have Gen. Norman Schwarzkopf make the information public two days later.

Browne's pique is understandable. But what does all this add up to?

271

A sanitized adjective, an altered airplane description, a story delayed for a day. Not exactly the Pentagon Papers.

Of course, had Browne not been forced to join a pool, he might have turned up far more interesting material. I doubt it, though, judging from the work of those reporters who did manage to slip their minders and make it to the front. Telling of loneliness and boredom, cold nights and bad food, their stories offered moving glimpses of soldiers preparing for battle. Unfortunately, they added little to our understanding of the war itself.

Too often, American correspondents seemed to be fighting the last war. Where there was sand, they saw rice paddies, and, like latter-day David Halberstams, they instinctively headed for the front. This was no guerrilla war, however, but a high-intensity, fully conventional conflict, and it required something other than traditional on-the-ground reporting. In particular, it required an ability to digest and make sense of the huge amount of data generated by the conflict.

Take the air war. The general lack of access to Iraq made gathering firsthand information all but impossible. And the press briefings in Riyadh and Washington, with their *Top Gun* videos, offered little help. Yet the sheer number of bombing raids indicated that something extraordinary was going on over Iraq. The Pentagon insisted it was targeting only military-related facilities, but the attacks on power plants, oil refineries, and other elements of the country's infrastructure suggested a far more destructive plan—one designed to return Iraq to "a pre-industrial age," as a UN report subsequently put it. What was the Pentagon's purpose in all this? And was it consistent with the UN resolution authorizing the use of force to liberate Kuwait? Reporters—busy talking their way through military checkpoints—never bothered to ask.

Nor did they ponder the extent of the killing being carried out by allied forces. True, it was mostly enemy soldiers who were being killed, and that's what war is all about. Yet many of the victims were hapless conscripts sent to the front against their will, and the policy of slaughtering them seemed to demand some analysis. This was not a simple task, given the refusal of U.S. briefers to estimate enemy KIAs. Yet, by extrapolating from the number of sorties flown, the amount of ordnance dropped, and the "killing box" strategy pursued by the B-52s and other aircraft, reporters could have offered some rough estimates of their own. Busy interviewing grunts at the front, they just didn't have the time.

Similarly, the press failed to scrutinize the types of weapons deployed by the allies. While reporting endlessly on the chemical-weapons threat from Iraq—a threat that never materialized—correspondents showed little interest in America's own fearsome weapons. Like napalm. For the first time since Vietnam, the U.S. forces used this flesh-searing substance, mostly to kill Iraqi troops in bunkers. In light of the outcry over the use of napalm in Vietnam, one might have expected questions to be raised about its use in the gulf. Yet the few stories that mentioned the subject seemed entirely perfunctory in nature. "Allies are said to choose napalm for strikes on Iraqi fortifications" ran the headline over a story in *The New York Times* on February 23. Only eight paragraphs long, the article explained that a wave of napalm-fueled fire splashed across the mouths of a system of caves or trenchworks may fail to burn the occupant but can remove so much oxygen from the air that the defenders suffocate. For this reason, some opponents of its use have argued that napalm should be classified as a chemical weapon and banned.

Nevertheless, napalm remains a mainstay of armies and air forces throughout the world, and has been used in many wars and minor conflicts since it was introduced in World War II . . .

That article was written by Malcolm Browne.

To get the real story in the gulf, reporters did not have to travel to the front. They did not even have to travel to Saudi Arabia. Most of the information they needed was available in Washington. All that was required was an independent mind willing to dig into it. In short, this war needed fewer David Halberstams and more I.F. Stones.

Newspapers, Getting It Late but Right

Howard Kurtz

In a war in which each F-14 raid, each Scud missile attack, each Pentagon briefing is broadcast live and in color, daily newspapers almost seem a quaint anachronism as their noisy presses churn out news that is six or eight hours old by the time it reaches people's doorsteps.

As *New York Post* editor Jerry Nachman put it in his inimitable tabloid style: "In a CNN war, whither newspapers?"

But if the networks have owned the Persian Gulf story, newspapers have nevertheless managed to find an eager audience for extra editions and beefed-up press runs. The *New York Post*'s 300,000 extra copies a day are "selling like bialys," Nachman says.

Newspapers have always offered greater depth and detail—*The New York Times* published 50 gulf-related stories and columns yesterday—but they have taken on another function in the fast-moving Gulf War. On Thursday night, for example, television was filled with conflicting accounts of the Iraqi missile attack on Israel, including false reports that some victims had suffered nerve-gas damage and that Israel was on the verge of retaliation.

"It was very dramatic," says Brookings Institution analyst Stephen Hess. "We learned an awful lot of what it must feel like to be there. We saw reporters with gas masks on, we heard the sirens.

"But almost all of the facts were wrong—the number of missiles, the numbers of casualties, the prospect of Israeli counterattack, the question of the use of nerve gas. Reporters were giving us their work sheets, their raw data. Newspapers by their very nature give us processed news. They've sorted out what's true and what's not true."

If the morning papers can't match the drama of Cable News Network anchor Bernard Shaw describing how he hid under his bed in a Baghdad hotel room, they can offer a bit of perspective, a

274

historical record, plus such useful details as the war's impact on gas prices and airline safety. Some liken it to fans devouring the Monday sports section after already having watched the Redskins game.

"You're giving people a chance to look at it the second or third time, to really study the map, to read the beat writers, the defense analysts, the Pentagon bureau chief," Nachman says. And then there are the local angles. Yesterday's *New York Post* included such stories as "Jews in New York Want an Eye for an Eye" and "Cardinal O'Connor: 'I Prayed All Night.'"

The Washington Post published two extra editions Thursday—the second one was distributed just before noon—and some readers were buying them from delivery trucks. The paper increased its press run by 180,000 beyond its normal 800,000 circulation. Other papers that boosted their Thursday press runs were *USA Today* (by 500,000), the *Los Angeles Times* (230,000) and *The New York Times* (50,000).

Albert Hunt, the *Wall Street Journal*'s Washington bureau chief, says the morning after the war began, "I had the feeling of a Chinese meal until I finished the *Post* and the *Journal*. It's a great television story, and what CNN did was wonderful, positively riveting. But there is a certain shallowness about television."

In a moment that seemed to underscore the value of print coverage, CNN Pentagon correspondent Wolf Blitzer read from a newspaper report detailing how a 2,000-pound U.S. bomb leaves a crater 36 feet deep and 50 feet wide.

But the fact remains that newspapers are filled with yesterday's news at a time when nearly everyone is watching the war unfold on prime-time television. Had the Scud missiles landed in Tel Aviv a few hours later, the morning papers would have already published their original stories about how Israel was relieved that no attack had taken place. Even some reporters and news junkies say they are merely skimming the coverage after each bleary-eyed night of CNN-watching.

Still, critics say the networks have filled the airwaves with hours of tiresome blather, which Hess describes as "speculation, innuendo, rumor, and plain misinformation."

"You have this endless parade of rather mediocre experts, retired generals, and others who are out of it, and banter between anchors and people in the field," says Everette Dennis, director of the Gannett Center for Media Studies. "There's a dulling and numbing sameness to it. Watching CNN was like reading the AP wire—it was disconnected, it was pieces. People want packages that make sense."

Ed Turner, CNN's vice president for news, agrees that television has not yet made print journalism obsolete. "This story has such impact that even though people have seen it, they want to turn around and read about it," he says. "People are hungry for analysis and commentary. You [newspapers] can provide stuff we can't."

Both television and print journalists have been up in arms for weeks over the Defense Department's coverage rules in the gulf, including requirements for military escorts and advance review of all stories. But in Saudi Arabia, where more than 100 reporters in 10 press pools have fanned out with U.S. forces, reporters seem pleased with their degree of access.

Molly Moore, a *Washington Post* reporter in Dhahran, says there have been some logistical problems, such as a pool report from the battleship USS *Wisconsin* that was delayed more than 12 hours. But she says military officials have made only two minor deletions in 118 pool reports.

"They've censored almost nothing," Moore says. "They got us some pilots pretty quickly. It's gone a lot smoother than any of us thought."

Some news executives have criticized the military for refusing to release casualty figures and other details.

Howell Raines, the *New York Times* bureau chief here, says Defense Secretary Richard B. Cheney and other officials have provided "very scanty information. There's a full range of information they could have given out that the public is entitled to."

But *USA Today* editor Peter Prichard says the Pentagon has acted reasonably. "Obviously, they're not being very forthcoming, but they're in the middle of a military operation," he says.

What the Media Missed

Eqbal Ahmad

For more than two decades, I have been harshly critical of the authoritarian and mindless minorities that rule the Middle East. Fortunately, this dissent has cost me much less than it has those patriotic intellectuals who have stayed on to confront the tyrannies. For those of us who identify with Middle Eastern civilization, care for the well-being of its peoples, and take pride in its achievements, opposition to the minority regimes has been a question not of expedience, but of moral and political obligation. That is why it has been so painful for me, no less than anyone I know from the region, to read and watch the media since President Saddam Hussein committed his wanton aggression against Kuwait.

What follows then is a brief listing of eight ignored aspects of the present crisis that, taken together, have the effect of denying the American public an overall perspective on events in the gulf.

One: There has been an absence of discussion of what compelled President Saddam Hussein's extraordinary ambition. After all, he has been in power for two decades. If this question had been explored, the 1978 Camp David accords would inevitably have emerged as a defining event. Camp David worsened the plight of the beleaguered Palestinians and isolated Egypt—since the early nineteenth century the political center of the Arab world—from its Arab milieu. Smaller players attempted to fill the resulting vacuum. Saudi Arabia tried, in 1981, when in partnership with the United States it mediated a cease-fire between the PLO and Israel; it failed when Israel invaded Lebanon in 1982, killing an estimated 20,000 people and destroying Beirut, the cultural and commercial capital of the Middle East. Saddam Hussein betrayed his ambition to lead the region when he invaded Iran. The United States encouraged him; the Saudis and Kuwaitis financed his aggression. The monster, if that is what President Hussein is, was nurtured by U.S. policies in the region.

Two: The media have noted that there is significant popular sentiment throughout the Middle East against the U.S.-led military intervention in the gulf. But scant attempt has been made by reporters and columnists to explore its rationale. It has usually been dismissed simply as xenophobia. In a rare departure from this pattern, one *New York Times* reporter did venture to investigate the matter and asked some experts in Washington why Arabs might oppose military intervention. One interviewee was described, I hope without his consent, as an "expert on the Arab mind." All spouted supercilious bromides about insecurity, anti-Westernism, and fundamentalism.

The simple answers have been strenuously avoided: No sane Middle Easterner can possibly take seriously President Bush's assertion of the unacceptability of territorial acquisition by force or of the necessity to uphold the UN Charter. After all, the United States has been sustaining Israel's occupation of Palestinian, Syrian, Jordanian, and Lebanese territories, and has continually frustrated UN efforts to uphold its charter in the Middle East. Furthermore, few informed Middle Easterners are unaware that for two decades now the United States has been enlarging its military presence in the gulf and seeking a permanent presence there.

Indeed, the complex answer would involve inquiring into the patterns of 14 centuries of antagonism and collaboration between Western and Islamic civilizations, and into the nature of the more recent colonial encounter in the Middle East. But perhaps it is unfair to expect such experts to enter into complexities.

Three: It is curious that there has been no discussion of the meaning and uses of America's much-invoked but suddenly forgotten "strategic alliance" with Israel. More than $60 billion in U.S. aid went into the making of one of the world's strongest military powers, and all of it was justified on the ground that Israel was our "strategic ally" in the Middle East. The media have reported that, at the outset of the gulf crisis, Washington requested Israel—please—to do nothing, and Israel complied. There have been suggestions in the press and in

278

Washington that Israel ought to be rewarded with increased military aid for accommodating the United States in keeping a low profile. Whatever the merit of Israel's case for more arms, we have in this instance a historically unique situation involving a possible revolutionary redefinition of the concepts both of "strategic" and "alliance." It merited at least some discussion in the media.

Four: Equally curious has been the absence of reporting and commentary on the politics and economics of oil, which underlie this conflict and the U.S. involvement in it. Oil prices have fallen more consistently and drastically than other commodities since 1980, reaching a low in 1990 of $18 a barrel of crude. Iraq wanted a higher OPEC price—around $25 a barrel; Kuwait resisted. Why? How could the interests of Kuwait, Saudi Arabia, and their client emirates be better served by low oil prices? One answer is that they are countries with small populations, large oil reserves, their own offshore refineries, and massive investments in the Western, especially American, market. They have to feed fewer people, and plentiful crude oil is only one of several sources of their income.

Five: There has been no discussion in the media of this crucial Middle Eastern anomaly: The larger and more populous countries have small oil reserves; and the small kingdoms and sheikhdoms rule over massive reserves. The rulers of the gulf know the significance of this issue, which is one reason why many, including Saudi Arabia, do not hold census counts and do not publish population figures. Could there be any truth in the popular belief that the imperial powers, which drew the boundaries of the nation states in the region, purposely delinked the wealth from the people of the Middle East? The answer may not change one's judgment of Iraq's invasion of Kuwait, but it could provide a better understanding of why neither the Kuwaiti sheikhs nor their Western allies elicit much support among the majority of the people in the region.

Six: There has been an absence of inquiry into the purposes of this unusually forceful U.S. intervention in the gulf. The media have noted that official justifications have run from the sublime to the ridiculous—from the defense of Saudi Arabia to the protection of American jobs. Every publisher and producer also knows that, starting in the early 1970s, the focus of American military and diplomatic attention shifted toward the Middle East. With Iran on its eastern flank and Israel to the west playing the role of Kissinger's "regional influentials," the Middle East became the centerpiece of the Nixon doctrine. Throughout the 1980s, more than 75 percent of total American military and economic aid went to three countries in the region— Israel, Egypt, and Pakistan. Deployments of the modernized U.S. Navy were concentrated in the Mediterranean and in the Indian Ocean; the Rapid Deployment Force was created and remained geared for intervention in the Middle East. Decades-long planning and investment suggests purposes greater and more complex than have been allowed in the media's discourse.

Seven: When the "costs" of the gulf crisis are raised, what is invariably meant is simply the cost to the United States in possible casualties in a war, or to the U.S. or Western economies in a prolonged standoff. A disregard for—in fact, a lack of the least thought about— Arab lives is evident in the current discussion of the possible costs of war in the gulf. Mention is rarely made of, and estimates never offered for, what a war might cost the Iraqi or Kuwaiti people. American casualties can be minimized, we have been told repeatedly, by maximum use of air power, by the sort of carpet bombing that might cause untold tens of thousands of non-American casualties. Similarly, American "hostages" in Iraq and Kuwait were in the headlines daily. Yet there was hardly any reporting on or analysis of how an embargo on food and medicines could affect the lives of Iraqi civilians.

Eight: Officials have invoked, and some columnists have repeatedly emphasized, the menace to world security posed by Iraq's imminent possession of nuclear weapons. The media, however, have failed to discuss soberly the issue of nuclear proliferation. Nuclear arms threaten human survival. They should not be a subject of polemic and propaganda. A superpower that possesses an awesome nuclear arsenal bears a special responsibility to deal with this issue

280

honestly and equitably. And this is precisely what is not happening in this country either at the governmental or public level.

Official and academic experts in Europe and the United States estimate that Iraq is years away from acquiring an operational nuclear capability. Pakistan is closer. India is nuclear capable (that is, while it may not have manufactured the bombs, it has the capability to produce and deliver them). In all of South Asia and the Middle East, Israel alone actually possesses a nuclear arsenal of up to 200 bombs and, thanks to U.S. arms supplies, the capacity to deliver them to distant targets. There are American laws prohibiting aid to countries that engage in proliferation. They were invoked early this fall when Congress cut off U.S. aid to Pakistan. Various dailies, including *The New York Times*, editorially praised the congressional action; but none even noted that the biggest violator, Israel, remains above the law.

To the best of my knowledge, no newspaper or magazine has thought it important to find out how the people in the region feel about living under the shadow of Israeli nuclear weapons. If the United States makes war on Iraq, it would certainly cite Baghdad's nonexistent nuclear weapons as one justification. When the guns are silent, millions shall mourn the dead and walk the ruins knowing that a nuclear power next door remains the only country in the world without declared boundaries.

Press Failed to Challenge the Rush to War

Gene Ruffini

Former Undersecretary of State George Ball is said to tell the following story about how the United States got drawn into the Vietnam War: A man takes a little boy to a zoo and, pointing to a long-legged, long-necked creature, says, "This is a giraffe." The boy asks, "Why?"

The failure to ask the giraffe question, Ball rightly concludes, led to the rush toward war.

Then as now. In the face of the administration's well-orchestrated campaign for war in the gulf, the media, print as well as broadcast, didn't ask the giraffe question loud enough or long enough—whenever, that is, they bothered to ask it at all.

The healthy, feisty skepticism of government hoopla that is supposed to characterize a free press never came into play. ABC's Sam Donaldson told *The Wall Street Journal* in August, "It's difficult to play devil's advocate, especially against such a popular president as George Bush."

Dallas billionaire H. Ross Perot told the *Los Angeles Times* on January 12, that the press had been "as limp-wristed as any time I can remember" in not challenging the strategy of the Bush administration. This is the same H. Ross Perot who had been a strong supporter of the American solider in Vietnam. But he vowed afterward to work against any conflict that didn't have the support of the American public. "If the press had been on its toes in August," he said, "we wouldn't be here right now."

Perot is not the only American who believes that, during the months when the Bush administration was maneuvering us relentlessly from economic sanctions and the defense of Saudi Arabia toward the crushing of Iraq's military power and probable ground warfare, the mighty American press refused a fair hearing to the case for peace.

282

With some notable exceptions, the media chose to ignore clear and early signs that the administration was preparing for a full-scale war against Iraq—and when that prospect could not be denied, helped make it appear to be inevitable through the business-as-usual transmission of the war whoops of the administration.

Those who argued for sanctions as a proper and effective response to the criminality of Saddam Hussein got relatively little air time on TV, which for many is the only medium of news, information, and opinion. The reading public could be slightly better informed if they made the effort. Critical columnists argued from isolated corners, and news of other naysayers was, as a rule, tucked within the inside pages of newspapers. Meanwhile the administration's public relations cavalry galloped unfettered up front.

Trampled in the dust, for the most part, were arguments that America's real interest in Iraq's brutal conquest of Kuwait was to control the price of oil and maintain the gusher of profits for the petroleum industry and the financial community.

According to a January 16 survey by Fairness & Accuracy in Reporting (FAIR), a liberal-oriented press watchdog, "nightly network news programs largely ignored public efforts to oppose the Bush administration's military policies in the Persian Gulf."

FAIR said that of 2,855 minutes of TV coverage of the gulf crisis from August 8 to January 3, only 29 minutes, roughly 1 percent, dealt with popular opposition to the U.S. military buildup in the gulf.

Jeff Cohen, FAIR executive director, pointed out that: "None of the foreign policy experts associated with the peace movement—such as Edward Said, Noam Chomsky, or the scholars at the Institute for Policy Studies—appeared on any nightly network news program during the period scrutinized. While the stories on Jesse Jackson's trip to Iraq were counted as antiwar coverage, none of these stories included any quotes from Jackson."

Alex Molnar, a University of Wisconsin professor and founder of the Military Families Support Network, also encountered a network stonewall. Molnar is the father of a 21-year-old marine in Saudi

Arabia whose open letter to President Bush strongly questioning his policy was printed in *The New York Times.*

The Cable News Network and three network-owned stations in Washington all turned down a 30-second commercial paid for by Molnar's group. Station representatives said that the commercial was "exploitive" and "sensational," that it made unsubstantiated charges, and that the whole issue was better served in newscasts that (supposedly) told both sides of the story.

The *San Jose Mercury News* reported January 12 that CNN and the Los Angeles and New York affiliates of ABC and CBS also rejected a paid antiwar spot sponsored by the Los Angeles chapter of Physicians for Social Responsibility. NBC stations in Los Angeles and New York and some small market stations around the nation ran the spot, the paper said.

While the antiwar voices were struggling to be heard, Arab interests and the well-heeled minions of the administration were pumping out their snake oil. The Kuwait government, for instance, spent millions trying to influence the American government through the media.

Jack O'Dwyer, who publishes a newsletter on the public relations industry, reported last December 5 that Citizens for a Free Kuwait, a group founded by 13 Kuwaiti exiles in the U.S., "stepped up its PR efforts" before the United Nations took its vote on the use of force to oust Iraq from Kuwait. The group paid the firm of Hill & Knowlton $5.6 million for the period August 20 to November 10, according to records filed with the foreign agents registration office.

H&K organized a photo exhibit for presentation to the UN Security Council and assisted Kuwaiti refugees in telling stories of torture to council members. The firm also helped to arrange interviews, button-holed and cultivated government officials and educators, and sent out a blizzard of mail to Congress on the issue. And it helped to arrange Free Kuwaiti Day. H & K was reportedly among seven firms handling the lucrative Kuwaiti accounts. H & K said it didn't know the other six.

Martin Tolchin reported in *The New York Times* last December 17 on another major campaign to influence the American government through the media. The Coalition for America at Risk, supposedly an ad hoc group of conservatives, paid for a commercial supporting the president's military stance.

The commercial showed an American solider in the desert writing to his family at home and saying: "All of the people here are behind us, and I hope the folks back home are, because we deserve their support."

The commercial was shown on 17 local stations from New York to Los Angeles. The group has also run full-page advertisements in *The New York Times, The Wall Street Journal*, the *Los Angeles Times, The Washington Post*, and other papers.

Tolchin reported last December that a former cochairman of the group is William R. Kennedy, Jr., a registered agent for the Kuwaiti Emergency Relief Fund, which oversees the finances of Kuwaiti officials and businessmen. He denied to Tolchin that his connection with the fund had anything to do with the coalition.

Rep. Jimmy Hayes (D-La.), a critic of the Kuwaiti PR campaign, said, "When all of this is over, I think we should reassess the lines we have blurred on allowing other governments to have enormous influence on our political process through money, which is what it boils down to—media is the result, money is the generator."

On the Sunday talk shows, popular repeat guests in the critical period from August 5 to January 6, when the administration was selling war like soap, were Secretary of State James Baker, Defense Secretary Richard Cheney, National Security Adviser Brent Scowcroft, White House Chief of Staff John Sununu, and Rep. Les Aspin (D-Wis.), chairman of the House Armed Services Committee. Throughout that same period, former Attorney General Ramsey Clark, a peace activist, appeared only once on a Sunday show, and other protest group representatives were equally as rare.

FAIR reported in its November/December newsletter "Extra" that it studied the first month of the gulf crisis "when a wide-ranging debate—including both supporters and opponents of the military buildup—could have affected policy.

"But we did not find such a debate; not a single U.S. guest on 'Nightline,' for example, argued against the U.S." presence. "Nightline" disputes this claim. FAIR also found that "nearly half of the U.S. guests on 'Nightline' and the 'MacNeil/Lehrer NewsHour' were current or former government officials."

"Extra" also pointed out that after the period involved in the study, guests on "MacNeil/Lehrer" did include critics of administration policy.

Most of the nation's newspapers, *The Washington Post* in particular, joined in the administration's "war is inevitable" sing-along. Vincent Carroll, editorial page editor of the *Rocky Mountain News*, reported in *WJR* (January/February), "Of the 25 largest U.S. newspapers . . . only one—the *Rocky Mountain News* in Denver—has argued for the most part against military action even as a last resort to dislodge Saddam Hussein's troops from Kuwait."

Media analyst Ben Bagdikian, author of *The Media Monopoly* and professor emeritus of the Graduate School of Journalism at the University of California, Berkeley, attributes whatever support sanctions received to the "safe authority figures who were citing that position very strongly, such as a former chairman of the Joint Chiefs of Staff [Retired Adm. William Crowe] before the Senate Armed Services Committee and Sen. Sam Nunn." As for the networks, he said, they are "cautious of straying from White House policies."

Moreover, the curse of television coverage is that it is predicated on objects that move. Therefore, Bagdikian said, television news producers have "an ingrained dislike for talking heads—words as opposed to action." The use of action pictures "increased the impression that this was essentially a military confrontation and not an . . . economic one."

Thus there was "the usual down-grading on TV of important policies and information not accompanied by dramatic action."

It's Bagdikian's opinion that if the public had been exposed to more opposing views, the vote in Congress approving U.S. troops in the gulf might have been affected.

"I don't think there is any question about it," he says. "The opposition in Congress was substantial, and it began when they started to hear from constituents."

To Everette E. Dennis, executive director of the Gannett Foundation Media Center in New York, there was more media coverage of debate than in any prior conflict. But still it was far from perfect, he added.

"Generally, when it comes to matters of national security and matters of war and peace, basically it is what the government says is happening [that] is the predicate and subject of the story," he said.

He pointed out that while "it is the role of the press to be critical, to make sure that things are done correctly—surveillance is one of the principal functions of the press—the reality is that role has not been played out very well in times of war. [It has] not been one of the press's finest hours."

In an age when media manipulation has become an art, more newspapers must balance official positions with opposing points of view either high in the same story or in prominent sidebars. Broadcasters should also present balancing opinions.

Then when some little boy asks "the giraffe question," he will get a fair and balanced answer.

Better still, he may never have to ask it.

Times Mirror Poll

The American public gives high marks to media coverage of the war in the gulf at the same time as it calls for increased military control of how the news is covered. A 57 percent majority believes that the military should increase its control over reporting of the war, while 34 percent believe that such editorial decisions should be left to the media itself. Nearly 8 in 10 Americans (78 percent) say they believe the military is not hiding bad news from them and is telling as much as it can under the circumstances, and a similar percentage (72 percent) believe that news organizations are attempting to deliver to the public an objective picture of the conflict. The press gets a positive rating for its coverage of the Gulf War from 8 in 10 Americans, with 36 percent rating its performance as excellent and 42 percent good. Sixty-one percent feel that news coverage of the war has been for the most part accurate, with only 18 percent saying that too many mistakes have been made.

Somber News

Americans of all ages, from all parts of the country and all walks of life, offer somber views of the war and its effects as the conflict entered its second full week. But the conflict in the gulf appears to be taking a far heavier psychological toll on women than on men. Overall, the percentage of Americans who described themselves as not happy with things these days rose from 9 percent a year ago to 33 percent currently. Among women, 41 percent said they were not happy compared to 23 percent among men. America's unhappy mood reflects in part the effects of massive television coverage of the first war in history to be brought into peoples' living rooms on a real-time basis.

288

Watching the War

As higher news ratings and newspaper sales indicate, the American public is staying extremely close to news of the Gulf War. Eighty-one percent of the public says it is keeping TV or radio tuned to the news, and 51 percent say they are reading newspapers more closely. Sixty-seven percent reported following the war *very closely,* 28 percent fairly closely, and 5 percent not closely. For many, news about the gulf is akin to an addiction—50 percent agreed with the statement that they can't stop watching news about the war. Among this half of the public, reports of war-related stress are twice as high as among those who don't feel a compulsion to watch Gulf War news:

- 21 percent of war news addicts say that because of the war they have had trouble concentrating on their jobs or normal activities (versus 9 percent among others).
- 18 percent cited war-related insomnia (versus 8 percent among others).
- 18 percent reported being fatigued by the way they feel about the war (versus 7 percent among others).

Younger people, who generally have followed the situation in the gulf less closely than older people, are more apt to say they can't stop watching—58 percent among those under 30 years of age versus 42 percent among those over 50 years of age. While half of the public feels compelled to watch war news, the most prevalent reactions to viewing the war on TV are feelings of sadness (74 percent), fear (67 percent), and sometimes confusion as to what's going on (65 percent). Significantly fewer but still sizable numbers report that the war doesn't seem real (33 percent) and that the coverage tires them out (34 percent). Women are much more likely than men to say they feel fear (80 percent versus 52 percent), sadness (87 percent versus 59 percent) and confusion (71 percent versus 58 percent) while watching the war on TV.

War Mood of Men and Women Vastly Different

Reactions to war coverage are just one indication of how differently men and women are experiencing the war in the gulf. Overall, half of the public reported they were feeling depressed by the war (50 percent). However, the gender gap on this measure is 31 percentage points, with 33 percent of men reporting depression, compared to 64 percent of women. Manifestations of war-related stress as measured in the survey are three to five times as great among women as among men:

- 21 percent of women report trouble sleeping because of the war, compared to 4 percent among men.
- 21 percent of women report difficulty in concentrating, compared to 8 percent among men.
- 19 percent of women report being tired or fatigued because of their feelings about the war, compared to 5 percent among men.

Women also express more fear-related behavior. Eighteen percent of women say they are considering canceling an airplane trip, and 14 percent are considering canceling a trip to a major city. Among men, these figures were 10 percent and 8 percent respectively.

The "War in the Gulf" Channel

For most Americans, Cable News Network's performance sets the pace for war coverage. CNN is seen as the network doing the best job of covering the gulf by a margin that is twice as great as it achieved for gulf coverage in a Times Mirror survey conducted three weeks ago. Over six in ten Americans (61 percent) think that CNN is doing the best job of covering the war, compared to 12 percent for ABC, 7 percent for CBS, and 7 percent for NBC. In Times Mirror's January 3–6 survey, CNN was chosen as the network doing the best job by 30 percent.

Despite public admiration for CNN, ABC's anchor Peter Jennings is most often selected as the journalist doing a particularly good job in reporting the war; 16 percent cited Jennings, 9 percent Dan Rather, 8 percent Tom Brokaw, 6 percent Bernard Shaw and 5 percent Peter Arnett.

Broadcasts of Iraqi-censored news is the only American media practice that comes under fire from the public. A 45 percent plurality of the public disapproves of news organizations broadcasting news from Iraq that has been censored by the Iraqi government, while 43 percent approve. Majority approval for this reporting is evident only among college graduates, whose opinions divide 53 percent approve, 39 percent disapprove. Among people who choose CNN as the network doing the best job of covering the war, opinions divide 45 percent approve, 43 percent disapprove.

If Vietnam was America's first TV war, the war in the gulf may be TV's first military exclusive. By a margin of 75 percent to 7 percent, the public thinks television reporters are digging harder to get the news than newspaper reporters. And among people who say they have read accounts in newspapers of events in the gulf that they have previously seen on TV, 73 percent say newspaper accounts pretty much cover the same ground, while 23 percent say they have been given a better understanding of what they have seen on TV.

Overall, 79 percent approve of the way George Bush is doing his job, and 73 percent feel that the U.S. made the right decision in using force against Iraq. Among women, Bush's approval rating is 76 percent, and 72 percent of women think the U.S. made the right choice in pursuing the military action.

The climate of opinion about the conflict and news coverage has sharply changed since January 15, 1991, as illustrated in the way people now feel about dissenting voices. In September 1990 and January 1991, Times Mirror surveys found pluralities of the public saying they wished to hear more about the views of Americans who opposed sending forces to the gulf. In the current survey, a 47 percent plurality say they have heard *too much* about the views of Americans who oppose the war in the gulf.

On a much smaller scale, the number of Americans who say they have attended a peace rally (3 percent) is one third the number who say they have attended a rally in support of the U.S. war effort (9 percent).

Public Confident of Victory—Worried about Casualties

Seventy-seven percent of the public say they are not worried much that the U.S. will lose the war with Iraq, while only 8 percent say they worry a great deal and 12 percent say they worry a fair amount about this. In contrast, 57 percent of Americans worry a great deal that U.S. forces will sustain a lot of casualties and 30 percent worry a fair amount about this. One in three said they worry a great deal about a terrorist strike in the U.S. and 38 percent worry a fair amount about this. A comparable level of public concern was expressed over the possibility that many Iraqi civilians will be killed (33 percent a great deal, 35 percent a fair amount).

People 50 years of age and older expressed more fears about both American and Iraqi casualties than younger people—61 percent of those 50 and older worry a great deal about U.S. military casualties and 38 percent a great deal about Iraqi civilian casualties. Among people under 30 years of age, these figures were 48 percent and 30 percent respectively.

Many Report Fearful Children

Two in three Americans with children aged 5–12 report that their children are following the war in the gulf closely. Only one in three say they are restricting how much war coverage their children watch, and 43 percent reported that children in the household have expressed fears about the war. As was the case with their own fears, female respondents were more likely to report fearful children than were men (49 percent versus 36 percent). Women also reported more often than men that they were praying more frequently because of the gulf war (77 percent versus 50 percent).

Forum Discussion at the National Press Club

Scott Armstrong

The primary debate . . . is not about unfettered access to the battlefield. By and large, the press is willing to live within the sorts of rules and restrictions that we lived with during Vietnam and that were outlined in the Sidle report. The fundamental issue is whether the press can remain the independent eyes and ears of the public during a time of war.

The free and independent press which our Founding Fathers nurtured does not guarantee that all reporters will get the same information or carry the same stories. Indeed, the principle is quite different. Our Founding Fathers stressed the diversity of viewpoint, the independence of journalists and publishers to follow their own interests and curiosities. From a more modern systems analysis point of view, the effect might best be characterized as a sort of probability theory within a universe of free access. Normally, hundreds, indeed thousands, of reporters will look for, or stumble on, an important story which informs the public. If they do so, if they unearth an appropriate sample of what is actually going on, the public is best served. Every branch of government, including the executive branch, learns a great deal it wouldn't have otherwise learned. In short, when we required defined answers to our own questions, we are—collectively at least—we do a pretty good job, and in many respects individuals did such a good job in the Persian Gulf War, on the ground, in Saudi Arabia, despite the restrictions.

Where we get into trouble, however, is when we get put into the position of being fed answers to which we must [pose] a challenging question. The briefing and pool system of Saudi Arabia had exactly these characteristics. Instead of a thousand reporters chasing hundreds of stories, we became a thousand reporters chasing a half dozen stories each day. The result was predictable by the Pentagon at least.

293

We learned less than we might have otherwise learned about the reasons for the decisions being made, and the public was poorly served.

We still know far too little about the predecessor events to the Iraqi invasion, particularly regarding the negotiations between Iraq and Kuwait. We still know too little about the U.S.-Saudi secret arrangements which allowed us very successfully to project force into the region in unprecedented numbers. We still know relatively little about the extent to which we defeated a significant Iraqi fighting force or virtually all of the nearly 500,000 Iraqis that were already in Kuwait, or if they had already fled, if, in fact, they were there to begin with. And we know relatively little about the amount of the loss of life in Iraq and in Kuwait of both the Iraqis and the fleeing Palestinians who were caught up in the final strafing and bombing along the major escape routes.

But the greatest challenge to the press was not the failure to adequately cover combat operations. The greatest press failing was not caused by pools or escorts or censors, the Pentagon, or the White House. Our greatest shortcoming was in Washington, where for seven months there was virtually not one sentence in print from a significant adviser to the president that had quote marks around it.

Two weeks ago we began to see glimpses of the first stories about the decision making in the round of stories about how the war was won. These stories raised more questions than they answered. They are fundamental and disturbing questions. Did the president and his key advisers distort the terms of the Soviet peace proposal in order to make it publicly rejectable? Did the Gorbachev proposal come closer to fulfilling the intentions of the United Nations resolutions than the Bush ultimatum that was given to the Iraqis? Did the Soviet proposal call for the cancellation of UN resolutions clearly unacceptable or merely suggest that they could be rescinded by the United Nations if Iraq withdrew immediately, which appears to be the case? Remember that several of the resolutions called the attention of the Iraqis to other international laws, and by their rescission would not have changed international law; there still would be a possibility of future reparations, etc. . . . Did President Bush purposely choose counter terms which they believe were most likely to cause Saddam Hussein to want to fight? Were tales of Iraqi systematic executions of Kuwaitis exaggerated to justify the ground war? Did American and allied briefers report, as *The Washington Post* alleged in the last few days, that Iraqi troops were fighting on, when, in fact, the U.S. military perceived them to be fleeing? Did, in short, the president of the United States lie to the public to manipulate events to permit the otherwise avoidable slaughter of tens of thousands of Iraqis and Palestinians in order to humiliate Saddam Hussein?

Let's be clear. I am certainly not urging that we abandon relentless reporting of Iraqi atrocities, or that Saddam Hussein's persistent record of abuse of his people and his neighbors be forgotten. I am simply saying that rational discussion and examination of the war is no longer being persued by those in government, even those who initially voted against military action in the legislature. It is uniquely the obligation of the press, whether or not we agree with the president's course of action or even with its results, to pose and pursue the basic questions.

The administration won a military victory in Iraq; that portion of the war is closed. But the administration also launched an offensive against the press to close off access to information. That is a battle that is not over and should never be over in this country. We are a free press because we have repeatedly risen to the challenge of previous administrations. The war for American freedom of information is ongoing. It is here and now. It is tomorrow and it is evermore.

Forum Discussion at the National Press Club

Xan Smiley

[I'd just like to make some] counterpoints to some of what my colleagues have already [said]. Yes, of course, the pool system was extremely cumbrous—fifteen hundred, fourteen hundred people out there. It did not work very well, and in our experience, the so-called unilaterals—some of the people who went out on their own with less apparent military help—actually found out rather more than those who did not.

But I don't really see what the alternative is to the pool, and in the broader context, I don't really share the indignation that has been expressed widely in Washington and quite a bit already on this table. For example, Scott Armstrong raised a number of questions which it seems to me have nothing to do with war coverage as such. You mentioned the need for more knowledge about the diplomacy, the screw-up in the State Department, the run-up to the invasion of Kuwait, the business about U.S.-Saudi secret arrangements. I mean it seems incredible to me to expect that we would be told what U.S.-Saudi secret arrangements were in the middle of the Gulf War. Yes, we would like to know more about loss of life in Iraq, which is obviously very high. But all these things, it seems to me, come outside the context of how you actually cover the war.

I was more struck as an outsider by the indignation of reporters in the Pentagon, who, quite frankly, I thought a lot of them asked the most staggeringly stupid questions which were met by an array of stone walls from the military. Of course we know that the military are going to try and put their best sort of face on everything. But 9 times out of 10, I think they were dead right to err on the side of keeping everything to themselves, because their main interest, and the public interest, was to win the war. I am not quite sure what particular instances of nonknowledge we were really suffering under. Access is one. And I have mentioned it, and it is very difficult to work out how we could have gotten more effective access given the number of our fairly ignorant journalists scattered across the desert that there were. The second access was, I think, access to information about battle plans. I mean, again and again journalists wanted to know what was actually going on in the battle.

But again, this was not like Vietnam.

Vietnam was mentioned. I see no comparison really at all. Vietnam was a guerrilla war, a set of more or less random skirmishes with no fixed front line. Perhaps I could add no really fixed military strategy either. And in those sorts of circumstances, of course journalists can move around freely. On top of which it was not an electronic media war in the way that this one was. There was no chance, really very little chance that what journalists found could be conveyed quickly back to the Vietcong to make much difference to what was actually going on in the battle. Whereas practically anything in this war was watched by Saddam Hussein and his men in Baghdad, and not just to do with military combat but diplomacy, mood, tactics, and all sorts of things were obviously likely to be of some use to him. And it seemed to be perfectly normal that the authorities would err on the side of keeping their cards to their chest.

So I would like to ask my colleague what particular aspects of news were we deprived of? As for the seven months not getting any quotes from President Bush's advisers, again, I did not feel particularly deprived in that context. He spoke to the press very often. One got quite a lot of stuff from people in the National Security Council and the State Department. I don't have any particular complaints. I am sorry if that goes against the grain of the instinctive media desire to know all.

Kelly Exits with Praise for Media

Army Lt. Gen. Thomas Kelly, the blunt general who became known to millions of Americans because of his daily briefings at the Pentagon during the Persian Gulf War, announced his retirement yesterday with praise for the news media and a defense of the First Amendment.

"I've just got to say that, believe it or not, I've enjoyed this little interlude," the operations director of the Joint Chiefs of Staff said. "Got a lot of letters from people who really don't understand hurly-burly and give-and-take of a press briefing, and at no time were you ever impolite to me and at no time did I ever become offended. And as you know, I hold a lot of you in great respect."

"The last thing I'd like to say is that having a free press has served the United States well for 215 years," added Kelly, 58, whose last duty day after 34 years in the army is Friday. "It is a crucial element in our democracy. And if anybody needs a contrast, all they have to do is look at the country that didn't have a free press and see what happened there."

When Kelly finished, his audience of reporters broke into applause.

Chapter Eight

Baghdad: Reporting from the Other Side

Should the press have covered the war from Iraq? Was CNN's Peter Arnett able to send back significant and useful reports from the other side, or did he become a mouthpiece for Saddam Hussein's propaganda?

Baghdad: The Ugly Dateline

Ed Rabel

The ancient Boeing 707 slowly lifts off the desert runway, climbs to altitude, then heads out over the Jordanian wasteland bound for Baghdad.

There are 175 other souls aboard Iraqi Airways Flight 168—women wearing chadors, babies squalling, and, mostly it seems, men smoking foul-smelling Turkish cigarettes. Crumbs left on my food tray from a previous flight spill onto my lap.

Through the window I can see the Amman airport disappear, and I am filled with foreboding. The words of friends tumble out of my memory: "Are you crazy, volunteering for Baghdad? They'll take you hostage there, or do something worse." It is mid-September, six weeks after the Iraqis' August 2 invasion of Kuwait.

I think of the 90 American men, nonjournalists, being used by the Iraqis as "human shields" at strategic locations. Maybe I'll end up like them. But reporters have been traveling in and out of Iraq for weeks at the behest of the Iraqi government. No problem, I figure, barring an attack on Baghdad. To report from Baghdad today, I decide, is to play Russian roulette. Western reporters in Iraq have always worked under severe restrictions, if they could gain access to the country at all.

Now conditions are even worse. From the moment of arrival in Baghdad until the government "invites" you to leave, usually after no more than a week in the country, a government agent dubbed a "minder" by British reporters hovers. No picture is taken, no interview conducted, no traveling done until the minder approves, or clears it with the government.

Our minder, from the Ministry of Information and Education, is a functionary named Najah. A slightly built man in his 30s, polite and personable, Najah seems embarrassed about all the restrictions he

300

must impose. He is a veteran of the Iraq-Iran war who served at the front for eight years. He speaks very little English, making it difficult to establish much rapport with him. Most of our more lengthy conversations are filtered through the interpreter who accompanies us.

Our days begin and end with Najah in the lobby of the Al Rashid Hotel. We usually get started on our rounds shortly after dawn. All reporters are required by the government to stay at the Al Rashid, a modern high rise not far from Saddam Hussein's presidential palace. It was built a few years ago to house diplomats slated to attend the Conference of Non-Aligned Nations, which, because of the Iran-Iraq war, was never held. What a fine idea, I think, to be billeted in a luxury hotel. But there are drawbacks.

Iraqi officials surely must have wanted the conference to go off without a hitch, judging by the hotel's security features. The view from my room overlooking the pool isn't bad. But the windows are securely locked. And I can't find anyone with a key.

Then I discover that the 20-foot-high wall in front of the hotel completely encircles the building. What appears to be a high-voltage cable runs along the top, and TV cameras watch from every angle.

In addition to Western journalists, the hotel is filled with well-heeled refugees making their way from Kuwait to Jordan, as well as a delegation of Palestinians. They find, as we do, that most of the hotel's restaurants have been closed and the room-service menu pared. Maybe the UN embargo against Iraq is taking a bigger toll than I thought.

Our news team includes Najah, John Siceloff, my producer from NBC's Miami bureau, cameraman Aziz Akayavis, and sound technician Ugure Canta, both Turkish citizens. Najah stays with us into the night, until transmission of the day's story by government satellite at 10:30.

After we have grown comfortable with each other, Najah begins suggesting camera angles and shots. We realize that Najah, aware that government restrictions are making news gathering here almost impossible, is doing his best to be helpful by giving us shots that will pass muster. Siceloff quips that everybody—even a government agent—wants to be a producer.

Still, Najah's suggestions are well within the government guidelines, which prohibit pictures of potential military targets—in other words, just about everything in Iraq. To risk taking a picture without government approval is to risk going to an Iraqi jail for a very long time. And even if you did get away with it, putting the clandestine pictures on the air from outside the country would jeopardize other journalists still inside Iraq. We heard of one British journalist who made an unauthorized stop to take photographs on the road to the airport. He was arrested and interrogated for several hours, and his film confiscated.

After Najah's initial review, every story I transmit from Iraq is subject to censorship. Each word, each frame of videotape is monitored scrupulously by Dr. Saad Al-Hamadani, a high official of the Ministry of Information. The U.S.-educated Saad speaks flawless English and knows its American nuances. Nothing gets by Dr. Saad that he doesn't want to get by.

In the grimy government TV transmission station, Saad's face is eerily lit by the glow from the monitor on which the night's images pass. Since the conflict began, he tells me, he's screened at least a thousand reports by Western correspondents, picking over them to ensure the outgoing story does not make Iraq look bad. Criticism is cut.

When American refugees fleeing Kuwait complained about the behavior of the Iraqi occupying force, their comments were chopped immediately. The refugees had accused the Iraqi soldiers of looting homes and mistreating Kuwaiti citizens. One of the most damning charges was that the soldiers had killed infants by removing them from hospital incubators. The incubators were shipped back to Iraqi hospitals, according to refugees.

Saad's assistant is the elegant Mrs. Awatef, who shows up each night in the shabby transmission room inexplicably dressed for an evening on the town. We call her the "plug puller." When Saad sees or hears something he does not like, she yanks out the audio and video cables. That cuts transmission to the satellite. On Saad's cue, when the offensive section has passed, Awatef reinserts the cables, and the report picks up again.

The Saad-Awatef performance has its humorous side, but the implications are ominous. One night Saad heavily censors a TV interview with an American man who, unbeknownst to Iraqi authorities, had taken refuge in Baghdad at the residence of the U.S. ambassador. The interview had been conducted by another NBC reporter without the Iraqis' permission.

Saad demands to know where the American is located, but newsmen won't tell him. Within days of the interview, the Iraqi government announces that it will hang any American diplomat found to have hidden or given shelter to Americans. Later Iraq backs down, saying diplomats would not be subject to prosecution for sheltering would-be hostages.

Our NBC team operates on a very short tether. We cannot ride around on our own looking for things to shoot or cover. We must tell Najah exactly what we want to do, and, if he approves, we pile in the car and head for the scene. He readily permits us to shoot in the big marketplace, to conduct man-in-the-street interviews (in his presence, of course), to cover the civilian militia in training, and to film some anti-American demonstrations.

One demonstration occurs after President Bush's 11-minute speech is broadcast on Iraqi television. I watch the broadcast, and moments later people pour out into the street to protest, seemingly according to plan. We are permitted to shoot that.

As part of our story on the effect of the UN sanctions on civilians, we report the Iraqis' claim that there is a shortage of baby formula and that infants are suffering because mothers had to give them rice water to drink. We get pictures of dehydrated kids in the hospital and comments from English-speaking Iraqi doctors that the children are suffering. We could have gone to shoot in the hospital ourselves, but to save time we decide to use some excellent footage from the BBC, with whom we have a working arrangement. After viewing that footage and talking with other sources, I do the voice-over.

We are also able to get tape from Iraqi TV of Saddam Hussein on horseback and in various other scenes. In fact, pictures of Saddam are everywhere you go—on walls, billboards, office desks, easels—often dramatically lighted at night. He's shown in his military uniform, in leisure outfits, even wearing a beach outfit with a kind of Panama hat. Some of the poses are very somber, others show him smiling blissfully. But the cult of personality in Baghdad conveys nothing so much as a land in the steely grip of Big Brother.

The fact that groups of battle-ready soldiers with automatic weapons stand guard at virtually every major intersection adds to our feeling of unease.

As far as I know, nothing that can be considered by the Iraqis as damaging to them ever gets past the censor, no matter how cryptic TV correspondents try to make their stories. This and the real possibility of government reprisals makes self-censorship inevitable. If reporters uncover something unfavorable to Iraq, they have to think twice before trying to report it via TV from Iraq.

Within that context, the final paragraph of one of my stories from Baghdad for the "NBC Nightly News," while in hindsight absolutely benign, takes on enormous significance for me. I report that actions by the Iraqi government, as one Western diplomat put it, "seem bizarre considering the powerful diplomatic and military pressure against this country." Obviously, the censor thinks the line to be as innocuous as it is, because he lets it go. But in the atmosphere of suspicion that is Baghdad, I except to hear jackboots outside my hotel door at any moment.

The limitations on our movements make finding even such stories as that nearly impossible. We can go to the U.S. embassy on our own and do interviews with the people there. But we can't do a lot we want to do: We repeatedly ask to go to Kuwait, to get out of the city more, and to interview Saddam Hussein. Authorities decline.

I meet with Sadoon Al-Janabi, a high-ranking member of the

Information Ministry. He is holding court in his office, handing out permission slips to journalists who kowtow to him for access to important government people. Sadoon knows how competitive the American TV networks are and, savoring his power to grant some of their wishes, plays one network team against the other. Capriciously, Sadoon gives the go-ahead to one camera crew for an interview and then, without reading the request of another team, scrawls, "No, it does not suit us" in large letters on the request form.

We have given Sadoon a list of government officials we want to interview; he says no. With other broadcast reporters we sit in Sadoon's office literally for hours at a stretch, waiting for responses to our questions. More often than not, there are none.

For some time, NBC News has been seeking Saddam Hussein for an appearance on "Sunday Today." I reiterate NBC's request. Sadoon complains that the program is too short (30 minutes) for Saddam. Later, the government offers its foreign minister, Tariq Aziz, for the Sunday broadcast. NBC accepts.

For a network news team to succeed in Iraq these days, much depends on the amount of air time the network is willing to grant Iraq's leaders. Among Iraqi officials, CNN is considered the U.S. broadcast outlet most likely to air the government's position.

Because it is a 24-hour operation with much time to fill, CNN naturally recycles the news it gathers in Iraq and elsewhere, repeating it frequently in the same day. What is more, CNN has come to be looked upon as a conduit through which Iraq and the U.S. government can speak.

An awkward moment occurs for a CNN representative in the office of Naji Al-Hadithi, director-general of external information. Naji, a well-educated former diplomat who served in England, is talking with a group of American reporters, including CNN. The subject is Saddam's 76-minute speech, which is being offered by Iraq to the U.S. State Department for broadcast in America.

I remind Naji that, unlike Iraq, the U.S. government cannot demand that broadcasters air Saddam's speech. How, therefore, does he

305

propose to get the speech on television in the U.S. if TV stations refuse to run it? "Simple," Naji replies, "we'll give it to CNN, they'll run it."

Saddam's speech, on videotape, is delivered to the State Department, which turns it over to American broadcasters. It does get on the air: NBC's Tom Brokaw, for example, gives it a 45-second voice-over. CNN, as predicted, runs the entire speech, but late at night. Excerpts of it run throughout the next day.

After a frustrating week in Iraq, our team finally heads for Saddam Hussein International Airport to exit the country. We try not to reveal to Najah, our minder, how glad we are to be leaving; no reason to offend him.

Camera crews and correspondents are cycled into Iraq by the networks because the government generally will not allow the same personnel to remain longer than a week to 10 days. It is assumed the Iraqis maintain the policy to prevent correspondents from being in the country long enough to make personal friendships, establish contacts, and find chinks in the country's censorship armor.

Never in 25 years as a network news correspondent have I spent a week of such frustration and anxiety—not in Vietnam, not in El Salvador, not in Nicaragua. It is the not knowing that shakes you—not knowing whether you will ever get out.

Najah works feverishly to get us through the police and immigration bureaucracy at the airport. We pass what we think are the last of the officials who check and recheck our passports. Najah bids us farewell and walks away.

We turn and move the 50 yards or so to the door of the plane that is our escape. There at the doorway stand two men in plainclothes, no doubt agents of the powerful Interior Ministry, infamous for its secret police and brutality. They scrutinize each of our passports. One of the policemen leafs through mine slowly. As his baleful eyes meet mine, he says in halting English, "There no exit visa in passport. Please step aside." I try to hide the utter sense of doom I feel.

One by one, each member of the NBC team is plucked out of line because of a missing visa. We watch as all the other passengers board the plane. Now we are standing alone as the two plainclothesmen speak into their walkie-talkies in Arabic, which none of us understands. It takes minutes. It seems much, much longer. Suddenly, a hand signal—we are free to go.

I am deep in my seat aboard the Iraqi 727, my head buried in a book as we taxi out for takeoff. I don't look back.

Why I Stayed Behind

Peter Arnett

Last week, I set off on a walk I'd taken many times before—out from the American Colony Hotel, up Nablus Road to the old city among the teeming Palestinian fruit markets and the curbside vendors. I was mobbed. Buses stopped, disgorging passengers to shake my hand. The Palestinians embraced me as a brother who had shared the hell of war with their idol, Saddam Hussein.

Then I walked into West Jerusalem, to the Orthodox Jewish community of Mea Shearim—a 30-minute stroll through the front lines of ethnic and religious hatreds.

I was mobbed again. The Jews who pulled me into their little storefronts, patting me affectionately on the back, wanted details of the execution of Iraq, and greeted me as a survivor from an evil place.

I take note of this personally, this spontaneous reaction as I walked by, my dark glasses and raised collar inadequate protection against recognition. My initial reaction has been to yield to it, to be swept up in the emotion of the circus—to obligingly give every interview requested of me, to kiss my fiancée yet again for the photographers. My colleagues, with whom I covered this and other wars, are as astonished as I am that I am now the subject of their fervid pursuits.

But as my moment of fame ticks by, a more pertinent issue persists: What hath CNN wrought in the worlds of communications, of diplomacy, of politics? The debate that flared during the war about the social and political effects of an omnipresent video news service will only intensify with future crises, but in the meantime its personal effects still eddy around me. It's not just the passersby in the streets who want to share the postwar moment, it's Crown Prince Hassan of Jordan, or Israeli Defense Minister Moshe Arens, who are on the phone chatting about Baghdad and the future—while on hold are officials from Niger to New Zealand.

My weeks in Baghdad were spent oblivious to much of the reaction to CNN's war coverage; the information flow was necessarily one-way. It's only now that I am learning some of the depths of vindictiveness and slander that greeted my reportage—some from public figures with whom I've been acquainted for years.

The reason I stayed in Baghdad is quite simple: Reporting is what I do for a living. I made the full commitment to journalism years ago. If you ask, are some stories worth the risk of dying for, my answer is yes—and many of my journalist friends have died believing that. I revere their memories, and I would betray them if I did anything less than continue a full commitment to coverage.

There was no question about CNN staying in Baghdad—it became a question of who would do it. I had resigned myself to covering the Israeli side of the war—an important side of the story, though with less potential drama than the battlefield itself. I was summoned to Baghdad at the 11th hour unexpectedly when it became clear to CNN that the Iraqis might permit our coverage beyond the January 15 deadline. Would I help out?

Upon my arrival in Baghdad on the eve of war, I saw a repeat of what happened during the fall of Saigon. Reporters were bailing out for various reasons. I watched with wonder as this rich journalistic prize fell into fewer and fewer hands. Four days after the war began, only 17 journalists remained from the hundreds who had covered Baghdad.

Everybody out, the Iraqis said, except CNN. Even CNN isn't sure why they made that decision. Perhaps it is because CNN alone is seen globally. What the Iraqis told us is that they had found our coverage since August to have been "fair."

Eventually, there was only me; the growing intensity of the war made the continued presence of a CNN producer and technician dangerously superfluous. Also at the Al Rashid Hotel was a Palestinian team that provided a flow of videotape sent overland to Amman, Jordan.

My means of communication was the INMARSAT [International

Maritime Satelite] phone, a suitcase-sized link with the world that I'd drag out each evening and aim at the heavens, while dialing into the International Desk at CNN Atlanta. At my end, we crouched in the chill of the evening, "we" being myself and at least one Iraqi censor, or "minder" as these censors came to be called. I prepared a simple, two-minute script that the minder approved, and that I then read into the phone.

But from the first day I established a procedure that I believe saved my credibility and made my presence in Baghdad a valuable one. That procedure was a question-and-answer routine between the CNN anchor of the hour and myself that followed each prepared script. The Iraqis were uncomfortable with it from the beginning because they could control neither the questions nor my answers.

The only rule I followed in these Q&A sessions was that I would not discuss matters of military security. Thus I didn't talk about the Scud missiles I'd seen barreling northwards on camouflaged trucks; I didn't mention the antiaircraft weapons on buildings around the Al Rashid Hotel, and I gave no details on military targets.

But that left a gray area of social change, of city life, of political and economic insights that I could glean from the daily trips we were permitted to make under supervision in Baghdad and elsewhere in Iraq.

Why did the Iraqis allow these Q&A sessions? I told them from the beginning that I was risking my life in Baghdad, but I was not prepared to risk my credibility. I accepted the limitations of military security, I said, but I needed the freedom to better explore the phenomenon of being in a capital at war.

Our arguments were long and sometimes heated. I sometimes had my bags half-packed to leave. But my views prevailed and the Q&As continued right up to my last broadcast, when I talked about finally being ordered out of Baghdad.

Several of my stories were the subject of controversy in the West too. My coverage of a number of bombing incidents in Baghdad were, I have learned, the subject of debate. In time, I will address those and other stories.

310

But perhaps the most curious circumstances surrounding any story I did in Baghdad involved my interview with Saddam Hussein, conducted in the second week of the war. The promise of such an interview had kept Bernard Shaw in Baghdad during the war's opening days, and CNN president Tom Johnson had been urging me to pursue it.

I emphasized to officials from the ministries of foreign affairs and information the need for a coherent explanation of Iraqi policy at this stage of the war. We had been dependent on the patriotic tirades of Radio Baghdad, echoed in the daily press, for a sense of government direction.

Late one afternoon in one of the darkened recesses of the Al Rashid lobby, I was told I had an "important" interview. I presumed it was with the information minister, Latif Jassim, until five burly young men in suits and ties escorted me to a room on the second floor, asked me to undress completely, and began checking every pocket and seam of my clothing. My wallet, watch, pen and notebook, handkerchief, and comb were put into a plastic bag and taken away. They were even reluctant to return my trouser belt until I objected.

Now fully dressed, I was taken into the bathroom and my hands were immersed in a disinfectant carried by one of the group. This was either an extreme form of security, or else, I mused, Saddam Hussein has a Howard Hughes-like phobia of germs. Then I was escorted back to the lobby and instructed neither to talk to nor touch anyone.

As I waited in the gloom, my CNN colleagues arrived after a three-day overland trip from Amman with a portable satellite video transmitter and tons of other gear. As they joyfully descended on me, I had to shout, "Don't touch me!" When they later phoned CNN's international editor Eason Jordan and told him what had happened, he told them that maybe I was angry that they were late.

I was taken to a late model, black BMW and sat alone in the back seat as the driver crossed the July 14 Bridge and drove into the darkened city. It soon became clear he was checking to see if he was being followed, taking elaborate maneuvers to throw off any possible

311

pursuer, rounding traffic circles three and four times, weaving in and out of poor neighborhoods.

After an hour of driving, we pulled up at a comfortable bungalow on a prosperous looking street where all the houses looked the same. A single attendant came to the car and took me inside. The living room had been transformed into a makeshift presidential suite, with brocaded chairs, officials seals, and three Iraqi Television cameras—all brightly lit by power from a humming generator. Saddam's closest aides were there—his chief of staff, a nervous, obsequious young man; his personal secretary, who sported a hairpiece; his young interpreter, who was familiar from the 16 previous TV interviews Saddam had given the Western press.

While we waited for the president, the group discussed in English recent programming they'd seen on CNN monitors in government ministries in Baghdad, laughing at pictures they'd seen of me operating the satellite telephone in the garden of the hotel. Only the information minister knew my name. Saddam's secretary asked me to spell it twice before introducing me to the president when he arrived. Saddam shook my disinfected hand. I think that all he knew about me was that I was the man from CNN.

En route to the interview I resolved to be as tough in my questioning as the situation would allow. I was not intimidated by the prospect of encountering the man many had called "The Butcher of Baghdad." I figured he could do no worse to me than the constant bombing of Baghdad was threatening to do.

Saddam Hussein unsettled me initially when he appeared. I had expected him to be in uniform, but he wore a mohair topcoat over a well-tailored dark blue suit, set off with a fashionable flower-print tie. He made small talk by asking, through his interpreter, why I had stayed in Baghdad. I replied it had become a force of habit because this was my 17th war. He expressed the hope it would be the last I would have to cover, and asked if I had "a long list of questions" to present to him. I answered melodramatically that I intended to ask him the questions to which the world wanted answers. He smiled, nodded

312

his head and invited me over to the cameras. "Let's go," he said.

I sat down opposite Saddam Hussein knowing this would be the most important interview of my life. I had not based my journalistic career on interviews, but over the years I'd undertaken a variety of them, from Fidel Castro to Yasser Arafat to Pham Van Dong. The day before I traveled to Baghdad, I had interviewed Israel's Yitzhak Shamir. He shook his head in disbelief when I told him some CNN staffers intended to remain in Baghdad through the January 15 deadline for Iraq's withdrawal from Kuwait. "They want to write books or something?" he wondered. At the time I was not aware of my ow travel plans.

J ₁new the Saddam Hussein interview might shed important light on tae course of the developing war. It might also have an impact on the course of my journalistic career if I didn't set the right tone. As I began my first question, I locked eyes with him and stayed unblinking throughout. I was as undeferential as possible. From the corner of my eye I could see his aides stiffening and muttering, but the president seemed relaxed and at the end thanked me for the conversation, posing with me for pictures which aides sent over to the hotel a few days later.

After Saddam Hussein left the interview room, I had an argument over the videotape. There were three angles photographed by Iraqi TV cameras, and Saddam's secretary wanted to let me have them the following day. I wanted to take them with me immediately because I was concerned that they might try to censor the material. We compromised; I would take delivery of the tapes within two hours at the hotel, dub them, and return them to Iraqi TV.

We planned to transmit the interview as our first video feed from Baghdad, and our two technicians struggled through the night to assemble the equipment. But by late morning, I discovered that the Iraqi officials had changed their minds about using the up-link for the interview. One told me, "the moment you start sending pictures of Saddam from here the Americans will bomb the satellite and the hotel."

This was the continuation of the argument over whether we should stay in the hotel at all. I had resisted initial attempts to move me to a "safe house" somewhere in the suburbs because there was no way I would give up the panoramic view of the air war from the hotel terraces. The government had also attempted to resist my use of the satellite phone to transmit daily reports in the earlier stages of the war. I argued successfully that the allies were more interested in hearing Saddam Hussein than in silencing him, and by late evening the first pictures were beaming to CNN headquarters in Atlanta—and I was praying that my confidence in the coalition's curiosity was not misplaced.

Because I am still on my way back to the United States, I have not seen enough of the commentary on CNN's coverage of the Gulf War to react to it. I know I have been criticized, and that many colleagues defended CNN's decision to allow me to stay in Baghdad. For that I am sincerely grateful. Later, in consultation with CNN, I intend to make a thorough examination of the criticism, and if necessary, a defense.

Criticism I accept—and expect. It's the labeling that angers me. For covering the Vietnam War the way we did, many of us were labeled "enemy sympathizers," if not communists. For being in Baghdad when I was, I was again labeled a sympathizer, if not a fascist.

I'd go anywhere for a story if there was enough viewer interest and CNN wanted coverage. I'd go to Hell itself for a story if someone important down there wanted to be interviewed. But then, the labelers would probably declare I was down there because I was an atheist.

Speech at the National Press Club

Peter Arnett

. . . When I arrived in Baghdad from Jerusalem just a few days before the war began, I discovered there was no finely honed Iraqi information organization that was controlling our professional lives there. Basically, there were a group of conscripts from the *Baghdad Observer* newspaper, the English language newspaper, and from the information ministry, and they were assigned to handle the international press, and they were completely overwhelmed.

I think you probably know that in the first 17 hours, when CNN was broadcasting, a few [of these people] came up and tried to interfere with the programming. They disappeared. They never came back to the ninth floor. And we had an open season on reporting because they just weren't around. We overwhelmed them. Now, some of these individuals, our censors, had graduated from Western universities in Scotland and in Germany, and they were generally in their late 30s-early 40s. Most, I discovered, were not in Saddam Hussein's Baath Socialist Party. They entertained healthy reservations about the regime, and these became clearer the longer I stayed, particularly as the bombing campaign revealed the increasing impotency of the government. Some of these, whom we called our "minders," were diplomats expelled from Washington or Paris when the embassies were closed. They were generally amiable, sophisticated. They all lived at the Al Rashid Hotel. Their families were a long distance from Baghdad. They had no contact with their families. There were no phones. Mostly they spent every night in the bunkers downstairs because of the bombing. And each night as part of the, as part of my relationship with them, I would go down with a few bottles of whatever I could find in CNN's ample storage rooms and hand them around and talk long into the night.

315

I mean, basically they were gregarious, amiable, and amenable to discussion when it came to coverage. And they would talk of their foreign travels, future hopes, and of journalism. One of these individuals, Mr. Sadoon [al Janabi] . . . in fact, I have a picture of me here, it may be incriminating, some may think, from *Stern* magazine. They did a feature on me, and here am I in an embrace with a gentleman we all know and love, all [who] have been to Baghdad, Mr. Sadoon. Mr. Sadoon is a gentleman who we dealt with—[who] every journalist who went to Baghdad dealt with. He was the senior "minder." He talked to Tom Johnson and Eason Jordan about trying to find Bob Simons of CBS and the others. He was the man who, in the notorious incident, used our INMARSAT [International Maritime Satellite] telephone to call the embassy in Amman, Jordan, the Iraqi embassy. What he was calling for was to bring in 18 new journalists to join the few CNN people there. Anyway, that is Mr. Sadoon. I presume he is still in Baghdad bringing in more reporters.

I was asked sometimes on the air whether I was subject to any incriminating bonding with the "minders." And I mentioned a couple of times the "Stockholm syndrome," which was notorious in the Korean War, where apparently prisoners bonded with their jailers, and would this be detrimental to balanced coverage. Since I have come out, I have been asked about how was balanced coverage affected by this.

But I would think the Iraqi government had far more concerns about my and our other journalists' relationships with the "minders" in the *U.S.* government. I mean, here we are. We arrived with up-links, satellite up-links, with telephones, rooms filled with cookies and good things to eat. We had abundant flashlights in a society where electric light is no more existent. We had expensive taxis poised to take us to the border anytime we wanted to go. They did not know about the "hundred grand" [sewn into] my jacket, but it was clear that we were affluent, it was clear that we had contacts. And I think as time went on they were aware of our special access to the outside world—an access that they knew was diminishing as each day of bombing continued and

316

as the ground war approached, and as it became clear in radio broadcasts from abroad that Saddam Hussein was indeed the pariah of the whole world. I think a coverage breakthrough that I made came early in the game when finally I was all alone. And we had the INMARSAT phone. I had a set of instructions on how to run it. Myself and Mr. Sadoon dragged the phone out into the yard in the evening. It was a chilly night. It was dark. I had a flashlight and I had fashioned a brief, approved script that I had written about a visit to Baghdad that day.

So, I read it over the air and anchorman Reid Collins at the conclusion of it asked me some questions: "Well, how did it look?" "What about this, that, or the next thing?" I was chatting to him and talking for about 15, 20 minutes and Mr. Sadoon was listening. At the end he said, "Who were you talking to?" I said, "Reid Collins." He said "Not Eason Jordan?" Because he knew Eason Jordan and he knew that we only did business with Eason. I said "No, he is the anchorman." "Well, who is an anchorman?" I explained. He said, "You mean you are on the air?" (Laughter)

But that was the breakthrough. Because later we discussed it at night. He brought the other minders around. We talked of this. He said, "But there is no censorship. How can we do this?" I talked to him about the need for credibility. That was the important factor. I said there was no point in me being in Baghdad if all that I could deliver each evening was a brief, approved dispatch. I had to have the question and answer. By miracle of miracles, I was able to get through to them, and so they accepted it. They wanted to listen to the questions. They could hear the answers, but I literally did not know how to connect the audio up for them to listen to. That came later.

So for the first eight or nine days I was able to communicate quite freely beyond that initial dispatch. And I think that helped enormously to diminish fears that somehow I was a robot being manipulated, or simply reading material that I had been either forced to write or had written under the most difficult circumstances.

I mentioned they did not like the Q & A, and when Tom Johnson insisted that with the up-link, the video up-link, we would continue with this method, there was even greater concern. First of all, they were concerned about the up-link being used in the Al Rashid Hotel. They were concerned that the moment it was used, it would be targeted by the U.S. Air Force. Then [also about] the idea of answering on live television questions that became increasingly demanding, or increasingly detailed, which I did not mind.

I wanted every kind of question. What we had was, I would be on the air and I would be looking and trying to give measured responses and there would be Mr. Sadoon or others that would be gesticulating, that would be cutting their throats, like they would like to do to me. They would be searching for the plugs to pull out and Vito [Maggiolo, the CNN producer in Baghdad] made it clear that they never found the plugs. And we had great scenes. Occasionally, one would make the mistake of straying into the camera orbit and attempting to hold his hands to say things like "no pictures," or he would wrestle with me, and that gave great entertainment. They soon learned not to do that.

But again, it was negotiation. What would a typical question be? I made note of a couple of them here. Bob Cain, our anchor, would be on the line. I had been to Basra and I would say I could not talk about any military information at all.

He would say, "Peter, on the road to Basra was there much military traffic?" You know. "Was there much military traffic?"

I said, "Well, Bob, there was much traffic on the highway, but very little of it was civilian." (laughter)

Then he would say things like "Peter, are the Iraqis moving tanks and antiaircraft emplacements into civilian areas?"

And I remember saying, "Bob, if I was to answer you, what I know about that question I would be pulled off the air." A little more subtle.

What did these reports finally add up to? This is, of course, in addition to our visual reports — a video of the obvious stories, the civilian casualties, the atmosphere of Baghdad on the streets, the many quotes we got from people along the way. I think what these reports finally added up to: We were able to chart the rapid deterioration of Iraqi society and the frustration of the average man on the street, and eventually the very negative comments of the "minders" themselves. They were increasingly unhappy. I mean the whole CNN crew were being pulled aside in hallways and given complaints about what was going on in the government.

We had to be very careful about how we handled all this information. My concern was agents provocateurs making up remarks. It was an attempt to test us. It was always each day, you know, how much of this information could we go with? How much could we prove? That was the criteria.

Eventually, the final, the ultimate of all this maneuvering, discussion, and, to a certain amount, freedom, came in the last night when we were eventually told that CNN had to depart Baghdad with the rest of the press corps. This was about several days after the war ended. I was waiting to go on live in the Al Rashid garden to talk about this at 11:00 at night, and Frank Sesno was summing up the news developments over the audio, I was listening to him. And a "minder" arrived. He was a young man. He was a Christian. I had talked to him before. He was concerned about the fate of his minority in the future.

I turned to him and I said, "Look, I am going to be very frank tonight. This is my last broadcast. I am sorry, but I will be frank."

He sort of looked at me and backed off and as we started to talk he just looked into the middle distance, into the sky, and Frank Sesno asked me questions like "What about the bunker? You are about to leave, tell us about that so-called civilian bunker."

I was able to say, "Well, the hot rumor here is that Saddam Hussein was in it two hours before it was hit. But I can't prove it."

Another question: "Is there any unrest in Baghdad?"

I was able to say that "We have got unconfirmed reports there was blood in the streets earlier today."

The "minder" was looking into the distance, and on we went for 35 minutes of it. Finally it was over, and I walked over to him and I shook his hand, and he sort of smiled at me and walked off into the middle distance. And that was that. So, to sum up, I think the Q & A saved my reputation. I was able to elaborate enormously on the information. Other newspeople coming in could use it. ABC used it eventually. CBS used it. ITN [Independent Television News] used it with various degrees of success. There was a subtle way to do it. You didn't want to rub their faces in information. But all the same I think it was integral . . .

Q: Can you tell us some of the things your chief "minder" deleted or altered in your copy?

Arnett: A good point. From the beginning they said no military information. So we could not . . . There were two aspects of what we gave to the minders. One was the written script. Nothing military could be referred to unless it was a quote from Radio Baghdad [or] was from the local newspaper. And these quotes basically extolled the virtues of the Iraqi military [and] predicted bloodshed in the upcoming mother-of-all-battles.

From the beginning I decided that there wasn't even any point fighting this restriction. Some of my colleagues on principle, when they later came to Baghdad, would do a script [with] three paragraphs on the antiaircraft guns in the buildings near the hotel, or that mentioned the Scud missiles seen driving by toward the Syrian border on their way into Jordan. Invariably these were deleted.

Basically I just did not go into this whole military issue. Now in Saudi Arabia and, of course, in Israel you were able to handle the military issue under censorship. They did allow some references to it. That was a total no-no in Baghdad from the beginning.

One aspect of it that did not concern me too much was that the real war was happening in Kuwait. We could visually see the destruction of the air war and even though after the first day where we talked freely of targets, we couldn't really refer to later targets. We could allude to it simply in our travels to the countryside and in our comments on civilian casualties. Kuwait—we couldn't get anywhere near it. I tried day after day to get to Kuwait City or to somehow get access to that area. We knew nothing about the Kuwait war, what happened, what went on there. And nothing was available on that area until our colleagues in Saudi Arabia were able to cross the border with the allied forces.

The political aspects of the coverage altered interestingly. After the first few days, and as the bombing of Baghdad and other cities increased, and as civilian targets increased along with it, the population was unhappy about it. We were told, "You can give any political comment you like on what the people of the country feel." So we could quote them politically.

It was, of course, impossible in the earlier days to find anyone who would criticize Saddam Hussein. But as the war went on we did have those who would criticize Kuwait. And it came up that we would do four or five times in a news story, talk about it, have people quoted with Kuwait.

As the war came to [a] close, however, and as this local or civil unrest developed at home, we were told we could not talk about politics. So, the censorship was fairly tough, but as I explained earlier we did try to circumvent it with the Q & A.

Q: Do you think most Americans understand why you had to stay behind in Baghdad to cover what you could even with censorship?

Arnett: Tom Johnson has told me that the mail, while initially negative, was later positive. I have to thank my professional colleagues for coming in and supporting CNN and myself for being there. I think the attempts by David Halberstam, *Newsweek* magazine, *The Washington Post*, and television critics throughout the country started to explain what it was really all about.

Actually, it was interesting to me that we had been covering both sides of wars for 25 years that I know of, from the first time we went out with the Viet Cong in the early 1970s, when they allowed us to visit their encampments for the first time. Then it was in Central America [El Salvador] with the FMLN and the government, [in Nicaragua] with the Sandinistas and Somoza's people. In Afghanistan with the Russians and the Mujaheddin.

I guess the American people weren't quite clear about what we

321

were doing. As I suggested in my prepared remarks, I don't think the U.S. public really has a real concept of what the press does. Part of it, we are to blame. Vietnam was a, it was a—I had better choose my words carefully here—it was not easy for the press.

I have talked earlier in the 1980s about how there were really no press heroes from Vietnam. That most of those who worked with me in Vietnam dropped out of journalism. I remember when I joined the Associated Press in 1961–1962. It was wonderful. The whole management lineup were World War II veterans: Wes Gallagher, Dan DeLuce, Hal Boyle was a top columnist—all of these great names of World War II. I mean 20 years after that, I don't think the AP had any Vietnam veterans in the top management, or in any other organization. Because it had not been the kind of war that created good management potential.

Because of those negative feelings about it all I think maybe the U.S. public didn't realize what the press has been doing all these years. I have got so many colleagues who have been to distant places and they [have been] doing wonderful work in the last 20 years. Maybe what we have been doing in the whole Gulf War will better illuminate what Americans think.

Just one point to add, I was really amazed to learn in Baghdad [of] the impact on the Third World of our coverage. Algerian journalists, Tunisian, Malaysian, Korean, and also the developed world, Japanese and Italian, were coming to interview me. And they were telling stories about how CNN was so important and powerful in their countries and how everyone was watching it. I was really amazed to see that Ted Turner's idea of a global village was actually coming to pass. I don't quite know how this translates into politics or what it really means for the fate of the world, but it is here.

Q: What is the real story behind the baby-formula factory? And was there a fence and military guards around the baby-milk plant?

Arnett: During the Vietnam War, I went to a town called Binh Tre during the Tet offensive, and I quoted an Army major as saying that, "We have to destroy the town to save it." And I think the baby-milk

322

factory is my, quote, "Binh Tre" of the Gulf War because that will follow me wherever I go.

The baby-milk factory. I was simply taken there one morning with WTN, which is a British news organization, actually a television film organization. They stayed behind with me, Palestinians. We went along and were shown this factory with a fence around it, a simple fence, a small road into it, a guard tower in the distance, a picture outside of Saddam Hussein caressing a crying child and on the fence was in Arabic and English "Baby Milk Factory." We went in there and I met two men in white smocks who talked about CNN having been there in September and they had done a story on it and how it was terrible that it had been bombed. So we spent an hour going over this plant. We walked up to our ankles in baby-milk powder and I was asking them where does it all come from and what was it all about. So, I went back to the hotel and reported it. WTN sent the video overland, and it appeared the next day. And I have been hearing about it ever since.

I thought it was just some insights into what it was all about. The Iraqis, basically they showed us it. There was no big hoopla. We spent a couple of hours and then they took us away. The next morning they took some people [over there] from the Gulf Peace Team, who were in the hotel, over there.

The Pentagon started talking about it being a biological testing plant, and the Iraqi government got very interested, increased their visits of everyone, tried to make me go back again, started sending diplomats over and others. And figured they had a really good thing going. They gave me documents allegedly about the development of this factory, how the builder had gone into debt, lots of details about financing from abroad, and I did eventually go back one week later with our own crew, and they came with the CNN people. I went back with David Rust, our cameraman, to get another look at the baby-milk factory. At that point, it had become a resource at our hotel. Lots of children of diplomats or other kids in the shelter. So whoever went was obligated to bring back one of these things.

This [holding up a small bag] is the infant formula from the factory. There were vats of it. I mean whole buckets of it laid out. And this was the product they claim. It is "al-Ban Sweetened Milk." They say it is for kids between the ages of three weeks and one year. And I got a few packets and I gave it with some hesitation to the children in the shelters. They ate it—they liked it. I was at a children's hospital a few weeks later where they pointed out, they were saying that their medicine had been put back 50 years, and they just could not get infant formula. I talked about the factory, and they said, "Well, we want it from the factory."

What it was, I don't know. I went all over the place twice. It was a small, about half-acre building. There were several big vats. It had been totally demolished in the bombing—other than these plastic containers which had dozens of these [bags] in [them]. I don't know. I did not see any evidence of biological testing, but then I don't know what biological testing would have looked like. But, anyway, that is my story of the baby-milk factory.

And if you believe me, you will join me later, we will open this packet. And we will put it in our coffee.

Q: Tell us your reaction and your response to Senator Simpson's attack on you as a sympathizer.

Arnett: Well, I was amused, frankly, because in April last year I was one of a handful of journalists in Jerusalem who were called to the U.S. consulate to be upbraided by Senator Simpson and others, Senator Metzenbaum, Senator Dole, and a few others.

Why were we upbraided? We were misrepresenting *Saddam Hussein*. At that point, of course, he had threatened to incinerate half of Israel and the stories we were doing from Israel were very negative toward Saddam Hussein. We were upbraided for referring to this paragon of virtue, an American friend, a future power in the gulf. We did not understand Saddam Hussein. So Larry Register, the CNN bureau chief, came back and said, "We have got to do something with this."

"I said, "Well, what *can* we do with it?" I think we offered it to

Atlanta or we suggested we would ship it. But already they had gone their own way. And there had been comments about the Palestinian situation.

So it sort of fell between the cracks. But we do still have the video, Senator!!

Just one further comment. My son Andrew, who is an aspiring rock star (more aspiring than a star), unbeknown to me, wrote a small commentary that was published in *The New York Times*, about defending his mother and me. And I think that does stand as my defense.

Now in addition to CNN, our executives, my colleagues, without number, have gone to my defense. And I don't think I need to say any more other than the fact that I have known Senator Simpson for 10 years. I have interviewed him many times, and I was sort of surprised to hear that sort of comment and how it was sort of a total lack of understanding of what I was about, what CNN was about, or what we are all about.

Bernard Shaw: Wasn't it really stupid, Peter?

Arnett: What?

Shaw: Wasn't it really stupid?

Arnett: Bernie Shaw said it was really stupid, and I have always admired and appreciated what Bernie has said.

Q: If you have the opportunity what do you plan to say to Senator Simpson?

Arnett: Just play the C-Span version of what I just said.

Q: Peter, to be specific, did you ever feel your life was in danger during your broadcast? Was there ever an AK-47 aimed at your head?

Arnett: Cruise missiles were aimed at my head. These are areas that I haven't really thought too much about, and I'm not trying to hedge it, because I haven't been out of Baghdad long and the implications of a lot of what we did, particularly in the garden at night and while we were waiting to go on the air and the sirens are going and there is other competing broadcasts. So do you go? Did Bob Fernad go with the Saudi briefing? Does he go with the Scud attack on Tel

Aviv? When does he pick up Baghdad? At what point does it become so pressing in Baghdad that we have just got to go to air. I mean it was a surfeit of journalistic joys that was facing CNN so often. I am sure you have seen a lot of this.

So, at times we would be out in the garden waiting and I remember one time a cruise missile hit a conference center 200 yards away, a huge building almost the size of the Al Rashid. It basically demolished the auditorium of that building and at times I was wondering how far with this do we go. What basically is this all meaning? Is this theater? I mean, what do we have here? Are we playing sort of a war game?

But on the other hand I was thinking, these things *are exploding*. The bombs *are* coming near. There *is* competing information. If we can stay up, if our equipment is working, and if my crew and I have the strength to remain rooted in place, fine.

One of the biggest problems was that our "minders" were reluctant to stand there with us. They didn't have the future of journalistic freedom on their minds. They didn't want to get killed. So often, they attempted to force us to leave or just left us anyway.

But I remember on one occasion, Bob Cain was talking on the air and it was very, very noisy. And I heard Bob come up with a comment to the viewers, "Well, we are having . . . There has been some heavy bombing in Baghdad. So it is possible we may lose the signal. So you will know what is happening there."

And I felt like saying, "You are also going to lose your correspondent and crew, Bob."

In terms of fear, one of our technicians sat in our tent, where we had the video satellite equipment, with a steel cooking pot over his head. But he stayed sitting there. Fear? What is fear when you are going live to the whole world and it is happening around you? I don't think we sort of considered that. Fear was not an option when it came to going live from Baghdad at times like that.

Q: Could you comment on the observation attributed to someone in the inner circle of the administration, that they found your reporting from Baghdad very valuable when reading between the lines and that

326

on-the-record sniping at you was encouraged to enhance your credibility with Saddam, to increase the likelihood that you would be permitted to stay on?

Arnett: I don't buy that argument. However, of course what we were observing was of benefit to observers of the scene. Many times in Israel before the Gulf War, one of the intelligence chiefs, *the* chief of intelligence, would say that CNN is absolutely essential for us to know what is happening in the world and in the gulf. In fact, one of his assistants told me one day that when they would start briefing him, when they would start briefing, they would hand around notes saying "we have seen the CNN broadcast today also—why does he bother talking about it."

So, from that point of view when you have got instant communications and widespread elaborate communications, sure it was valuable. I made a point of fighting to get pictures on the air of the bridges that were down, of installations that I argued that were not really military, were not command and control, like a bank, like the telecommunications center. I mean, these officials, they eventually went along with it.

I knew that, in fact, after we published pictures on the air of these three bridges of Baghdad, I had a message from Charles Jaco from Saudi Arabia, "Congratulations from the Stealth guys," who had apparently blown up the bridges. And they said, "Great pictures. Thanks. Keep up that heads-up performance." So, of course it was beneficial to everyone. But my purpose there was to be beneficial to the viewers of CNN and anyone who picked up our broadcast. And anything else was simply peripheral.

Q: What can you tell us about collateral damage and the public health effects of bombing of the water and sewer system, hospitals, electrical systems, etc?

Arnett: Well, they were all targeted earlier on in the war. We pointed it out that they were targeted. They did not make the people of Baghdad very happy. The government was not happy. I presume it was a planned targeting procedure. And we reported on it fully at the time. The possibilities of disease—of course. But then that is a consequence that I don't think military planners could essentially follow through on—determining if, indeed, the lack of running water will ultimately harm the population more than is necessary to bring the government down or to alter their particular policy course.

I was interested to read in the *Herald Tribune* yesterday in Paris, and I presume it was in the American press also, an official quote as saying that 70 percent of the non-smart bombing basically missed the targets. So the kind of stories that I was reporting on initially—saying that I saw 42 craters, each 25 feet deep and 50 feet across, and they looked to me like aerial bombardment.—this would suggest that the implications of this were simply shells from antiaircraft weapons falling to ground was not really accurate and that a lot of bombs did miss their targets. I mean from the beginning, I think I said in one of the earliest broadcasts, we were talking about civilian casualties and I said to whoever was asking me, "You know, we got to get used to the fact that [when] you launch this kind of bombing you are going to have some collateral damage. Civilians will get hurt. Face up to it."

Talk about the successes of the smart-bombs, which we did talk about. But I felt that our viewers, the American public, could come to terms with a degree of civilian casualties. I thought it was interesting, however, as the war did proceed, and as the bombing became more intense, leading into the bombing of the shelter, which I called "civilian" for a while, which we just call "shelter" now because we don't really know what it was. We almost had a sense of it going to happen, though, because the bombing was getting closer. It just was getting almost more desperate. The bridges were going down. And when the shelter was hit, it was as though it was another whole element in the air war. It was as though it was taking it a degree further, that the policy had shifted towards a policy of actually targeting the civilian population.

I think our reportage of that helped, I think, Gorbachev to come to the conclusion to try and launch his peace initiative, because Gorbachev apparently is an ardent CNN viewer, as people are in Moscow. And

I think that maybe the reporting of that tended to alter the political picture to some degree.

On the other hand, I think the bombing was aiming more and more at civilian—well, if not civilian targets, targets that were aimed at the structure of the country. What I have read suggests that maybe someone at the Pentagon said they were aiming at senior officials of the Socialist Baath party who may have been there. As I said, I heard a rumor that Saddam Hussein may have been there. But there were also 270 women and children and old men there. So I think it became a question then of, "Is Saddam Hussein or members of a government worth that many civilian casualties?" I think that was the question we raised in our coverage, and I have no apology for that.

Q: About those bottles you referred to in storage in the CNN office which you shared with Iraqi diplomats and press. How did you get those into an Islamic country, and did the Iraqi acquaintances have any problems consuming alcohol?

Arnett: Iraq has come to Islam sort of later than others. It is a secular country; at the duty-free store at the edge of town, which remained open throughout the bombing, five hours a day, you could get all the booze you would ever want to drink. And so we acquired it. It was part of a, it was simply a way to relax. I am not a heavy drinker, but I must admit that on a regular basis myself and, dare I mention his name, Vito Maggiolo would descend to the bunker and we would pass the bottle around.

And in the terms of Islam and the propriety, it was basically lost in the hotel because there were families, women and men, sharing the shelter floor together. So while they do exercise propriety there, under those conditions there was less. So, the idea of relaxing after a long, hard day with a bottle or two became part of the more pleasing chores of the press corps there, I guess. I don't want to go into that too much. Our executives are here. And I want to pretend that I was clear-headed the whole time.

Arnett

Walter Goodman

Peter Arnett spent the days and weeks after leaving Baghdad early in March, when all Western reporters were invited out, answering the criticisms that his presence there throughout the war had brought down on him and his employer, the Cable News Network. By turns defiant and defensive, the correspondent upheld his role even as he acknowledged that the sort of journalism he had practiced, or been permitted to practice, had been severely circumscribed.

What exactly was the role that Arnett and the other correspondents in Baghdad played and why did it create its own desert storm? Much of the abuse was strictly political. The Scuds came mainly from the right, from Reed Irvine of Accuracy in Media, whose mission it is to expose what he deems to be the prevailing leftism of press and television, and Sen. Alan K. Simpson, the Wyoming Republican, who evidently did not like having pictures of civilian victims of the American bombings on the tube, lest they get in the way of public support for the administration. As even Simpson seemed belatedly to have recognized, their attacks were personal and nasty. (Arnett told an audience at the National Press Club that when he was reporting from Jerusalem before the war, Simpson and other senators had upbraided him and other correspondents for being too critical of Saddam Hussein.)

A surprisingly high-pitched comment came from Jim Wooten, a columnist for *The Atlanta Journal* (not the ABC correspondent), who drew a distinction between CNN, which broadcasts to the world, and networks that serve mainly the United States, where viewers have access to a range of information. He wrote: "CNN, however noble its intentions, while in Iraq is part of the controlled press and could be a legitimate target for electronic jamming by the

330

allies." Then there was sniping from competitors against the man who had the beat to himself for a considerable period. When other network reporters were allowed into the city, however, their dispatches were not all that different from Arnett's.

Arnett's champions, such as his friend David Halberstam, rebutted with credential-mongering. They reminded us of Vietnam, where Arnett won a Pulitzer Prize, and spoke of his integrity and his courage. The nature of his current coverage was hardly mentioned. Opponents of the war (yes, there really were some back in January) also came to the defense, in hopes perhaps that reports like Arnett's might produce a Vietnam effect. In any case, the concentration on the individual drew attention away from the predicament: Should American journalists be in enemy territory, sending home dispatches under the eye of the enemy censor? Is there any way to do that without abetting the enemy? Is there value to an American audience in hearing even inherently loaded reports?

The first and last questions seem to me easy. By remaining in Baghdad, Peter Arnett was doing what any journalist would do, and by trying to get into the city, the other network news departments were doing likewise, and good luck to them. As Arnett told Larry King after he left Iraq, "I was in Baghdad for the people who look at CNN," not for the United States government.

An on-the-ground presence in Baghdad was particularly valuable given the nature of the air campaign (how do you report it if you can't see where the bombs land?) and the Pentagon's control of information. Applying the tactics that had kept reporters at bay in Grenada and Panama, the military effectively shaped coverage from the beginning to the end of the Gulf War. That encouraged the natural wartime disposition to celebrate Our Brave Men and Women and censure, or even censor, anyone who didn't pitch in heartily enough.

The notion of American correspondents reciting reports approved by the enemy is uncomfortable, but noncoverage is not an attractive alternative. The best the journalist can do in enemy territory is to make

331

plain to viewers and readers the conditions under which he or she is permitted to operate and try to slip in more information than the minders have in mind. Which gets us back to Baghdad.

Accompanying every dispatch from Iraq on all networks were notices that censorship prevailed. It also prevailed to some extent in Saudi Arabia, Israel, and Washington. Yet what bothered even friendly critics of Arnett and his colleagues was their failure to make clear enough that they were being used expressly to report on civilian casualties. Some did try. As the CBS screen was taken up with a child in a hospital bed, for example, Betsy Aaron said, "In a hospital, the most innocent of victims is shown to the cameras." In the nature of things, the picture overwhelmed the wink, but the wink was there.

Talking with Frank Sesno of CNN as he was leaving Baghdad on March 6, Arnett conceded that the authorities had allowed him to stay so that he could tell about civilian casualties. He said he had lobbied for more information, but to little avail. In an interview with Sam Donaldson on ABC's "Prime Time Live," Arnett spelled out just how tight the control was: "From the beginning I accepted the constraints that the Iraqis laid down. They said, 'Anything you do, you put on paper. We go over it, and we alter it. We change it if we wish to, and that's what you're going to use.'"

To viewers around the world, it must have seemed that Saddam Hussein could have nothing to complain about in Arnett's performance. Whether it was a description of a bombed milk factory (could it have been a laboratory for bacteriological weapons?) or of what he called a civilian air raid shelter (could it also have been a military control center?), his reports never contradicted the Iraqi line.

Taken to a neighborhood where he was told that 24 civilians had been killed and the screen showed a framed photograph of a child in the debris of a house, he said he had seen only homes and a school, no mention of any munitions depot or military communications site or chemical-warfare plant that the Pentagon said were in the vicinity. But, of course, it was understood that military targets must not be mentioned. As Wooten wrote: "Take a reporter to a scene where civilians are suffering, tell him to say anything he wants about it, so long as he does not convey information of military value and you have ground rules that make fair and accurate reporting impossible." Describing hits near Iraqi holy places, Arnett went so far as to use the verb "targeted," as though pilots had been aiming at them.

In a self-gratulatory apologia that appeared in *The Washington Post* when he had left Baghdad, Arnett wrote that his daily question-and-answer exchanges with the CNN anchor after he had delivered his Iraqi-approved script "saved my credibility and made my presence in Baghdad a valuable one." For example, he was able to report on what he could see along the way to the destinations that had been selected for him. In his National Press Club talk, he gave the impression that his minders grew panicky over these Q & A's. His hints about the presence of military vehicles and his observations of daily life were welcome, but even here, it seemed to this viewer, he either did not see much of interest or was reluctant to try the patience of his hosts. The questions, which alerted viewers to how closely Arnett was controlled, were more informative than the answers.

For a time, ABC's Bill Blakemore was going around Baghdad interviewing residents. They were all amiable, serving coffee and so forth, and he said he felt they were speaking frankly despite the presence of an Iraqi official who, he assured viewers, was not in uniform and who stayed in the background. The men on the street and on camera said nothing unkind about their regime or its invasion of Kuwait.

Now, listen to Arnett as he is being kicked out of the country: "We don't get any really honest appraisals on camera because when we give an—have an interview in the street, there is a Ministry of Information official standing with us. You know, the conversation is being monitored." Only at the end, with his monitor "being very, very tolerant," was he able to say that once President Hussein had suggested a conditional withdrawal, "the public, to a person, was commenting that they didn't really need to be in Kuwait, that they wanted an end to the war."

333

Some of the correspondents in Baghdad apparently got to be on friendly terms with their minders, so much so that toward the end Arnett told his CNN interviewer that he would prefer to hold off talking about public feelings in Iraq until he reached Amman, "where I don't necessarily have to embarrass any local official, Frank." A reporter reluctant to embarrass a local official? The delicate concern wore off as soon as Arnett was out of the country. If Baghdad was monitoring his talk to the National Press Club, those minders might have been highly embarrassed, since he referred to their criticism of the Hussein regime and singled out one who, he said, allowed him to deliver an uncensored report on his final night in Iraq.

Set aside the cheap innuendos of disloyalty. And set aside, too, Jim Wooten's proposition that CNN reports from Iraq should be blocked lest they force a shift in military strategy for political reasons, which is an invitation to a censorship party—an invitation that is all the more disturbing coming from a newspaperman. A journalist who decides that his job is to help win a war, rather than just to describe it, is better off enlisting.

It was important for Arnett, Blakemore, and the others to be in Baghdad. It was important that people see something more of the consequences of the bombing than the photographs through targeting cross hairs beloved of Pentagon warriors. Nothing is harder or more essential to remember in the heat of war than that the other side is made up of human beings, too.

What was missing from most of the Baghdad reports was a degree of distance from the approved material, a touch of the skepticism that Washington reporters lay on when talking about American politicians. Wherefore the untypical deference? Were the correspondents afraid they would be kicked out if they hedged their reports a bit? Were they carried away by the professional temptation to squeeze emotion from scenes of pain? Were they feeling normal sympathy for people under attack?

As he was leaving Baghdad, Arnett replied to critics that he felt "very proud to be an eyewitness so the rest of the world would know how its policy was being implemented." That's nice. And he added, "I think the record will show the policy was implemented pretty effectively." His stint in Iraq over, was Arnett doing some repositioning?

All right, the coverage from Baghdad was only part of television's effort; Washington and Riyadh supplied most of the news. And judging Arnett and Blakemore and the other television reporters in Baghdad from afar is an easier assignment than the one they carried out, under tough conditions and with admirable perseverance. Yet aspects of their performance remain troubling, not from a patriotic point of view but from a professional one. The question nags, whether they adapted too readily to their host's scenario, whether they might not have found more ways to talk to viewers over, behind, beneath, and around those friendly minders.

In his *Washington Post* piece, Arnett told of "long and sometimes heated" arguments with the Iraqis and added, "I sometimes had my bags half-packed to leave." It's a close call: I can't fault any correspondent for staying on, but if Arnett had in fact been ejected for doing the journalist's job instead of the regime's, well, that would have been illuminating, too.

Peter Arnett: Anti-Hero of Baghdad

Bill Monroe

Behold Peter Arnett reporting from Baghdad. See him irritating millions of Americans who view him as shilling for Saddam Hussein. Note the "Disinformation" rebuke he draws from Marlin Fitzwater: That bomb-busted factory was for biological warfare, not for baby formula. Watch him send a normally sane senator, Simpson of Wyoming, boinng! up the wall. Listen to him coolly probe the limits of Iraqi censorship. Observe the legend taking shape—the legend of Peter Arnett, go-to-hell war correspondent.

In Saudi Arabia 700 or 800 reporters are jostling to get at little military-fed bites of the story. In Baghdad this rumpled character Arnett has staked out for himself the entire other half of the war.

Peter Arnett, the perfect symbol of the beleaguered press in the Scudded world of February 1991: He lives and breathes the story. He subsists on quantities of canned tuna. He sleeps in a bomb shelter under friendly fire that sometimes shakes the ground. He spends his days "minded" by agents of a murderous dictator. He keeps the window to Baghdad open a crack. And for his pains he nets, most visibly, a chorus of alarm, invective, and challenges to his patriotism.

Half the American people, judging by a poll or two, don't think Arnett should be there. What's an American reporter *doing* in the enemy capital? Get him outta there, he's doing propaganda for Saddam Insane.

Explaining how the First Amendment permits an American to hang out in wartime Baghdad filing Iraqi-cleared reports is not easy:

Arnett is producing some useful nuggets of information. . . .

Get him outta there.

He lets us know he is censored, so we can judge for ourselves. . . .

Get him outta there.

If Arnett wasn't there, Saddam would still be getting his message

336

out through Baghdad Radio or Spanish reporters or Soviet diplomats. . . .

Get him outta there.

The whole paradox of it all so scrambled Alan Simpson's cerebellum that he fired off a cruddy old piece of Cold War artillery. Arnett was a "sympathizer," he told an astonished group of reporters.

Peter Arnett, Simpson explained, "was active in the Vietnam War." Well, yes. Arnett, in fact, committed prodigious activity in Vietnam. Terry Smith of CBS recently told Ken Ringle of *The Washington Post* that "in Vietnam if you ever got caught up in a firefight and Arnett wasn't already there, he would be along shortly."

Former AP Foreign Editor Nate Polowetzky recalled Arnett, then with AP, messaging him in New York in 1975 "that the Viet Cong had just walked into the (Saigon) bureau with him. I told him to pull the plug and get out of there. He told me, in effect, to go screw myself."

Arnett, Simpson continued his indictment, "won a Pulitzer Prize in Vietnam largely because of his antigovernment material." Here the senator inflicted what the Pentagon calls collateral damage. He was aiming at Arnett, but in the process he revealed the nasty business of the entire Pulitzer board caught in antigovernment depravity.

It gets even worse. Arnett, said Simpson, "was married to a Vietnamese whose brother was active in the Viet Cong."

Vietnamese wife? Ah so. Brother-in-law with the Viet Cong? Double ah so.

Obviously (in case the senator's hand at this point was quicker than your eye), he's a sympathizer with Saddam Hussein. BIG ah so, sometimes rendered in English as ah CHOO.

"Malice in Wonderland" by Alan Simpson. A pity, because in real life we find Simpson to be a genial senator, only rarely so short of fuse that he blows himself up. And over there in the real life of Baghdad we find—what so proudly we hailed before Simpson's red glare—Peter Arnett, unmarked and still talking into his handy-dandy portable satellite telephone.

And who is this fellow Arnett?

He is the hero that journalists deserve, that's who he is, sent by the Lord to comfort us in our time of affliction and gross unpopularity. He is neither hunk nor jock nor leader of the free world to the limousine born. Unlike Secretary Cheney, he does not look as if he could reel off the answer to 3.2 trillion dollars compounded daily for six months. Unlike General Powell, he is starkly bereft of majesty. Unlike General Schwarzkopf, he does not give that solid impression of being built on treads.

Arnett has that special charisma that is visible only to journalists. He is bald. He wears a previously used face. By the testimony of old colleagues, he is ornery—possibly, one speculates, because once he had to contend with the New Zealand class structure. He is skeptical of all officialdom. He believes nothing he can't see for himself and not all of that. And, particularly endearing to journalists, he is effortlessly offensive to the vast millions who believe that the Pentagon will tell us when our bombs miss the target, that President Bush once met a secret he didn't like, and that the First Amendment is the sweet reunion after a first lovers' quarrel.

Our man in Baghdad. Our own anti-hero hero. May the fierce, battered god of press freedom protect him.

Senator Simpson Calls Arnett "Sympathizer"

Howard Kurtz

Sen. Alan Simpson (R-Wyo.) charged yesterday that CNN correspondent Peter Arnett is "a sympathizer" with Iraq, that his reporting during the Vietnam War was biased, and that he has a brother-in-law who was "active in the Viet Cong."

At a Capitol Hill luncheon with reporters, the Senate minority whip assailed Arnett for his censored television reports from Baghdad. He said the reporter is "what we used to call a sympathizer . . . He was active in the Vietnam War and he won a Pulitzer Prize largely because of his antigovernment material. And he was married to a Vietnamese whose brother was active in the Viet Cong. I called that 'sympathizers' in my early days in the Second World War."

An Arnett family member, who asked not to be identified, said the Viet Cong allegation is "completely untrue." The family member said Arnett's wife, Nina, from whom he has been separated for several years, had two brothers—a heart doctor who was forced into early retirement by the Viet Cong and died in the 1960s, and a math professor in Hanoi who was not politically active during the war and who has not been allowed to leave the country.

Friends and colleagues of Arnett reacted angrily to Simpson's remarks.

Simpson, known for his outspoken and acerbic style, said in a telephone interview after the lunch that he was given the information "by an AP man who was involved in reporting during the Vietnam War . . . a man of great repute . . . a friend I've known for 30 years." He said he did not know the brother-in-law's name or the nature of his supposed Viet Cong activities.

Asked if he felt it was proper to make such an allegation public without attempting to verify it, Simpson said: "I find a lot of those [kind of allegations] used in your line of work . . . They slap guys like me around day and night [with such charges].

"This is what I was told by a source I consider to be reputable . . . To me, it has not been refuted."

Simpson said the source gave him the information about Arnett last week after the senator debated columnist Jack Anderson in Cheyenne, Wyoming. Anderson, in a column published Wednesday, reprised some controversial remarks Simpson made when he visited Saddam Hussein with a Senate delegation last April.

"I believe your problems lie with the Western media and not with the U.S. government," Simpson told the Iraqi leader. "As long as you are isolated from the media, the press—and it is a haughty and pampered press—they all consider themselves political geniuses. That is, the journalists do. They are very cynical. What I advise is that you invite them to come here and see for yourselves."

Author David Halberstam, who also won a Pulitzer for his Vietnam coverage, said yesterday he was "stunned by the ugliness" of Simpson's remarks about Arnett. "I like Alan Simpson. I think he's smart as hell, funny as hell," Halberstam said. "But the ugliness of him even mentioning someone like Nina, and connecting Peter's extraordinary coverage, as if that made him a sympathizer to the other side. . . . He's dead wrong. I know the family and that charge is particularly painful for them."

Terry Smith, a CBS News reporter who was *The New York Times* Saigon bureau chief, said, "It is ludicrous to suggest [Arnett] is a sympathizer with Saddam Hussein, or that he was in any way sympathetic to either the North Vietnamese or the Viet Cong. He makes crystal clear in every report that he was taken to thus or that site on a guided tour by the Iraqi government.

"People are intelligent enough to hear that and understand exactly what he is telling them. I just find this sort of personal attack outrageous," Smith said.

Ed Turner, CNN's executive vice president for news, said he was "flabbergasted" by Simpson's remarks. "CNN is fortunate to have on site, in the most difficult circumstances, a seasoned combat correspondent, Peter Arnett, who has been tested by time and in so practicing his craft received the highest honors journalism can bestow. Arnett and CNN are there so all our viewers can be there—as imperfect, restricted, and dangerous as the conditions are."

Arnett has been criticized, by White House spokesman Marlin Fitzwater among others, for reporting on allied bomb damage in residential neighborhoods to which he was taken by Iraqi authorities. Saddam granted him an interview several days ago.

At the luncheon, Simpson acknowledged that he was putting "my foot clear down in my mouth." But he said "our greatest problem right now in this conflict" is that "now there is an entire convoy of media people crossing the desert to get to Baghdad, with their satellite dishes and all their antennas, and we've got to protect them. And who the hell who has any imagination knows what they're going to feed us . . . .

"Maybe I'm from the old school, that we can't spend our time trying to protect people who are there at the invitation of an enemy government."

In the interview, Simpson said it was "good for the American people" to know of Arnett's personal history. He said Arnett, who remained in Vietnam for a time after U.S. forces withdrew, "was able to have free range of the country in a communist regime."

The senator called Arnett's reporting from Baghdad "repulsive," citing his report that allied forces had bombed what the Iraqs claim is an infant formula factory but which the White House says is a biological weapons plant. "My question is, why is he the only one there? . . . Here is a man who is reporting from a country with which we are at war, the same people who are trying to kill our young men and women," Simpson said.

Simpson's Scud Attack

Jim Hoagland

When it comes to the press, Sen. Alan Simpson has the aim, skill, and humanity of an Iraqi Scud rocketeer. The verbal warhead the gentleman from Wyoming flung at CNN's Peter Arnett in Baghdad exploded well short of its target, showering Simpson with its noxious fallout.

Simpson's intemperate outburst calling Arnett an Iraqi sympathizer is in itself not very important. The senator's reputation as a judge of character and of the press shrank to Smurf size after he journeyed to Baghdad last April to pay court to Saddam Hussein.

The Iraqis later leaked a transcript showing Simpson and the Iraqi dictator agreeing that journalists are the scum of the earth. Far from denying the Iraqi version, the senator responded to the transcript as Indonesia's Sukarno is said to have responded to a KGB attempt to blackmail him with compromising photographs of him and blondes during a visit to Moscow: Send dozens of copies to my people. This will really impress them.

But Simpson touched a nerve about the role of the press in war, and that is important. Reporters become pawns not only for editors and for the politicians they normally frequent in symbiotic servitude, but also for war makers dealing in life-and-death decisions that journalists affect through their presence and their coverage.

In peacetime, a newspaper or a network is manipulated every day in hundreds of little ways by publicists, governments, and hidden sources with hidden agendas. In war, the manipulation is big, crude and unrelenting. How the journalists respond is certain to become an issue itself in this contentious electronic age.

Iraq has developed a deadly new wrinkle in "using" journalists. A dozen Western reporters were forced to leave Baghdad Friday after only a week there. The bureaucratic pretext was that their visas had expired. A new team of journalists was admitted, presumably for an equally brief stay.

The incoming and outgoing journalists have to travel in convoy along the heavily bombed Baghdad-Amman road. The Iraqis have been using convoys to mask travel by Scud mobile launchers which dart out to fire and then weave back in line to hide, according to Pentagon officials.

The Iraqi's media plan is a twofer: They hope that journalists traveling on the road will buy them a pause in U.S. raids, and they count on the newly arrived journalists to convey fresh horror and outrage over civilian casualties and bombed-out schools.

That is where Simpson's Scudlet aimed at Arnett falls into the desert.

Throughout his lonely, dangerous stint in Baghdad, Arnett has been meticulous in conveying information, not emotion or propaganda. I watch each of his broadcasts with growing admiration, not only for his bravery but also for the way in which he brings his intelligence and experience to bear and tell us more about what is happening in Iraq than the censors standing in front of his flashlight-illuminated nose realize.

Arnett has made a point of repeatedly saying that the Iraqis are refusing to take him to see the military targets that the bombing raids are hitting. In a dozen other subtle ways he reminds us that the United States is concentrating on military targets and is not conducting a terror campaign against defenseless citizens.

Those who listened carefully to Arnett in the opening days of the bombing raids on Baghdad heard him suggest that civilian casualties in Baghdad must have been remarkably low, since the Iraqis had been able to show him so few for filming. More recently, as conditions worsen, Arnett has begun to emphasize the plight and anger of the people of Baghdad. He shows us that the pressure is getting to the Baghdadis, if not yet to Saddam.

The controls that the Iraqis have clamped on Arnett and his colleagues are not unusual for Arab regimes at war. When Israel struck Egypt in 1967, Western newsmen were arrested and interned in Cairo before they could file on the military disaster Egypt was experiencing (Egyptian officials later complained that Western media had refused to report that the Israelis had struck first.) Those of us who covered the 1973 war from Syria spent much of our time on the roof of the Semiramis Hotel in Damascus watching dogfights and Israeli air raids in the distance.

We were not used by the Syrians, who snickered at our demands to go to the front. We were ignored. The Iraqis are more skillful. They limit foreign access to a single story—civilian casualties. But good reporters like Arnett can get more of the story out and do so.

Simpson was wrong about Saddam last April, and he is wrong about Arnett now.

Letter to Editor

Sen. Alan Simpson

March 15, 1991

To the Editor:

At a Washington luncheon during the height of the air war against Iraq, I told a group of reporters that I thought Peter Arnett of CNN was a sympathizer for staying in Baghdad and for allowing Saddam Hussein to use him for Iraqi propaganda.

I also repeated a rumor that seems to have followed Mr. Arnett for more than 20 years—a rumor that indicated that because of his marriage to a Vietnamese woman, who was reported to have a brother active in the Viet Cong, Mr. Arnett decided it was safe to stay in Saigon long after the evacuation of United States forces. It is a matter of record that he was granted permission by the Communists to continue reporting for the Associated Press after the fall.

While I still strongly criticize him for his reporting from Baghdad during the Persian Gulf war, I do feel the deep personal need to apologize for repeating the rumors about Mr. Arnett's family connection to the Viet Cong. I said from the outset that if it couldn't be proven, I would apologize. In the absence of concrete evidence to corroborate the family situation, I wish to do so now. I greatly regret any hurt, pain, or anguish that I have caused his family.

Furthermore, I admonish all who have engaged in this item of gossip over Mr. Arnett's past to put up or shut up. I regret being part of it. Just as Operation Desert Storm has healed many wounds left from Vietnam—it is also time to allow that wound to heal. So, I direct this expression particularly to Peter Arnett's son, Andrew, who wrote so eloquently and poignantly in "The Truth About My Family" (Op-Ed, March 13).

I have not changed my opinion of Peter Arnett's presence in

345

Baghdad. I felt the bunker incident reporting was repugnant. The baby-formula factory story only slightly less so.

Several journalists delivered reports on the bunker-bombing. What was most disturbing about Mr. Arnett's report was that it seemingly condemned the United States for carelessly bombing civilian targets, and yet, it was mostly based on what his Iraqi handlers told him about the event. He reported that civilians had routinely been sleeping in the bunker, without ever confirming this assumption. He did not make an attempt to determine if the bunker had military markings. Yet only reporters who made the effort to climb upon the bunker did find evidence of military camouflage paint on its roof.

Saddam Hussein may have placed civilians in the bunker with the conjecture that the United States would target it and reward him with a significant propaganda victory. Or it may have been one of those random events of war, unplanned by President Hussein. What is certain is that Mr. Arnett reported the event in a tone and manner that was helpful to the government of Iraq and harmful to the United States. He reported hearsay evidence—just as I had done with regard to his family—and did little to investigate Iraqi claims.

I happen to know firsthand of Saddam Hussein's obsession for propaganda and disinformation from how he manipulated and abridged the transcript of a meeting I had with him last April. All references to our criticism of his government, from the gassing of the Kurds to the hanging of a British journalist, to possessing nuclear triggering devices and the big pipe-gun caper, all went unreported. He did report that I said that some of the Western press in that area of the world were a "haughty and pampered press—they all consider themselves political geniuses. They are very cynical." And the news media will be wrapping that one around my head like a tire iron for lots of years to come.

Yet it is my firm belief that if Western reporters had not been in Baghdad—behind enemy lines, if you will—Saddam Hussein might not have been tempted to indulge himself in the photo opportunities that were presented to the world. He knew devilishly well the consequences of his actions. Unfortunately, the news media naively overlooked theirs.

My choice of the word "sympathizer" was not a good one. I wish I could have snatched it back and rephrased my remarks. The word "dupe" or "tool" of the Iraqi government would have been more in context with my original comments. However, I do know when I am wrong and stubborn—and for that I apologize. I would also hope the news media might acknowledge their serious mistakes on the coverage of the Gulf War from Baghdad. But I sure won't hold my breath on that one.

Al Simpson
U.S. Senator from Wyoming
Washington, D.C.

Chapter Nine

Press Neutrality?

Should and can the press be "neutral" in wartime? What do we mean by "neutral" and "objective"? As they assert independence from their government in wartime, must journalists distance themselves from their nationality as well? Do all viewpoints deserve media coverage in wartime even if the government asserts that some will undermine morale at home and at the front? Should the media present opposing views from small segments of the population?

CNN's Breakthrough in Baghdad

Jeff Kamen

After the three major networks had somehow lost their signals out of Iraq, there they were, the high-flying Baghdad Boys of the Cable News Network. Bernard Shaw, Peter Arnett, and John Holliman, their own "four-wire" line still hot, went on describing the story outside their hotel window: the criss-cross of tracer fire, the explosions of bombs or missiles uncomfortably nearby, the first hours of a war. Later Arnett would become the lone Western correspondent *permitted* to file from Iraq's capital.

Their spectacular scoop and the public adulation that followed are only the surface elements of the most important media story of the year—Global Village War I.

One week later, shortly past 8 p.m. on January 24, Bernard Shaw is back at the CNN anchor desk in Washington for the first time since the triumph in Baghdad, and he is furious. "Where is the attribution in this copy? Who says three Iraqis were killed? This sounds like a sports report. Where is the attribution?" Writers hustle to make the copy conform to Shaw's standard. Everyone on the staff knows that their star has hardly begun to catch up on his sleep, let alone recover, from his tense time in Saddam Hussein's capital, where he tried to reassure himself that the ordnance falling around him was harmless. "They're not bombs," Shaw told himself, "it's just thunder and lightning, just thunder and lightning."

Only minutes before he roared his displeasure at his support team in Washington, Shaw had been quiet and reflective, musing to an interviewer that his anchor chair didn't feel quite right after weeks in the field. CNN's premier Washington anchor had been overseas interviewing world leaders when, by an accident of timing, he got stuck in the Al Rashid Hotel with Arnett and Holliman as the allied bombardment began. For the first time U.S. reporters—the CNN team and correspondents of other networks—were *inside* an enemy capital when a war started.

"What is new in this war is not censorship—Vietnam was the exception, a noncensored war," says Stephen Hess, a media expert at the Brookings Institution. "What is totally different is an instantaneous, continuous, and international network. CNN really *is* the story. And it's clear that we all have a lot to learn about this new phenomenon."

The Baghdad Boys' narration of the first attacks on Baghdad, 17 hours of live, radio-style drama, put them in the pantheon of broadcast celebrities. Their instantaneous journalism did indeed usher in a new phenomenon: war-as-it-happens TV reporting beamed simultaneously to all the nations in conflict. But the adventure of Arnett, Holliman, and Shaw also raised troubling issues about the nature of war reportage in the age of global television, especially as practiced by Ted Turner's CNN, still the only worldwide 24-hour all-news service.

The 10-year-old network has a six-continent audience. Until the allies hit Baghdad on January 16, CNN rarely had drawn more than a million viewers in the U.S. during any sustained coverage. At the height of the Baghdad bombing, CNN was reaching more than 10 million in the U.S. alone.

Turner's burgeoning baby seeks to be all things to all viewers, a complex reflection of its founder's world view. His philosophy is embodied in a memo he wrote last year in which he banned the word "foreign" from his network. Henceforth CNN would have an "international" desk. Writers and reporters were warned: Repeated use of the banned word would result in cash fines, or worse.

This one-world philosophy was severely tested by the brutal Iraqi invasion of Kuwait, with its rape, butchery of civilians, and organized looting extending even to hospital incubators. Saddam Hussein seized thousands of Western hostages who were unable to escape Kuwait and Iraq, including about 800 Americans. The horror of Ayatollah Khomeini's abuse of 50-odd American diplomats was now being revisited on a scale 16 times larger.

When Iraqi TV told CNN that it would make available Saddam's meeting with some of the hostages, the network decided to take it live. ("Live," in this case, meant airing the tape as it was received. The Iraqis had recorded the scene earlier.) The grotesque images of kidnapper and hapless victims stirred bitter condemnation from people in and out of the media who felt that Turner had turned CNN into a propaganda vehicle for a madman.

Interviewed the next day by the Canadian Broadcasting Corporation, CNN Executive Vice President Ed Turner (no relation to Ted) said that airing Saddam's hostage meeting was the "same as airing a live speech by the president, or a football game."

Informed of that comment and its context, Robert Lichter of the Center for Media and Public Affairs said, "God, did CNN say that? Ouch! . . . to say that covering a Bush speech live is like covering a Saddam speech live is to ignore the differences between a democracy and a dictatorship. You have to make judgments. There is such a thing as international aggression. You have to understand the context of what you're covering. What if Edward R. Murrow had tried to be totally objective about Hitler bombing London? Is that what we really would have wanted?"

Walter Cronkite defended CNN's practice of airing unedited Iraqi propaganda. "I don't know any reason why we shouldn't listen to Saddam unedited . . . if we are in such a delicate state in our democracy that we can't afford to let our people listen to that, we should look to our own [democratic] credentials."

At Brookings, Stephen Hess also supported CNN's put-it-on-live policy but underlined the necessity of providing context, "something which CNN doesn't do well . . . Most of CNN's anchors are traffic directors."

During his first hour back in the anchor chair, Shaw seemed highly irritable much of the time he was not on camera. When the red light went on, he uncharacteristically stumbled through some of his stories. When he had a break, Shaw tore through the Gulf War updates brought to him. Three times he crossed out the word "enemy" and replaced it with "Iraqi."

Later, Shaw told *WJR* that his work is seen and heard in 105 countries and must be free of bias: "There's no 'enemy,' there's no 'friendly'; I can't take sides and I don't take sides. As an American, how I feel privately, that's personal. But professionally, I do not take sides. . . . As a reporter I am neutral." Asked if there is a moral equivalency between President Bush and President Saddam Hussein in the way they are treated on CNN's air, Shaw said, "I don't make moral judgments." Reminded that his personal heroes, Edward R. Murrow and Walter Cronkite, both referred to "enemy" actions in their broadcasts, Shaw said, "That was Murrow and that was Cronkite. I'm Shaw."

But Cronkite told *WJR*, "The question of being neutral, in the sense of trying to remove yourself from being an American, I think is an impossibility; further, I think, the identification of the 'enemy' is accepting the national definition of the moment. It's also a useful synonym."

Lichter is worried by the Ted Turner/Bernard Shaw approach: "Even if you see yourself as a citizen of the world, you're still a representative of the human race and you have to be against things that are inhuman. By refusing to take sides you can be on the side of inhumanity. Journalists say that all the time when they're doing hard-hitting documentaries. I'd hate for them to forget it when they want to insure access to a foreign dictator. . . . That is a legitimate concern that CNN needs to allay."

CNN congressional correspondent Bob Franken, now in Dhahran, passionately defends CNN's approach: "We cannot assume that one side has a corner on the truth, and there is a tremendous jingoistic pressure to choose sides."

Cronkite concurs: "It is not a duty of journalists to conform to the government line."

If he could do it all again, CNN's Holliman said he would not report where the American bombs and missiles struck. "The day after, our Iraqi minders told us the military had been furious about our being so specific." Unwittingly, CNN had become a forward observer for

Riyadh and Washington, providing information hours before data was available from satellites or videotape from bombers.

During a Pentagon news conference Defense Secretary Richard Cheney called CNN's coverage the best, and Joint Chiefs Chairman Colin Powell referred almost affectionately to information he was getting from "Bernie" in Baghdad. Cheney and Powell, who properly expect journalists to protect the security of soldiers, were not being sensitive to the problems of journalists. Their praise for the CNN correspondents could have angered Saddam Hussein and gotten them into trouble with Iraqi officials.

When the exhausted Shaw resumed his Washington duties in late January, his colleague Peter Arnett, the Pulitzer Prize-winning combat reporter, remained in Baghdad—the only Western journalist to continue to cover the war from the enemy's capital. But his reports, subject to Iraqi censorship, were creating a flap among some viewers stateside.

White House spokesman Marlin Fitzwater sharply criticized an Arnett dispatch that said U.S. planes had attacked what the Iraqis identified as a baby-formula factory. "Disinformation," said Fitzwater. "That factory is, in fact, a production facility for biological weapons." (In his report, Arnett had described the extensive damage to the facility he had seen—"the steel girders . . . twisted and blackened"— adding the curious fact that "The intact signboard at the entrance of the factory read 'Baby Milk Plant' in English and Arabic.")

In Atlanta, CNN's Ed Turner issued a statement that said Arnett reported "what the Iraqi claim was [that it was a milk plant] and his own observation on site. . . . CNN believes it is in the interests of our viewers to maintain the only Western journalist to watch and report from Baghdad."

The next morning Arnett turned on his gasoline-powered satellite telephone and, surrounded by Iraqi censors, defended the story: "I learned in Vietnam to believe only what my eyes have seen as [opposed to] anything I hear from any official of any government or from any person. I have an inborn skepticism because I'm a journalist.

So we are dependent on what officials tell us about what is going on. . . . I can only confirm what my eyes see, and I can't always say that I am seeing exactly what I think I'm seeing."

Live, with a world of both friendly and hostile witnesses listening in, the anchorman in Atlanta asked Arnett if he were being instructed (by Iraqi officials) to report the Iraqi line. Arnett replied, "I plead to use the phone as often as I can, which is maybe twice a day, and nothing that I'm telling you on this phone is being forced for me to say because I am constantly worrying officials and pushing them to give us information about what's going on. . . . Nothing I am saying I am being told to report."

After the White House charged CNN with spreading enemy disinformation, a CNN anchorwoman told viewers, "We ask our viewers to keep in mind Peter Arnett's reports from Baghdad are based on official statements by the Iraqi government and whatever personal observations he is able to make. His movements are, of course, restricted by the Iraqi government, and he has no access to outside independent sources of information."

CNN is the network Saddam and his deputies watch. Like other world figures, they use it to signal and track their friends and foes, especially the United States. Iraqi leaders regard CNN as "impartial," Arnett once reported from Baghdad, when asked why CNN alone was allowed to remain on the story.

Media-watcher Robert Lichter, usually a CNN fan, says it was "dangerous for CNN and dangerous for journalism to have the only reporter—even if he's the world's best war correspondent—working in the shadow of guns that could be aimed at his head. . . . In a way he's a hostage, and you have to treat his statements as those of hostages. A short-run advantage can turn into a long-run debacle if we later learn that Arnett has either unwittingly or unwillingly served as a propaganda organ for Saddam Hussein."

Independent Television News of London's Washington correspondent, David Cass, hailed Arnett's courage and said of his exclusive interview with Saddam, "That's why the Iraqis allowed him to stay."

Less than three weeks into the war, the CNN ratings bonanza had settled into a 500 percent increase over prewar audience shares; the company was charging $20,000 for the same 30-second commercial that went for only $3,500 before the bombs began to fall and the Baghdad Boys made history.

Meanwhile, the Times Mirror Center for the People and the Press reported January 30 that 61 percent of those surveyed believed CNN was doing the best job of covering the war. The closest runner-up was ABC with 12 percent; NBC and CBS trailed dismally with 7 percent. However, 45 percent of the 924 adults questioned by Times Mirror disapproved of American news organizations sending censored dispatches from Iraq, while 43 percent approved.

What emerges from the fog of warfare is that TV's raw power is growing as more of the planet becomes able to tune in to the same newscast. CNN is the first worldwide TV news organization to follow other giant multinational companies—thinking less like Americans and more like citizens of the world. If there's a loss of national identity, there may be a paradoxical gain to the nation. What the whole world is watching is not a Japanese or German or Soviet network, but an American network whose anchors live and work in Atlanta and Washington. The political—and journalistic—consequences of a 24-hour global news network headquartered in America are uncharted and uncontrollable.

Army of Experts on the Attack

As Operation Desert Storm continues its nonstop march across the nation's TV screens, news producers and guest bookers are under attack by an army of military experts, would-be crisis negotiators, and publicity-hungry authors and college professors eager for their 15 minutes of fame. While the onslaught of hopeful talking heads has actually yielded some telegenic interviewees, most didn't make it past the fax machine.

"Everybody's got a comment and everybody wants to make it on

356

television," says Gail Evans, vice president of network booking for CNN. By the beginning of the war's second week, Evans figured she had been phoned by a thousand would-be guests and faxed by 200 more. "It's not just off-the-wall people—it's very respectable people who feel they can end the war. And they're very insistent."

Among the CNN hopefuls:

- Academics from Mt. Holyoke College (available "around the clock")
- Academics from the University of North Carolina (as listed in "Tarheel Tipsheet")
- The four Bolano brothers (all Vietnam veterans)
- Three astrologers (bearing star charts of Saddam Hussein)
- Creators of a Desert Storm commemorative map

Spokespersons at the other networks say they've also been offered an unprecedented range of possibilities, from Arab groups, Jewish groups, and peace groups, to T-shirt merchants and music tape vendors, not to mention:

- Nixon-aide-turned-prison-reformer Chuck Colson
- Comedian-activist Dick Gregory
- A sales training expert (expounding on President Bush's Persian Gulf War "sales techniques")
- The creator of a Saddam Hussein voodoo doll

And—who else?—Dr. Joyce Brothers.

Bashing the Media: Why the Public Outrage?

Stephen Aubin

"Just whose side are they on?" a *Time* (February 25) magazine headline asked. *Time* was referring, of course, to U.S. journalists covering the Gulf War. In the accompanying article, reporter Richard Zoglin noted that "media bashing has been on the upsurge since the start of the war." In describing public sentiment, he added, "Why, goes the common cry, is the press trying to undermine the war effort? What are they first—journalists or Americans?"

Wall Street Journal (February 11) reporter Dorothy Rabinowitz pointed out that in World War II "the view of reporters as independent operators above the fray of battle was not the sort of thing reporters of Edward R. Murrow's era were used to . . . Murrow, one of the earliest most potent of [the Germans'] wartime enemies . . . took sides. It is as difficult to imagine his younger colleague Eric Sevareid espousing the view that in covering the war his first allegiance was to the principles of journalism." Yet, today, she notes, CNN's Bernard Shaw states quite categorically that a journalist must remain neutral, "which inspired Charlton Heston to retort . . . 'Who does he think he is—Switzerland?'

Such naïveté on the part of reporters, and the cheap shots that it evokes, like Sen. Alan Simpson's description of CNN's Peter Arnett as "a sympathizer," is understandable, but still unfortunate. The real issue has nothing to do with patriotism. In a recent hearing before the Senate Governmental Affairs Committee, Assistant Secretary of Defense for Public Affairs Pete Williams said he had no doubt about the patriotism of the journalists he had seen in action. Most had been extremely careful about what they reported, and few, if any, took issue with the need to maintain military operational security and to protect the lives of American troops.

The real issue goes beyond name-calling and other forms of

"shooting the messenger." It comes down to the dramatically constrained role of the media in wartime. Like it or not, the media are more hamstrung than ever, and there is little popular support for cutting them loose. Why? Because the media are not neutral observers—they are players, maybe even weapons of war. The media may be doing their best to get behind the story, to chase after the truth, and to nobly inform the American public, but when it comes right down to it, they are being used.

Jonathan Alter of *Newsweek* (February 25) writes: "In theory, reporters in democratic societies work independent of propaganda. In practice they are treated during war as simply more pieces of military hardware to be deployed. While the allies play it straighter than Iraq, much of the information they release has propaganda value, too." Alter is close to the mark, but the subtlety of his point about the allies playing it straighter than Iraq should not be understated. After all, the U.S. media on the allied side may not have much firsthand military information, but they can tap into government sources, including intelligence sources (ask Bob Woodward), consult experts, and track what Western colleagues are reporting around the world. In other words, they are not isolated, and they are much harder to manipulate than their brethren in Baghdad.

Additionally, behind the information being put out by both sides are two distinctly different governments and societies. It is exactly this difference that the vast majority of the American public seems to understand far better than some journalists. For instance, on February 10, UPI correspondent Leon Daniel stated, "Arnett remains on the job in Baghdad, reporting as best he can under tight restrictions. The Iraqi government evidently decides what the media may report from the other side of the war. Since both governments so tightly manage news coverage of the war, it is important to have journalists of integrity such as Arnett at every possible vantage point."

There is in Daniel's naive statement the same kind of moral equivalence that conservatives railed against during the early 1980s, when the U.S. and Soviet military establishments were treated as equal threats to world peace. This even-handed, "neutral" approach was wrong then, and it is wrong now. As for today's Gulf War, here's a news flash: there is virtually nothing in common between Iraq's practiced attempts to manipulate world opinion and the U.S. government's attempt to protect its operational security. Even the U.S. government's efforts at "spin control" are a far cry from the totalitarian control of society through a secret police apparatus that makes the KGB look amateurish. U.S. reporters can permeate their government, and, in the end, they can write what they want.

If U.S. reporters deserve the public's ire for anything, it is for their pathetic failure to provide context when conveying information from both sides. Why not paint the truth in vivid terms. For instance, a reporter could say, "Baghdad Radio, the mouthpiece of Saddam Hussein's government, reported today that . . ." Television reporters could also add context to video coming out of Baghdad. Instead of flashing "cleared by the Iraqi government," why not point out that the reason reporters stationed in Iraq have had to travel so far for so few pictures of civilian casualties is that the allies are taking pains to avoid such casualties. In the case of the U.S. bombing of an Iraqi bunker on February 13, Stephen Hess of the Brookings Institution told the *Washington Times* (February 14), "Journalists have not accepted the basic distinction that Saddam Hussein's targets were civilians while the U.S. targets were military, in which unfortunately civilians may have died." Professor Ted J. Smith of Virginia Commonwealth University added, "We've seen throughout the impossibility of journalists functioning as journalists from an enemy capital in time of war. By being there and insisting on Western standards of journalistic neutrality . . . not objectivity . . . they've set themselves up for use in war propaganda."

Newsweek's Alter provides one clear example: "Iraq has been polishing up its propaganda game for years. A woman wailing in TV-perfect English about civilian casualties turned out, as CNN later reported, to be an Iraqi official. (She also showed up on French TV wailing in French.)" Did the "seasoned, professional" Arnett not suspect that he was being set up? Maybe the Iraqis gave him no choice. But then again, Arnett does have a choice: he can turn off the camera and not file at all when he realizes he is being manipulated.

On ABC's "World News Tonight" (February 11), Bill Blakemore, reporting from Baghdad, stated, "The script process is very normal for wartime, I would say . . . We write our scripts, we find one of the censors who's down in the hotel lobby, and we show it to the censor, who reads it, and sometimes there's a slight change of a word here or there. Very often you may say something you didn't realize would touch a sensitivity, but there's not been any kind of heavy censorship in my experience here so far. It's a fairly easy understanding we have." Reporters have no such "easy understanding." If they did, they would understand the need to make distinctions, provide context, and to realize that they are being manipulated—a lot more on one side than on the other. Moreover, nothing is normal in wartime.

The Issue of Neutrality

John Corry

Almost unremarked, we have passed a turning point in journalism, particularly as journalism is practiced on television. Exactly when this happened is unclear—although by the 1980s there were hints—but American broadcasts from Baghdad while American warplanes flew overhead finally made it certain. The old journalistic ideal of objectivity—the sense that reporting involves the gathering and presentation of relevant facts after appropriate critical analysis—had given way to a more porous standard. According to this new standard, reporters may—indeed should—stand midway between two opposing sides, even when one of the two sides is their own.

This is no academic matter. Neutrality is now a principle of American journalism, explicitly stated and solemnly embraced. After Dan Rather of CBS reported from Saudi Arabia last August that "our tanks are arriving," *The Washington Post* gave him a call: wasn't it jingoistic, perhaps xenophobic, to say "our tanks"? Rather apologized and promised he would never say such a thing again. He should have known better in the first place. After all, Mike Wallace, Rather's CBS colleague, made the new standard clear well before the gulf crisis started. At a conference on the military and the press at Columbia University on October 31, 1987, Wallace announced that it would be appropriate for him as a journalist to accompany enemy troops into battle, even if they ambushed American soldiers. And during the war itself, Bernard Shaw of CNN, explaining why he had refused to be debriefed by American officials after he left Baghdad, declared that reporters must be "neutral."

As it happens, Shaw once said that the late Edward R. Murrow of CBS was his great hero. Indeed, a whole generation of television newsmen regard Murrow as their hero, invoking his name every time they give one another an award. They ought to go back now and listen

362

to his broadcasts. In the Battle of Britain and other engagements, Murrow was outspoken about which side he was on, and he was never a neutral reporter. It would have been unthinkable for him in 1944, say, to make his way to Berlin, check into the Adlon Hotel, and pass on pronouncements by Hitler.

Still, this is the New World Order, and rules everywhere are changing. The great place to be for television journalists this winter was the Al Rashid Hotel in Baghdad, in the basement of which, according to the Pentagon, was a command-and-control center, although the journalists holed up there were (neutrally) unable to find it.

Colleagues did complain when Peter Arnett of CNN stayed on in Baghdad after other journalists had been expelled; the complaints, however, were not so much about whether CNN (which has outlets in 104 countries) was acting as a broadcasting service for Saddam Hussein as about whether it was taking advantage of its competitors. When CBS, ABC, and NBC got their own correspondents into Baghdad, the complaints ended.

"You must avoid the appearance of cheerleading," Ed Turner, the vice president of CNN, said during the war. "We are, after all, at CNN, a global network." Turner, no relation to his boss Ted Turner, although obviously they think alike, went on to stress that CNN wanted to be fair to *all* nations. But the truth was that CNN had a mission. Speaking from Baghdad, Arnett told us what it was:

> I know it's Ted Turner's vision to get CNN around the world, and we can prevent events like this from occurring in the future. I know that is my wish after covering wars all over and conflicts all over the world. I mean, I am sick of wars, and I am here because maybe my contribution will somehow lessen the hostilities, if not this time, maybe next time.

Old-style journalists grew sick of wars, too, although few thought their presence would prevent them. New-style neutral journalists, however, have their conceits, and the constraints that bind fellow citizens are not necessarily binding on them. At the Columbia conference, Mike Wallace was asked if a "higher duty as an American citizen" did not take precedence over the duty of a journalist. "No," Wallace replied, "you don't have that higher duty—no, no." But if a neutral journalist does not owe a higher duty to citizenship, where does his higher duty lie? Old-style journalists seldom thought about that. A story was a story, and a reporter went out and reported it. Our age is self-consciously moral, though, and higher duties now weigh on us all. Arnett was clear about his higher duty, even without being asked. "I don't work for the national interest," he asserted in another broadcast from Baghdad. "I work for the public interest."

And it may be here that neutral journalism flies apart and breaks up into shards. What is this public interest, and who determines it, anyway? The national interest is determined by consensus and people are elected to serve it. The recent consensus was that the U.S. national interest lay in driving Iraq out of Kuwait and decimating its war machine. But the public interest is amorphous and usually it turns out to be closer to the interest of its advocates than to that of the public.

Consider the performances in Baghdad. The correspondents there could not gather relevant facts, and if they had tried, they would have been expelled, or worse, from Iraq. What the correspondents did was listen to government-controlled Baghdad Radio (with a translator, presumably; none of the correspondents seemed to speak Arabic), tour Baghdad neighborhoods (with government guides and monitors), and in the fashion of journalists everywhere, pick up what they could from other correspondents they met.

There is not much chance to do real reporting in a situation like that, and most of the time, one suspects, the correspondents knew it. Anchormen pressed them on questions they could not possibly answer. Tell me, Peter (or Bill, or Tom, or Betsy), an anchor would ask, how do Iraqis feel about this statement from President Bush? And Peter (or Bill, or Tom, or Betsy), from a cubicle in a hotel, an eight-

364

hour time difference away, in a country whose language he did not understand, would reply as best he could.

The most accurate reply would have been, "I don't know," but you cannot say that very often and keep your job in television. So the reporting from Baghdad inevitably turned into an exercise by the correspondent in appearing to know something when he probably did not know much, while bearing in mind that he could not offend the host government.

Obvious questions arise: what if a correspondent in Baghdad had discovered something the host government did not want revealed? What if a correspondent had uncovered news about a party purge, or an outbreak of civil disorder, or the whereabouts of Saddam Hussein? Or—and this is not far fetched—what if a correspondent, being bused from Baghdad to Basra, had come across an artillery battery with shells loaded with nerve gas and pointed toward U.S. Marines? The profession was uncomfortable with questions like that. Nonetheless, they could not be entirely ignored, and obliquely the correspondents in Baghdad addressed them. Were they, for example, holding back information?

"There are lots of things that you can't report," Betsy Aaron of CBS acknowledged. "If you do, you are asked to leave the country, and I don't think we want to do that. I think you do a very valuable service reporting, no matter what you are allowed to report."

No matter what you are allowed to report? Imagine Ed Murrow saying that. Neutral journalism assumes that what the reporter reports is not nearly as important as the fact that the reporter is there to report it. Journalism becomes a symbolic act, distinguished by form and not content. Operate under that standard, and censorship will not be a problem. Here is Bill Blakemore, speaking over ABC from Baghdad:

> The script process is very normal for wartime, I would say. We write our scripts. We find one of the censors who's down in the hotel lobby, and we show it to the censor who reads it, and sometimes there's a slight

change of a word here or there. Very often you may say something you didn't realize would touch a sensitivity, but there's not been any kind of heavy censorship in my experience here so far. It's a fairly easy understanding we have.

Clearly, the "fairly easy understanding" between correspondents and one of the world's most repressive governments meant that the correspondents simply censored themselves. If they were uncertain how to do this, they could always get help. Here is Blakemore again, in an exchange with his anchorman, Peter Jennings:

"Bill, are you operating on a completely uncensored basis?" Jennings whimsically asked.

No, Blakemore responded, "we got organized just now and managed to get somebody over here to listen and make sure we don't have any military or strategic information."

Neutral status means that a journalist does not report objectively; he reports selectively. Arnett, visiting what had been Baghdad's two main power plants, now destroyed by bombs and missiles, spoke of "relentless attacks on civilian installations." He did not mention that those installations had been covered in camouflage paint. When he reported on the famous target that the Pentagon said was a biological-weapons factory and the Iraqis claimed was a "baby-milk plant"—"innocent enough from what we could see," observed Arnett—he did not notice the camouflage there, either. (Visiting German peace activists, of all people, did notice it and talked about it when they got back to Europe.) After being taken to another bombed-out site, Arnett reported that "while we were there, a distraught woman shouted insults at the press and vented anger at the West." Then we saw and heard the woman, who was standing next to a crater. "All of you are responsible, all of you, bombing the people for the sake of oil," she screamed in perfect English. She also turned up on French television speaking perfect French. Several days later, a CNN anchor in Atlanta identified her as an employee of the Iraqi Foreign Ministry.

Arnett, an old hand at covering wars and seeing through propaganda, presumably knew that when the "distraught woman" was shouting. Surely he at least noticed that her jogging suit had "United Nations" printed down one leg. A neutral journalist must narrow his vision and report with one eye closed.

The Baghdad correspondents, as individuals or as a group, most likely will sweep this year's television-journalism prizes. A claque formed almost immediately for Arnett, heaping encomiums on his head (especially after his patriotism was questioned by Sen. Alan Simpson). He was a "dukes-up guy," "brave" and "independent," and an ornament to his profession. In the true spirit of neutral journalism, government-controlled Iraqi newsmen joined the claque, too. "The Iraqi press wrote favorably about me," Arnett told Larry King, the CNN talk show host, who interviewed him when the war was over. Arnett also said he had become a "third-world hero."

Certainly Arnett and the other Baghdad correspondents displayed physical bravery in placing themselves in a war zone; and they did report, loosely speaking, to the best of their abilities. On the other hand, the correspondents as individuals were incidental. If there had not been Peter, Bill, Tom, or Betsy, there would have been John, Morton, Arthur, or Susan, and the "reporting" would have been much the same. For them, the great thing was that anyone was in Baghdad at all, and it did not matter that a great many other Americans were disturbed. When a *Washington Post*-ABC News poll asked if we should bomb a communications center in the Baghdad hotel where the reporters were staying, 62 percent of the respondents said we should issue a warning and then bomb even if the reporters were still there; 5 percent said we should forget the warning and just go ahead with the bombing.

In fact, the press as a whole did not come off well in the war. Television tarred more reliable print, and polls showed a huge dislike of the media. The essential reason was captured by the headline over a story in *Time* about disenchantment with the press: "Just Whose Side Are They On?" The "they," of course, were journalists, and simply by raising the question *Time* went a long way toward providing the answer, even though the story itself predictably took a different position: "The attacks from both sides probably mean that the press is situated just about where it usually is: in the even-handed middle ground."

Well, perhaps, but the even-handed middle ground becomes an increasingly elusive place in the television age. There were no American reporters in Kuwait when Iraq salted and pillaged that country; it was not in Iraq's interest to have them there. It was in Iraq's interest, however, to have reporters in Baghdad; when the war was over, Iraq kicked them out. Could the press have found a more even-handed middle ground here? Why, yes. It could have insisted that if it was going to be in Baghdad it must also be in Kuwait. Obviously, no network did insist on that.

The principal signs of television's search for a middle ground were "cleared by censor" titles; they were even-handedly applied to film approved by either American or Iraqi censors, showing skepticism of both sides. But the new neutral journalism also went a long way toward suggesting which side it was the more skeptical of. As long ago as last August, Michael Gartner, the president of NBC News, in a piece for the op-ed page of *The Wall Street Journal,* had alerted us to danger: "Here's something you should know about the war that's going on in the gulf: much of the news that you read or hear or see is being censored."

Actually, the American part of the war had not begun yet, but that did not deter Gartner. He went on to quote, disdainfully, from a list of things the Pentagon did not want us to know. They included:

(1) Number of troops
(2) Number of aircraft
(3) Number of other equipment (e.g.,artillery, tanks, radars, trucks, water "buffaloes," etc.)
(4) Names of military installations/geographic locations of U.S. military units in Saudi Arabia
(5) Information regarding future operations
(6) Information concerning security precautions at military installations in Saudi Arabia

And so on, ending with "(9) Photography that would show level of security at military installations in Saudi Arabia" and "(10) Photography that would reveal the name of specific locations of military forces or installations."

While it would be easy to dismiss Gartner as merely frivolous, it may be assumed that his peculiar ideas about censorship and war and the military and the press got passed on to his reporters. Surely they were reflected in an NBC special, "America: The Realities of War," when Arthur Kent, the NBC correspondent in Saudi Arabia, took on Pete Williams, the Pentagon spokesman in Washington.

"Why are you trying to put your hands so far into our business?" Kent asked peevishly. "We're not trying to tell you how to run the war. We're just trying to cover it. Why do you want to control us so completely?"

Williams did not mention Gartner's laundry list of complaints, although if he had he would have made a reasonable argument not just for controlling the press but banning it altogether. Williams did not say either that some of the television coverage was so goofy the Pentagon might have thought its higher duty was to straighten it out. In an interview when the war was over, General H. Norman Schwarzkopf remarked that he had "basically turned the television off in the headquarters very early on because the reporting was so inaccurate I did not want my people to get confused."

On the same program in which he attacked Williams, Kent also offered a choice specimen of the reporting General Schwarzkopf probably had in mind:

"Saddam Hussein is a cunning man, and nowhere does he show that more clearly than on a battlefield when he's under attack," Kent told Faith Daniels, who was anchoring the special.

"And that, Arthur, really seems to be this administration's greatest miscalculation," Daniels replied.

"That's right, Faith," Kent continued. "He is ruthless, but more than ruthless. In the past 11 days, he's surprised us. He's shown us a capable military mind, and he still seems to know exactly what he's doing."

With "reporting" like that, is it any wonder that 57 percent of the respondents in one poll said the military should exercise more, not less, control over the press, and that 88 percent in another poll supported censorship? For, in addition to the other problems—moral, political, and professional—it has created, the neutrality principle has evidently turned many otherwise intelligent people into fools.

Hindsight: Can the Press Be Free in Wartime?

Katharine Seelye and Dick Polman

When Cable News Network anchor Bernard Shaw returned home from Iraq soon after war broke out in the Persian Gulf, he found the U.S. military eager to debrief him. He refused. He was a reporter, he said, and reporters are neutral.

"Who does he think he is?" scoffed Charlton Heston. "Switzerland?"

In a nation at war, the mere claim of neutrality can sound like an act of treason. But despite the common public perception that the news media undercut the allied effort in the gulf, many analysts now insist that most journalists served as virtual mouthpieces for the Pentagon.

Routinely, they say, newspapers and television focused on Defense Department videos of "surgical" strikes—only the successful ones, none of the mishaps—and relied heavily on retired officers reborn as military experts—including, on CNN, Richard V. Secord, who pleaded guilty to perjury in connection with the Iran-contra scandal. One media critic, columnist Richard Reeves, suggested that CNN call itself PNN—the Pentagon News Network.

All this was no accident; it was military strategy. "In Vietnam, the one weapon in the arsenal that the military had no control over was the press," says Bill Kovach, curator of the Nieman Foundation for journalism at Harvard and former Washington bureau chief of *The New York Times*. "But since 1973, every senior officer in the military who had any command responsibility spent time war-gaming on how to control public opinion through controlling the information the press presented."

The payoff came in the gulf.

The military simply overpowered the media from the start, curbing reporters' access to the battlefield and clipping their claws.

"Everybody has been trying to manipulate the media to their side, and the U.S. military has been much better at it than Hussein," said Daniel Hallin of the University of California at San Diego.

"The networks have treated this war as a technical military exercise," which is just how the White House wanted it, said Andrew Tyndall, a former NBC research consultant who publishes a newsletter analyzing network news.

Some of the stuff on the news has been beyond belief: 'We' and 'our troops.' It's symbolic of the whole problem," said Jeff Cohen, director of Fairness & Accuracy in Reporting (FAIR), a left-of-center media-monitoring group. He blamed this coziness in part on what he called the networks' pro-establishment bias.

During the war, Cohen said, the networks "filled air time with one of the most one-sided lists of experts I've ever seen . . . Their idea of 'balance' is to bring in Democrats who support the war, like Stephen Solarz, Les Aspin, and Lee Hamilton."

After monitoring ABC, NBC, and CBS nightly news shows during the first five months before the war, FAIR also concluded that only 1 percent of the gulf coverage dealt with grass-roots opposition to the troop buildup.

Newspapers heard, too, from readers who complained that antiwar activities got short shrift compared with Pentagon war briefings. "There have been numerous antiwar demonstrations throughout Europe, including daily demonstrations in Germany," Karel Kilimnik of Philadelphia wrote *The Inquirer* last week. "Why is this coverage missing from the pages of *The Inquirer*? The U.S. government does not want us to know, but why are journalists accepting these restrictions?"

With as many as 1,400 members of the media in the gulf, the military had a good excuse for imposing order and for imposing restrictions it had been refining since the Grenada invasion of 1983. It denied access to the front, limiting coverage of combat to a greater degree than ever before. All stories were "reviewed." Breaking with tradition, the Pentagon barred media coverage of bodies at Dover Air Force Base.

The military got the coverage it wanted—and won the battle of public opinion as well.

In their defense, media executives say there was a practical reason for using military analysts: The war was a military story. "We go and find the experts who can make sense of it for the viewer," said Ed Turner, vice president for news gathering at CNN. It may have been less apparent in print, but newspapers and magazines often relied on think tanks staffed by former military officers.

Working with the military, on the military's terms, was a necessity. "It's for lack of any other way to get the story out," said Michele Stephenson, picture editor of *Time* magazine. She acknowledged that the media had put themselves in this bind. "We're at fault—we agreed to do it," she said. "But I don't think it will happen again. It's too compromising."

Some analysts suggest that the media also bent over backwards to avoid criticism of a popular war.

"The networks don't want to be caught on the 'wrong' side of this war," Tyndall said.

The networks don't disagree. George Watson, vice president and Washington bureau chief of ABC News, said: "The media are not sitting on another planet. They are American citizens who have opinions, emotions, and beliefs that are generally common in our society. There's a great feeling of pride and patriotism in the country. People in the media share that, by and large."

Until Vietnam, the only war America lost, a patriotic press was the norm in wartime. In World War II, wrote John Steinbeck, reporters were "part of the war effort . . . Not only that, we abetted it . . . The foolish reporter who broke the rules would not be printed at home, and in addition would be put out of the theater by the command."

But in Vietnam—where rosy government reports often conflicted with battlefield realities—reporters' loyalties were called into question. The defining moment came after the 1968 Tet offensive, when a reporter asked Secretary of State Dean Rusk whether Americans had been outfoxed by the Viet Cong. Rusk blew up and yelled, "Whose side are you on, anyway?"

Today, in the wake of the Gulf War, Vietnam looks like an aberration.

"In Vietnam, the press became skeptics because they were being lied to," said Stephen Hess of the Brookings Institution. "This time, I don't think they feel they [were] lied to. It's more a question of just not getting enough information."

Still, many Americans simply don't believe that reporters shilled for the military in the gulf—and if they did, what's wrong with that?

Public opinion, measured by polls and letters to editors, overwhelmingly was that the media were antiwar and had little regard for troop safety.

When *The Inquirer* published a seven-year-old photo of downed navy pilot Jeffrey Zaun of Cherry Hill, scores of peopled phoned to complain that the newspaper had no right to violate an order from the Pentagon to withhold the picture.

To Hess, the public sentiment was easily explainable: "Freedom of the press, freedom of information, is an abstraction. Another basic right—the freedom to defend yourself from death—is not an abstraction. . . . For most people, the priorities aren't very mysterious: First you win the war, *then* you have a free press."

The Republican National Committee traded on these sentiments. It sent 500,000 antipress letters to party contributors, urging them to forward them to their local newspapers.

CNN's Peter Arnett, reporting from Baghdad, served as the lightning rod for much of the public criticism. A massive letter-writing campaign to get Arnett out of Baghdad, where some felt he was a propaganda tool of Saddam Hussein, was orchestrated by Accuracy in Media (AIM), a conservative watchdog group. AIM mailed 100,000 postcards to supporters urging them to demand Arnett's removal.

Reed Irvine of AIM called Arnett's broadcasts "a betrayal of the troops." It was preposterous, he said, for reporters to cling to the quaint idea of a free press while soldiers were risking their lives.

374

Irvine quoted the famous decision by Oliver Wendell Holmes: "When a nation is at war, many things that might be said in time of peace are such a hindrance to its effort that their utterance will not be endured so long as men fight. No court could regard them as protected by any constitutional rights."

The same goes for the press in wartime, Irvine says. "One of the best ways to undermine the home-front morale is to show the horrors of the battlefield. The press is insisting on its right to undermine home-front morale."

To many in the press, Irvine misses the point.

"If we stop asking questions because they might hurt morale," says columnist Reeves, "then we've lost it all. The 200 years have been wasted."

The gulf, for him and others, has become a cautionary tale.

"The press side," says Kovach of the Nieman Foundation, "had better get . . . thinking about how it can do the job it has to do. Otherwise we'll wind up as part of the vast entertainment network."

These issues might not be so difficult for the media if the war hadn't been so popular. "When confidence in the government goes up, confidence in the press goes down," said William Schneider, an analyst with the conservative American Enterprise Institute. "Our national self-confidence, our self-esteem, have gone up enormously. When things are going well, the press looks like it's tearing things down."

Chapter Ten

Implications
for the
Future

What does the Gulf War experience mean for the future of war coverage? Are restrictions similar to those in the gulf to become the standard, and are "pools" to remain the primary means for journalists to cover American forces in combat? Are there lessons for the future? Should we modify old rules, develop new ones, or reexamine how and whether we restrict the press in wartime? How then should the press be managed in wartime, and why did the media not offer any alternatives to the pool system in the Gulf War?

Letter to the Secretary of Defense

Representatives of the Press

April 29, 1991

Dear Mr. Secretary:

Please consider this letter as the first step in a process that we hope will lead to improved combat coverage and improved understanding between the military and the media over our respective functions in a democracy.

The Defense Department seems to think, as Pete Williams put it, that "the press gave the American people the best war coverage they ever had." We strongly disagree.

Our sense is that virtually all major news organizations agree that the flow of information to the public was blocked, impeded, or diminished by the policies and practices of the Department of Defense. Pools did not work. Stories and pictures were late or lost. Access to the men and women in the field was interfered with by a needless system of military escorts and copy review. These conditions meant we could not tell the public the full story of those who fought the nation's battle.

Our cooperation in Pentagon pool arrangements since the Sidle Commission has been based on an understanding that pools would provide emergency coverage of short duration. Clearly, in Desert Storm, the military establishment embraced pools as a long-term way of life. The pool system was used in the Persian Gulf War not to facilitate news coverage but to control it.

We are deeply concerned about the abridgement of our right and role to produce timely, independent reporting of Americans at war. We are apprehensive that, because this war was so successfully prosecuted on the battlefield, the virtual total control that your department exercised over the American press will become a model for the future.

Our organizations are committed to the proposition that this should not be allowed to happen again. We are seeking a course to preserve the acknowledged need for real security without discarding the role of independent journalism that is also vital for our democracy.

We are intent upon not experiencing again the Desert Storm kind of pool system. In fact, there are many who believe no pool system should be agreed to in the future. We cannot accept the limitations on access or the use of monitors to chill reporting. Nor do we want a repeat of the disaster that resulted from unacceptable delays in the transmission of our stories and pictures because of security review requirements.

We have made, and will continue to make, commitments to unilateral coverage. Pentagon coverage guidelines should recognize and facilitate this open coverage, including open access to all American troops and the ability to file expeditiously, without censorship or review.

The signers of this letter met informally at ABC News on April 15 to begin a postwar assessment. The group is not meant as a self-appointed commission to represent all media. We simply felt we had to start somewhere, with a group of manageable size.

We have problems of our own to work out and news organizations are not used to working together. Indeed, an important safeguard to press freedom is that we are so competitive. Nevertheless, we are committed to restoring our general ability to function on the battlefield and we hope that a more sensible method of operating can be achieved.

We hope within the next several weeks to arrange a meeting with you to make our points as specifically as we can, to document them and to offer workable changes.

Sincerely,

Stan Cloud, *Time*; Nicholas Horrock, *Chicago Tribune*; Howell Raines, *The New York Times*; Barbara Cohen, CBS News; Albert R. Hunt, *The Wall Street Journal*; Timothy J. Russert, NBC News; Michael Getler, *The Washington Post*; Clark Hoyt, Knight-Ridder, Inc.; Evan Thomas, *Newsweek*; Andrew Glass, *Cox Newspapers*; Charles Lewis, *Hearst Newspapers*; George Watson, ABC News; William Headline, Cable News Network; Jack Nelson, the *Los Angeles Times*; Jonathan Wolman, Associated Press.

cc: Pete Williams, Marlin Fitzwater, Gen. Colin L. Powell, Adm. Frank B. Kelso II, Gen. Merrill McPeak, Gen. Carl E. Vuono, Gen. Alfred M. Gray

Keeping the News in Step: Are Pentagon Rules Here to Stay?

Jason DeParle

Midway through the air war against Iraq, two words began to reappear in the press, spooking White House aides with ghosts from conflicts past: "credibility gap."

Reporters who had spent months complaining about strict new press restrictions were taking their concerns public, asking what the government was trying to hide. The aides, determined to quell comparisons to Vietnam, began to talk of easing the restraints on what reporters could see or say.

Then reassurance for the administration came from an unlikely quarter—"Saturday Night Live." The NBC show, known for its lampooning of President Bush, began its February 9 broadcast with a skit depicting reporters in a briefing room as comically self-absorbed, with little understanding of national security and even less concern.

After coming in Monday morning, John H. Sununu, the White House chief of staff, picked up the talk of the office and quickly ordered a tape. By the afternoon, aides had hurried a copy to President Bush, offering it as evidence that the public was on their side.

Sole Moment of Doubt

"It was not a trivial component," said a senior White House official, referring to the skit. He said the program "gave us an indication that things weren't being handled too badly."

That closed the book on what government officials have called their only moment of doubt in placing dramatic new restrictions on the way the nation's press covers military operations.

According to interviews and documents examined by *The New York Times* in a six-week review of the press policy, President Bush

381

and his inner circle had vowed from the start of the deployment to the Persian Gulf in mid-August to manage the information flow in a way that supported their political goals. They punctuated that determination on the war's eve with a Pentagon rule limiting all press coverage of combat to officially escorted pools.

Now, when the air bombardment began on January 17, officials turned their attention from formulating the restrictions to putting them into effect, surprising even themselves with the control the system provided.

A Divisive Argument

The details of how that system worked during the six weeks of actual combat, and how officials moved to capitalize on it, have formed the starting point of a divisive argument between the Pentagon and the press over the policy's merits.

"I look at it as a model of how the department ought to function," said Defense Secretary Dick Cheney, the primary architect of the policy, who has said the system provided "better coverage" than "any other war in history."

But representatives of 15 major news organizations complained in a letter to Mr. Cheney last week that "the flow of information to the public was blocked, impeded, or diminished" by the policy.

The signers, who included representatives of *The New York Times*, *The Washington Post*, the Associated Press and the four major television networks, requested a meeting and told Mr. Cheney, "We are intent on not experiencing again the Desert Storm kind of pool system."

Changes and Delays

As the war began, reporters found that censors changed and delayed their copy, while escorts kept them far from the action, and the military police arrested those trying to operate independently. Access to real action was so limited that even when public affairs officials tried to get reporters airborne in B-52s, to curry favorable publicity for the fearsome machines, they were thwarted by suspicious commanders.

With few opportunities to gain first-hand reports, the press responded by giving increased prominence to the official statements and government-issued videotapes being promulgated in briefing rooms in Riyadh and Washington.

Administration officials said that even they had failed to anticipate the power the briefings would take on in shaping public opinion. But they were quick to capitalize on that power, staging elaborate rehearsals for key Pentagon briefers, like Lt. Gen. Thomas W. Kelly. General Kelly recalls that one day's preparation was so complete that he turned to an aide and asked in jest "if they'd passed out the questions in advance" to the journalists, who seemed to be dutifully reading them back to him.

The choreographing of public opinion was in mind even when commanders chose names for the operation's two phases, as Gen. H. Norman Schwarzkopf, the mission's commander, and Gen. Colin L. Powell, chairman of the Joint Chiefs of Staff, huddled with aides and swapped suggestions by telephone. "Desert Sword," "Desert Thunder," and "Desert Strike" all hit the discard before the commanders settled on "Desert Storm."

"'Storm' was appropriate to the type of operation we were planning," said General Powell. "And it kind of had a cute angle to it with 'Stormin' Norman,'" General Schwarzkopf's nickname.

The Rules

Control Exercised Through Pools. The decision to restrict all combat coverage to official pools brought a fundamental tilt in the balance of battlefield power, taking the most basic journalistic decisions out of the hands of correspondents and giving them to commanders.

One set of complaints focused on the review of copy for security violations—a reversal of the Vietnam practice of trusting journalists to comply and expelling those who broke the rules. While Pentagon guidelines stated that escorts would not suppress material "for its potential to express criticism or cause embarrassment," reporters sometimes found otherwise. When the Associated Press reported that navy pilots were watching pornographic films before leaving on missions, an escort deleted it.

A second problem, acknowledged by the military, concerns delays in the military's transmission of reporters' copy. Some dispatches did not arrive until after the war's end.

But the journalists say the most important power the military exercised was the decision over where to send the pools. As Deborah Amos, a correspondent for National Public Radio, put it, this turned officers into assignment editors, determining story lines by dictating what reporters could see.

Circumventing the System

Six days into the air war, for instance, Judd Rose, a correspondent for ABC News, was part of a pool pressing for interviews with pilots. Instead, the reporters were shuttled to the military motor pool, whose commander complained that his "unsung heroes" had not been receiving the publicity they deserved.

As the war progressed, an increasing number of reporters tried to circumvent the pool system, despite some detentions by the military, and their efforts produced some of the war's most memorable reporting. After linking up with the Saudis, Forrest Sawyer, a correspondent for ABC News, became the only reporter of the war to accompany a pilot on a bombing mission.

Mr. Sawyer faults reporters for not resisting the rules sooner and in greater numbers. "I think we were too docile for too long—all of us," he said.

The Briefings

Key to Success: Preparation. The military briefings spoofed by "Saturday Night Live" were so popular with the public that some critics have wondered whether they were part of a preconceived strategy. But Marlin Fitzwater, the White House press secretary, said, "We had no idea how that was going to work."

The cameras seemed to spotlight the reporters' weaknesses, since many had little previous experience with the military. At the same time, the sheer length and frequency of the briefings made the military seem candid, even when the long lists of innocuous statistics, like number of missions flown, added little real knowledge. As one admiring White House official put it, the briefings made the Pentagon seem to be making public "much more information than it was."

Among those staying tuned on a daily basis was the president himself. "There weren't many where he didn't see at least a piece of it," said Mr. Fitzwater. And when the Riyadh briefings got off to a shaky start, with junior officers who seemed to lack confidence and candor, the White House was quick to complain to Pete Williams, Mr. Cheney's chief aide for public affairs. "I did mention that to Pete, and he got higher-ranking guys in there," Mr. Fitzwater said.

Praise for the Performance

In tapping General Kelly for the duty at the Pentagon, General Powell was turning to an officer whose performance as a briefer during the American strike against the Panamanian government had already won White House praise.

By 8 each morning, General Kelly's staff would start to assemble lists of questions that they expected journalists to ask. They were aided by the journalists themselves, who were walking the Pentagon halls and asking such questions all day. Public affairs aides began quietly appending the inquiries to their lists, which they used at the 2 p.m. rehearsal. "I never let on to any of them," said one aide.

With the briefing room's power now clear, other officials also prepared carefully. While rehearsing his important January 23 briefing, General Powell had a nagging concern.

In a few hours he would step in front of television cameras and deliver one of the most confident predictions in American military history. Of the Iraqi Army, he promised, "First we're going to cut it off and then we're going to kill it."

But first he tested the line on an aide, asking, "What do you think?"

"He was concerned it would seem too harsh, too severe," the assistant said.

The War Images

The Bombs Never Missed. Perhaps the most enduring image of the war is the remarkable gun-camera footage of precision bombs, produced not by journalists but by the military. While 90 percent of the bombs dropped on Iraq were the highly inaccurate "dumb bombs," only the precision weapons produced videos, and the American government, unlike the British, never showed one that missed.

"Those videos had an enormous impact on the American public," said David Gergen, who as an aide in the Reagan White House helped pioneer the use of images to form public opinion. Mr. Gergen, now editor at large of *U.S. News & World Report,* said the military set a benchmark for disseminating "a kind of video press release."

Mr. Cheney said he did not think of the tapes as a press release, but added, "I will admit we did clean it up," by removing the audio portions that disclosed the raw sounds of "guys in combat."

Faced with requests for footage of errant bombs, American spokesmen used the same reasonable tone that worked to their advantage throughout the conflict, avoiding a flat No. Mr. Williams, for instance, told journalists on January 21, "I will look into giving you some of that footage."

In recent interviews, officials adopted a tone of innocent forgetfulness.

Mr. Cheney said such tapes would have been "pretty dull, boring stuff."

Mr. Williams said, "That's one that fell through the cracks."

Capt. Ron Wildermuth of the navy, General Schwarzkopf's chief public affairs aide, said the item "was not high on my priorities."

Copter Video Barred

The military also refused to make public vivid videotape of Apache helicopter attacks on Iraqi positions, although when several reporters arrived at a forward unit without their escorts they got an unauthorized viewing from a commander proud of the machines' performance.

John Balzar, of the *Los Angeles Times*, said the tape showed Iraqi soldiers "as big as football players on the T.V. screen." He added: "A guy was hit and you could see him drop and he struggled up. They fired again and the body next to him exploded."

But after his article about the tape appeared, Mr. Balzar said, he was never again allowed near an Apache unit. And top commanders refused repeated requests by other reporters to see the tape.

Capt. Mike Sherman of the navy, who ran the military's Joint Information Bureau in Dhahran, Saudi Arabia, until December, said there was no deliberate attempt to sanitize the war, but agreed that battle footage was scarce. "I didn't see the images I thought I was going to see," he said. "I haven't seen a tank battle yet, have you? Why there weren't any video teams there is beyond me."

Cheney's Rare Blunder

Beyond the briefing room, several official policies also helped keep disturbing images from the television screens, including one that banned cameras from Dover Air Force Base as military coffins arrived.

Another Pentagon policy forbade any spokesman from appearing on television programs beside any of the 16 plaintiffs from a lawsuit challenging the pool system.

387

One of the few blunders in briefing performances acknowledged by administration officials occurred February 23, the night the ground war began. With what struck his colleagues as excessive zeal, Mr. Cheney sternly announced a 48-hour information blackout.

Mr. Fitzwater said he immediately thought it was a mistake. "I watched him on camera, and I said, 'My friends in the press are going to find that a little eager.'"

So did General Schwarzkopf, who called the next day and said, "I got to brief."

By most accounts, Mr. Fitzwater weighed in heavily and got Mr. Cheney reversed. He declined to confirm that directly, but added, "If there are things you can't say, you just go out and say you can't say them. But it's not proper for government to run and hide."

To some in the press corps and some senior officials, however, the memory of that night lingered as a moment when Mr. Cheney's true attitude toward journalists seemed to pop through his habitual Western reserve.

"I think it was uncharacteristic," concluded Mr. Fitzwater. "I'm glad it didn't last."

What Next?

Second Thoughts on Restrictions. Some analysts, like Bill Kovach, curator of the Nieman Foundation at Harvard, have called the policy a watershed that will change the flow of official information not only in the military but throughout the government, increasing officials' power to bend public opinion to their will.

Mr. Kovach argues that such power has been growing for a decade. He cites as other examples Mr. Gergen's work in the Reagan White House, and the use by Mr. Bush's media consultant, Roger Ailes, of negative campaigning during the 1988 presidential election.

The Gulf War policy, Mr. Kovach said, "worked so clearly, so well, and the public accepted it so fully, I think it has established a new standard in terms of the amount of information the government is willing to give its people."

But others see the government's success as a product of particular circumstances unlikely to be repeated. Reporters were unusually constricted in getting to the action, they say, since most of the fighting being done in the air and most of the dying occurred behind enemy lines. After just four days of ground fighting, they say, the pool system was on the verge of collapse. Pool reporters, angered by how long it took the military to review and transmit articles, started filing them directly to their home offices, and reporters not in pools raced into Kuwait and hooked up with American forces on their own.

News Executives Wary

"The way this war was made up made this policy possible," said Rep. Les Aspin, chairman of the House Armed Services Committee, who worked in the Pentagon in the early days of the Vietnam War. "This thing would have blown up in their face if the war had dragged out or you had a lot of casualties."

Since the war's end, the administration's pubic relations professionals—Mr. Williams and Mr. Fitzwater—have said that they now find some of the gulf rules overly restrictive.

Mr. Fitzwater said he was uncomfortable with having officers review articles before publication, adding that he blamed himself for letting such provisions take effect.

"There's something wrong with that," he said. "I don't like the idea of anybody in the government ever reading a piece of copy by a reporter."

Mr. Williams, who also now professes some discomfort about reporters' copy being read by escorts said, "I think the presumption in the future should be against pools." He said they inevitably produced complaints from reporters and headaches for the government.

But some news executives, who are meeting among themselves to forge a counterproposal to the Pentagon press policy, view such talk with suspicion.

"They believe that by saying some nice things about freedom of the press the whole thing will just sort of blow over," said George Watson, Washington bureau chief of ABC News.

Appearing at a recent meeting of the American Society of Newspaper Editors, Brig. Gen. Richard Neal of the Marine Corps, a main briefer in Saudi Arabia, said bluntly, "I can tell you: the pool system is here to stay."

And Mr. Cheney said, "If we had to do it tomorrow, I would start with what we've just done," adding, "We'd be willing to listen to recommendations on how to improve it."

But he went on: "Bottom line is—you've got to accomplish your mission. You've got to do it at the lowest possible cost in terms of American lives. And that takes precedence over how you deal with the press."

Excerpts from the Plaintiff's (Press) Lawsuit Brief

Introduction

This action is about one word: *access*. It does not seek to establish a new right; rather, relief is sought to protect a right which has always existed and which defendants have only recently, and very effectively, denied. Nor does this action seek to establish new legal frontiers. It seeks a declaration that defendants may not impose new restrictions upon a right which has always existed, which defendants until 1983 never questioned, but which defendants now assert does not and has never existed.

Nor do the plaintiffs seek assistance from defendants. They seek only that defendants not prevent them from exercising freedom of the press.

Defendants have imposed a blanket prior restraint on the collection of news in the Persian Gulf. They have set up a system where journalists in the Persian Gulf have been forbidden to gather news about overt activities of U.S. forces unless they are in news pools organized, escorted, and under the control of defendants. Defendants also require that dispatches be subject to censorship in the form of a "security review" prior to filing.

It is an absolutely basic constitutional principle that no prior restraint may be imposed on the press without an overwhelming reason. A prior restraint comes before a court "with a 'heavy presumption' against its constitutionality validity." *New York Times v. United States*, 403 U.S. 722, 724 (1971).

The Defense Department defends the prior restraint based upon plenary military authority under Article II of the Constitution (Defendants' Brief, pg. 23). Their reasons for exercise of the authority are set forth in operating procedures (Defendants' Brief, pg. 2): They are administrative convenience and military security.

As will be elaborated below, the administrative justification for the press restraints is without merit and cannot tip the balance of the presumption against the restrictions.

Nor do defendants satisfy the burden of showing a bona-fide security justification for the press restraints. The evidence before the court, to the contrary, shows that battlefield-tested ground rules used when press had wide and unrestricted access to the battlefield, particularly in Vietnam, met military needs for operational security and safety of the troops, and at the same time the needs of the press.

Here, as in the Pentagon Papers case, the government rests its position on inherent executive powers to protect the national interest. That there "could," "might," or "may" be prejudice to Operation Desert Storm. "But the First Amendment tolerates absolutely no prior judicial restraints of the press predicated upon surmise or conjecture that untoward consequences may result." *New York Times v. United States, supra,* at 726.

Here the government's justification of a security need has been made with no *proof* of a real and existing threat to security. Only such proof can justify a prior restraint. Mere rhetoric cannot overcome the presumption against validity of prior restraints. Evidence is the only commodity which can tip the balance which favors the right of the press to be free of hindrance to access. Defendants have presented none. "In no event may mere conclusions be sufficient . . ." *New York Times v. United States* at 728.

Background

In a drastic departure from the practices observed throughout the history of this nation, including the era of modern warfare and reflected in World War II and the Vietnam War, defendants and their recent predecessors have imposed restrictions on press access to overt military operations of United States armed forces which had formerly been open to the media.

This action seeks to restore press access to the form in which it existed prior to defendants' recent infringements by *inter alia* enjoining restrictions on coverage of the Persian Gulf War issued by the

Department of Defense during the week of January 7, 1991. These restrictions are the most recent of a series of infringements on press freedom by defendants which began with the exclusion of reporters during the United States invasion of Grenada in 1983.

The media pools organized by defendants are rigidly controlled. The pools can accommodate only a fraction of the members of the press who are in the region and wish to cover the war. Membership in the pools has been limited to major media. Even media who qualify to participate in pools must wait weeks, and in some cases months, to rotate through the pools.

Management and selection of pools has been delegated to members of the press, allowing private citizens to exercise governmental authority, sometimes against their competitors.

This system is a drastic departure from the system of open access practiced by the military prior to the Grenada invasion. Most recently, in Vietnam, correspondents had full access to the field, and dispatches were not subject to censorship. Correspondents followed ground rules developed by the Defense Department to protect the security of military operations and the lives of combatants, rules which the press gladly accepted. The military agreed that in observing the "ground rules," the press satisfied the needs of operational security.

Restrictions on press access began with the total exclusion of the press during the United States invasion of Grenada in 1983. Objections to the military's press blackout of the Grenada invasion resulted in a Directive of the Secretary of Defense to provide press access to all future United States military operations. Where circumstances entailed the need for military secrecy or surprise, a Department of Defense Media Pool would be used in the first waves of operations until full press access could be accommodated.

However, in the two major military operations following the Grenada invasion and creation of the Pool, the invasion of Panama in December, 1989, and the dispatch of forces to the Persian Gulf in August, 1990, the Department of Defense failed to mobilize the Pool despite its public pledges and internal directives. . . .

Excerpts from the Defendant's (Pentagon) Lawsuit Brief

... DoD's Motion to Dismiss. DoD has not moved to dismiss the amended complaint. We contend that NATION has failed to state a claim under the First Amendment upon which relief can be granted, and that its Fifth Amendment claims are nonjusticiable under Article III.

Argument

I. The creation and use of news media pools to provide combat coverage of U.S. forces during the initial stages of Operation Desert Storm does not abridge "NATION'S" First Amendment rights. NATION contends that DoD's creation and use of news media pools to cover U.S. military operations under Operation Desert Storm restricts its access to news, in violation of the First Amendment. Since DoD's guidelines and operating procedures make it clear that the pools have been established "to provide initial combat coverage of U.S. forces," and apply "during the initial stages of U.S. military activities in the Arabian Gulf," the premise of NATION's facial challenge to the pools is that it has a constitutional right of personal "access" to U.S. combat operations in the Gulf whenever and wherever they may occur. See NATION's Memorandum in Support of Motion for Leave to Accelerate Discovery, dated January 16, 1991 ["Pl. Memo"], pp. 4–11. However, as we shall now demonstrate, the First Amendment does not grant NATION such a broad right of access. Therefore, the creation and use of news media pools is not unconstitutional.

A. The First Amendment Does Not Obligate the Government to Provide the Press with "Access" to All Newsworthy Events. The First Amendment protects and maintains the freedom of the press by preventing government intrusion ("Congress shall make no law * * *"); it bars government interference with publication in order "to preserve an uninhibited marketplace of ideas in which truth will ultimately prevail * * *." *Red Lion Broadcasting Co.* v. *FCC*, 395 U.S. 367, 390 (1969). The First Amendment, however, is not defined by convenience of the press. It does not obligate the government affirmatively to assist the press to improve its news gathering or news distribution techniques and methods or to increase the volume or quality of the information it furnishes to the public. The decisions of the Supreme Court teach that otherwise valid government action is not invalidated under the First Amendment merely because it makes more difficult either the obtaining of information by the public or the performance by the press of its functions. . . .

Limitations upon access by the news media to judicial proceedings [such as those referred to in *Branzburg*,] have long been accepted, even though such limitations may make it more difficult for the media to obtain and distribute to the public the fullest information about such proceedings, or may even have the practical effect of excluding certain media entirely. For example, there is little doubt that full television coverage of an important trial would give the public a more graphic, more accurate, and more complete idea of what happens than a mere written or verbal description of the events, particularly because a courtroom has limited space and not every person who wishes to attend can be accommodated or can arrange to be present. But, because of the threats that such coverage poses to a fair trail, court rules prohibiting television coverage consistently have been upheld by the Second Circuit and others courts of appeals against First Amendment challenge. . . .

Even greater restrictions have been sustained in cases dealing with access to government facilities which, unlike courtrooms, normally are not open to the public. In *Pell* v. *Procunier*, 417 U.S. 817 (1974) and *Saxbe* v. *The Washington Post*, 417 U.S. 843 (1974), the Supreme Court held that state and federal regulations which barred press interviews of specific prison inmates did not violate the First Amendment. In reply to the media plaintiffs' assertion in *Pell* that the press has "a right of access to the sources of what is regarded as newsworthy information," 417 U.S. at 829–830, the Supreme Court said (*id.*, at 834–835):

> The First and Fourteenth Amendments bar government from interfering in any way with a free press. The Constitution does not, however, require government to accord the press special access to information not shared by members of the public generally. It is one thing to say that a journalist is free to seek out sources of information not available to members of the general public, that he is entitled to some constitutional protection of the confidentiality of such sources, * * * and that government cannot restrain the publication of news emanating from such sources. * * * It is quite another thing to suggest that the Constitution imposes upon government the affirmative duty to make available to journalists sources of information not available to members of the public generally. That proposition finds no support in the words of the Constitution or in any decision of this Court (footnote omitted). . . .

1. *The historical record.* During the Revolutionary War there was no established "press corps" covering military activities, and newspapers relied almost exclusively on letters from the battlefront and government pronouncements for information. Organized war correspondence similarly was "unheard of" during the War of 1812, although reporters living in the Washington, D.C., area were present when the capital was captured and burned.

The extension of press coverage into actual theaters of war first emerged during the Mexican-American War of 1846–1847. But despite the absence of legal restrictions on reporting this war, almost all the reporters were fighting soldiers who participated in the battles they wrote about.

Civilian war correspondents appeared in large numbers during the Civil War. However, they often stayed behind the lines and gleaned information from officers' conversations. Major battles were fought without any accredited reporters present, and both Northern and Southern generals banished journalists from their camps at one time or another. When General Grant prohibited communications with reporters during the bloody Wilderness Campaign, "[i]t was understood that war correspondents as a class were so far under the authority of the commanding general of the army which they accompanied that he might issue rules and regulations to govern their conduct."

While Civil War reporters usually were able to publish what they pleased, their reports were occasionally censored. Indeed, in 1862 President Lincoln ordered that all telegraph lines be placed under military control, thereby restricting the ability of correspondents to file their stories without submitting to censorship. Some censorship and exclusion of reporters from combat zones occurred during the Spanish-American War as well.

At the beginning of World War I, the English and the French decided to exclude reporters from their armies. Although these policies were relaxed by the time the American Expeditionary Force arrived under the command of Gen. John J. Pershing, American correspondents did not have open access to military activities. General Pershing restricted coverage by initially limiting the number of accredited reporters to 31 and barring travel to the front lines. Censorship was imposed, and reporters who failed to clear their stories had their credentials revoked. Only toward the end of the war were correspondents permitted to accompany American troops into battle.

Immediately after the United States entered World War II, President Roosevelt ordered the creation of an Office of Censorship which published a "Code of Wartime Practice" for the press and broadcast media. The "voluntary" censorship imposed by the codes "meant some sacrifice of the journalistic enterprise of ordinary times." Overseas, the military services censored all dispatches from the theaters of war, using "public information officers" to transmit reporters' stories over lines controlled by the military. Logistics problems limited reporters' access to major battles. "Many—perhaps most—of the war's major actions were, initially at least, reported from rear-echelon headquarters—including the massive D-Day landings of June 6, 1944, in Normandy, when only a handful of reporters went ashore." No reporters covered the Battle of Midway, the successful defense of Bastogne during the Battle of the Bulge, or the dropping of the first atomic bomb on Hiroshima.

The three major picture agencies (Associated Press, Acme, and International News Photo) and *Life* magazine created a photographic pool in early 1942. "Under it, they were to pool their resources, supplying photographers for the war fronts from the staffs of all four organizations, whose pictures were then available to all four."

During the Korean War, correspondents were at the mercy of the military command. Before full censorship was imposed in December, 1950, the command expelled reporters at will. After the correspondents requested, and were made subject to, full and compulsory censorship, they "were placed under the complete jurisdiction of the army, and for any violation of a long list of instructions they could be punished by a series of measures beginning with a suspension of priveleges and extending in extreme cases, to deportation or even trial by courtmartial."

Journalists had much freer access to military activities during the Vietnam War. Nevertheless, of the hundreds of accredited journalists, perhaps 40 were in the field with American troops at any given time. Moreover, reporters occasionally were forbidden to enter operational areas, and their accreditation depended on compliance with guidelines on the release of combat information. Pressure by the government of Thailand resulted in a general ban on access to Thai bases.

In more recent conflicts, press access to military activities has been constricted. When the United States embarked on Operation Fury in Grenada on October 23, 1983, to rescue American medical students and help restore a democratic government, the press was barred from joining the initial assault force. Adm. Wesley McDonald, commander-in-chief of the Atlantic fleet, later explained that "media participation in the operation was restricted initially based on the military assessment of the importance that the element of surprise played in the successful execution of the mission and the consideration of the lives of both hostages and servicemen involved in the operation." On the third day of the operation, 15 pool reporters escorted by the military were permitted to go to Grenada, and that number was expanded the following day. By the fifth day, access restrictions were lifted by the military.

After the Grenada operation, the Chairman of the Joint Chiefs of Staff Media-Military Relations Panel (known as the Sidle Panel) was created to make recommendations on how to conduct military operations in a way that maintains operational security and protects the troops while keeping the American public informed through the media. The chairman of the panel, Maj. Gen. Winant Sidle, U.S.A. (Ret.), recommended among other things that "[w]hen it becomes apparent during military operational planning that news media pooling provides the only feasible means of furnishing the media with early access to an operation, planning should provide for the largest possible press pool that is practical and minimize the length of time the pool will be necessary before 'full coverage' is feasible." He also recommended that DoD study whether to use a "pre-established" pool for certain military operations, and that "a basic tenet governing media access to military operations should be voluntary compliance by the media with security guidelines or ground rules established and issued by the military."

Acting on the recommendations of the Sidle Panel, DoD established a national media pool in 1984. This pool was activated shortly after the United States intervened militarily in Panama on the morning of December 20, 1989.

In sum, the historical record shows that combat operations have not been open to the general public. Rather, access to the battlefield has been limited to accredited correspondents, and even they frequently have been denied access to certain areas and often been subjected to censorship.

The courts, too, have acknowledged the nonpublic nature of military activities. In *Greer* v. *Spock*, 424 U.S. 828, 838 (1976) the Supreme Court observed that it is "the business of a military installation like Fort Dix to train soldiers, not to provide a public forum. A necessary concomitant of the basic function of a military installation has been 'the historically unquestioned power of [its] commanding officer summarily to exclude civilians from his area of command.'" *Accord, Cafeteria Workers* v. *McElroy*, 367 U.S. 886, 890 (1961) ("[t]he control of access to a military base is clearly within the constitutional power granted to both Congress and the President").

Since there is no tradition that the initial stages of U.S. combat activities, such as the combat activities in Operation Desert Storm, "historically ha[ve] been open to the press and general public" (*Globe Newspaper, supra*, 457 U.S. at 605), NATION cannot claim a First Amendment right of personal access to these combat activities. Consequently, DoD's use of news media pools to cover these activities is not unconstitutional. . . .

2. *DoD's decision to use news media pools to cover U.S. combat activities during the initial stages of Operation Desert Storm is an exercise of the plenary authority of the President as Commander-in-Chief in a theater of military operations.* The guidelines, ground rules, and operating procedures that govern the pools are therefore entitled to exceptional deference.

The operating procedures explain the reasons for the pools. The pools "are designed to balance the media's desire for unilateral coverage with the logistics realities of the military operation, which makes it impossible for every media representative to cover every activity of his or her choice, and with CENTCOM's responsibility to maintain operational security, protect the safety of the troops, and prevent interference with military operations." Furthermore, the "purpose and intention of the pool concept is to get media representatives to and from the scene of military action, to get their reports back to the Joint Information Bureau-Dhahran for filing —rapidly and safely—and to permit unilateral media coverage of combat and combat-related activity as soon as possible." The operating procedures emphasize "[t]here is no intention to discriminate among media representatives on the basis of reporting content or viewpoint," and "[f]avoritism or disparate treatment of the media in pool operations by pool coordinators will not be tolerated."

These stated reasons for DoD's use of news media pools are facially legitimate and bona fide. In light of the President's express constitutional authority as Commander-in-Chief to direct military efforts during war, and the traditional limited judicial inquiry available for decisions made with that authority, it is not necessary for this Court to apply the traditional "balancing test" of weighing the importance of news media pools against NATION's claimed First Amendment rights, to decide whether the pools are constitutional. Rather, following the rationale of *Kleindienst* v. *Mandel,* 408 U.S. 753 (1972), the Court's inquiry should end with the threshold determination that the pools are being administered under guidelines, ground rules, and operating procedures that are facially legitimate and bona fide. . . .

III. DoD's use of media pools is necessitated by compelling military interests and is narrowly tailored to serve those interests.
. . . DoD's use of news media pools to cover U.S. combat operations during the initial stages of Operation Desert Storm does not shut off access by the press to these operations. Rather, it controls press access by initially limiting forward area entry to nine newsgathering pools composed of eighteen or seven members each, which all news media are welcome to join. Such control in a war zone plainly is a "compelling governmental interest." There are obvious logistical problems of transportation, communication, and safety which, as the operating procedures state, 'make it impossible for every media representative to cover every activity of his or her own choice." More importantly, with more than 900 media representatives currently in the Arabian Gulf area, unlimited access by every media representative to all combat operations would make it impossible for the military to fulfill its overriding responsibility "to maintain operational security, protect the safety of the troops, and prevent interference with military

operations." It is hard to imagine a more "compelling governmental interest" than this.

Similarly, the news media pool guidelines do not ban publication. Public affairs officers review media pool material before it is released solely to determine if it complies with ground rules protecting "sensitive information about military plans, capabilities, operations, or vulnerabilities." Surely there is a "compelling governmental interest" in taking steps to prevent the publication of this information in wartime.

The use of news media pools is "narrowly tailored" under the guidelines, ground rules, and operating procedures to meet these compelling interests. The use of pools is not intended to be a permanent feature of media coverage of hostilities in the Persian Gulf. The stated intention is "to permit unilateral media coverage of combat and combat-related activity as soon as possible. Furthermore, although the use of pools limits the number of media representatives who will, at any given time, have actual access to the front lines, positions in the pools rotate every two to three weeks. Finally, the rules explicitly state that the review of pool material conducted before release is "solely for its conformance to the attached ground rules, and not for its potential to express criticism or cause embarrassment."

Accordingly, even if the Court were to apply the traditional "balancing" test to DoD's news media pools, they must be sustained against NATION's challenge. As a result, NATION's First Amendment claims must be dismissed.

Excerpts from the Court Opinion

Judge Leonard B. Sand, U.S.D.J.

Introduction and Summary

This is an action by various members of the press challenging regulations promulgated by the United States Department of Defense ("DoD") to govern coverage of military activities of American armed forces overseas during periods of open hostilities. These regulations, adopted after the Vietnam War, were in effect in some form during the Grenada and Panama military operations. In revised form, they were in effect during American military operations Desert Shield (American military presence in the Persian Gulf) and Desert Storm (open hostilities). They were lifted on March 4, 1991, upon the informal cessation of hostilities in the Persian Gulf.

The NATION plaintiffs, in an action commenced on January 10, 1991, prior to the transition from Desert Shield to Desert Storm, have challenged these regulations as being violative of the First and Fifth Amendments. While these regulations are challenged on various grounds, plaintiffs' fundamental claim is that the press has a First Amendment right to unlimited access to a foreign arena in which American military forces are engaged. Plaintiffs urge that the DoD "pooling" regulations, which limit access to the battlefield to a specified number of press representatives and subject them to certain restrictions, infringe on news gathering privileges accorded by the First Amendment. The primary focus of plaintiffs' challenge is on the question of access and not primarily on those restrictions which limit, for national security reasons, the information that pool members may publish.

DoD argues that the First Amendment does not bar the government from restricting access to combat activities and that the regulations are narrowly tailored and necessitated by compelling national security concerns. No party or amicus questions the applicability of the First Amendment to regulations imposed on American press representatives by the DoD governing actions overseas.

The issues raised by this challenge present profound and novel questions as to the existence and scope of a First Amendment right of access in the context of military operations and national security concerns. Those few precedents which have discussed First Amendment issues in the context of national security have been "prior restraint" cases. See *Near v. Minnesota*, 283 U.S. 697, 716 (1931) (prior restraint presumed unconstitutional, though "no one would question but that a government might prevent actual obstruction to its recruiting service or the publication of the sailing dates of transports or the number and location of troops"); *New York Times Co. v. United States*, 403 U.S. 713, 722–23 (1971) (the Pentagon Papers case). Cases addressing a right of access have arisen in the context of such fora as a courtroom, a prison, and a campaign headquarters. . . . No previous cases deal on the merits with a right of access to a battlefield. The closest, but hardly controlling analogies, are those cases which have upheld the exclusion of the press and public from military bases. See, e.g., *Greer v. Spock*, 424 U.S. 828, 838–40 (1976).

The basic question of access to the battlefield raised in this case is a significant matter of first impression. However, before a federal court may adjudicate an issue on the merits, various threshold questions must be resolved in plaintiffs' favor. Indeed, DoD asserts that for several reasons this Court should dismiss the complaint without reaching the merits. DoD's first contention is that plaintiffs have no standing to raise these issues since there has been no showing that they were in fact excluded from admission to any media pool. The Court finds this argument to be without merit. Whatever validity this claim may have had at the outset of this litigation was dissipated when, as discussed below, Agence France-Presse ("AFP") was in fact excluded from a pool and joined this suit.

The second ground on which DoD suggests this Court should decline to hear the merits of the controversy is the political question doctrine. DoD urges that the questions presented are non-justiciable because the United State Constitution designates the President as the Commander-in-Chief of the Armed Forces. For this reason, DoD claims that a federal court may not review determinations made by the Executive Branch in a military context, even when First Amendment rights are implicated. The Court rejects this contention for the reasons stated below.

Third, and most strenuously, DoD urges that once the regulations were lifted this controversy became moot and therefore non-justiciable. In resolving the question of mootness, a court must answer two discrete questions. First, is there in fact an ongoing controversy? This may be found to exist if the challenged conduct is either continuing or is "capable of repetition, yet evading review" ... To meet the "capable of repetition, yet evading review" requirements, the court must find that the challenged action was too short in its duration to be fully litigated and that there is a "reasonable expectation" that the party bringing the suit will "be subjected to the same actions again" . . . For the reasons discussed below, we conclude that this controversy survives a challenge of mootness on these grounds. However, this conclusion resolves only the first of the two mootness issues present in this case—namely, that the Court has jurisdiction and the power to determine the questions presented.

The second, more delicate and troublesome mootness inquiry is whether, in an action such as this, where plaintiffs seek both declarative and injunctive relief, the court should in its discretion exercise such power to adjudicate the merits of the dispute. For a number of reasons more fully stated below, we conclude that such power should not be exercised in this case. We base this conclusion primarily on the abstract nature of the important issues now before the Court. We conclude that this Court cannot now determine that some limitation on the number of journalists granted access to a battlefield in the *next* overseas military operation may not be a reasonable time, place, and manner restriction, valid under the First and Fifth Amendments. Since we find the issues as here presented to be too abstract and conjectural for judicial resolution the Court, on this ground, grants DoD's motion to dismiss the complaint. . . .

Discussion

. . . In this case, the question is whether any constitutional right asserted by the plaintiffs involves the activities of the United States military, and if so, whether this Court's review of the claim on the merits would conflict with separation of powers principles, which assign this country's military matters to the legislative and executive branches of government. There is a long line of cases addressing the role of the judiciary in reviewing military decisions made by the Executive Branch pursuant to its Article II powers under the Constitution. The message is clear. Civilian courts should "hesitate long before entertaining a suit which asks the court to tamper with the . . . necessarily unique structure of the Military Establishment." *Chappell v. Wallace*, 462 U.S. 296, 300 (1983).

. . . In cases evaluating whether the political question doctrine bars review of military decisions, the Supreme Court has almost always declined to reach the merits of these cases. Yet, each of the cases involved direct challenges to the institutional functioning of the military in such areas as the relationship between personnel, discipline, and training. . . .

In this case, there is no challenge to this country's military establishment, its goals, directives or tactics. As such, the President's Article II powers as Commander-in-Chief are not implicated because resolution of the question does not impact upon the internal functioning and operation of the military. Certainly this Court would have neither the power nor the inclination to review a military determination that the presence of a large cadre of press representatives at a particular time and place would jeopardize the covert nature of a military operation. This might occur, for example, if all of the press corps suddenly left one area where amphibious landings were being practiced to deceive the enemy and moved to another area where a

406

flanking ground action was poised to take the enemy by surprise. But here the press is not challenging exclusion from covert operations. Rather, it claims that the regulations do not represent a fact-specific tactical or strategic decision, but rather are "blanket" regulations which apply with equal force to access to battlefields where overt actions are in progress.

Accordingly, this Court concludes that the question of what restrictions may be placed on press access to combat zones is not "committed by the text of the Constitution to a coordinate branch of government" . . . Nor does the question impact upon the foreign relations power by interfering with United States relations with a foreign sovereign, such as Saudi Arabia. The two central issues in this case—press access and inequality of treatment of different press organizations—relate primarily to CENTCOM management of the United States press covering United States military operations and have only an incidental relationship to American policy towards Saudi Arabia or other nations.

Furthermore, it cannot be said that plaintiffs have failed to allege a judicially enforceable right, or that enforcement of the rights raised by plaintiffs would require this Court to move beyond areas of traditional judicial expertise. The historic competence of the federal judiciary to address questions of First Amendment freedoms and equal protection is clear. . . . What is alleged by members of the press is the violation by the United States government of a judicially enforceable right under the First and Fifth Amendments. Plaintiffs seek to be freed from government interference in gathering and reporting news involving events that occur during an overt military operation, such as that in the Persian Gulf.

The Court concludes that plaintiffs' complaint alleges claims that are judicially enforceable under the First and Fifth Amendments. We find unpersuasive DoD's primary argument that the political question doctrine bars an Article III court from adjudicating any claims that involve the United States military. Under this theory of separation of powers, a court would lack jurisdiction to hear any controversy that involved DoD, including any government actions that violated the rights of nonmilitary personnel. This reasoning is inconsistent with large bodies of constitutional law. . . .

The most difficult of the justiciability questions raised in this action is whether the case may survive a mootness challenge. Defendant has the burden of proving that a case has become moot by virtue of events subsequent to the filing of the complaint. DoD urges that this has occurred. DoD, furthermore, claims that none of the well recognized exceptions to the mootness doctrine are applicable in this case. Finally, defendant suggests that even if the Court determines that the case is not moot, plaintiffs' request for equitable relief in the form of a declaratory judgment, which is at all times a matter within the Court's discretion, should be denied since the claims are not presented in a concrete and focused manner. For reasons that require some exposition, we conclude, based on all the circumstances of the case, that this controversy is not now sufficiently concrete and focused to permit adjudication on the merits.

Generally, a case becomes moot when the issues "presented are no longer live or the parties lack a legally cognizable interest in the outcome" . . . In other words, a case fails to meet Article III case and controversy requirements and to satisfy related prudential concerns when the passage of time has caused it to lose "its character as a . . . controversy of the kind that must exist if [the Court is] to avoid advisory opinions on abstract propositions of law" . . .

The question for this Court is whether any of plaintiffs' outstanding claims survive under the "capable of repetition, yet evading review" test. The war in the Persian Gulf, like many recent military conflicts involving the United States, was short and swift. Even with efforts by all parties, the judicial process often will not be able to resolve legal controversies such as this before hostilities have ceased. . . . As such, this Court concludes that the controversy engendered by the CENTCOM regulations did not "last long enough for complete judicial review" . . . Because of the speed with which recent wars have terminated, as is clearly documented by the sequence of events in

Panama and Grenada, the "evading review" test outlined in *Weinstein*, 423 U.S. at 149, is satisfied.

The more difficult question is whether there is a reasonable expectation that the "same parties" will be "litigating the same issues" when the United States next engages in a military operation overseas. DoD has admitted that the CENTCOM regulations have been "lifted" but remain in place and may be reactivated. In fact, during the last three military efforts of the United States abroad, various types of pooling arrangements were utilized and the government concedes it is likely to follow this format in the future. . . . Given these facts, it is not unreasonable to suppose that in future military activities DoD will behave in a manner that is susceptible to the same challenges as those raised in this complaint. Furthermore, it takes little imagination to assume that the NATION and AFP, both of which have a long history of covering wartime stories, will be seeking to report the news during the next conflict.

There is, however, a caveat. No two sets of pooling regulations will be identical nor will their application be the same since the nature of modern warfare is such that each conflict is different. DoD has asserted that its press regulations are under review now, as they were after Panama and Grenada, and that revisions will reflect, to the extent DoD deems appropriate, suggestions made by the press. Thus, the possibility exists that precise repetition may not occur. . . .

At issue in this action are important First Amendment principles and the countervailing national security interests of this country. This case presents a novel question since the right of the American public to be informed about the functioning of government and the need to limit information availability for reasons of national security both have a secure place in this country's constitutional history. In short, this case involves the adjudication of important constitutional principles. The question, however, is not only which principles apply and the weighing of the principles, but also when and in what circumstances it is best to consider the questions. In determining whether to exercise its power to hear plaintiffs' claims for declaratory relief, the

Court must evaluate each of the underlying claims in the context of existing First and Fifth Amendment doctrine to consider if the issues, at this time, are presented in a "clean-cut and concrete form." *Rescue Army*, 331 U.S. at 584.

... **Right of Access.** The gravamen of plaintiffs' complaint is that, under the First Amendment, the press has a right to gather and report news that involves United States military operations and that DoD's pool regulations are an unconstitutional limitation on access to observe events as they occur. Plaintiffs suggest that this action does not seek to establish a new right or open new constitutional frontiers since no access is sought that involves military plans, secrets, operational information, or strategic sessions. In other words, plaintiffs claim that no affirmative assistance from the government is being requested, only the freedom from interference to report on what is overtly happening in an allegedly open area. Contrary to what plaintiffs suggest, this Court finds the question to be one of first impression, the answer to which would require charting new constitutional territory.

The Supreme Court has on a number of occasions considered the relationship between the First Amendment and national security. See *Near*, 283 U.S. at 716; *New York Times Co.*, 403 U.S. at 722–23; *Snepp v. United States*, 444 U.S. 507, 514–15 (1980). None of these cases, however, has addressed directly the role and limits of news gathering under the First Amendment in a military context abroad. Nonetheless, there is no dearth of case law on questions involving the access rights of the press and public in other circumstances. As in most cases involving novel issues, the Court must reason by analogy. It is certain that there is no right of access of the press to fora which have traditionally been characterized as private or closed to the public, such as meetings involving the internal discussions of government officials. See *United States v. Nixon*, 418 U.S. 683, 705 n.15 (1974). Limitations may also be placed on access to government controlled institutions, such as prisons and military bases. . . .

On the other hand, there is an almost absolute right of access to open places, including such fora as streets and parks. . . . In recent times the Supreme Court has been particularly generous in interpreting the scope of the public's right under the First Amendment to know about government functioning, at least in such fora as a criminal trial. See *Richmond Newspapers, Inc.*, 448 U.S. at 564. In these cases, there appears to be some indication that the basis for such a right of access could apply more broadly. See *Globe Newspaper Co. v. Superior Court for County of Norfolk*, 457 U.S. 596, 606 (1982).

A fundamental theme is the importance of an informed American citizenry. As the Court wrote, guaranteed access of the public to occurrences in a courtroom during a criminal trial assures "freedom of communication on matters relating to the functioning of government." *Richmond Newspapers*, 448 U.S. at 575. Learning about, criticizing, and evaluating government, the Supreme Court has reasoned, requires some "right to receive" information and ideas. *Martin v. City of Struthers*, 319 U.S. 141, 143 (1943). In *Globe*, the Court devoted extensive attention to the importance of this "checking function" against abuse of government power. See Blasi, "The Checking Value in First Amendment Theory," 1977 Am. B. Found. Research J. 521, 593. This theme has been echoed by the Supreme Court even when the government has suggested that national security concerns were implicated. See *New York Times Co.*, 403 U.S. at 728 (Stewart, J. concurring) (". . . [w]ithout an informed and free press, there can not be an enlightened people.")

Given the broad grounds invoked in these holdings, the affirmative right to gather news, ideas, and information is certainly strengthened by these cases. By protecting the press, the flow of information to the public is preserved. As the Supreme Court has observed, "the First Amendment goes beyond protection of the press and the self-expression of individuals to prohibit government from limiting the stock of information from which members of the public may draw." *First National Bank v. Bellotti*, 435 U.S. 765, 783 (1978). Viewing these cases collectively, it is arguable that generally there is at least some

411

minimal constitutional right to access. See *Branzburg v. Hayes*, 408 U.S. 665, 681 (1972) ("without some protection for seeking out the news, freedom of the press could be eviscerated.")

If the reasoning of these recent access cases were followed in a military context, there is support for the proposition that the press has at least some minimal right of access to view and report about major events that affect the functioning of government, including, for example, an overt combat operation. As such, the government could not wholly exclude the press from a land area where a war is occurring that involves this country. But this conclusion is far from certain since military operations are not closely akin to a building such as a prison, nor to a park or a courtroom.

In order to decide this case on the merits, it would be necessary to define the outer constitutional boundaries of access. Pursuant to long-settled policy in the disposition of constitutional questions, courts should refrain from deciding issues presented in a highly abstract form, especially in instances where the Supreme Court has not articulated guiding standards. See *Rescue Army*, 331 U.S. at 575–85. Since the principles at stake are important and require a delicate balancing, prudence dictates that we leave the definition of the exact parameters of press access to military operations abroad for a later date when a full record is available, in the unfortunate event that there is another military operation. Accordingly, the Court declines to exercise its power to grant plaintiffs' request for declaratory relief on their right of access claim.

Pooling as an Access Limitation. The second claim which this Court must determine whether it will decide on the merits involves the question of limitations on access. Plaintiffs suggest that the government gave some members of the press preferential treatment in the form of financial assistance and more extensive access to events as they occurred. Again, the Court is being asked to provide declaratory relief that a set of regulations, though lifted, are unconstitutional on their face. It is questionable whether any inquiry would be sufficiently focused to pass muster under *Rescue Army*. *Id.* A brief discussion of the underlying law is useful to identify the difficulty facing this Court were it to decide this portion of the case on the merits.

In the instant case, the government chose to grant some access to the press for purposes of covering military activities in the Persian Gulf. By opening the door, albeit in a limited manner, the government created a place for expressive activity. Establishing pools for coverage of the "initial stages" of the Persian Gulf conflict, the government, in essence, determined that the war theater was a limited public forum. ... Regardless of whether the government is constitutionally required to open the battlefield to the press as representatives of the public, a question that this Court has declined to decide, once the government does so it is bound to do so in a nondiscriminatory manner. ...

Once a limited public forum has been created, the government is under an obligation to insure that "access not be denied arbitrarily or for less than compelling reasons." *Sherrill v. Knight*, 569 F.2d 124, 129 (D.C. Cir. 1977); ... Restrictions on newsgathering must generally be no more "arduous than necessary, and ... individual news [persons] may not be arbitrarily excluded from sources of information." *Sherrill*, 569 F.2d at 130; ...

The right of the press to be free from regulations that are discriminatory on their face or as applied, however, is not synonymous with a guaranteed right to gather news at all times and places or in any manner that may be desired. ...

The activities of the press are subject to reasonable time, place, and manner restrictions. ... In reviewing regulations, such as those that are written by DoD for use in a military operation, the Court would inquire whether they are "justified without reference to the content of the regulated speech, that they serve a significant governmental interest, and that in doing so they leave open ample alternative channels for communication of the information." *Heffron*, 452 U.S. at 648.

There is little disagreement, even from plaintiffs, that DoD may place reasonable time, place, and manner restrictions on the press upon showing that there is a significant governmental interest. Yet, when asked at oral argument about how the government may design appropriate non-content-based regulations that had reasonable time, place, and manner restrictions, counsel for the NATION responded, "Fortunately, I don't have to make that decision." Transcript, March 7, 1991, at p. 46. When the Court posed a hypothetical case involving an amphibious landing in a foreign land which assumed the presence of more press representatives than boats to accommodate them, counsel for the NATION had no suggestion on how to decide which members of the media should be included. Instead, arguing that no limitations whatsoever should apply, he explained, "I dare say that if NBC rented [a luxury private yacht] . . . it doesn't impede the [amphibious] military operation." Transcript, March 7, 1991, at p. 53.

Of course plaintiffs' espousal of the view that any journalist wishing access to a battlefield may have such access avoids the necessity to provide for some selection process when either logistics or security concerns may mandate limitation of the number of journalists who may be present. But surely a court ruling on the possible appropriateness of such a restriction for some future military conflict must consider the possibility that at times such circumstances may be present. Who can say that during the next American overseas military operation some restriction on the number of journalists granted access at a particular time to a particular battlefield may not be a reasonable time, place, and manner restriction? Who today can even predict the manner in which the next war may be fought?

The Court, repeatedly and unsuccessfully, pressed plaintiffs to propose specific alternatives to the DoD regulations that the press believe would pass constitutional scrutiny. Except for AFP, whose request for relief is specific but moot (i.e., that it be admitted to the photo pool), plaintiffs' only response was that the press be allowed unlimited unilateral access. Although specifically alerted at an early pretrial conference to the Court's concern about the lack of specificity in the NATION plaintiffs' prayer for relief in the original complaint, and that the Court would carefully scrutinize the then-anticipated amended complaint for proposed specific remedial measures, the

414

amended complaint still lacks specificity. Rather than make specific proposals, such as suggesting that any regulations must include provisions for a speedy administrative review process for those who claim they were improperly excluded from a pool, plaintiffs have adhered to an absolute "no limitation" approach.

In a case of such moment, involving significant and novel constitutional doctrines, the Court must have the benefit of a well-focused controversy. See *Army Rescue*, 331 U.S. at 584. The Court should not now be evaluating a set of regulations that are currently being reviewed for probable revision, to determine their reasonableness in the context of a conflict that does not exist and the precise contours of which are unknown and unknowable. For these reasons, the Court declines to grant plaintiffs' application for declaratory relief on their First and Fifth Amendment equal access claims.

Conclusion

In the Court's view, the right of access claims, and particularly the equal access claims, are not sufficiently in focus at this time to meet the *Rescue Army* requirement that "the underlying constitutional issues [be presented] in a clean-cut and concrete form." See 331 U.S. at 584. For the reasons articulated throughout the Opinion, prudence dictates that a final determination of the important constitutional issues at stake be left for another day when the controversy is more sharply focused. Accordingly, the complaint is dismissed.

Argument

I. Freedom of the Press Is a Fundamental Right and There Is a Presumption Against a Prior Restraint of the Press

The long historical tradition of U.S. press access to overt operations of the U.S. military is uncontroverted. It was never questioned by defendants until 1983.

For the first time in U.S. history, the government suggests in this case that there is no right of access (Defendants' Memorandum pgs. 6, 7, 12). But defendants' arguments are qualified: "The First Amendment . . . does not obligate the government *affirmatively* to assist the press to improve its news gathering or news distribution techniques and methods or to increase the volume or quality of the information it furnishes to the public." (Defendants' brief, pgs. 7–8) (emphasis added). Defendants make further qualifications: "There is no tradition of public 'openness' to the initial stages of U.S. combat operations, and public access to those operations does not serve the type of purpose such access serves with connection with criminal trials." (Defendants' brief, pg. 14).

This action does not seek the government's affirmative assistance to cover overt operations. It seeks to enjoin defendants' interference in media coverage of overt military operations. . . .

Defendants leave the meaning of "initial stages" undefined. The Gulf War operation has been building for seven months. Defendants concede the impropriety of their limitations by saying it is their intention to liberalize their press restraints "as soon as possible" (Defendants' brief, pg. 2). But their promise has neither a date nor substantive description.

This action does not seek to establish a new right or open new constitutional frontiers. Plaintiffs only want to protect a right which has always existed, which defendants always acknowledged (and apparently continue to acknowledge).

416

This action seeks to enjoin government interference with plaintiffs' access to overt events. Not access to plans, not access to secrets, not access to operational information, not access to televise military planning sessions on C-SPAN. Freedom from interference to make one's own way to see what is overtly happening in an open area.

Defendants have recognized that First Amendment rights are fundamental. In both the Sidle Report and the Hoffman Report, as in the repeated statements of official spokespersons, and the challenged regulations themselves, the Department of Defense has enunciated a preference for wide press access. Defendants repeatedly assert that they favor a policy facilitating access by the press. This wisely recognizes the importance of Freedom of the Press. ("[F]reedom of speech and of the press—which are protected by the 1st Amendment from abridgment by Congress—are among the fundamental personal rights and 'liberties' protected by due process clause of the 14th Amendment from impairment by the states." *Gitlow v. New York*, 268 U.S. 652, 666 (1924)). . . .

Defendants here argue the Courts should not become involved (Defendants' brief, pgs. 23, 26, and 31). However, the Defense Department's Sidle Panel left no doubt that it is for a court to decide when an issue about the press's First Amendment rights arises when covering overt activities of the U.S. military . . .

The right of access to news and information about overt combat is a fundamental First Amendment issue. "When the question before the court is a basic confrontation between the First Amendment right to freedom of the press and national security," the information to be published must be looked at in terms of whether there is a "grave and irreparable injury to the public interest." *New York Times v. U.S., supra.*

The application of the doctrine of a right of press access to a courtroom established in *Richmond* and *Globe* is based on the far-reaching concept that the American people have a fundamental right to information about the activities of their government. An ill-informed citizenry is incompatible with effective democracy. Information about the government's conduct in war is no less vital to the process of democratic government. . . .

II. Defendants' Restrictions on the Press Deny Equal Protection of the Law

A. Plaintiffs Have a Right to Equal Access to Cover Military Activities. The denial of access to press in the Gulf violates plaintiffs', their readers', and listeners' constitutional rights guaranteed by the First and Fifth Amendments. . . .

The press pool system set up by defendants as the only means of press access in the Gulf is hopelessly flawed.

The pools' operating procedures set up nine pools, and pool products can only be shared within that pool.

But qualifying to get into one of the pools is "limited to media . . . that have had a long-term presence covering Department of Defense military operations. . . ."

On its face, that criteria excludes all press which do not originate daily spot news in time of peace. If a radio network has relied on a wire service to report Pentagon news in peacetime rather than having its own on-the-scene Pentagon correspondent, it is eliminated from participation in the pools. This restriction excludes *inter alia*, analysis, or feature media . . .

What remains is a pool plan open only to a portion of the U.S. media . . .

B. The Defendants Refusal to Accord Plaintiffs and Other Media Equal Access to Overt Military Activities Violates the Due Process Clause of the Fifth Amendment. The defendants' refusal to accord plaintiffs and other press access to public news sources equal to that which could be had by a tourist traveling in Saudi Arabia, other pool members or "hometowner" invitees, is a denial of equal access . . .

In the present instance, newsgathering has been limited to pools, the pools' membership is limited to an undefined "major" media, those media cannot participate unless they regularly have covered a peacetime Pentagon beat, and even then, media cannot participate in the pools until they have been in the Gulf for at least three weeks.

Journalists conceded a need for operational security and protection of the lives of American troops. But battlefield experience has demonstrated that those legitimate concerns are amply addressed by the Vietnam ground rules which are very similar to those contained in the defendants' 14 Jan. 91 "Operation Desert Shield Ground Rules." While the Vietnam rules may not be the least restrictive means, they are *considerably* less restrictive than the restrictions on access and the censorship provisions of the defendants' 14 Jan. 1991 "Guidelines for New Media." The Vietnam rules have been proven to be sufficiently accommodating of the competing interests of press coverage and tactical security.

Especially in view of the practices in existence prior to October, 1983, it simply cannot be shown that a legitimate governmental interest has arisen to warrant greater restrictions than those used in Vietnam.

The defendants' restriction of plaintiffs to coverage through pools should be declared a denial of equal protection of the law.

Appendices

Appendix 1: Map of the Persian Gulf War Zone

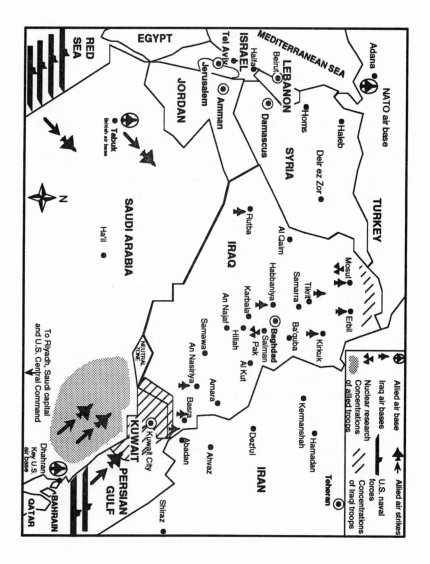

Appendix 2: Gulf Crisis Chronology

July 1990–March 1991

1990

July

18 Broadcast reports accusation by Iraqi Foreign Minister Tariq Aziz that Kuwait had stolen $2.4 billion of Iraqi oil and had built military installations on Iraqi territory.

24 Thirty thousand Iraqi troops are reported to have massed on the Kuwaiti border, rising to 100,000 by the end of July.

26–27 Organization of Petroleum Exporting Countries (OPEC) holds emergency meeting.

August

2 Iraqi forces invade Kuwait. UN Resolution 660 demands the withdrawal of Iraqi forces.

3 Fourteen Arab League states condemn the invasion, as does a joint statement by U.S. Secretary of State James Baker and Soviet Foreign Minister Eduard Schevardnadze. Both the United States and the United Kingdom announce they will send naval forces to the gulf.

6 Saudi Arabia invites allies to reinforce defenses against Iraq. UN Resolution 661 imposes economic sanctions.

7 U.S. troops are committed to the gulf.

8 Iraq annexes Kuwait. France sends naval forces to the gulf.

9 UN Resolution 662 declares Iraq's annexation of Kuwait "null and void" under international law.

10 Twelve of 20 Arab League members approve sending forces to Saudi Arabia.

12: Iraqi President Saddam Hussein links Kuwaiti "occupation" with other Middle East "occupations."

15: Iraq accepts Iranian peace terms ending the Iran-Iraq War.

16: U.S. and U.K. citizens are ordered to surrender to Iraqi authorities, as a "human shield" policy is launched.

18: UN Resolution 664 demands immediate release of all foreigners in Iraq and Kuwait, and insists that Iraq must repeal its order sealing foreign embassies in Kuwait.

25: UN Resolution 665 calls on UN members to join a naval armada to enforce economic sanctions against Iraq.

28: Iraq declares Kuwait the 19th governate of Iraq. Iraq offers to free women and children detainees.

September

1 UN Secretary General Perez de Cuellar and Aziz meet in Amman.

9 President Bush and Soviet President Mikhail Gorbachev meet at the Helsinki Summit.

11 The United Kingdom commits ground forces to the gulf.

25 UN Resolution 670 extends land and sea blockade to include air traffic, except authorized humanitarian aid.

27 Iran and the United Kingdom resume diplomatic relations.

October

9 Oil prices reach $40 a barrel.

29 UN Resolution 674 calls for an immediate end to Iraqi hostage taking and reminds Iraq that it would be liable for "restitution or financial compensation."

November

8 Iraqi chief-of-staff is dismissed and is reported to have been executed. U.S. forces are doubled. Bush explains on November 9 that this will give the United States an "offensive capability."

18 Iraq announces it will free all hostages after December 25. Releases begin earlier.

19 Iraq mobilizes 250,000 more soldiers, bringing the total number of Iraqi forces in southern Iraq and Kuwait to an estimated 700,000.

26 Aziz visits Moscow.

28 Syria and the United Kingdom resume diplomatic relations.

29 UN Resolution 678 authorizes allies to "use all necessary means" to implement UN resolutions on Kuwait if Iraq does not withdraw by January 15, 1991.

30 Bush offers to hold direct talks with Iraq to "go the extra mile."

December

1 Iraqi Revolutionary Command Council accepts Bush proposal for talks but says Israeli problem must be "at the forefront" of discussions.

6 Saddam Hussein orders the release of all Western hostages in Iraq and Kuwait.

10 Algerian President Chadli Benjedid initiates Arab mediation effort, but Saudis on December 16 refuse to see him. Israeli Prime Minister Yitzhak Shamir visits the United States.

12 Saddam Hussein dismisses Iraq's defense minister.

16 British embassy in Kuwait, last remaining open, is closed.

18 Bush confirms the cancellation of planned Bush-Aziz talks in Washington after controversy over the timing of the visit.

24 Saddam Hussein announces that Israel would be the first Iraqi target if war breaks out.

26 Israel pledges not to attack Iraq without consulting the United States.

1991

January

4 European Community foreign ministers invite Aziz to talks in Luxembourg, but this and an offer on January 9 for talks in Algiers are rejected.

6 Saddam Hussein promises "the mother of all battles" if war breaks out.

9 Baker-Aziz talks take place in Geneva.

10 Perez de Cuellar flies to Baghdad.

12 U.S. Congress authorizes the use of force against Iraq. Last U.S. diplomats leave Baghdad. France is the only Western country to keep diplomats in Baghdad.

14 Last-minute French peace proposals are blocked. Iraqi National Assembly unanimously supports Saddam Hussein's handling of the crisis and calls for a *jihad* (holy war).

15 Perez de Cuellar makes a final appeal to prevent "a conflict none of the world's peoples want." UN deadline for Iraqi withdrawal from Kuwait expires at midnight New York time.

16 Operation Desert Storm begins shortly after midnight, Greenwich mean time.

17 First Iraqi Scud missiles hit Israel. Price of oil drops from $30 to $18 on perceptions of overwhelming allied military strength. Military briefings reveal first combat losses: 1 U.S. aircraft, 3 other allied aircraft.

19 United States sends Patriot missiles to Israel.

20 First Iraqi Scuds against Riyadh are launched. Iraqi television shows men identified as captured allied airmen. Bob Simon and CBS crew are captured by Iraqi troops.

24 Japan increases contribution to allied war effort at Group of Seven meeting.

25 United States accuses Iraq of pumping oil into the gulf.

26 Peace demonstrations take place in Bonn, Washington, San Francisco, and Paris.

27 Iran announces that 12 Iraqi aircraft are being held. The number reaches 100 by the end of January.

29 Iraq captures the Saudi town of Khafji. Baker and Soviet Foreign Minister Aleksandr Bessmertnykh meet in Washington. French Defense Minister Chevenement resigns. Germans increase contributions to the war effort.

30 First U.S. soldiers—11 marines—are killed in ground combat. On February 3, U.S. briefers confirm that their deaths were due to friendly fire.

31 Allies recapture Khafji.

February

2 Iranian peace initiative presented to Saddam Hussein, whose rejection is made known on February 10.

6 Iraq severs diplomatic relations with Egypt, France, Italy, Saudi Arabia, and the United States.

13 At least 300 Iraqi civilians are killed in an allied air attack that hits a Baghdad bomb shelter.

15 Iraq announces it will withdraw from Kuwait but sets conditions.

18 Gorbachev meets with Aziz in Moscow and announces peace plan.

22 After second meeting with Gorbachev, Aziz announces Iraqi acceptance of the Soviet peace plan. Bush ultimatum demands that Iraq begin troop evacuation of Kuwait by midday on February 23.

22–25 Iraq destroys Kuwaiti installations, burning oil pumping stations.

23 A new, stricter Soviet plan is accepted by Aziz, but does not meet the terms of the Bush ultimatum.

24 Ground campaign begins at 1:00 a.m. Greenwich mean time.

25 Iraqi Scud missile kills 28 U.S. troops in a barracks in Dhahran, Saudi Arabia.

26 Saddam Hussein announces Iraqi "victory" and the start of the withdrawal of Iraqi troops from Kuwait.

26–27 Kuwait City is liberated and Iraqi forces are overwhelmingly defeated.

27 Iraqi government announces the unconditional acceptance of all UN resolutions on Kuwait.

28 Allies suspend military operations.

March

1 First reports appear of a revolt against Saddam Hussein in Basra.

2 UN Resolution 686 sets out terms for a formal end to the conflict. Bob Simon and crew are released from captivity in Baghdad.

3 Iraq agrees to "fulfill its obligations" under UN Resolution 686.

5 More than two dozen journalists are reported missing near Basra in southern Iraq.

Appendix 3: Contributors

Eqbal Ahmad teaches Middle Eastern politics and international relations at Hampshire College, writes a weekly syndicated column for South Asian and Middle Eastern newspapers, and is a writing fellow of the MacArthur Foundation Program in Peace and International Security.

Henry Allen is a reporter for *The Washington Post.*

Scott Armstrong is a former reporter for *The Washington Post* and a visiting scholar of international journalism at American University's School of Communication. He is also the founder of the National Security Archives.

Peter Arnett is a correspondent for Cable News Network and a Pulitzer Prize winner for his reporting in Vietnam.

Stephen Aubin is managing editor of *Defense Media Review,* a publication of the Center for Defense Journalism at Boston University.

Stuart Auerbach is a reporter for *The Washington Post.*

Frank A. Aukofer is a reporter for *The Milwaukee Journal.*

Malcolm Browne, a science writer for *The New York Times,* has covered military affairs and conflicts on several continents and won a Pulitzer Prize in 1964 for his coverage of Vietnam.

Dick Cheney is U.S. Secretary of Defense.

Steve Coll and **William Branigin** are reporters for *The Washington Post.*

John Corry teaches at the College of Communications at Boston University and is former television critic for *The New York Times.*

Walter Cronkite is the former anchor of "CBS Evening News."

Jason DeParle is a reporter for *The New York Times.*

Gen. Michael J. Dugan, U.S. Air Force (retired), was chief of staff of the air force from July 1 to September 17, 1990.

430

Robert Fisk is a veteran Middle East correspondent for the London *Independent*.

Barton Gellman is a reporter for *The Washington Post*.

Michael Getler formerly covered military affairs and is currently assistant managing editor for foreign news for *The Washington Post*.

Walter Goodman is a television critic for *The New York Times*.

Christopher Hanson, who writes under the pen name William Boot, is a contributing editor of the *Columbia Journalism Review* and Washington correspondent for the *Seattle Post-Intelligencer*.

Chris Hedges is a reporter for *The New York Times* who has covered several wars and regional conflicts.

Caspar Henderson is a reporter for *New Statesman & Society*.

Jim Hoagland is a columnist for *The Washington Post*.

Jeff Kamen is a television correspondent and author based in Washington, D.C.

Howard Kurtz is a reporter for *The Washington Post*.

Gara LaMarche is executive director of the Fund for Free Expression, a division of Human Rights Watch in New York.

Lewis H. Lapham is editor of *Harper's Magazine*.

Robert Lichter is editor of *Media Monitor*, a publication of the Center for Media and Public Affairs in Washington, D.C.

Thomas W. Lippman is a reporter for *The Washington Post*.

Arthur Lubow is an author and freelance magazine writer.

Ann McDaniel and **Howard Fineman** are correspondents for *Newsweek*.

Michael Massing is a contributing editor of the *Columbia Journalism Review* and a writer for *The New York Review of Books* and *The New York Times Magazine*.

Bill Monroe is editor of the *Washington Journalism Review*.

Burl Osborne is president and chief executive officer of the *Dallas Morning News* and president of the American Society of Newspaper Editors. **Larry Kramer** is executive editor of the *San Francisco Examiner* and chairman of the Press, Bar, and Public Affairs Committee of the American Society of Newspaper Editors.

Richard Pyle is a reporter for Associated Press.

Ed Rabel is a Washington-based correspondent for NBC News.

Gene Ruffini is a freelance writer based in New Jersey and a veteran newspaper and broadcast reporter.

Sydney H. Schanberg is a columnist for *New York Newsday*. He won a Pulitzer Prize in 1976 for his coverage of the fall of Cambodia.

Eric Schmitt is a reporter for *The New York Times*.

Katharine Seelye and **Dick Polman** are reporters for the *Philadelphia Inquirer*.

Maj. Gen. Winant Sidle, U.S. Army (retired), is former Chief of Information of the Army and former Deputy Assistant Secretary of Defense (Public Affairs).

Alan Simpson is a U.S. Senator from Wyoming.

Xan Smiley, Washington bureau chief of the London *Sunday Telegraph,* has worked with the BBC, CBS Radio, the *Times* of London, the *Economist*, and the London *Daily Telegraph*. He has covered more than a dozen wars around the world.

Maj. Gen. Herbert Sparrow retired from the U.S. Army in 1973 after a career that began with horse-drawn cannon and extended to the close of the Vietnam War.

Col. Harry G. Summers, Jr., U. S. Army (retired), is with the Army War College in Carlisle, Pennsylvania.

Lt. Gen. Bernard E. Trainor, U. S. Marine Corps (retired), is Director of the National Security Program at the Kennedy School of Government, Harvard University, and former military correspondent for *The New York Times*.

Richard Valeriani is a freelance journalist and former NBC News correspondent.

Tom Wicker is a columnist for *The New York Times*.

Pete Williams is Assistant Secretary of Defense (Public Affairs) in the U.S. Department of Defense.

Barry Zorthian was the government spokesman in Vietnam and is former chief of the Central News operation of the Voice of America and former president of Time-Life Broadcast.

Appendix 4: Sources and Permissions

Many of the entries in this book are reprints of material that originally appeared in other sources. Sources and permissions are listed below.

The Rationale of Policy: Pros and Cons

"Military Decisions Leading to Gulf War News Censorship" by Jason DeParle originally appeared as "Long Series of Military Decisions Led to Gulf War News Censorship," *The New York Times*, May 5, 1991, p. 1. Copyright © 1991 by The New York Times Company. Reprinted by permission.

"What Is There to Hide?" by Walter Cronkite, from *Newsweek*, February 25, 1991, p. 43. Reprinted by permission of Mr. Cronkite.

"Censoring for Political Security" by Sydney H. Schanberg, from *Washington Journalism Review*, March 1991, pp. 23–26, 53. Reprinted by permission of *Washington Journalism Review*.

Clash of Cultures: The Press Versus the Military

"Generals Versus Journalists" by Michael J. Dugan originally appeared as "Generals vs. Journalists, Cont.," *The New York Times*, May 24, 1991, p. A31. Copyright © The New York Times Company. Reprinted by permission.

"The Military and the Media: A Troubled Embrace" by Bernard E. Trainor, reprinted from *Parameters*, U.S. Army War College Quarterly, vol. 20 (December 1990), pp. 2–11.

"Rusk to John Scali: Whose Side Are You On?" by Bill Monroe, from *Washington Journalism Review*, January/February, 1991, p. 8. Reprinted by permission of *Washington Journalism Review*.

"The Briefers and the Press: Cobatants on This Side of the Line" by Thomas W. Lippman, from *The Washington Post*, February 21, 1991, p. A19. © 1991, *The Washington Post*. Reprinted with permission.

Government Control of Information: Precedents and Parallels

"Read Some About It" by Arthur Lubow, from *The New Republic*, March 18, 1991, pp. 23–25. Reprinted by permission of *The New Republic*, © 1991, The New Republic, Inc.

"General Sought to Avoid Past U.S. Mistakes with Media" by Richard Pyle, from *The Dallas Morning News*, April 22, 1991, p. 6. Reprinted with permission of Richard Pyle.

"In Bad Company" by Gara LaMarche originally appeared as "In Bad Company: Censorship in the Gulf War," *The New York Times*, May 18, 1991, p. A22. Reprinted by permission of Gara LaMarche.

"The Filtered War" by Caspar Henderson from *New Statesman & Society*, April 5, 1991, p. 16. © *New Statesman & Society*, April 1991.

How the Government Policy Worked During Combat

"The Pool" by Christopher Hanson. Reprinted from the *Columbia Journalism Review*, May/June, © 1991. Reprinted by permission of Chris Hanson.

"Out of the Pool" by Robert Fisk, from *Mother Jones*, May/June 1991, pp. 56–58. Reprinted by permission of *The Independent*, © 1991.

"The Unilaterals" by Chris Hedges. Reprinted from the *Columbia Journalism Review*, May/June, © 1991. Reprinted by permission of Christopher Hedges.

"The President's 'Spin' Patrol" by Ann McDaniel and Howard Fineman, from *Newsweek*, February 11, 1991, p. 31. © 1991, Newsweek, Inc. All rights reserved. Reprinted by permission.

"U.S. Lets Some News Filter Through 'Blackout'" by Howard Kurtz, from *The Washington Post*, February 25, 1991, p. A18. © 1991, *The Washington Post*. Reprinted with permission.

"Do Americans Really Want to Censor War Coverage This Way?" by Michael Getler, from *The Washington Post*, March 17, 1991, p. D1. © 1991, *The Washington Post*. Reprinted with permission.

435

What We Missed

"An Unknown Casualty" by Tom Wicker, from *The New York Times*, March 20, 1991, p. A29. Copyright © 1991 by The New York Times Company. Reprinted by permission.

"U.S. Bombs Missed 70 Percent of Time" by Barton Gellman, from *The Washington Post*, March 16, 1991, p. 1. © 1991, *The Washington Post*. Reprinted with permission.

"U.S. Relied on Foreign-Made Parts for Weapons" by Stuart Auerbach, from *The Washington Post*, March 25, 1991, p. 1. © 1991, *The Washington Post*. Reprinted with permission.

"U.S. Scrambled to Shape View of 'Highway of Death'" by Steve Coll and William Branigin, from *The Washington Post*, March 11, 1991, p. 1. © 1991, *The Washington Post*. Reprinted with permission.

"Army Is Blaming Patriot's Computer for Failure to Stop the Dhahran Scud" by Eric Schmitt, from *The New York Times*, May 20, 1991, p. A6. Copyright © 1991 by The New York Times Company. Reprinted by permission.

"U.S. Military Faces Probe on Performance" by Frank A. Aukofer, from *The Milwaukee Journal*, May 5, 1991, p. 1. Reprinted from *The Milwaukee Journal*.

Washington and Saudi Arabia: How Good Was the Press?

"The Instant Replay War" by Robert Lichter, from *Media Monitor*, V, 4 (April 1991), pp. 2–6.

"Talking Back to the Tube" by Richard Valeriani. Reprinted from the *Columbia Journalism Review*, March/April, © 1991. Reprinted by permission of Richard Valeriani.

"The Media Impact on Foreign Policy," from *Cosmos Journal* 1991.

"Trained Seals and Sitting Ducks" by Lewis H. Lapham, from *Harper's*, May 1991, p. 10. Copyright © 1991 by *Harper's Magazine*. All rights reserved. Reprinted from the May issue by special permission.

436

"The Gulf Between the Media and the Military" by Henry Allen, from *The Washington Post*, February 21, 1991, p. D1. ©1991, *The Washington Post*. Reprinted with permission.

"Another Front" by Michael Massing. Reprinted from the *Columbia Journalism Review*, May/June, © 1991. Reprinted by permission of Michael Massing.

"Newspapers, Getting It Late but Right" by Howard Kurtz, from *The Washington Post*, January 19, 1991, p. C1. © 1991, *The Washington Post*. Reprinted with permission.

"What the Media Missed" by Eqbal Ahmad, from *Deadline*, Vol. VI, Number 1 (January/February 1991), pp. 12–13. Reprinted with permission of *Deadline*, which is published by the Center for War, Peace, and the News Media at New York University.

"Press Failed to Challenge the Rush to War" by Gene Ruffini, from *Washington Journalism Review*, March 1991, pp. 21–23. Reprinted by permission of *Washington Journalism Review*.

"Kelly Exits with Praise for Media" from *The Washington Post*, March 5, 1991, p. A14. Reprinted with permission.

Baghdad: Reporting from the Other Side

"Baghdad: The Ugly Dateline" by Ed Rabel, from *Washington Journalism Review*, December 1990, pp. 26–28. Reprinted by permission of *Washington Journalism Review*.

"Why I Stayed Behind" by Peter Arnett, originally appeared as "Why I Stayed in Iraq, and How I Got That Interview with Saddam," *The Washington Post*, March 17, 1991, p. D1. Reprinted by permission of Peter Arnett, CNN correspondent.

"Arnett" by Walter Goodman. Reprinted from the *Columbia Journalism Review*, May/June, © 1991. Reprinted by permission of Walter Goodman.

"Peter Arnett: Anti-Hero of Baghdad" by Bill Monroe, from *Washington Journalism Review*, March 1991, p. 6. Reprinted by permission of *Washington Journalism Review*.

Press Neutrality?

Implications for the Future